Organizational Change for
the Human Services

Organizational Change for the Human Services

THOMAS PACKARD

OXFORD
UNIVERSITY PRESS

OXFORD
UNIVERSITY PRESS

Oxford University Press is a department of the University of Oxford. It furthers
the University's objective of excellence in research, scholarship, and education
by publishing worldwide. Oxford is a registered trade mark of Oxford University
Press in the UK and certain other countries.

Published in the United States of America by Oxford University Press
198 Madison Avenue, New York, NY 10016, United States of America.

Library of Congress Cataloging-in-Publication Data

Names: Packard, Thomas Roy, author. Title:
Organizational change for the human services / Thomas Packard.
Description: New York : Oxford University Press, 2021. |
Includes bibliographical references and index.
Identifiers: LCCN 2020053303 (print) | LCCN 2020053304 (ebook) |
ISBN 9780197549995 (hardback) | ISBN 9780197550014 (epub) |
ISBN 9780197580707
Subjects: LCSH: Human services—Management. |
Organizational change—Psychological aspects.
Classification: LCC HV41 .P263 2021 (print) | LCC HV41 (ebook) |
DDC 361.0068/4—dc23
LC record available at https://lccn.loc.gov/2020053303
LC ebook record available at https://lccn.loc.gov/2020053304

DOI: 10.1093/oso/9780197549995.001.0001

1 3 5 7 9 8 6 4 2

Printed by Integrated Books International, United States of America

For Leslie and Adam, of course, with unlimited love and gratitude.

Contents

1. OVERVIEW

2. CHANGE LEADERSHIP

3. A CHANGE MODEL

5. CHANGE METHODS FOR HUMAN
SERVICE ORGANIZATIONS

Foreword

This book is unique, timely, and important. Its uniqueness captures the important role of organizational change skills needed to respond to the internal and external challenges faced by human service organizations. This skill set is relevant for staff working at the line level as well as those carrying out management roles. The book captures the rich history of organization development (OD) principles and practices. Woven throughout the volume are the lifelong experiences and expertise of the author, who is a talented educator, researcher, and consultant.

The chapters reflect many of Professor Packard's strengths. They feature his research and practice experiences related to assisting organizations with the process of promoting organizational change. His emphasis on the practical "how to" features of practice is complemented by a unique combination of chapters that are descriptive, prescriptive, and theory informed. The book reflects his deep commitment to case-based teaching and learning as reflected in the four cases that he incorporates throughout the chapters. Rarely do we find such a combination of perspectives in one volume.

The core principles and practices of OD are located in the central chapters (Assessment and Goal Setting, Launching the Change Initiative, Implementation Systems and Processes, Support and Resistance, and Institutionalization and Evaluation). These chapters are followed by descriptions of other change methods (using consultants; data collection and assessment; change interventions; advancing diversity, equity, inclusion, and social justice; quality and efficiency improvement processes; organization redesign; and changing organizational culture). The book concludes with chapters specifically relevant to improving and changing human service organizations.

One of the book's most intriguing chapters involves the use of an OD consultant. Since agency staff are often overloaded with the delivery and management of client-centered services, the use of a consultant can be the key to success when addressing organizational issues that are barriers to improved services. OD-related skills include the development and refinement of help-seeking behaviors, such as developing reflective questions and insights into one's own cognitive and affective domains. The help-seeking process involves overcoming a variety of concerns such as (1) appearing ignorant or incompetent, (2) feeling unclear about the assistance being sought, (3) being unsure of how to gather and utilize alternative perspectives, (4) fearing that more assistance will simply add confusion, and/or (5) worrying that asking for assistance takes too much time.

While help-seeking behaviors tend to focus on individual or group dynamics related to seeking OD consultation, other timely chapters feature the larger context of organizational change, namely, leadership and organizational culture. They highlight Professor Packard's considerable consulting and research experience. As he reminds us, organizational change is nearly impossible without leadership from inside or outside an organization. Leadership from outside an organization can take the form of philanthropic foundations seeking to strengthen organizational capacities or legislation calling for the restructuring of services. The mandate for organizational change can also emerge internally from staff feedback or senior management observations.

In addition to the central role of leadership, the book also focuses on the importance of organizational culture, the most common barrier to successfully implementing organizational change. It emphasizes the important distinction between understanding organizational culture and organizational climate by drawing on the pioneering research and practice related to these essential features of organizational life.

This Foreword is another example of the different ways that Professor Packard and I have collaborated over the past several decades. We have written articles and a casebook together and consulted extensively with each other on issues of management practice and education in human service organizations. We share a deep commitment to the social work values and ethics that underlie effective OD practice. I greatly appreciate the opportunity to contribute to this important book about a unique form of practice that is essential for all levels of staff working in nonprofit and public human service organizations.

Michael J. Austin,
Mack Professor of Nonprofit Management Emeritus
Founding Director, Mack Center on Nonprofit and
Public Sector Management in the Human Services
School of Social Welfare
University of California, Berkeley
June 2020

Acknowledgments

I must start by acknowledging the huge amount of undeserved privilege into which I was born, giving me too many advantages to count that helped me reach this point in my life and career. I had all the typical advantages of being born into the white suburban middle class in the early years of the postwar baby boom. In addition to those important demographics, being a first-born cisgender male and having two college-educated parents provided additional advantages. At least equally important, I had an advantage that not all such children did: devoted parents who not only provided sustenance and safety but also gave me unconditional love and support. My parents also served as valuable role models for how to be good parents and manage careers (Dad occasionally reminded us that "your mom has two full-time jobs").

Similarly, my five siblings were loving and supportive companions during my formative years and remain dear and valued friends. Each of them has also made unique contributions to my career in social work administration teaching and research. I have had valuable discussions with Steve and Mark regarding our shared experiences teaching college students and their earlier work in telecommunications and restaurant management, respectively. Anne and Mary, with their careers in nonprofit financial management and international nongovernmental organization capacity building and development, respectively, have offered valuable insights on actual work on the ground that enriched my teaching. And many of my social work administration students may remember examples of my "meatpacking brother" Dwight's excellent leadership and management activities as an executive and later as a turnaround manager in the beef-processing industry.

I have had the good fortune to have had many jobs that were interesting and enriching, giving me an appreciation for the good that formal organizations can do for customers, clients, patients, and staff. Nearly all of my supervisors also had valuable positive impacts on my development and thinking.

My first role model as a leader was my high school swimming coach, Ray Obermiller. Decades later I realized that he had demonstrated how a low-key, supportive, and results-focused leadership style could pull (not push) people to higher and higher levels of performance. At my first job during high school, my manager at McDonald's, Gary Goodwin, created a positive and supportive work environment and showed me the good aspects of scientific management—high-quality products and efficiency—without the common negatives of dehumanizing work. For two other summers, Andy (can't remember his last name), the supervisor on a gas construction crew, had created another positive work environment for digging ditches and repairing gas mains. For another summer, Joanne Brody saw some potential in me and hired me for my first supervisory job—managing a municipal swimming pool. At Bellevue Hospital, my head nurses—Joanne Albus on the Prison Ward and William Gillette in the Psych Hospital—saw in me potentials beyond my lowly role and gave me rich opportunities to learn and contribute.

At San Diego Youth Services, founding executive John Wedemeyer was a fantastic role model for competent and dedicated management behavior and a supportive and inspiring leader and friend. My other bosses there–Kathleen Armogida, Randy Mecham, and Nancy Smith—were similarly supportive and became lifelong friends. Also at that time, our "community consultant" Anne Dosher, older and wiser than all of us, exposed us to new thinking about the potentials of alternative human services.

In my master's in social work program, Percil Stanford was a fantastic role model as a teacher and administrator, and Jack Stumpf showed great passion in putting community practice and advocacy into action in San Diego.

At UCLA, my advisor Alex Norman was most supportive, pushing me and exposing me to new ideas in the most good-natured way. Nathan Cohen was intellectually challenging and also jovial and humble—another fantastic role model. Jim Taylor and Lou Davis in the Graduate School of Management and the Center for the Quality of Working Life exposed me to fascinating vistas in sociotechnical systems and treated me with much appreciated support and respect.

In the city of San Diego's Organization Effectiveness Program, I had colleagues who showed amazing skills, positive energy, and admirable commitment to improving the operations of city programs and work teams. My colleagues on our fire department project, Robin Reid and Daryl Grigsby, not only were fantastic team members but also became lifelong friends. My bosses Rich Hays and Trudy Sopp were supportive and passionate about our work. Also on the fire department project, Fire Chief Earle Roberts was the best client imaginable, showing vision and passion for changing the culture of the fire department and trusting us as we suggested all kinds of organization development interventions. Two of the department's internal OD coordinators, Michael McCormick and Perry Peake, also became valued colleagues and friends. Firefighter Union President Ron Saathoff shared Earle's passion for change and became another great collaborator and friend.

I also have great appreciation for a wide range of clients, from the city to small nonprofits, who welcomed me into their work worlds and trusted me to explore with them ways to improve their operations and work relationships.

Many of my students in over 30 years of teaching have been eager and com-mitted learners, forcing me to apply concepts and theories to actual organiza-tional and community life. Some have become valued friends and colleagues, enriching my life. I particularly appreciate my students over the past 6 years who dealt with earlier versions of this manuscript and were helpful in its refinement.

I have appreciated working with many in the social work administration field who have enriched my work. In particular, Rino Patti has been a valued mentor for decades, and I have greatly appreciated being able to do research and write with him. The same goes for Mike Austin, always positive, supportive, and im-possible to say "no" to. They both saw in me potential that I did not see for myself.

Jennifer Tucker-Tatlow, the chief executive officer of the Academy for Professional Excellence in our School of Social Work, has been a wonderful col-league, research collaborator, and friend. Several of her staff, especially James Coloma, Carrie Gibson, Karissa Hughes, and Patti Rahiser, have been helpful to me on research and training collaborations, as well as being delightful to work with.

My colleagues at the national and local levels of the Network for Social Work Management, too many to list, have given me validation and support, lifting my confidence along the way.

I greatly appreciate CEO Walter Philips at San Diego Youth Services and the staff who allowed me to study organizational change at their agency. Julie DeDe and her staff at Father Joe's Villages were similarly helpful and much appreciated.

I must also acknowledge, beyond the citations, writers, too many to name, who influenced my work, with their knowledge and sometimes inspiration, and some through valued discussions at professional conferences.

Publisher David Follmer, a valued presence at professional conferences, connected me with the Oxford University Press and provided helpful suggestions and support. At the Oxford University Press, Dana Bliss was constantly helpful and supportive on this project. I also greatly appreciated the anonymous reviewers and a committee member who gave me very valuable feedback to improve my work. Mike Austin also provided very useful feedback and suggestions for the final version of my manuscript. I appreciate the Oxford staff, especially Kate Brown, who did exceptionally helpful editing, and Poonguzhali Ramasamy, who guided me through the publication process Of course, I take total responsibility for all that is in this book, including the ways I used and cited the work of others.

I should also acknowledge the value of the music of John Coltrane, which never failed to help me get through rough spots in my thinking and writing process.

And last but certainly not least, my wife, Leslie, has been a constant loving companion and source of support, even during her decades of demanding work as a teacher. Our son, Adam, has given us unending joy, enabling me to give at-tention to my work when needed, sometimes at the expense of time with him.

SECTION 1
OVERVIEW

Introduction

I see myself more like a real good journeyman. And that's fine; you
do your job real good, you pass on some part of the flame . . . and you
stir things up a little bit if you can.
—Bruce Springsteen (*Bruce Springsteen: The 1984 Music Awards.*
Rolling Stone Magazine, Loder, 1985)

Welcome to what I hope will be for you a delightful and enriching, although perhaps sometimes challenging and frustrating, adventure to explore the potentials
of organizational change and your role as a change agent, whatever your position
in an organization.

Anyone who has worked in a human service organization (HSO) for some
amount of time has probably said or thought, "If I were in charge around here,
I would definitely change . . . " followed by an idea that probably would, in fact,
change the organization for the better. Those who are officially "in charge"—a
chief executive officer (CEO) or some type of general manager with a good deal
of autonomy—definitely have ideas for changing their organization. And those
in between, from front-line supervisors to middle managers, have some amount
of authority to initiate change and probably wish they could initiate change beyond their own position. I hope this book offers some guidance and support
to anyone who wants to initiate change in any aspect of an organization's functioning or performance.

Because there are so many perspectives from which to look at an organization
and its functioning, this Introduction begins with a discussion of some of the
common ways of viewing organizations, which can give you some frameworks
and grounding to understand and make sense of what you see from your position
in an organization. To the extent that you can use empathy to try to understand
the perspectives of others in the organization, this can also help you as a change
agent who will try to encourage others to engage in change. Change in this sense
will apply at the individual and organizational levels: You and any other employee will need to change as the organization goes through larger changes.

Next, I discuss the purpose of the book, including potential audiences and
how you may use this in your educational or work setting. I also briefly address
how I used evidence to guide what I have written. I then describe four cases that
will provide examples of the concepts and materials I cover, followed by an overview of the sections and chapters.

Organizational Change for the Human Services. Thomas Packard, Oxford University Press. © Oxford University Press
2021. DOI: 10.1093/oso/9780197549995.003.0001

Making Sense of Organizations

People's views of an organization can vary based on both their overall worldviews and their work experiences. Over a career working in organizations, people develop assumptions that frame how they look at things. Given the importance that one's prior experiences in an organization affect how they assess an organization, I think it will help for me to share my personal perspectives here. This is especially relevant regarding organizational change, which can be approached in widely varying ways depending on one's assumptions about how organizations work.

I've had the good fortune to have worked mostly in organizations that were at least adequately functioning and in some cases functioning at some levels of excellence, and to have had bosses, team members, and coworkers who were generally positive, respectful, and in some cases truly outstanding. I do know that for many people who work in HSOs, this is not common. In spite of the good intentions and positive values of those doing human services work, some factors—many external to the organization—create conditions that can lead to bad morale, cynicism, and burnout. I, with my generally optimistic view of formal organizations, assume that a lot of these problems are correctable, hence my interest in organizational change and my secondary interest in policy advocacy to change conditions that HSOs address.

So, I lay out here some perspectives for viewing organizational life and share which ones have influenced the ways I look at organizations. I end this introduction by reviewing plans for the book.

Throughout my work career (starting while in high school, at McDonald's) I've been fascinated by formal organizations: the people who work there; how employees work together; what the organizations accomplish; and organizations' impacts on their employees, their customers, clients, and communities. The more I reflected on what the organizations actually accomplished, the more I thought about how these organizations could be improved. During my master's in social work program, my thinking became better crystallized, focusing on how to define and then measure how these organizations were performing and finally how to improve them.

At various times in my career, I have been a consultant and an academic. The term *pracacdemic* fits well for me: Since my doctoral education I have paid special attention to how practitioners can use academic knowledge and how academics can discover and share new knowledge that is relevant and useful. An image that I like is "practitioners in the mud of organizational change, academics in the ivory tower of analysis, and consultants running up and down the stairs to connect the two" (Benschop & Van Den Brink, 2018, p. 193), with all playing valuable roles. I hope this book addresses some of the challenges in connecting research to practice regarding organizational change (McBeath et al., 2019).

Human service organizations have complex and often nonroutine technologies, from how services are delivered to how office administrative procedures are done. That makes them both more challenging and more interesting than some for-profit organizations. And compared to a factory or a retail store, the stakes are a lot higher when you are working with human beings who are facing significant challenges. These people enter our organizations in varying conditions of vulnerability, stress, and/or oppression, and also with inherent strengths and capacities. They deserve the best and most appropriate services and other support that we can provide. That principle has been a major driving force for me and led me to studying and practicing organizational change. I have been very fortunate to have been able to help organizations by facilitating, guiding, and supporting planned organizational change. Teaching has given me an even greater opportunity: to train and educate students who can become the change leaders of the future.

Gareth Morgan, in his recent minor classic *Images of Organization* (2006), used metaphors to give members of organizations ways to "read" and make sense of an organization, including its culture, climate, values, and priorities. I add some detail that might help you understand an organization with which you are familiar.

The organization as a *machine* applies to a bureaucracy in which there are clearly defined roles and procedures. Scientific management, where management knows the "one best way" to do something, is an example. This is valuable where precision is required, such as an operating room or an accounting system. There are obvious limitations regarding responding to a changing environment or tapping creativity and innovation of staff.

An organization as an *organism* suggests an open system that adapts to an environment and goes through life cycle stages. This fits well with ecological and open system theories that are common in social work theory courses, but cannot be taken too literally.

The organization as a *brain* sees organizations as information-processing systems. Environmental scanning in strategic planning and learning organizations are examples.

An organization as a *culture* is a common metaphor, looking at an organization's norms, values, symbols, and generally "the way we do things around here." This has special relevance for organizational change, where the next three metaphors are also useful to frame the need for organizational change. An organizational culture that devalues, even subtly, the perspectives and contributions of non-dominant groups is a clear target for organizational change. Such a culture also suggests opportunities to create more egalitarian or client-oriented cultures or to implement evidence-based practices.

An organization can be seen as a *psychic prison* if it is excessively bureaucratic or oppressive in its structure, does not allow power sharing, and does not allow criticism of an existing culture of control. This presents huge opportunities for organizational change, but those in power in such an organization may be resistant to change, creating feelings of hopelessness for staff.

An organization as a *political system* considers the formal and informal power dynamics that can exist in any organization, which might receive varying amounts of attention. Dynamics of discrimination based on race, gender, and other factors are relevant here, with organizational power traditionally residing with white males. A related perspective, *critical theory*, was mentioned by Morgan within his psychic prison metaphor, where he suggested that this is a good framework for organizational change. However, I believe the political and power perspective provides a stronger basis for applying critical theory to organizational change. Critical race theory, and feminism, discussed later in the book, can help frame organizational problems of discrimination so that they can be addressed at a systems level. In organizational change more broadly, the particular interests of various staff groups will need attention, and conflict must be recognized and addressed.

Organizations as *instruments of domination and exploitation* are represented by excessive applications of bureaucracy and exploitation of staff. Some HSOs might be seen as reflecting this theory, regarding various aspects of marginalization, discrimination, and power imbalances affecting underrepresented populations in a workforce. This perspective has shown up more often in the literature on staff-initiated organizational change (covered in Chapter 19), but it can also be useful to change agents in power positions in the organization. In fact, it may be even more important for an executive-level change leader, particularly white males who still are overrepresented at this level, to use this perspective to guide change initiatives, particularly in areas including changing an organizational culture to make it more inclusive, advancing social justice within the organization, and changing human resources practice to address systemic mistreatment of women and other underrepresented segments of the workforce.

Flux and transformation is a more abstract metaphor that includes dynamics of feedback loops, chaos and complexity theory, and, interestingly, the current notion of innovation as creative destruction.

My most common frame of reference is to see an organization as an open system, and I can easily see the dynamics of bureaucracy, with its strengths, including the principle the every position should be occupied by someone with proper qualifications, and its potential limitations of rigidity and resistance to change. I'm also attuned to an organization's culture, as a force sometimes even more important than bureaucratic aspects such as structure. I sometimes am not as alert to political dynamics that should be recognized, and I know from my consulting, particularly in public sector bureaucracies, that some employees see their organization as instruments of domination or psychic prisons. And, as a white male, I probably need to pay more attention to critical theory, and more specifically feminist theory (Netting, Kettner, McMurrtry, & Thomas, 2017, pp. 214–216) when assessing organizational conditions and opportunities for change.

Employees may believe that more than one of Morgan's (2006) metaphors applies in their organizations, and different employees may see the same organization in different ways. In terms of change leadership, allowing discussions about how staff see their organization, program, or unit can be valuable assessment tools. Human services leadership scholar Jean East has put it this way: "One important understanding for leadership is embracing the multiple realities of our daily experience" (2019, p. 6), adding that "leaders need to create spaces and conversations that allow multiple viewpoints to be articulated" (p. 9).

Another valuable framework for me is O'Connor and Netting's term *organization practice* (2009), which gives employees of an organization some tools for thinking about their work and the nature of their organization, suggesting opportunities for change. Knowledge of an organization's environment, in particular the demands and expectations of outside stakeholders, including clients, community members, and funders, and of its internal dynamics, including its structure, culture, and decision-making processes, can give staff insights regarding why their organization does some of the things that it does. According to O'Connor and Netting,

> disorder and chaos are the way many of our systems creatively solve the problems associated with human service work. Organization practice, therefore, requires one to constantly be assessing and reassessing situations. (2009, p. 8)

Being able to make sense of your organization can help you to more effectively work within it and, for our specific purposes here, participate in or lead a change process that will make the organization more effective or a better place to work.

Purpose of the Book

With that background, I now share my thinking on the need for and the purpose of this book on organizational change. For several years I have used varying combinations of books, articles, and other readings to teach organizational change. I finally decided that one book, with a coherent conceptual model, a solid theory base, extensive use of current best practices research, relevant practice wisdom, and opportunities for readers to reflect on themselves as potential change leaders, would be a useful basis for learning in a classroom, an administrator's office, or a management team setting.

Recognizing that HSOs should always be adapting and improving, and that such changes cannot always happen without conscious attention and leadership, the purpose of this book is to provide, in one place, a package of theory, research, and practice that can offer guidance to anyone working in an HSO who sees opportunities to improve some aspect of an organization's functioning. I use the word *guidance* very precisely here. Much of the organizational change literature is written with a tone of "I'm an expert, so do all these things I recommend." Having practiced as an organization development consultant full time for 6½ years and part time for many more, and having researched it for 15 years, I approach this work with some confidence about what I have not only found and learned, but also with some humility, skepticism, and curiosity. I do feel confident in being a guide, rather than being someone who gives orders on what to do. A guide, in settings from a forest to a museum, can point things out to you and offer some expert knowledge, but would typically then let you assess things for yourself and draw your own meanings and conclusions.

I provide here the *best available* evidence that I could find, from a small number of randomized controlled trials to cross-sectional surveys, case studies, and practice wisdom. You can use the context in which something is presented to determine for yourself its value. An appraiser of art provenance said that "his success was due not to the belief that he was necessarily right but to the knowledge that, of available opinions, especially on great artists, his was least likely to be wrong" (Kaiser, 2013, p. 13). I have a similar aspiration.

When I was growing up in Iowa, I was familiar with the greeting of "What do you know?" I occasionally heard a variation that in retrospect has deep wisdom that has affected me in my work. That greeting, "What do you know for sure?" was followed by the response, "Not a whole heck of a lot." While many of the books of the "management by bestseller" or "guru literature" type display overwhelming confidence that all you need to do is follow their advice and you and your work will be fantastic, I am more thoughtful here, sometimes not knowing things "for sure."

A lot of what I say here is based on material from refereed journals, which adds another layer of credibility, even when the studies described may not have used the highest levels of evidence. And I have greater confidence in some of my assertions that represent convergences from multiple sources, even if not done through a meta-analysis or full systematic review.

Essayist Michele de Montaigne said in the sixteenth century, "It could be said of me that in this book I have only made up a bunch of other men's [people's] flowers, providing of my own only the string that ties them together" (Ratcliffe,

2017). In many respects, that is what I've done here: used a lot of the work of others, with some additions from my own work, and presented it within my own worldviews about and experiences with organizations.

The main audiences I have in mind for this book are those working in a medium-to-large HSO (very roughly, 100 to 1,000 employees) or those (especially students) expecting to soon be working in such a setting. While those at a middle or upper level of management should be able to most easily relate to this material, even lower level managers or supervisors could benefit from learning more about how they could develop as change leaders and could then suggest opportunities for change in their organizations. Organizational consultants and perhaps human resources staff may find this material valuable to the extent that their roles involve facilitating and supporting organizational change.

Readers currently at the front-line level can benefit from this book in several ways. First, it can give you some useful exposure to the ways administrators think about their organizations. Having such insights will better enable you to try to influence change upward: To the extent that you show your supervisor or other administrators that you understand the challenges of administrative work, they will likely be more receptive to your proposals or ideas for improvement that meet their needs, such as improved services or decreased expenses. If you hope to promote into administrative positions, having such insights will help in your growth and development as a future administrator. And, if you plan to remain at the front-line level, the chapter on staff-initiated organizational change may be particularly useful to you and your colleagues.

In my teaching with graduate students, I have found that almost all of them have worked in at least a medium-size HSO, often at a front-line staff level, or are in an internship that would give them a frame of reference to work from. I have also found that graduate students have typically had experiences in some other type of work setting, from being a server at a restaurant to working in a law firm.

Cases We Will Study

Before providing an overview of the rest of the book, I introduce here some case examples of change leadership: executives and staff in their organizations who saw opportunities or challenges and addressed them. These are used to illustrate the application of change leadership principles and change technologies (sometimes known as techniques or interventions) discussed in later chapters. Two of these cases of nonprofit organizations are based on research colleagues and I have done (Packard, 2017, 2019). Another case, a county human services agency in Northern California, is adapted from a case study that coauthors and I used in a book (Austin, Brody, & Packard, 2009) and from a later publication (Borland, 2019). The information here is from the director's point of view when she prepared the case. Of course, there would be other perspectives from those involved regarding that change process, and we have little follow-up on what has happened since then. The final case is based on a consulting project with the San Diego Fire Department that I worked on when I was in the Organization Effectiveness Program (OEP) in the city of San Diego (Packard & Reid, 1990).

Father Joe's Villages

Father Joe's Villages (http://my.neighbor.org/) includes a range of programs for homeless people and encompasses several city blocks and multiple sites near downtown San Diego. The project described here was in St. Vincent de Paul Village, which included many of the agency's programs. At the time of this study, those programs were serving over 12,000 people annually. Their programs housed nearly 900 families, single men, and single women every night and prepared more than 3,000 meals each day. Programs included rapid rehousing, transitional housing, permanent supportive housing, and affordable housing. Ancillary services included employment and education services, therapeutic child care, a state-licensed community clinic, a federally qualified health center that provided integrated behavioral and physical healthcare, a state-certified outpatient addiction treatment program, multidisciplinary team case management, and veterans' assistance. At the time of the change initiative described here, there were approximately 180 staff in all programs and in administrative and other support functions.

Julie DeDe, the director of programs, and the managers in charge of case management saw some opportunities to make significant improvements in their service delivery system through a major programmatic and structural change to create integrated co-located multidisciplinary teams. They initiated an organizational change process that lasted about 8 months.

After the change process had concluded, my colleague Carrie Gibson and I surveyed their staff, and I interviewed the Julie DeDe and two other staff, and examined agency documents to learn about this change process.

San Mateo County (California) Human Services Agency

San Mateo County is located in the southern San Francisco Bay Area between the Pacific Ocean and San Francisco Bay. At the time of this change process, their County Human Services Agency had approximately 750 employees and a budget of approximately $213 million. It provided a typical range of services, including child and family services, employment services, and public assistance programs.

When Maureen Borland arrived in San Mateo in 1992 to assume the position of director of the agency, one of the members of the county board of supervisors (elected officials) shared a concern with her about the number of families who had complained to her about the fact that there didn't seem to be a single point of contact for somebody who had any kind of a social service need. This led to a major organizational change process that, along with some other related initiatives, occurred over a period of several years.

San Diego Youth Services

San Diego Youth Services (SDYS) (https://sdyouthservices.org/) is a highly regarded and highly successful human services organization in San Diego County in California. The agency has been a major provider of comprehensive services at 14 locations for homeless, abused and at-risk youth, and their families and communities, serving over 10,000 youth and their families per year with a budget of over $12 million and approximately 200 staff. In spite of the agency's 40-plus years of outstanding service provision, challenges in the agency's environment required large-scale changes in the agency's operations. Agency CEO Walter Philips had led ongoing growth and innovation in the agency for over 10 years and recently concluded that the agency was facing new major challenges to which it would need to respond.

This change process actually had three components: a significant restructuring activity affecting upper and middle management staff, a shift in client service delivery methods to trauma-informed care, and a "rebranding" process in which the agency changed its name and developed a new marketing plan. After the process had been completed, I surveyed their staff, interviewed Walter Philips, and held a focus group to gather data on people's views of this process.

San Diego Fire Department

A fire department may seem to be an unusual case example to be used in a book about HSOs. While it does, of course, differ from even a large governmental HSO, there are important and relevant similarities. Both types of agencies operate within traditional principles of public administration and governance, and have missions to provide essential services to the community as a whole. Both face challenges due to increasing public demand for quality services and inadequate resources. Both have their share of bureaucrats, good and bad; excellent and poor leaders; and workforces that include very committed staff and those who may have become cynical or negative. More importantly for our purposes here, it is a case that represents a quite full use of organizational change technologies that have also been used in HSOs and that offer promise for improving any large HSO.

The San Diego Fire Department, hereafter referred to as the SDFD, was by all accounts a very typical bureaucratic organization that used a top-down management philosophy and a classic bureaucratic culture. In 1979, Earle Roberts was brought in as the first fire chief hired from outside the department. The San Diego city manager was hopeful that Chief Roberts could develop a more progressive, change-oriented culture in the SDFD. At the time of this change initiative, the department had about 820 employees and a budget of over $26 million.

Chief Roberts made a request for consulting services to the OEP, where I worked. Located in the city's Financial Management Department, OEP had 14 professional staff—half organization development consultants and half productivity analysts—and offered a wide array of consulting services from team building to workflow analysis. Two other OEP consultants and I worked with the SDFD for 3 years, with ad hoc follow-up after that.

Plan for the Book

There are six sections in the book.

Section 1 provides an introduction and two chapters. Chapter 1 discusses some of the challenges and opportunities, external and internal, that an organization may face when considering and implementing planned change, including assessing the extent to which planned organizational change can really make a difference. It ends with some definitions for planned change itself and for leading and managing change. Chapter 2 presents a conceptual model for organizational change that will provide a framework for the remainder of the book, briefly touching on the various steps and technologies that can be used.

Section 2 has two chapters that address what may be the key variable in a successful organizational change initiative: the change leader. Here, *you* are the target of assessment and change. This brings to mind a famous quotation often attributed to organizational systems change expert Peter Senge: "People don't resist change; they resist being changed." Usually, someone suggesting a need for organizational change is looking at people above or below the person wanting change as the main targets of the change. This addresses the notion that, "I don't need to change; others need to change." Chapter 3 focuses on a change leader's self-assessment and introspection, particularly looking at how you as a change leader can benefit by looking at yourself and then what you can do to further develop your own skills. Chapter 4 covers some leadership theories that have particular relevance and value for change leaders.

Section 3, really the core of the book, has five chapters that walk through the phases of an organizational change process. It covers in some detail the steps of the change process outlined in Chapter 2, with particular attention to change tactics. Examples from the cases are inserted to show applications of change principles.

Section 4 covers a menu of generic organizational change technologies that can be used as appropriate in the implementation of a particular change initiative. Since organizational change can often be more successful with the assistance of a qualified consultant, Chapter 10 covers two major types of consultation and offers considerations in acquiring and using a consultant. Such a consultant may be a traditional "external" consultant engaged by the organization, but may also be "internal" to the organization as a staff member, perhaps a human resources or quality improvement professional with the needed competencies.

Chapters 11 through 16 cover generic organizational change technologies that can be used within the framework of the model covered in Section 3. These technologies, which have been used in general business organizations as well as occasionally in the public sector and in some cases in nonprofit organizations, include team building, action research, employee attitude surveys, role clarification, force field analysis, and conflict management. A chapter on advancing diversity, equity, inclusion, and social justice is included in this section because it is a content area in which virtually any organization can and should make improvements. The next chapter covers quality improvement methods such as Total Quality Management, Continuous Quality Improvement, and Lean Six Sigma—generic change methods that are becoming increasingly popular in HSOs.

A major organizational change method, organization redesign, more commonly referred to as "restructuring," is such a common change method that it is covered in its own chapter. This not only includes the very common technique of restructuring the boxes of programs, functions, and staff, but also addresses key organizational processes such as decision-making, communication, and organizational culture. Because organizational culture and climate are such important issues for organizational change, they are also covered in a separate chapter.

Section 5 describes some change technologies that have been designed specifically for HSOs. Included here are capacity building, best practices and benchmarking, cutback management, implementing evidence-based practices, implementation science, and creating learning organizations. Specific change models, including the ARC (availability, responsiveness, and continuity) model, the sanctuary model, getting to outcomes, and the design team model are also summarized.

The model covered in Chapters 5 to 9 is based on the assumption that the leaders of the change initiative are in administrative positions—typically at an executive level or at management level with executive support—with the authority to support and direct the effort. Another model of organizational change is one that is initiated by lower level staff to influence upward to create organizational change. This model, generally referred to as *staff-initiated organizational change*, is covered in Chapter 19.

The final section summarizes what we have covered in this book and gives you an opportunity to pull together and reflect on what you have learned and how you can use your new knowledge now or in the future.

Most chapters end with some reflection and focusing questions.

While Chapters 5 to 9 should be treated as a coherent whole—a phase model of implementing organizational change—subsequent chapters can be used in an as-needed or menu format, within the context of a change process. I see Chapters 3 and 4 regarding you as a change leader as relevant throughout, with hopes that in the process of implementing an organizational change, you will maintain your self-awareness and be alert to what you yourself need to be doing to change.

The Appendices include an item covering organizational change history, some details on the evidence regarding organizational change in HSOs and other organizations, and some of the literature regarding organizational change in particular fields. Another item includes detail on research that colleagues and I have done on organizational change tactics and offers some suggestions for advancing even further the knowledge, practice, and research in this area. These items are intended to show both what we do know about organizational change and what we don't yet know, offering evidence to guide practice and suggesting opportunities for additional research. The Appendices also include some other resources, including the Organizational Change Tactics Questionnaire used in my work.

I also include in many chapters occasional quotes from Jaiya John, a most energetic and compassionate change agent for the human services. Much of what I present comes from an academic, analytical point of view. I augment this with some of my own reflections and experiences, delivered, I hope, with both thoughtfulness and a touch of feeling, including empathy for the administrators and staff of HSOs who face a range of challenges big and small every day, and with appreciation for the work that they do in service of people, many of whom are among the most disadvantaged or challenged in our society. Beyond that, however, I have found Jaiya to be able, as a speaker and writer, to address administrators and staff with a depth of feeling, compassion, and energy that I can't match. I hope his words will enrich what I present, which is often in the form of descriptions and statements of practice principles that have some evidence in the literature.

For example, he gives a lot of attention to the principle of caring. Some of his thinking is worth quoting at length. Here is how he puts it:

> A prime ingredient in any relational space is caring. We don't have to know each other well, or even like each other. But we must care. And this caring must be mutual. It must extend in both directions across authority lines. . . . *Caring is motivational.* It requires a sincere motive to support the needs and wellness of another. *Caring is attentional.* The motive to support should naturally manifest as genuine attention to the signs and signals that another is communicating, and to the circumstances in which that other person exists. Even if those conditions are beyond that person's awareness. *Caring is active.* Motive and attention should lead to action on behalf of the other person's needs and wellness. *Caring is receptive.* It is more motivated to receive from another (insight, sincerity, story, perspective, expression) than it is to dictate. (John, 2016, pp. 64–65, italics in original)

My wanting to help people improve the functioning of their organizations is, for me, an act of caring: caring about the quality of working life of staff at all levels and caring about the clients and communities that our agencies serve. Staff, in whatever position, deserve careers of fulfillment, where they can use their knowledge and skills and see the impacts they are having. Clients and communities, regardless of their status in our society, deserve the best and most effective services possible. The larger social policy issues that have huge impacts in terms of what and who society values and supports, and what our agencies have to work with in terms of resources, are beyond the scope of this book. I do hope that making our agencies more effective in service delivery will help lead to positive outcomes for those we serve, and that evidence of the positive impacts of our programs can be used to advocate for greater support at policy levels.

Summary

Anyone in an organization has the potential to become an organizational change agent. Staff at all levels and all parts of an organization can see opportunities for organizational improvements. This book should offer some guidance and support to anyone who wants to initiate change in their organization.

Everyone has their own unique perspective for looking at and trying to make sense of how an organization is operating. Such perspectives can be shaped by one's implicit theories about how organizations work as well as by prior experiences at work. Being aware of one's perspectives can provide a foundation for assessing an organization's functioning and developing ideas about what should be changed.

Several theories are particularly valuable for someone assessing an organization's need for change. An organization can be seen as a *machine*: a bureaucracy with clearly defined roles and procedures. Seeing an organization as an *organism*—an open system—can help one examine an organization's processes and its relationships with its environment. Viewing the organization as a *brain* can help examine how information is gathered, processed, and shared. Organizational *culture* is a commonly used term for assessing the beliefs, values, and norms of the organization. An organization can be seen as an oppressive *psychic prison*, a *political system* where power dynamics predominate, an *instrument of domination and exploitation*, or, more abstractly, a system of *flux and transformation* that can include chaos and innovation. More broadly, *critical theory* can be used to assess political or power dynamics and also examine dynamics of diversity and discrimination within organizations.

This Introduction discussed the purpose of the book: essentially to offer an evidence-based model that includes the various dimensions and technologies of organizational change that can be used by practicing administrators; students; consultants; and, really, anyone working in an HSO. I then described the four cases what are used as examples in some of the chapters and reviewed the overall layout of the book.

Reflection and Focusing Questions

1. What are your current perspectives and views for how you describe an organization: what it is doing and what effects it is having on its staff and outcomes in terms of services to clients?
2. Have you ever experienced a formal organizational change process? If so, what happened? What were the goals and how successful was it? What activities contributed to the success or lack of success of the initiative?
3. At this point, what would you like to learn about organizational change?
4. How can your increased knowledge of organizational change make you a better change agent and a more valuable member of your organization?

1

Challenges and Opportunities

> People hate change, and with good reason. Change makes us
> stupider, relatively speaking. Change adds new information to the
> universe; information that we don't know. Our knowledge—as a
> percentage of all the things that can be known—goes down a tick
> every time something changes.
>
> —Dilbert (Adams, 1996, p. 198)

This chapter begins by framing our discussion of organizational change, focusing on *planned* organizational change that can happen at the level of a program, a division, or the entire organization. I'll cover some current conditions in society that require organizational change and how these can be seen as opportunities. Leading and managing organizational change are presented as complementary and essential skills. I'll present some challenges in implementing organizational change and finally define the concept.

Framing Organizational Change

Human service organizations (HSOs) are constantly changing. At the broadest level, organizational change can be planned or unplanned. Unplanned change can be radical, due to events such as a major cutback in funding; moderate, when staff morale gradually declines; or minor, when staff make small changes in a procedure. Organizations can change by becoming worse or less effective through deteriorating morale, inattention to the operation of programs or management processes, or other factors. Planned change, the subject here, occurs when members of the organization take conscious steps to move the organization to a more desirable future state or to address and resolve current or expected challenges or problems. Changes can originate within the organization, when executives, teams, supervisors, or individual workers have ideas for implementing a new strategy or service delivery model or improving something, such as an intake procedure or the way paperwork is processed. Sometimes, change is forced on the organization by something in the environment, such as a government policy change.

Organizational Change for the Human Services. Thomas Packard, Oxford University Press. © Oxford University Press 2021. DOI: 10.1093/oso/9780197549995.003.0002

The focus here is on *planned* change, employing rational adaptation approaches (more on this in Chapter 2), that see managers and others as change agents who can assess their environments and other conditions and then purposefully drive change within their organizations. This is distinct from organizational change, which *happens* to organizations, such as when funding is cut or environmental conditions seem to dictate that change must occur. This latter dynamic, unplanned change that comes without organizational intent, can, however, be followed by purposeful, planned organizational change to deal with new environmental demands or any negative conditions affecting an organization.

Another variable regarding planned organizational change is the size of the organizations that would be appropriate for this model. Planned organizational change can be used for an entire organization, in our case, most likely a nonprofit agency; a for-profit HSO; or a unit of a larger entity, such as a department or division of a city or county government. Any such organization may be at one physical site or could have multiple facilities or programs in regional offices or other dispersed sites. Most of the organizational change literature in HSOs, and my own research and practice experience, is at these levels.

So, when I say "the organization" I mean all the staff and programs or units that will be involved in the process. I can add that the principles in the model I use here are pretty well aligned with those used in much larger organizations, although there are hugely significant differences in scale. A small agency of fewer than, say, 50 or 100 staff would probably not need to use the full set of techniques discussed here, but the basic change tactics and principles should be relevant regardless.

I have done some short-term consultations with nonprofit organizations (NPOs) and for-profit organizations of fewer than 20 paid staff and found that, even with such small organizations, tactics ranging from clear problem identification and goal setting, getting staff involved, having a clear change process, to evaluating results can all be relevant. At the upper end for me, when I was with the Organization Effectiveness Program in the city of San Diego, we did two citywide projects that each involved a good number of employees, but not nearly all, in a workforce of about 10,000.

Some Conditions Requiring Change

One concept that is now popular in the general organizational literature is VUCA (volatility, uncertainty, complexity, and ambiguity), which certainly applies to the human services. Gibbons (2015, p. 77) said that volatility "means greater frequency and scale of the uncontrollable, unpredictable events that alter the competitive landscape." These conditions clearly apply to the environments of HSOs.

In a VUCA environment, many organizational changes are, of course, based on outside forces. Because many such forces and trends are pretty well known to most people who work in HSOs and because, at the time of this writing, there are so many unknowns in the policy environments of HSOs, I don't attempt to create a comprehensive list, but simply mention some major themes. Suffice it to say that there seems to be more uncertainty than ever, in areas ranging from racial justice, immigration policy, and healthcare to broader effects on at-risk populations, from environmental policy and regulatory changes to programs for the homeless.

Human service organizations have been facing massive changes in client populations, including new immigrant and refugee groups from around the world, that require agencies to become much more culturally competent and humble and to recognize and value the diversity of not only their clients but also their staff and volunteers. HSOs will continue to be faced with funding challenges along with growing demands for new and more effective and efficient service delivery programs.

At this writing, the COVID-19 crisis is a vivid example of opportunities, and in some cases necessities, for organizational change. A recent study by LaPiana Consulting (LaPiana, 2020) found that NPOs were already facing serious funding challenges, dealing with the effects of teleworking, and needing to become more nimble and innovative. Any HSO must be dealing with these challenges, and some, especially those that are providing essential services that often have to occur in person, face the additional challenges of preventing the possible transmission of the virus. COVID-19 is having a proportionately greater impact on low-income and ethnic and racial minorities, who are often low-wage workers in "essential" work, increasing their health risks while they are already vulnerable due to their economic and demographic status. These conditions will place increased demands on HSOs serving low-income and otherwise disadvantaged populations, creating the need for organizational changes that not only can protect workers but also give them the organizational support they need to be effective.

This will also create new opportunities. HSOs that provide health services, especially those in vulnerable communities, have connections and relationships with community members that can be very valuable to public health officials needing qualified personnel to do outreach to community members regarding education on the disease and to help with essential functions such as testing, contact tracing, and vaccination. All HSOs will probably continue to be faced with serious decreases in revenues. State and local governments are already facing significant cuts due to decreased tax revenues during the economic slowdown. This will present opportunities, if not demands, for cutback management strategies as well as for innovation and intrapreneurship. For example, school social workers and other counselors might see opportunities to start or augment mental health programs in schools to respond to the effects of COVID-19 on students and families (Brennan, 2020). All of these processes are more likely to be successful if planned organizational change strategies and tactics are used.

In the midst of the COVID-19 crisis, the United States was also faced with the killing of George Floyd by police in Minneapolis, Minnesota, sparking demonstrations not only across the country but also around the world. The video of a police officer with his knee on the neck of George Floyd for nearly 8 minutes brought issues of police brutality and racial inequities, particularly regarding African Americans, to a most vivid and undeniable level of crisis. This created huge and unprecedented organizational change opportunities (actually demands) for culture change within police departments, from a "warrior culture" to a "guardian-style approach that rewards problem-solving engagement between officers and the communities they protect" (Rice, 2020). I hope that police departments will be hiring qualified organization development and diversity and inclusion consultants to help them make these changes.

Related organizational change opportunities for HSOs specifically will be in designing and implementing new strategies and practice to collaborate more deeply with communities, other organizations, and law enforcement to jointly implement collaborative initiatives to substantively address racial justice issues, not only in policing but also for overall life in poor communities. The scope of such change could range from new program designs to overall strategy changes and possible revisions of an organization's mission. HSO leaders can take these opportunities to refine and develop their organizations' capacities to advocate for change at the policy level and also to develop evidence-based programs for law enforcement and community collaboration. For some HSOs, this will be a culture change for them, from staff seeing law enforcement as hostile or negative forces to developing a culture of collaboration with law enforcement, while maintaining appropriate commitment to demands for system change. There are already well-developed models for HSO staff working with law enforcement on psychiatric emergency response teams and homeless outreach teams.

Some HSOs will be expected to attack more deeply the issues of systemic racism and other forms of discrimination in their own organizations as well as in society at large. Going beyond cultural competence and cultural humility training to addressing deep issues of discrimination within the workforce will create both challenges and opportunities for change leaders to articulate visions and plans to substantively address these longstanding concerns.

More broadly, at the macro level, the social work profession has developed 13 "Grand Challenges for Social Work" (https://grandchallengesforsocialwork. org) that are appropriately focused on broad policy in areas from health and homelessness to social and economic justice and harnessing information technology for social good. Embedded in their action recommendations are many that will require HSOs to engage in transformational changes in their operations.

In terms of effects more focused on organizational practices and operations, Schmid (2013) noted several trends facing NPOs (but that also apply to government and for-profit HSOs) that may suggest strong needs for organizational change. *Devolution and decentralization* of power from the federal to local levels may create significant challenges for NPOs in conservative states that will be less constrained by federal policies of past administrations that have provided support for the poor and disadvantaged. Privatization of formerly government services is a trend that began decades ago but is creating new challenges as more for-profit organizations are engaging in government contracting for human services.

New public management (NPM), and the related concept of *new managerialism* (Spitzmueller, 2018), both with an emphasis on applying business principles to government organizations, represent another trend that, while not new (dating to at least the reinventing government movement in the United States in the 1990s), continues to present challenges for HSOs, which are expected to use better management practices, including clearly defined outcomes with data and accountability mechanisms, to increase program efficiency and effectiveness (Germak, 2015). NPM has clearly had mixed effects on HSOs. A fuller use of effective management technologies may enhance an organization's effectiveness, but NPM may also complicate or challenge client-centered values and practices of HSOs (Hasenfeld, 2015). Spitzmueller (2018), in a study of the effects of NPM on a mental health clubhouse, asserted that "new public management is not only an instrument for monitoring and coordinating human services, it also changes the implicit conditions of work by transforming organizational incentives, resources, and demands" (p. 128). A special issue of *Human Service Organizations* (Mosley & Smith, 2018) presented several cases of the challenges that NPM has created for HSO managers, including increased demands for service integration and collaboration, the fostering of increased user choice and competition, and increased interest in social enterprise and social impact bonds (Mosley & Smith, 2018). All of these challenges force agencies to engage in organizational change.

Regardless of a HSO's mission and environmental context, a competent and proactive administrator, particularly at the executive level, as well as managers and other staff at program levels, will need to be monitoring the environment to identify any strategic issues that may impact the organization or one's own program area.

While advocacy is not the subject of this book, I believe that proactive administrators and managers should, in order to ensure that their organizations remain viable and relevant, also be engaging in advocacy to shape policies that affect their agencies, clients, and communities. For example, David Sanders (2016) described the work of Casey Family Programs to "connect the dots between what we were learning from [our] partnerships, the research, and the innovations that were being tested in the field . . . to ensure that child welfare leaders and partners had this cutting-edge knowledge and the support to change policy and practice to respond to the changing landscape" (p. 303). They worked to influence national conversations through symposia; dialogue with national, state, and local policymakers; white papers; and testimony before Congress to impact funding and support demonstration programs.

Within an organization, every new client creates opportunities for staff to provide different (better or worse) services. Every new grant or contract brings new expectations and requirements, such as new accountability mechanisms, new program models, enhanced cultural competence, and expectations for better documentation of client outcomes and increased cost effectiveness.

Growing expectations for quality improvements (e.g., better outcomes in child welfare services) and increased efficiencies (e.g., in programs such as Medicaid and Medicare) are especially prominent for local government agencies. New or revised government policies at the federal and state levels require new programs and policies at the local level, which typically require changes in practice models, training and development of staff, and modified information systems.

Newly elected local elected officials may create or modify policies regarding social problems such as homelessness, drug abuse, or mental illness that require changes in not only the city or county they oversee but also local agencies that receive funding from them through grants or contracts.

Such externally mandated policy or program changes can be implemented most simply through the development of new policies and procedures that show at least minimal compliance with new requirements, followed by the issuance of new procedure manuals and perhaps some level of training. There is growing evidence, however, that the use of planned organizational change strategies and tactics, along with effective change leadership, can result in more complete and efficient implementation and longer lasting improvements in the organization.

Particularly in the nonprofit sector, foundations and other stakeholders are increasingly interested in seeing changes through strategies including "social innovation, social entrepreneurship, social enterprise, design thinking, social impact bonds, b-corps, crowdfunding, impact investing, [and] social entrepreneurship" (Berzin & Camarena, 2018, p. xi). All of these initiatives represent organizational change, sometimes at a transformational level. The work of Berzin and Camarena regarding what they called "innovation from within" represents a specific subset of organizational change strategies and tactics to implement initiatives in these areas. I cover key principles of their work in Chapter 18.

Many funding organizations (including governments and foundations) are expecting the use of evidence-based practices (EBPs), best or promising practices, or innovative service delivery methods that need to be documented with new information systems and evaluation designs. Good research on EBPs continues to accumulate, and I discuss some of these advances in Chapter 17 as they are applicable to organizational change. Nevertheless, a lot more needs to be done, including continuing research and, at least as importantly, disseminating new knowledge to organizations in ways that they can and will use to fully implement new EBPs. Referring to an Institute of Medicine (2015) report, Enola Proctor (2017), a major leader in the EBP field, noted that the report concluded that

> too few evidence-based practices have been found to be appropriate for low-resource settings or acceptable to minority groups. Second, existing interventions do not adequately reflect the breadth of social work practice. We have too few evidence-based interventions that can inform effective community organization, case management, referral practice, resource development, administrative practice, or policy. (p. 338)

In addition to change demands from outside the organization, internal organizational dynamics such as the devaluing or unfair treatment of staff with particular demographic characteristics—ranging from race, ethnicity, and gender to age and ability status—create opportunities, or implicit demands, for organizational change. Besides enhancing cultural competence of staff and programs to better serve client populations, much still needs to be done to rectify deficiencies regarding workforce diversity, especially at the management and executive levels. This requires adoption of not only cutting-edge human resources policies but also executive leadership in supporting systemic efforts to combat discrimination and increase equity, inclusion, and empowerment of underrepresented staff in areas including race, ethnicity, gender, sexual orientation, age, and abilities.

Staff burnout and turnover continue to be ongoing problems, particularly in HSOs with very demanding expectations from external funding organizations coupled with inadequate financial support. Executives in these organizations need to be advocating externally for adequate support to fulfill mandated expectations for quality services; they can also work internally to create changes that can better support staff and improve their quality of working life.

Our organizations thus face challenges on several levels related to organizational change: learning more about how to identify and adapt appropriate evidence-based programs, learning about and adopting best practices in management and leadership systems, and also learning more about organizational change methods. This book focuses mostly on the last: finding and using the best available evidence regarding implementing organizational change, whether to implement a new EBP (including important work in the implementation science field) or create change in a different area, such as improving an information system, redesigning an organization, or increasing the cultural competence of staff.

Within an organization, a newly hired executive brings fresh perspectives and new ideas for possible implementation. A manager promoted to the executive level similarly will have ideas for changes that were perhaps not seen as possible under the former leadership. Through their regular activities, management teams will identify problems that need to be addressed or opportunities to which the organization can respond by changing policies, procedures, or programs. Individual staff members who notice procedures that are inefficient or out of date and that could be changed to improve service quality or efficiency can initiate organizational change. Staff members are acutely aware of an organization's culture and climate and probably have many ideas on how these could be improved, leading to a higher quality of working life, enhanced staff retention and job satisfaction, and ultimately better service delivery.

Even if these examples do not apply to a particular HSO, an executive who does not see other needs for organizational change should consider the words of management guru Tom Peters, who asserted that "If it ain't broken, you just haven't looked hard enough" (Peters, 1988, p. 3).

This review of the conditions and challenges facing HSOs is intended to stimulate you, dear reader, on a regular basis, to be alert to opportunities for change. You may already be aware of some of the conditions, dynamics, and demands highlighted here, and you are probably aware of other conditions or situations that suggest the need for organizational change. I expect that you and your colleagues or classmates are already addressing some of them.

While I intended this review to be brief, it now seems a bit overwhelming. I don't expect that society as a whole will adequately address everything I mentioned, at least not in the next few years, and these challenges are clearly beyond the capacities of any one organization. Individual staff members can feel overwhelmed by having to address even one of these challenges, so it will be important for you to make realistic assessments about what you and your organization can do and address challenges in a way that will not overwhelm you or the system in which you are working. If right now you could use some encouragement and validation of the important work that leaders (quite possibly including you) are doing to address these challenges, you can jump to the quotation by Meg Wheatley in Chapter 20.

Leading and Managing Change

Planned organizational change used to be commonly described as *change management*. Recently, the term *change leadership* has been more frequently used. For a little conceptual clarity, it might help here to briefly review the distinctions between *management* and *leadership* in organizations. Both are relevant to organizational change. In its most basic sense, management can be seen as doing the best you can to get through a difficult situation. Many organizations probably deal with demands for change in this way, not consciously using specific techniques or models for change, but operating based on past experiences and instincts.

More precisely, management is often seen as using traditional processes and systems, including planning, budgeting, designing, staffing, controlling, and problem-solving. Common technologies include strategic plans, budgets, Gantt charts, organization charts, and logic models. Leadership, in contrast, includes establishing direction through visioning, aligning people with the vision and strategies, and motivating and inspiring staff. In this conceptualization, change *management* would include activities such as project planning, coordinating people and resources, and developing and tracking goals and objectives. Change *leadership* typically starts with executives or other administrators, who articulate visions for improving the organization and inspire and support staff as they take on the challenges of change. Both management and leadership are needed for organizational effectiveness in general and also for effective organizational change. With that context, I briefly describe here some examples of approaches to change leadership.

At a broad level, a recent survey by McKinsey and Company (Jacquemont, Maor, & Reich, 2015), gathered data from 1,713 executives whose organizations had experienced major transformations. They ranked 24 "practical actions" that, according to McKinsey, are associated with successful implementation of an organizational change initiative. These are ranked in terms of their perceived impact. Their analysis suggested that no single action impacts success of an initiative, but "the more actions an organization takes, the more likely its transformation is to succeed" (p. 1). Many of these are in alignment with the tactics that have been seen as success factors in the research I've described here.

  Senior managers communicated openly across the organization about the transformation's progress and success
  Everyone can see how their work relates to organization's vision
  Leaders role-modeled the behavior changes they were asking employees to make
  All personnel adapt their day-to-day capacity to changes in customer demand

Senior managers communicated openly across the organization about the
transformation's implications for individuals' day-to-day work

Everyone is actively engaged in identifying errors before they reach customers

Best practices are systematically identified, shared, and improved upon

The organization develops its people so that they can surpass expectations for
performance

Managers know that their primary role is to lead and develop their teams

Performance evaluations held initiative leaders accountable for their transformation contributions

Leaders used a consistent change story to align organization around the
transformation's goals

Roles and responsibilities in the transformation were clearly defined

All personnel are fully engaged in meeting their individual goals and targets

Sufficient personnel were allocated to support initiative implementation

Expectations for new behaviors were incorporated directly into annual performance reviews

At every level of the organization, key roles for the transformation were held
by employees who actively supported it

Transformation goals were adapted for relevant employees at all levels of the
organization

Initiatives were led by line managers as part of their day-to-day responsibilities

The organization assigned high-potential individuals to lead the transformation (e.g., giving them direct responsibility for initiatives)

A capability-building program was designed to enable employees to meet
transformation goals

Teams start each day with a formal discussion about the previous day's results
and current day's work

A diagnostic tool helped quantify goals (e.g., for new mind-sets and behaviors,
cultural changes, organizational agility) for the transformation's long-term
sustainability

Leaders of initiatives received change-leadership training during the
transformation

A dedicated organizing team (e.g., a project management or transformation
office) centrally coordinated the transformation (Jacquemont et al., p. 3)

Additional broad strategies—specifically as applied to HSOs—for addressing
the huge environmental challenges listed previously come from the fields of social entrepreneurship (Linton, 2013) and innovation (Berzin & Camarena, 2018;
Berzin, Pitt-Catsouphes, & Gaitan-Rossi, 2015). These writers have paid particular attention to *intra*preneurship: members of an organization who apply
entrepreneurial principles within their organizations, including "enterprise"

initiatives such as creating businesses that employ clients and improving efficiency and effectiveness of existing programs. As I noted above, this is such an important aspect of organizational change that I cover it in more detail in Chapter 18.

Another broad strategy that HSOs can consider to adapt to dynamic and demanding environments is to increase their *agility*. In a recent article from McKinsey and Company, one of the top management consulting firms, Rieckhoff and Maxwell (2017), noted the increasing volatility, uncertainty, complexity, and ambiguity of organizational environments (VUCA, as mentioned above) and asserted that in such environments "companies that survive and grow seek the attributes of agility: the power to be both dynamic and stable at the same time" (p. 4). While they were focusing on public sector organizations, these ideas apply easily to nonprofit HSOs as well. They suggested that public sector organizations can become more agile by having "a backbone of stable elements—for example, a simple organizational structure or operating norms" (p. 5) plus the ability to use on a regular basis dynamic qualities such as those used successfully in the face of a crisis, such as law enforcement and intelligence agencies did after the 9/11 attacks.

Their research pointed to four core areas that organizations should attend to in order to enhance their agility. First, they suggested that a clear strategy, including vision and purpose, can provide both stability and, with ongoing analysis of the environment, the ability to react quickly to external changes. In a similar vein, a simple structure provides stability, and when it is augmented with decentralized decision-making and autonomy in program operations, the organization can adapt quickly as needed. The same principle applies to organizational processes. Well-designed systems in areas including information technology, finance, and human resources facilitate efficient operations, and when there are also processes for continuous improvement, organizational performance can be enhanced on an ongoing basis. Finally, they noted that people (i.e., staff) appreciate a degree of stability and having shared values and organizational culture as well as the opportunity to create change so that "agile organizations focus on creating a culture of self-improvement and stretch goals in an atmosphere of open, honest feedback. Smaller, more dynamic teams test and refine new ideas together" (p. 6). They concluded by suggesting that the first step in becoming more agile is to assess current operations and then to identify a desired future state. These suggestions each have implications for organizational change that I address in later chapters, from creating a strategic plan and engaging in ongoing strategic management to ensuring that management systems are well functioning and that the organization has clear processes for continuous improvement.

Paul Gibbons, whose *The Science of Successful Organizational Change* (2015) is mentioned occasionally in this book, has provided additional detail on "change-agile" organizations. He says that change-agile organizations have these characteristics:

- change readiness and change capability, . . . particularly regarding learning and development capacity
- not being change-fatigued or change-overloaded
- having a dynamic flow of knowledge, ideas, problem solving, initiative, and innovation—including more bottom-up, and not just top-down change
- being operationally adaptable and strategically nimble—doing the disrupting rather than being disrupted. (p. 39)

Some of these, particularly the expectation of not being change-overloaded, may seem excessively aspirational for HSOs, which are typically underresourced and face increasing demands from stakeholders and even society at large. The challenges of dealing with homelessness, gun violence (particularly the mental health aspects), immigration and refugees, and child abuse and neglect are regularly covered in the mainstream press, with no comprehensive solutions in sight. As I implied above, issues such as these at the level of the Grand Challenges will require intensive actions at the macro policy level, but policy changes will also require HSOs to change their operations; increased organizational agility will certainly help.

To What Extent Can Planned Organizational Change Really Help?

So, assuming that you do recognize the importance of organizational change, and see that there are many viable ideas and strategies for creating change, let me add here two more points regarding the success (or not) of much organizational change activity.

First, there are countless books on organizational change, mostly in the popular management press but also as textbooks for classroom use. But, as I cover in more detail in Appendix 8, an analysis of this literature suggests that there is a lot of organizational change occurring that is not based on evidence-based principles and models but relies mostly on consultant advice and/or the practice wisdom and instincts of administrators and their staff as they struggle to cope with pressures to change or improve their organizations.

It has also become axiomatic in the organizational change literature (mainly in the popular management press, again covered in more detail in Appendix 8), that 70% of organizational change efforts fail. This is often followed by some version of "hire me as a consultant and I can help you have *successful* organizational change." Hughes (2011) persuasively challenged this 70% figure and then reviewed some of the complexities that are often overlooked in a simple statement of success or failure, including difficulties of identifying factors that are associated with the outcome, multiple perspectives on the change process and its results, and the measurability of organizational change.

In a more recent review, R. Hamlin recognized the continuing limitations of research on success, but nevertheless concluded that "there is little contemporary evidence to indicate there has been any substantial increase in the success rate of OCD [organizational change and development] programs during the first two decades of the 21st century" (2019, p. 4).

McKinsey and Company, whose earlier reports used the 70% failure figure and was criticized by Hughes, reported results of a later survey of nearly 2,000 executives who had experienced major transformations, finding that "just 26% of respondents say the transformations they're most familiar with have been very or completely successful at both improving performance and equipping the organization to sustain improvements over time" (Jacquemont et al., 2015, p. 1). Their research has at least one common weakness: using only organizational executives as the data source. For example, in one study of 13 child welfare organizations, colleagues and I (Packard, McCrae, Phillips, & Scannapieco, 2015) found that the perceptions of success of an organizational change initiative varied based on how involved an employee was in the change process. I say more about this issue and broader issues of evidence regarding organizational change in Appendix 8.

Even given the limits of the research on success or failure of formal organizational change initiatives, I think it's safe to conclude that success is not ensured. Nevertheless, the McKinsey study and other research suggest that there are specific factors—many included in the generic framework offered in this book—that can enhance prospects for success.

Challenges of Implementing Organizational Change

Given all the reported failures of organizational change, I note here some of the specific challenges that can face change leaders and preliminary thoughts on how to address them.

The examples above referred to the *content* of change: *what* needs to be changed. As I discuss in the next chapter, equally important, if not more important, are the dynamics of the *process* of change: *how* the change will occur. Whereas EBP mainly addresses the content of change, such as implementing a new service delivery model, the newer field of evidence-based *management* looks more at the process of change: how managers and leaders behave to help their organizations be as effective and efficient as possible. This involves "making decisions through the conscientious, explicit, and judicious use of four sources of information: practitioner expertise and judgment, evidence from the local context, a critical evaluation of the best available research evidence, and the perspectives of those people who might be affected by the decision" (Briner, Denyer, & Rousseau, 2009, p. 19). The challenge here will be to take the time to as thoroughly as possible gather data from multiple sources before implementing a change initiative.

Taking time to gather evidence is an example of a broader challenge for change leaders: resisting the temptation to do something too quickly, perhaps to satisfy impatient external stakeholders such as elected officials, community advocates, or board members. Those concerned with issues as serious as deaths of children under child welfare system care are understandably impatient for change. An old axiom in organizations is that, given the criteria of good, fast, and cheap, you can accomplish two at a time but not all three.[1] Change leaders should be as clear as possible with both external stakeholders and staff regarding how these trade-offs will be managed, adding that getting quality, impactful results will take both time and resources. One of my most valued mentors, the late John Wedemeyer, sometimes asked, "Why is it that no one has time to do it right but everyone has time to do it over?"

R. Hamlin (2019) listed several reasons for change program failure that represent challenges for a change leader. One, managers not knowing the fundamental principles of change management, can, I hope, be addressed effectively by those who have read this book and done other professional development work. He noted the temptation of the "quick fix" solution, similar to the good/fast/cheap expectation just noted. Change leaders may be able to educate stakeholders with such expectations by sharing data on what is really needed, ideally in evidence-based terms, for their goals to be met through planned change by the organization. Two of his failings, "managers not fully appreciating the significance of the leadership and cultural aspects of change" and "not appreciating sufficiently the significance of the people issues" (pp. 6–7) show the importance of dealing with not only the content of change, which may seem simple (e.g., implement an EBP) but also the complex dynamics related to organizational culture and addressing concerns of staff. For example, change efforts can fail because change leaders

---

[1] The NFP Developer Society offers some guidelines in addressing this dilemma regarding information technology development projects at https://medium.com/@devsociety_/good-cheap-fast-pick-two-and-how-ngos-can-play-the-triangle-like-a-pro-20d1380884a8.

don't "take sufficiently into account the internal politics and the strengths/resilience of the embedded cultures" (R. Hamlin & Russ-Eft, 2019, p. 39).

More broadly, in their summary of the literature, R. Hamlin and Russ-Eft offered this list of reasons for failure in organizational change:

> (a) the change management process takes more time than originally planned; (b) unexpected problems arise during the change process; (c) co-ordination of the various change agency activities is inadequate; (d) competing demands on managers' time and crisis events distract management from properly or fully implementing the decision to bring about the desired organizational change; (e) change agency competence and capability of the various managers and supervisors involved in facilitating/managing the change are not sufficient; (f) the training and instruction given to lower level employees is inadequate; and (g) uncontrollable factors in the external environment adversely affect the implementation. (p. 41)

While prospective change leaders cannot specifically predict any of these, this list is worth using as a checklist of things to possibly anticipate. Some, such as including buffer time in the schedule, planning coordination processes, and ensuring that involved staff get the advanced training they need, can be built into the design of the process. Others must just be noted as things that might come up, requiring contingency planning.

Popular change leadership author John Kotter (2012) found several commonalities in failed change efforts, including allowing too much complacency, undercommunicating the change vision, permitting obstacles such as existing systems to block the new vision, declaring victory too soon, and neglecting to anchor changes firmly in the corporate culture. The change model described in this book addresses these factors and others that contribute to failed efforts.

As overall guides to deal with these challenges, change leaders need to

> (a) to acquire a deep understanding of the particular organization being changed and developed, (b) to become involved in the development and implementation of a suitable OCD strategy, and (c) to evaluate the effectiveness of the strategy implementation in terms of the process and outcomes. (R. Hamlin & Russ-Eft, 2019, p. 39)

So, challenges for change leaders include not only content issues of properly identifying a problem or need and setting an appropriate goal, but also thoughtful choice of strategies, tactics, and methods that are likely to lead to success. Many of these considerations receive attention in this book.

Organizational Change Defined

Before we go much further, a specific definition is in order. Schmid (2010, p. 456) defined organizational change as "the process that occurs in an HSO as a result of external constraints imposed on it or as a result of internal pressures that cause alterations and modifications in the organization's core activity, goals, strategies, structures, and service programs." More specifically, I'll adapt a definition from my own field of organization development (French & Bell, 1995). In this book, planned organizational change is seen as involving

- leadership and the mobilizing of staff to explicitly address problems, needs, or opportunities in the organization's current state,
- to move the organization to a desired future state using change processes that involve both human and technical aspects of the organization.

This definition includes some normative biases, that, as I show elsewhere in the book, have some research support. First, planned organizational change involves not only management processes in which managers analyze a situation and decide to change some aspects of organizational functioning (e.g., proposing a restructuring of the organization and changes in managerial and staff duties), but also leadership: executives or others articulating a desirable future and inspiring staff to engage in the change effort. It is focused on solving a problem or addressing a need, of course; in addition it also focuses on a future that is seen by many in the organization as desirable. Technical aspects, such as work processes, job descriptions, information systems, and reporting relationships, are likely to be involved, but planned change in this sense also pays a lot of attention to the human factor, including how staff see the change, their concerns and more importantly their input and ideas, and how everyone will work together to create a culture of support and learning. These implications are covered in detail in Chapter 4 regarding leadership philosophy and style as applied to organizational change.

Finally, in the spirit of EBP, the following definition of *evidence-based* organizational change and development can be used to underpin the broader definition above.

Evidence-based OCD is the conscientious, explicit and judicious use of current best evidence and/or action research to inform, shape, critically reflect upon, and iteratively revise decisions made in relation to the formulation and implementation of OCD interventions and the associated change management processes. (R. Hamlin, 2016, p. 129)

The principles implied in this definition are addressed, in much simpler language, in the change model covered in Section 3.

Summary

Change is inevitable in organizations. *Planned* organizational change, involving administrators and other staff as change leaders, can use evidence-based principles to consciously design and implement a process for assessing a need or opportunity, determining a desired future state, and developing and implementing a process to reach a change goal, creating better conditions and outcomes for clients, staff, and communities. As we go through a set of stages and tactics, examples from successful organizational change initiatives are used to show how this can happen.

Clients and communities who are served by our agencies most certainly deserve effective services delivered by competent, compassionate, and committed staff members. Those who support our agencies, including taxpayers, donors, philanthropists, policymakers, and board members, deserve to have their support and contributions used to deliver programs that are not only effective but also efficient in their use of valuable financial and staff resources. Staff, from front-line workers and support staff to executives, deserve opportunities to have their unique competencies used in the service of the noble purposes of our organizations, so that they can experience professional fulfillment and help change the lives of those they serve. Change leadership and organizational change can be powerful forces to help fulfill all these aspirations. I hope that this book provides knowledge and encouragement to change leaders and staff that will enhance the prospects for the success of organizational change initiatives.

Reflection and Focusing Questions

1. What challenges in the environment are facing your organization?
2. What could you and others be doing to change operations to improve effectiveness, client outcomes, efficient use of resources, or staff morale?
3. To what extent could a planned organizational change process be useful to your organization?
4. What issues, problems, opportunities, or challenges need attention?

2

A Conceptual Framework

> In new science, the underlying currents are a movement toward
> holism, toward understanding the system as a system and giving
> primary value to the relationships that exist among seemingly dis-
> crete parts.... Disorder can play a critical role in giving birth to new,
> higher forms of order.
>
> —Margaret Wheatley (*Leadership and the New Science*,
> 1992, pp. 9, 11)

The conceptual framework presented here has two broad elements. The first element considers ways of looking at organizational change, including theories
of organizational change and, flowing from that, perspectives from which to
view change. The second element is essentially a model of steps to take when
planning, designing, and implementing organizational change. While particular sections of the second area offer the most promise for developing actionable practice principles, particularly in terms of organizational change tactics,
the overall conceptual model is important to ensure that new knowledge is adequately contextualized.

Key Theories of Organizational Change

At the broadest level, I'll highlight here several theories commonly used to
frame discussions of organizational change (Fernandez & Rainey, 2006; Garrow
& Hasenfeld, 2010; Schmid, 2010). These can shape a change leader's views of
organizational change and offer some things to consider when embarking on
organizational change. These theories also represent different perspectives for
seeing the same phenomena.

- *Life cycle* theories suggest that managers should anticipate normal stages of
  growth (e.g., needs for a new organization to create formal administrative
  systems), and that when an organization becomes "mature," it will still need
  to continue to change to avoid stagnation.

Organizational Change for the Human Services. Thomas Packard, Oxford University Press. © Oxford University Press
2021. DOI: 10.1093/oso/9780197549995.003.0003

- *Evolution theories* suggest that organizations will have to adapt to environmental challenges in order to survive.
- *Institutional* theory suggests that an organization will follow the trends in its field, such as, in the human services, incorporating evidence-based practices or developing advanced accountability systems, or following other relevant "rules" in the organization's environment.
- *Stakeholder* theories focus on how the organization adapts in order to satisfy key stakeholders, including funding organizations and community groups.
- *Political* theories suggest that interest groups within an organization compete and bargain with each other, and that these dynamics are part of organizational change processes.
- *Rational adaptation* approaches suggest that managers and other staff can use their human agency to respond to external and internal forces for change.

The emphasis here is on rational adaptation approaches that see managers and other staff as change agents who can assess their environments and internal conditions and then purposefully drive change within their organizations. Within this framework, however, dynamics related to other theories may operate. While many human service organizations (HSOs) have reached a life cycle level of maturity, with well-developed management systems, further changes will be needed to ensure that the organization continues to grow and adapt and does not become a rigid bureaucracy. Related to this, evolution and institutional theories can help an administrator continually monitor the agency environment, identifying trends to which the agency must respond in order to thrive. Stakeholder theory can provide specific focus on how the needs and expectations of external and internal stakeholders point to expectations for change. Political theory here applies to power dynamics within an organization and can remind a change leader to be alert to the key interest groups and factions that may support or resist change.

Within these theories, there are multiple perspectives from which to view organizational change. Each perspective can help change leaders assess the organization, make sense of what they are seeing, and develop plans for change.

Planned Versus Unplanned Change

At the broadest level, organizational change may be planned or unplanned. Change leaders, by assessing external trends and internal organizational dynamics, stakeholder expectations, and other forces, can identify an opportunity or need for change and put a change process in motion. On the other hand, organizations and staff constantly change in small ways, such as programs developing new procedures or staff becoming less satisfied at work, perhaps without even recognizing that change is occurring. The latter may be considered examples of *unplanned* change. Environmental forces such as funding cuts can simply *happen* to organizations, dictating that change must occur. Internal dynamics such as morale problems coming to a head, resulting in staff so dissatisfied that the work environment is clearly affected, can be another source of unplanned change. Such changes that come without intention from the organization can, however, be followed by purposeful, planned organizational change to deal with such negative developments affecting an organization

A most vivid example of unanticipated demands for change is the Covid-19 crisis that began in 2020. Leaving aside prevention and policy aspects such as the needs for ample supplies of necessary equipment and well-developed disaster plans, here we can consider how organizational change can occur in organizations that have been affected by Covid-19.

Such a crisis may precipitate *emergent* change, which can be "continuous, unpredictable, and essentially political in nature" (Livne-Tarandach & Bartunek, 2009, p. 5). Emergent change "should not be perceived as a series of planned linear events within a given period of time. Rather it is best viewed as a continuous, open-ended process of adaptation to changing circumstances and conditions" (Livne-Tarandach & Bartunek, 2009, p. 6). These authors described *transcendence* as a way of integrating the dichotomous elements of planned and emergent change, which involves understanding the tensions involved and critically examining existing assumptions in order to develop some kind of new synthesis of the existing crisis conditions and the use of more deliberate planned change processes.

The perspectives of *complex adaptive systems* (CASs), adapted from chaos and complexity theory, may offer guidance to change leaders facing particularly complicated, and sometimes crisis-based, situations such as hospitals dealing with the Covid crisis. This mindset can offer not only reminders to examine traditional assumptions and perspectives but also reassurance that the apparent chaos that an organization is experiencing can, in fact, be managed and successfully addressed, however erratic and unplanned the process may seem at the time. This perspective may be particularly useful in organizations where there are high amounts of interconnectedness and interdependence across units or functions. A CAS perspective is well suited to conditions of uncertainty, disagreement about causes of the problem, possible unanticipated consequences, and perhaps even a lack of clarity about a desired end state (Choflet, Packard, & Stashower, in press). Participative leadership styles, and in particular, adaptive leadership, covered in Chapter 4, and should be particularly useful in these situations, facilitating shared leadership in which potentially anyone can "contribute ideas and take action" (Khan et al., 2018, p. 4).

While recognizing such complex and challenging conditions as these may exist, the focus here is on *planned* change, whether proactive, based on anticipating a need or opportunity, or reactive, based on unanticipated forces. In either case, the material presented in this book can serve as a foundation for adopting effective change strategies and tactics that can be proactively used by administrators, other staff, and consultants.

While planned change happens within all types of organizations, particular attention is given here to change principles as they can be applied in HSOs, drawing on the general management, nonprofit management, and public administration literatures as needed.

Levels of Change

Change can range from minor or incremental to major or transformational, with the latter requiring a greater use of planned change principles. Anderson and Ackerman-Anderson (2011) and others have described three types, or levels, of organizational change.

Developmental change involves adjustments to existing operations or improving a skill, method, or process that does not currently meet the organization's standard: basically improving something that already exists. This level of change is the least threatening to employees and the easiest to manage. Examples include simple problem-solving, routine training, changing a hiring or accounting process, and improving communications. These are often handled within a program or unit and don't require involvement of agency leaders.

Transitional change involves implementing something new and abandoning old ways of functioning. This move through a transitional period to a new future state requires patience and time. Anderson and Ackerman Anderson (2011) have found in their consulting that transitional changes are likely to require some amount of extra leadership, in the case of an HSO, maybe from a program manager. This involvement may be as simple as being a "sponsor" (discussed in a later chapter; basically someone in a position of authority who shows support for the change, including as needed providing resources or staff time to work on it). Examples might include implementing a new information technology system, simple reorganizations of staff roles, and implementing a new program. Leader support (including perhaps some training and coaching of staff), forming a task group, identifying the goal, assigning roles, and developing and following a time-line will sometimes be adequate.

However, an agency executive should not underestimate the scope of change as seen from the point of view of staff. You may assume that implementing a new information technology system or a new performance appraisal system will be very simple, while staff involved will see the complexities and the time it will take as well as disruptions to their normal routines. If you are in doubt, consider treating the change as a transformational one, or at least build in more aspects of the planned change process that are presented in later chapters. Definitely consult with your relevant managers and perhaps supervisors and others in-volved to see how they perceive the change and develop a plan that will be most appropriate.

The most extreme form of change is *transformational change*, which requires, according to Anderson and Ackerman Anderson (2011, p. 55), "a radical shift of strategy, structure, systems, processes, or technology . . . so significant that it requires a shift of culture, behavior, and mind-set . . . to implement and sustain over time." This might evolve out of necessity, for example, as a result of major policy changes such as managed care or a shift to outcomes measurement or performance-based contracting required by funding organizations. This will be a nonlinear process, perhaps with occasional chaos; the use of a planned change process, with extensive involvement of many staff and comprehensive communi-cation tools, can make the process much more manageable. It could even involve the goal or implementation plans changing as people get into the process. The new state after such change, and even the change process itself, is likely to involve a new culture, new beliefs, and awareness of new possibilities. Because of these complexities, a participative leadership style will clearly be needed. It might be especially difficult for an executive to share power and control when the outcome and the way to get there are so undefined at the beginning. (In fact, one distinc-tion between transitional and transformational change is that for the latter, the new state might not be fully known until late in the process.) This will require that you as a change leader have high confidence in the skills and commitment of your staff, who will be engaging in lots of activities and decision-making in which you won't be directly involved.

For transformational change and some transitional changes, the use of the planned change process and change technologies in this book should enhance the prospects of the organization reaching its desired new state. Depending on the complexities of a need or opportunity, the tactics and methods for planned change may be applied selectively, with more or less formal use of specifics. Consultants may also be brought into any change process as appropriate.

Change Context, Content, and Process

Another set of concepts may help you make sense of a complex change process and be alert to things that will need attention along the way. Organizational change can be viewed in terms of its *context*, its *content*, and the change *process* (Armenakis & Bedeian, 1999). I'll start by looking at change context because this is what will drive many decisions to engage in a planned organizational change initiative. In a study of 33 organizations, Higgs and Rowland (2010) found that change leaders paid inadequate attention to "broader contextual factors involved in the change process" (p. 369). Many conditions, such as environmental forces and organizational characteristics can be considered when assessing for and planning a change process.

Change *context* refers to both external and internal factors, including the problem, need, challenge, or opportunity that will be the focus of the change process. External contextual factors include environmental changes such as new governmental policies, decreases in funding, expectations for greater accountability to funding organizations and, most broadly, any "public expectations" (Akingbola, Rogers, & Baluch, 2019, p. 6). Government and both nonprofit and for-profit HSOs can face competitive pressures from others providing the same or similar services. Developments such as the Affordable Care Act, evidence-based practice, and performance-based contracting have precipitated needs for organizational change, requiring that HSOs adapt to these new expectations and make changes to organizational systems. Internal contextual factors include leadership characteristics, organization culture and climate, and staff characteristics and attitudes. Human resource management practices can be important internal context factors (Akingbola et al., pp. 24–26). An organizational change may have impacts on job designs and performance management and reward systems, and will certainly involve some new staff training. Existing human resource policies may need to be considered while planning employee involvement in change activities.

Change *content*, according to Anderson and Ackerman-Anderson (2011), looks at "what in the organization needs to change, such as structure, systems, business processes, technology, products, or services" (p. 52). This typically includes the goals and targets for change (a desired future state) and the aspects of the organization that need to be changed. Any of the contextual factors just mentioned could be examples of content areas for change.

Change content can be further differentiated into *administrative* changes such as changing the organization's design or culture and *program* or *technical* changes to services, such as implementing a new evidence-based practice.

Change *process* includes assessment considerations, including staff readiness and resistance, organizational change capacity; leadership considerations;

change strategy and tactics; roles and systems for those involved in the change initiative; and methods such as Total Quality Management and organization development (OD). This represents the bulk of the change process and is discussed in detail in later chapters.

A Conceptual Model of Planned Organizational Change

Within these perspectives on organizational change, planned change can be seen as a series of steps, including identifying a need or opportunity, setting a change goal, assessing organizational conditions, choosing a strategy, implementing the change process using change tactics and specific change technologies and methods, institutionalizing the change, and assessing outcomes of the change process.

The model presented in Figure 2.1 is consistent with common planned change models, including those of Akingbola et al. (2019); Anderson and Ackerman Anderson (2010); Burke (2018); Hemmelgarn and Glisson (2018); Kotter (1996); Proehl (2001); Whelan-Berry and Somerville (2010); and Young (2009) and those summarized by Al-Haddad and Kotnour (2015); Palmer, Dunford, and Akin (2017); and Stouten, Rousseau, and Cremer (2018).

In the model used here, I include the essential elements that consistently show up, especially those with empirical support. Here are the steps in the process that I cover in this book. Most of these steps occur at the tactics stage, where the vast majority of change activities happen.

1. Identify the problem, need, challenge, or opportunity
2. Identify the desired future state: the change goal
3. Assess the present: context, content, and process (external and internal factors)
4. Determine an overall change strategy
5. Communicate the need for and desirability of the change
6. Create a sense of urgency
7. Communicate the change vision
8. Develop the action system
9. Implement the change
10. Develop and maintain support
11. Institutionalize the change
12. Evaluate the change

While this can be seen as a phase model suggesting sequential activities, it is in fact dynamic: Steps may be repeated or modified based on experiences during

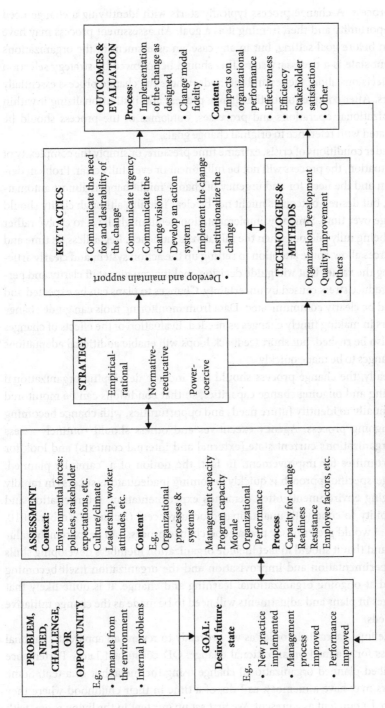

Figure 2.1 A conceptual framework for organizational change.

PROBLEM, NEED, CHALLENGE, OR OPPORTUNITY

E.g.,
• Demands from the environment
• Internal problems

GOAL: Desired future state

E.g.,
• New practice implemented
• Management process improved
• Performance improved

ASSESSMENT

Context:
Environmental forces: policies, stakeholder expectations, etc.
Culture/climate
Leadership, worker attitudes, etc.

Content
E.g.,
Organizational processes & systems
Management capacity
Program capacity
Morale
Organizational Performance

Process
Capacity for change
Readiness
Resistance
Employee factors, etc.

STRATEGY

Empirical-rational
Normative-reeducative
Power-coercive

KEY TACTICS

• Communicate the need for and desirability of the change
• Communicate urgency
• Communicate the change vision
• Develop an action system
• Implement the change
• Institutionalize the change
• Develop and maintain support

TECHNOLOGIES & METHODS

• Organization Development
• Quality Improvement
• Others

OUTCOMES & EVALUATION

Process:
• Implementation of the change as designed
• Change model fidelity

Content:
• Impacts on organizational performance
• Effectiveness
• Efficiency
• Stakeholder satisfaction
• Other

the process. A change process typically starts with identifying a change need or opportunity and then framing it as a goal. An assessment process may have begun before goal setting, but in any case, an assessment of the organization's current state is a necessary step. This should be followed by strategy selection and decisions about tactics and methods, where the change process essentially occurs. After completion of the change process and institutionalizing it within organizational operations and processes, outcomes of the process should be evaluated with reference to original change goals.

Under conditions of crisis, extreme time pressure, or simply the complexity of the situation, the process will not be fully linear or even fully clear. Problem definition and the need for and urgency of change might happen almost automatically, but desired outcomes might not be clear initially, although clarity should emerge over time. Similarly, implementation detail might have to evolve rather than being fully laid out when the initiative is launched. Regardless, as time and resources allow, some attention to setting up the action system and clearly articulating the values that will guide decision-making can give staff clarity and perhaps reduce stress caused by uncertainty. Changes to plans can be expected and should be clearly communicated. Data from monitoring tools can guide change leaders in making timely changes as needed. Evaluation of the effects of changes will also be rushed, but short feedback loops will enable additional adaptations or changes to be made quickly.

Ideally, the change process should also include developing organizational learning and ongoing change capacities, so that conditions can be monitored continually to identify future needs and opportunities, with change becoming an ongoing process. Agency executives and others should routinely assess the organization's current state (external and internal contexts) and look for opportunities for improvement. In fact, the notion of a "carefully planned, change-specific approach is quickly becoming inadequate as success in rapidly changing environments often demands experimentation, improvisation and the ability to cope with unanticipated occurrences" (Buono & Kerber, 2010, p. 10). I would prefer to say that a good change process can be extremely valuable, and that it should in fact include organization members developing skills in experimentation and improvisation and the organization itself becoming skilled at ongoing organizational learning and change. It is quite likely that changes in plans and adjustments will need to be made as the change initiative proceeds.

One final caveat is in order as we get ready to review an apparently rational process for planned organizational change. OD consultant Larry Porter once described planned organizational change using the metaphor of a tent. Some readers may have a memory, as I do, of a time in their childhood where they received a pup tent as a present. We first set up our tent in the living room, with little effort and much subsequent fun. However, in the "real world," a tent may be set up when the campers arrive after dark at a campsite, in the rain, on a hill with water running through, and ending up on a hard, lumpy surface and missing at least two tent stakes. (My wife and I had one such adventure near Yellowstone Park and ended up spending the night in a cheap motel near the park.) The process as described here is like setting up a tent in your living room, and actual organizational change is more like dealing with a dark, rainy campsite. The steps should all be done, but there will be inevitable complications and challenges that will need to be addressed.

And, while these steps are presented in the order that they should normally occur, there may be times when the order may change, or, more commonly, steps may need to be partly repeated based on new developments or on broadening the effort to new parts of the organization. For example, while this model positions assessment to occur after goal setting, at least some amount of assessment should be occurring as part of the initial analysis of a problem, need, or opportunity for change as a step before goal setting. Some other steps, particularly developing and maintaining support, may occur at the same time as another step.

As I go through these steps, I insert segments of a hypothetical case to briefly illustrate what can happen at each stage. I present this assuming ideal conditions in terms of executive and all staff commitment to the process, adequate resources (mainly staff time and fees for consultants), while recognizing that things are always more complicated and challenging than anticipated. This case is mainly intended to give you a feel for how a well-executed change process could look. Many organizational change concepts are identified here with italics and are fully explained in later chapters.

Problem, Need, Opportunity, or Challenge for Change

Before beginning to plan a change initiative based on a problem, need, opportunity, or challenge that you face, it might be worth stepping back a bit to look at your big picture. What is the context of the change idea that you are considering? Could it in fact be part of something bigger? You might quickly, and correctly, decide that what you want to address is, in fact properly framed, and dealing with broader contextual issues will not be relevant, but at least consider this before beginning. For example, you may conclude that your goal of implementing a new evidence-based program is a simple and appropriate way to deal with the fact that one of your funders is requiring an evidence-based program if you want to continue to receive funds from them. Or, a funder may require that you adopt a particular information system. In such a case, you may want to consider the information system for the program of interest to the funder, but you may also consider whether or not it would be appropriate to look at your overall agency information system and see if the scope of change should be for not only one program, but also the whole agency. It might make more sense to adopt a new system that works for all programs and also ensures data management for all of them as a whole. That would change the scope of the change initiative.

Beyond a basic situational assessment of a change idea, note that any change initiative should be driven by and be consistent with the organization's current and planned strategy. If the agency does not have a current strategic plan, a strategic planning process may be the first appropriate change activity. At a deeper level, if the absence of a strategic plan or any other management system deficiency is reflective of inadequate management capacity overall, a first change activity may involve building management capacity in general, through management consultation, training, and/or leadership development. If a current strategy seems in some way inappropriate or inadequate for addressing the current challenge, an update to the strategic plan may be necessary; this itself can become a formal organizational change process.

Assuming, then, that larger contextual or system issues are being adequately addressed, your organizational change process can begin. This typically starts when agency administrators or other staff become aware of a condition that requires organizational change. Several examples were mentioned above as part of the context of change, including external demands or challenges facing the agency or internal conditions such as substandard program performance, budget deficits, inadequate information systems or human resource processes, or employee morale issues.

A need or opportunity for change should also be assessed in terms of the level of change that will be needed. Developmental change can move forward without much particular attention to planned change processes, other than ensuring that relevant staff are involved and a problem-solving process is followed. Transitional or transformational change may indicate that it would be wise to initiate a more comprehensive planned change process.

Initial thinking and discussions may involve only an agency executive and a management team, but it may be useful, even at this early stage, to broaden the dialogue to include others in the organization. This may enrich the initial assessment through hearing other perspectives and should also begin to build staff commitment to working collaboratively and participatively on the challenges or opportunities facing the organization.

As I mentioned, what comes out of this initial analysis and discussion should be treated as being open to further thinking, analysis, and idea sharing that might lead to a redefinition of the situation. As is often the case, an initial focus may be on a symptom, and further analysis and discussion may lead to a more fundamental underlying cause that should be the target of action. In any case, more detailed analysis is built in to later stages as well.

I now introduce the hypothetical case to illustrate steps in the change process.

The Community Services Center (CSC) was founded in a working-class community in the 1940s to provide services to residents, including recent immigrants from rural areas moving to the city for employment opportunities. The demographics of the community have changed over the decades, from a primarily White population to more Black residents, and most recently there has been a large number of immigrants from Somalia.

While the demographics changed in the local communities being served by the CSC, the agency's workforce evolved more slowly, always maintaining a large number of White staff, especially in the upper ranks. Front-line staff had evolved to include more Black and Asian American employees. With the recent influx of a large number of refugees and other immigrants from Somalia, the agency was receiving increasing pressure from community residents to change their services not only to better meet the needs of new immigrants but also to be more understanding of and responsive to the cultural characteristics of more recent community members. Lower level staff were increasingly frustrated about limited advancement possibilities and the continued overrepresentation of White staff in the management ranks.

Change Goal

Next, the problem, need, opportunity, or challenge is framed as a change goal, connecting the problematic current state with a desired future state. Goals of organizational change are typically based on responses to external or internal pressures for improvement and can range from implementing new strategies or policies, such as welfare reform or evidence-based practices to internal concerns such as funding reductions, staff retention, weak management systems, or performance improvement. This stage may not initially involve a full assessment, or what consultants often call a "diagnosis," of the organization in terms of its current functioning and areas that need to be addressed or used to support the change. The initial goal may be simple and broad, with further analysis and detailing during the assessment stage.

Changing organizational culture is a common change goal. In HSOs, examples include creating a culture oriented to organizational learning (Austin & Hopkins, 2004) and implementing an evidence-based practice as culture change (Austin & Claassen, 2008). These receive more attention in Chapters 15 and 16.

Even in the apparent absence of an urgently needed change, a proactive agency executive may simply have a desire to improve the organization's functioning or outcomes in some way and may need to do a full assessment of the organization in order to identify specific areas for improvement, which can then be reframed as change goals. This more detailed assessment may follow the identification of a change goal and is addressed in the next section.

Once change goals have been identified, a more detailed assessment of organizational conditions can help to both identify leverage points and targets for change and identify additional change opportunities. Eventually, ideally after introducing the change goal to the rest of the organization, specific objectives, for both the outcome of the change and the steps in the change process, should be developed in collaboration with staff. This will help people maintain focus and commitment as well as aid in the evaluation of the change initiative.

The CSC's executive team realized that they would need to seriously address both of the identified areas of concern. They set *change goals* to (1) ensure that all front-line staff, supervisors, and even management had cultural competence knowledge and skills to effectively serve the current client populations and (2) address any issues of discrimination in the workforce to ensure high levels of diversity, equity, and inclusion (DEI) throughout the agency.

Assessment

By now, those initially involved in the change process would have done a fair amount of assessment of external and contextual factors and determined an overall change goal. Depending on the scope or complexity of the challenges being faced and the proposed change goal, it might help at this point to involve other staff in further assessment. If only the agency executive has been part of this thinking so far, it would be appropriate to bring this to the agency's executive team for further discussion, input, and analysis. In a nongovernmental organization, briefing of the board of directors may be appropriate, especially if it involves policy or financial issues. Depending on scope and focus, involving other staff at this early stage should help a lot.

You will see throughout this book that participative decision-making is a major interest of mine. As I explain in more detail in later discussion, there is some evidence that greater staff participation in decision-making can lead to not only more committed staff but also, maybe more importantly, improved decisions and outcomes. For example, if a funding organization has required that an agency's program must add extensive outcomes measurement to a program, perhaps in the context of performance-based contracting, it would make a lot of sense to quickly involve staff in the affected program and other relevant staff, such as data systems or evaluation specialists.

In addition to assessing the context for a potential change, doing an assessment as part of organizational change involves two layers: *content* and *process*. As noted above, assessment regarding *content* includes identification of problems, issues, or conditions in the organization that may benefit from organizational change. Assessment regarding the *process* of change looks at factors including the organization's readiness and capacity for change and possible sources of resistance. These are covered in detail in the chapter on assessment and goal setting.

Thanks to a generous grant from a local foundation, the CSC was able to hire two consultants: one from a firm specializing in DEI issues in HSOs and an *organization development* consultant with experience with nonprofit organizations.

To learn more about client complaints regarding inadequate language capacities and services as well as staff being deficient in their knowledge of the new immigrant cultures, the agency decided to conduct a comprehensive needs assessment and asset mapping process to ensure that they clearly understood the conditions in the community to which they could respond with services.

To assess their cultural competence capacities, the DEI consultant led staff in implementing a *cultural competence assessment*. Because there had also been complaints about unfair treatment of staff and occasional disrespectful comments about clients made by supervisors and managers, the consultant conducted *focus groups* with separate groups of staff based on their racial, ethnic, and gender identities and also assessed agency policies and procedures to identify areas that might reflect discrimination of any kind. The consultant summarized data and presented findings (anonymous major themes) to the executive team and then to any program staff who were interested.

The OD consultant held some individual meetings with the chief executive officer (CEO), and suggested that she take a specific look at her own leadership styles as they impacted staff. She arranged to have a *360-degree feedback process* for the CEO and also to interview key staff about her behaviors. The consultant fed back themes to the CEO to help assess her capacities to be a change leader on this change initiative. The OD consultant also worked with staff to assess their *readiness* and *capacity* (e.g., their commitment to change and feelings of self-efficacy regarding change) to engage in a significant organizational change process. The OD consultant fed back all these data at an off-site *team-building* session with the executive team, which included the directors of all programs and administrative functions such as human resources. After identifying their strengths and limitations in readiness and capacity, they conducted a *force field analysis* to examine factors that would support the change and those that might restrain the effort.

Strategies

Based on the change goals and assessment of conditions outside and within the organization, broad change strategies are selected. A change strategy may be defined as "the general design or plan of action," contrasted with tactics—"the concrete and specific actions that flow from the strategy" (Lauer, cited in Connor, Lake, & Stackman, 2003, p. 122).

One classic conceptualization of change strategies suggests that organizational change can be based on rational and analytical methods, attention to individual and interpersonal processes, or the use of power (Burke, 2018). Specifically, *empirical–rational* strategies assume that "people are rational and that they will follow their rational self-interest once it is made apparent to them" (p. 196). In this approach, research findings and analytical techniques are used by change leaders to show what needs to be done and what change processes should be used.

Normative–reeducative strategies assume that "people conform and are committed to sociocultural norms" (p. 198). This strategy is reflected in the use of extensive employee participation in the change process through techniques such as group problem-solving. Several of the leadership styles discussed in Chapter 4 would be appropriate styles to use with this strategy.

Power–coercive strategies suggest using power, for example, by applying "political and economic sanctions for noncompliance with the proposed change" (p. 199).

A change initiative could use more than one of these strategies depending on the particular situation. Change leaders should give thoughtful consideration to relevant contingency factors, including pressures and expectations from the organization's environment, organizational culture and climate, and the values of the organization and its change leaders.

With the preliminary assessments of the CSC's community, the issues related to cultural competence and discrimination or bias, and readiness to engage in this change initiative, the executive team chose overall strategies to guide them. They chose an empirical–rational strategy to share all the information they had gathered about changing community needs and internal morale problems related to diversity dynamics. They also planned to use a normative–reeducative strategy to frame the change effort in terms of the agency's mission, the values and ethics of their helping professions, and their commitment to provide the best possible services and support a high quality working life for staff.

Tactics

After a comprehensive assessment has been completed, goals have been set, and strategies are selected, change leaders should select specific tactics, or practice behaviors, to address the goals to take the organization to the desired future state. The steps covered so far are more likely to have been done by a relatively small group—maybe an executive team, selected managers, and representatives of affected parts of the organization. At this point, the change process becomes much more public, potentially involving all staff in the organization. This staff involvement can range from heavy, regular involvement in planning and making decisions regarding the project's change activities to working on change activities such as problem identification and analysis; group problem-solving; and team building; or to simply receiving training, briefings, or updates on the change process.

The relatively small size of the Key Tactics box in Figure 2.1 understates its importance. Three chapters are devoted to covering those steps in detail. You can see in the figure that *develop and maintain support* is inserted vertically to suggest that it should be happening at every stage of the process. As I cover in more detail later in the book, this suggests that the change leader should clearly support both the change process and the staff who will be working on it and should also work to ensure that staff support the change process.

Also, Figure 2.1 has evaluation as a separate step, showing the feedback loop returning to see if goals were accomplished and the initial conditions were adequately addressed.

And, partly so the figure will not be too dense and partly to accent the overall key tactics, some of the other tactics that have shown up in the research literature are not in that box in Figure 2.1. The full list of tactics is in Figure 2.2. All these are covered in Section 3.

There are several important points embedded in these steps. For example, change leaders need to clearly and persuasively communicate the need and urgency for change and the expected outcomes. Top management must show support and commitment through designating a senior individual or group to champion the cause for change and forming a broad-based team of staff to guide the change. Key individuals and groups affected by the change should be solicited for their support, and widespread participation of staff in the change process should be encouraged. Systems need to be designed to plan and monitor implementation of the change process, and all employees need to be kept informed regarding progress. Results of the change initiative need to be reported to staff and institutionalized through formal changes in policies and procedures, new or modified staff roles, permanent funding, or other mechanisms.

1. Clearly and persuasively communicate the need for and desirability of the change
2. Clearly and persuasively communicate the urgency for the change
3. Share information to document the change problem to be addressed
4. Clearly communicate the vision and outcomes for the change
5. Clarify the plan for how the change process will be implemented (including basic activities and who would be involved)
6. Provide top management support and commitment, including a senior individual or group to champion the cause for change
7. Select a cross section of employees for a team to guide the change
8. Provide for staff the information and training needed to implement the change
9. Involve and solicit for their support key individuals and groups affected by the change
10. Ensure widespread participation of staff in the change process
11. Provide adequate opportunities for team building and conflict management
12. Ensure support by political overseers (e.g., Board or CAO/CEO)
13. Ensure support by collaborating organizations and other community partners
14. Clearly communicate progress on the change process throughout the organization
15. Provide sufficient resources (staff time, necessary funding) for the change process
16. Ensure that any concerns of staff are addressed
17. Use monitoring tools to track progress and results
18. Revise project activities as appropriate based on new information or changing conditions
19. Institutionalize the results of the change process through formal changes in policies and procedures, training, new or modified staff roles, permanent funding, etc.
20. Evaluate the results of the change process using data (e.g., pre-post data)
21. Make staff aware of the results of the change process

Figure 2.2 Change tactics. CAO, chief administrative officer; CEO, chief executive officer.

A broader and equally important point is that these steps are not strictly linear. For example, one tactic, *communicate the change vision*, includes a brief description of the action system, which is more fully covered in a later stage. This suggests that initial planning by change leaders should describe, at least in general terms, plans for the overall process, all the way to how it will be evaluated. Knowing something about how the initiative will be evaluated can guide planning and implementation by ensuring that everything addressed in the evaluation, including data to be measured, will be built in early. The plan should be treated as organic and malleable. Changes in the plan are likely once the process gets underway.

The next big step for the CSC was to introduce the change initiative to the rest of the staff. The executive team and the consultants held all-staff sessions in each program and in the administrative office to launch the initiative. The CEO and other executive team members conveyed the *urgency* and the *need* to address these problems and challenges. They articulated a *vision* for how the agency would look when they had fully responded to new community needs and expectations as well as to concerns that had been identified by staff. They also described the *action system* for the change process. They would form a *change leadership team* consisting of representatives of all programs and all staff levels to oversee the change effort. The CEO was identified as the *sponsor* of the change process, who would, along with the executive team, provide ongoing support, including making staff time available for change activities and showing her personal investment in the process. She also emphasized that they had briefed the board of directors, and the board was fully supportive of this process. The head of human resources would be given some assigned time to serve as the *change champion*, who would coordinate overall change activities in conjunction with the OD consultant. Staff were told that they would have ample opportunities to participate through involvement in *action teams* that would analyze particular problems that had been identified and recommend solutions. The CEO realized that there might be *resistance* to change, and that staff might not feel they had the skills or time to participate. The executive team and other managers vowed to show ongoing *support* to staff and work teams throughout this demanding process. They would ensure that staff would receive any necessary training in areas such as *brainstorming*, *creative problem-solving*, and *conflict management*. The OD consultant outlined a process for *monitoring* all the change activities and providing *ongoing communication* with staff to both keep people informed and hear about any concerns or emerging issues. All the ideas for changes would be forwarded to the change leadership team for review and action, with items going to the executive team as needed.

Over time, many program changes were anticipated. The executive team expected that there may even be changes to the agency's mission statement, vision, and values. Additions to the strategic plan would be likely, leading to new or modified goals and objectives in program and administrative operations. As new processes or systems were implemented, they would be *institutionalized* through inclusion in policies and procedures documents and staff training. At the all staff meetings, the CEO would emphasize that this will be a long-term process, and attention to these issues would be ongoing to ensure that the agency achieves its desired levels of excellence in service to the community and treatment of staff.

Technologies and Methods

In an organizational change process, generic change tactics such as those just mentioned can be augmented with specific organizational change technologies, and methods, based on the organizational setting, conditions, and change goals. While no precise definitions contrast technologies, methods, and other related terms such as interventions, I offer some brief distinctions here. Change methods are broad conceptualizations of a set of tactics and/or technologies. Some of the main generic change methods, such as OD and those specific to the human services such as the ARC (Availability, Responsiveness, and Continuity) model, are described briefly here and covered in more detail in later chapters. Technologies are in fact much more broadly defined than the common example of information technologies. Most broadly, a technology is a transformation process—anything from turning raw materials into smartphones to, in organizational change, transforming a dysfunctional team into a highly functioning one. Team building, for example, is a change technology that, in OD, is sometimes referred to as an intervention.

Specific organizational change technologies include activities that typically happen in a workshop setting, such as team building, conflict management, and role clarification. Quality improvement methods such as Total Quality Management can be seen as change technologies. Employee surveys are a technology that can operate at the level of the whole organization. These and others are covered in Chapters 12 and 14.

Ideally, of course, thoughtful attention to issues of assessment and the selection of appropriate change strategies, tactics, technologies, and methods will be followed by full implementation of the plan, including institutionalizing the changes within the organization's management systems and culture, to achieve the change goals.

An often neglected step of the change process is explicitly reviewing what actually happened and what results are evident: evaluating both the implementation of the change process and the actual outcomes.

The OD consultant would administer an agency-wide *employee survey* to gather additional data on the concerns related to both services and internal organizational dynamics, including morale. Anonymous data summaries would be provided at sessions with all staff groups for identification of problems to address. The OD consultant would be available to conduct *team-building sessions* with staff groups and would facilitate *conflict management* sessions as needed.

Action teams would receive facilitation by the OD consultant regarding *brainstorming, problem-solving,* and other techniques such as *Continuous Quality Improvement* methods as needed.

Change technologies to address cultural competence and diversity issues would be used by the DEI consultant. As needed, these might include *a task force on racial disparities and disproportionalities, workshops on self-care and internalized oppression, racial affinity groups or caucuses, antiracism training* for all program managers, and changes in the agency's strategic plan, policies, and procedures, especially regarding hiring and promotions.

Eventually, changes implemented could include new cultural competence and humility training; revised human resources policies and procedures for hiring diverse staff; ongoing staff support, including mentoring; and equitable promotion and performance appraisal processes.

Outcomes of the Change Process

As you can see in Figure 2.1, the outcomes of an organizational change effort can be evaluated in terms of both process and content. Evaluation of the change *process* typically assesses the extent of implementation of the change process as designed (e.g., the extent to which the change process plan was followed). If a specific change model, such as ARC, was used, the change process can be evaluated in terms of model fidelity: the extent to which the model was implemented according to defined standards. Another important evaluation element is assessing the extent to which the results are institutionalized through formal changes in policies, procedures, staffing structures, or other changes in organizational operations.

Evaluating the content of an organizational change examines its impact in terms of some important aspect of performance, such as improved outcomes for consumers, client and/or stakeholder satisfaction, improved efficiency or cost savings, a better service delivery model, a more appropriate culture and climate, lower turnover, new staff knowledge and skills, increased organizational learning capacity, enhanced management capacity, or improved employee quality of working life. The challenges of validly measuring organizational performance, in terms of both outcomes and organizational processes, are well known but not insurmountable. Of course, clear measurable objectives will be helpful in evaluating results.

After all stated goals and objectives for the change process at the CSC had been addressed, a formal evaluation would have two elements. First, the extent of accomplishment of goals and objectives would be measured. These might address the extent of implementation of new or modified programs; changes in client outcomes; the cultural competence of staff; and perceptions of DEI throughout the agency.

The change *process* would also be evaluated by looking at the extent to which all the change plans regarding the action system were implemented and how effective the change processes and activities were. The executive team would thank staff for their hard work and make provisions for celebrating the accomplishments. The agency would also make a commitment to continuing their efforts to enhance DEI as well as to maintain a high quality working life for staff.

Essential Elements for Managing Complex Change

I add here one final perspective on organizational change: Another way to look at elements of a change process is to examine what may happen if any element is missing. This minimodel, from Knoster, Villa, and Thousand (2000), suggests that these elements (all included in the model used here) are each essential in managing complex organizational change:

- A *clear and compelling vision* of a desirable future state that will significantly improve organizational functioning
- *Necessary skills* of change leaders and all involved with the process, ranging from leadership and group dynamics skills to analysis and problem-solving
- *Incentives* that are appealing to participants: things that they desire that they can see will result from a successful change, such as feelings of empowerment or autonomy, better working conditions, better program outcomes, or improved leadership
- *Resources,* not only mainly staff time, but also materials, software, and new skills that can be imparted through training, and perhaps consultant support
- *An action plan*: detailed activities in a timeline with clearly defined roles and outcomes for each step

This model suggests that all elements are needed. The following are likely to result if one is missing, even if the others exist:

- If a vision is missing, *confusion* is likely.
- If managers and other staff do not have the relevant change management skills, *anxiety* is likely.
- If managers and other staff have no incentives to change, *resistance* is likely.
- If the change process lacks necessary resources, *frustration* is likely.
- If there is no action plan for implementation, *false starts or stagnation* are likely.

The implications are clear: To ensure best prospects for success, change leaders must ensure that each of these elements is fully addressed in the change plan and its implementation. During the process, change leaders can regularly check to ensure that each element is being addressed and to see if any of the negative outcomes are evident. Adaptations can then be made to keep the process on track.

Summary

In terms of theory, organizational change can be seen from several perspectives. For our purposes, a rational adaptation perspective reinforces the idea that organizations and staff are not simply passive recipients of change but that as members of the organization they can be proactive leaders and managers of change.

After organizational needs, problems, and conditions are assessed, change goals can point to the level of change needed, from minor or incremental to major or transformational. The processes mentioned here and covered in detail in later chapters would not all be needed for minor change, but pieces of the model may be relevant in any case. For transformational change, the processes and technologies covered here should be very useful.

A change initiative needs to be assessed in terms of both its content (the change goals, e.g., implementing a new program model or a new information system) and change process (the strategies, methods, and tactics used). Assessment of the organization will guide the choices made about the change initiative, considering environmental forces such as accountability expectations; content factors such as the state of the organization's current systems and operations as well as staff morale; and process issues such as organizational readiness and capacity for change, resistance, and organizational culture.

Based on these assessment factors, an overall strategy may emphasize empirical–rational, normative–reeducative, or power–coercive approaches. The first two strategies are in much better alignment with the change models and tactics suggested here than are power–coercive strategies.

Several chapters are devoted to change tactics such as demonstrating urgency, clarifying the change to the vision, providing a plan, developing communication processes, and providing for staff participation.

Methods and technologies to implement these strategies can include traditional OD tools such as employee surveys, process consultation, and team building as well as specific interventions, including quality improvement models and implementation science processes.

Outcomes of the change should be considered from the very beginning of the initiative to keep the process properly focused and also, of course, to see if the change process was successful. This has been a weak area in organizational change research and practice. Impacts on organizational performance are especially important to measure, and other factors such as changes in organizational culture and staff morale or quality of working life can also be important considerations.

Reflection and Focusing Questions

1. Which of the organizational theories covered here seem to fit with how you have seen organizational change happen in organizations with which you are familiar?
2. If you have experienced a significant organizational change,
   a. What were the key events?
   b. Were the change goals clear? Were they appropriate to address problems that you saw?
   c. Did you see the use of any of the steps that are part of the conceptual model here?
3. Which of the essential elements for managing complex change do you use in your organization?
4. What are your current thoughts on how planned organizational change could improve the functioning of your organization?

SECTION 2
CHANGE LEADERSHIP

3

You as a Change Leader

Assessment and Development

Feedback should be viewed as a gift, and if others offer you this gift
you should thank them.

—James Kouzes and Barry Posner
(*The Leadership Challenge*, 2002, p. 64)

This chapter focuses on you as a change leader, with specific attention to assessing yourself regarding key change leadership competencies and skills and how you can develop as a leader. We have a short discussion of change management versus change leadership and then review some of the competencies that have been found to be important for a change leader, including specific change leadership behaviors and influence tactics. After a discussion of ethics issues as relevant to organizational change leadership, some basics of leader development are reviewed, and suggestions are given on how they can apply to change leadership.

There is growing evidence of the direct importance of leadership and leader development to enable human service organizations (HSOs) to change to meet the complex challenges that they are facing (Vito, 2018a; Woolever & Kelly, 2014). And, as consultants from McKinsey & Company put it,

> Too often . . . senior executives overlook the "softer" skills their leaders will
> need to disseminate changes throughout the organization and make them stick.
> These skills include the ability to keep managers and workers inspired when
> they feel overwhelmed, to promote collaboration across organizational bound-
> aries, or to help managers embrace change programs through dialogue, not dic-
> tation. (De Smet, Lavoie, & Hioe, 2012, p. 1)

It should be easy for you to assume that you are or will at some point be a change leader.

Change leaders do not need to be chief executive officers (CEOs), and they do not always need to even have a formal role as a manager in charge of an organizational change initiative. Staff-initiated organizational change, covered in

Organizational Change for the Human Services. Thomas Packard, Oxford University Press. © Oxford University Press
2021. DOI: 10.1093/oso/9780197549995.003.0004

Chapter 19, involves lower level staff becoming ad hoc change leaders. A manager or, in fact, any employee may become a change leader when performing a role such as a problem-solving group chair or facilitator. So, whatever role you occupy in an organization, you may have opportunities to be a leader on a change initiative.

As I noted in Chapter 1, there will always be plenty of organizational change opportunities in an HSO. Whether the change opportunity seems to require developmental, transitional, or transformational change, it will benefit from the involvement of a change leader who has both good self-awareness of personal skills, styles, and preferences and knowledge of change leadership principles.

Assessing Yourself as a Change Leader

It has occasionally been noted by those in the quality improvement or organizational change fields that W. E. Deming, who was a major leader in the founding of the quality improvement movement, was alleged to have said that anywhere from 85% to 97% of an organization's problems were caused by management. His main point was that problems were mostly caused by systems, not by individual people, and that management is the main designer of systems. This brings to mind for me a notation by social work management writer Gary Grobman (2008), who suggested with, I assume, tongue in cheek, that for some employees "change management" should start with changing *management*. Management can of course change through turnover and replacement, but more importantly, you as a manager and leader can change *yourself* to help improve the operation of your organization or a subunit of it.

Most of this chapter covers formal aspects of leadership competencies and leader development, but I think it is important to begin by framing this from the point of view of you as a leader and how you can engage in self-examination and self-assessment to become a better leader and, more specifically here, a better change leader. I'm not asking you to reflect on how many of the problems in your organization were caused by you and/or other managers, but rather that you take some time to reflect on your own visions for yourself and your organization and what you can do to develop yourself in order to better help develop your organization. You could treat the ideas in this chapter as ministimuli that you can bounce off yourself, considering what aspects of the competencies and behaviors here you would like to develop further.

Some of this thinking was put very well by Carucci (2016):

Diligent leaders often devote countless resources to planning out the perfect change management initiative. To raise the odds of success, however, my experience suggests the place that leaders need to begin their transformation efforts is not their organizations: It's themselves . . . .

A leader's ability to affect change across the organization depends on their ability to affect change within themselves. Accepting this will fundamentally shift how one leads. Such introspection is an active process. Leaders should take notes, spot trends, correct course. They should solicit feedback from others, tracking the impact their behavior has on others and how closely their actions match intentions.

Leaders should start a transformational journey accepting that the organization will have to transform them as much as they will have to transform it. The more a leader knows how they will react during change, the better equipped they'll be to foster real change in themselves, others, and the organization.

A final thought here that relates both to your own development as a leader and also how you can role model development for your workgroup or organization comes from Jaiya John (2016, p. 43; italics in original), who suggested using storytelling to talk about development and change:

> Story renovation addresses *language, content, structure, and spirit.* All four determine our internal message. And while we're at it, we might as well scrub away at our team or unit story, and our larger subsystem story. We need to ask certain questions: *What am I telling myself about this work? Who do I say I am in this work? What am I saying is the point of this work? What worth or value do I recognize in this work?* The same questions apply to the collective [e.g., the organization]. Honesty is required in answering these questions. We may not like some of the answers. These are the ones that can offer us the most value. They reveal changes we need to make to our story.

Change Management and Change Leadership

Before we begin the discussion of competencies, we should make a distinction between *change management* and *change leadership*. In the field of administration, distinctions can be made between *management* and *leadership*. In HSOs, management can be seen as having to do with functions including program design, finance, information systems, and human resource management; leadership is concerned with visioning, inspiring and empowering staff, strategy development, and culture management (Lewis, Packard, & Lewis, 2012, p. 279). These together comprise *administration*. Put another way, in the general management field, Kotter (1990) said that management produces predictability, order, and consistency regarding key results, while leadership produces change.

Both, of course, are needed for effective organizational functioning. Regarding organizational change specifically, Kotter has asserted (1996) that successful organizational change involves 70%–90% leadership and 10%–30% management.

In a parallel way, organizational change *management* involves planning, monitoring, control, and resource allocation (Gill, 2003). Gill also asserted that, "Change efforts that are purely 'managerial' in nature, especially those that are mismanaged, result in a lack of dedicated effort, conflict between functional areas and resistance to change" (p. 308), adding that "the human and political aspects of change are often not well thought through in change management initiatives" (p. 309).

Change *leadership*, then, augments effective change management through articulating a compelling vision and its relationship to the organization's mission and values; developing viable strategies to achieve change goals; and involving, motivating, and empowering staff. Clearly, then, effective organizational change requires both good change management and good change leadership. Both of these processes are addressed in the change model covered in later chapters. The focus in this chapter is on the change *leader*.

Change Leadership Competencies

Management and leadership competencies have long been seen as fundamentals of leader development. It is important, however, to start not with competencies but with personal and organizational *outcomes* that are needed and then determine the specific competencies that can lead to desired organizational results (Woolever & Kelly, 2014). This thinking parallels my previous (and ongoing) point that change or development should be in the context of organizational strategy: what is needed to continually enhance organizational performance. With that contextual background, we'll start with change leadership *competencies* and then cover traits, skills, and talents, which are behaviors that can be judged with reference to competencies.

In the general field of leadership studies, there are varying definitions of traits, abilities, skills, and competencies. The general view is that of these, some traits, such as intellectual intelligence, are mainly (but not totally) given, whereas abilities, skills, and competencies can obviously be developed. The term *competencies* has become much more commonly used in recent years in both general leadership and human services practice, with the Council on Social Work Education's (CSWE's) Educational Policy and Accreditation Standards as a major example. Their nine competencies are defined to include "knowledge, values, skills, and cognitive and affective processes that comprise the competency" and "behaviors that integrate these components" (CSWE, 2015, p. 7).

The CSWE model and other conceptualizations used to reflect the way professionals perform can become confusing, with the terms competencies, abilities talents, traits, skills, and behaviors sometimes used interchangeably. For example, one leadership scholar (Northouse, 2019, p. 48) listed problem-solving skills, social judgment skills, and knowledge as competencies, bracketed by *individual attributes* (cognitive ability, motivation, and personality) and *leadership* outcomes (effective problem-solving and performance). From a social work perspective, Woolever and Kelly (2014) used the terms traits, styles, abilities, practices, competencies, and characteristics when describing leadership.

One leadership scholar makes the distinctions this way:

> Competencies are often used to describe qualities considered relevant for managers in a particular organization or profession. . . . *Trait* refers to a variety of individual attributes, including aspects of personality, temperament, needs, motives, and values. . . . *Skill* refers to the ability to do something in an effective manner. Like traits, skills are determined jointly by learning and heredity. . . . The term *competency* may involve traits or skills, and *competencies* often include a combination of related skills and traits. (Yukl, 2013, p. 136; italics in original)

Regarding change leadership in HSOs specifically, the National Child Welfare Workforce Institute (NCWWI),[1] identified change leadership as a major competency area. Their model has five "domains": Leading Change, Leading People, Leading for Results, Building Collaboratives, and Fundamental Competencies (e.g., effective communication, integrity/honesty) (2011).

The NCWWI definition of leading change is notable for being grounded in an outcome: strategic change:

> This domain involves the ability to bring about strategic change, both within and outside the organization, to meet organizational goals. Inherent to this domain is the ability to establish an organizational vision and to implement it in a continuously changing environment. (2011, p. 7)

The specific competencies are defined as follows:

- *Creativity and Innovation Competency*: Develops new insights into situations; questions conventional approaches; encourages new ideas and innovations; designs and implements new or cutting edge programs/processes.

---

[1] The NCWWI mission is to build the capacity of the nation's child welfare workforce and improve outcomes for children and families.

- *External Awareness Competency*: Understands and keeps up to date on local and national policies and trends that affect the organization and shape stakeholders' views; is aware of the organization's impact on the external environment.
- *Flexibility Competency*: Is open to change and new information; rapidly adapts to new information, changing conditions, or unexpected obstacles.
- *Strategic Thinking Competency*: Formulates objectives and priorities, and implements plans consistent with the long-term interests of the organization in a global environment; capitalizes on opportunities and manages risks.
- *Vision Competency*: Takes a long-term view and builds a shared vision with others; acts as a catalyst for organizational change; influences others to translate vision into action (NCWWI, 2011, p. 7)

Their model has been used nationally in training and capacity-building programs (Bernotavicz, McDaniel, Brittain, & Dickinson, 2014; Dickinson, 2014).

The Network for Social Work Management (Wimpfheimer et al., 2018, p. 10) has developed a guidebook with a set of 21 management competencies. Under the domain of Executive Leadership, the competency *initiates and facilitates innovative change processes*, the following performance indicators are listed:

7.1 Remains current on trends and identifies shifts that require an innovative response.

7.2 Presents innovations to appropriate decision-makers and stakeholders to inform decisions.

7.3 Assists staff with implementing positive change.

7.4 Supports staff in risk taking, following thorough analysis.

7.5 Supports innovative practices to improve program-related issues and services.

Their guidebook has suggestions to enable you and your supervisor to review your current performance with reference to each indicator and also has some suggestions for skill development.

Leadership Traits

Early discussion of traits suggested that these were inherent within a person—something they were born with. Current work frames traits more as characteristics, many of which can be developed. Little is known about how combinations of traits may impact effectiveness or how traits affect organizational outcomes (Northouse, 2019, p. 31), but researchers do agree that traits are important only to the extent that they are relevant to a particular leadership situation.

Northouse (2019, pp. 23–25) summarized trait research with five major leadership traits: intelligence; self-confidence; determination (e.g., desire to get the job done, including initiative, persistence, dominance, and drive); integrity; and sociability. He also included with trait theory emotional intelligence, which has two major components: personal competence (self-awareness, self-control/regulation, conscientiousness, and motivation) and social competence (empathy and social skills, including communication and conflict management).

A summary by another leadership researcher (Yukl, 2013, p. 139) listed the following traits that have been associated with managerial effectiveness:

- High energy level and stress tolerance
- Internal locus of control orientation
- Emotional maturity
- Personal integrity
- Socialized power motivation (using power for the good of others and the organization)
- Moderately high achievement orientation
- Moderately high self-confidence
- Moderately low need for affiliation

In addition to these traits, leadership effectiveness has recently been associated with being "authentic." Grounded in positive psychology, the authentic leader "[is] . . . confident, hopeful, optimistic, resilient, moral/ethical, future-oriented, . . . gives priority to developing associates to be leaders . . . is true to him/herself . . . [and] exhibits behavior [that] positively transforms or develops associates into leaders themselves" (Luthans & Avolio, 2003, p. 243).

Finally, from a social work perspective, Woolever and Kelly (2014) listed these traits: an ability to adapt, self-awareness, the ability to promote and elicit the innovative talents of their personnel, decisiveness, collaborative skills, and emotional intelligence.

The term *talent* can even come up in this context. Buckingham and Clifton presented this typical definition of a talent: "a special natural ability or aptitude" (2001, p. 48), which sounds like a trait. They then took a different approach, suggesting that a talent is "any recurring pattern of thought, feeling, or behavior that can be productively applied (2001, p. 48). This, they say, suggests that even a "negative" trait such as obstinacy can be a talent if it is productively applied, such as "sticking to your guns" when necessary.

Self-awareness is an important aspect of leadership in general and change leadership in particular. Warner Burke, one of the major figures in the organization development field since the 1960s.suggested (2018) that a change leader should begin a major organizational change initiative with self-examination, focusing on one's self-awareness, motives, and values, and use insights from this assessment when deciding on change tactics.

According to Burke (2018), a change leader should have a tolerance for ambiguity, accept not being able to control everything, understand how feelings affect behavior, and be open to shared decision-making. Tolerance for ambiguity is important because organizational change can sometimes become chaotic and is not totally predictable. This also applies to the extent to which you have high control needs. A participative management philosophy, as discussed in the next chapter, will be of immense help on this.

Finally, summarizing other work in this field, Burke concluded that "effective change leaders need to have an above-average level of energy and be capable of (1) working long hours when needed, (2) interacting with lots of people, and (3) energizing others" (p. 324).

Others have identified competencies that are particularly relevant to change leadership. Battilana, Gilmartin, Sengul, Pache, and Alexander (2010) noted the importance of competencies including person-oriented behaviors such as interpersonal skills and emotional intelligence, and task-oriented behaviors, including a focus on goals and outcomes of the change process. Gilley, McMillan, and Gilley (2009) identified coaching, motivating, communicating, and team building as characteristics of leadership effectiveness in organizational change.

In the HSO field, a study by Carnochan and Austin (2004) of county HSO directors who had recently been involved with the 1996 welfare reform legislation gathered some valuable lessons learned from the directors. As an example of the control issue mentioned above by Burke, the directors found that "control must be replaced by influence, featuring the participatory styles of negotiating, educating, and persuading" (p. 9). Consistent with another of Burke's assertions, they noted that "massive and rapid change cannot be completely planned" and "change takes time and requires patience, incremental steps, and some agreement on the value of change" (p. 9). This point about showing the value of change will be a major element of the change process discussed in the next section. The directors also noted that staff "have limits on the amount and pace of change they can tolerate" (p. 10), and that therefore change leaders need to have realistic expectations. And, perhaps particularly important for a government organization, the directors noted that attention needs to be paid to external relations with community stakeholders and political leaders. Finally, they noted that "fundamental organizational change often requires a change in the organization's culture" (p. 15). Culture change is often stated as a change goal in its own right and is sometimes seen as essential to facilitate other changes, such as implementing evidence-based practices or developing a culture that values the use of data in monitoring and evaluating client change.

I now review some change leadership behaviors, which can also be considered as skills, which are often simply manifestations of competencies.

Task, Relationship, and Change Behaviors

Early leadership theories, and more recent models including the leadership grid and situational leadership, put a heavy emphasis on task and relationship behaviors. Those aren't reviewed here except to note the basic principles that, in situations where leadership may help, such as in a task group or team, a leader can assess what the group needs and make an intervention through a task or relationship behavior. A task behavior such as suggesting a process for goal setting and problem-solving may help if a group or team is unfocused, and process behaviors such as supporting group members or facilitating conflict resolution can help when a group is having problems working together (Northouse, 2019). A change leader at any level, from the CEO in an executive team meeting to a facilitator of a problem-solving group, can consciously assess a situation and use task or relationship behaviors as needed.

In his comprehensive book about leadership, Yukl (2013) added another dimension to task and relationship behaviors. The following change behaviors would obviously be especially relevant in organizational change.

- Monitor the external environment to detect threats and opportunities.
- Interpret events to explain the urgent need for change.
- Study competitors and outsiders to get ideas for improvements.
- Envision exciting new possibilities for the organization.
- Encourage people to view problems or opportunities in a different way.
- Develop innovative new strategies linked to core competencies.
- Encourage and facilitate innovation and entrepreneurship in the organization.
- Encourage and facilitate collective learning in the team or organization.
- Experiment with new approaches for achieving objectives.
- Make symbolic changes that are consistent with a new vision or strategy.
- Encourage and facilitate efforts to implement major change.
- Announce and celebrate progress in implementing change. (Yukl, 2013, p. 52)

Influence Skills

One final skill or competency area is worth mentioning here: the use of influence in organizational change. Influence is often associated with power. Generally, power or influence is defined as the ability to get others to do things that they would not otherwise do. Power is often considered to be coercive, while influence is considered to be persuasive. Using the overall organizational change strategies discussed previously, the power–coercive strategies would obviously be associated with the use of power, which in an organization is often based on one's position—being able to give orders—or the ability to use rewards or punishment (through desirable or undesirable assignments, etc.). On the other hand, normative–reeducative strategies use noncoercive influence strategies. Table 3.1 lists a few influence tactics that are used in organizations. Some of these would have application in organizational change situations.

A contingency approach is usually best: using the tactics that are likely to be successful in a given situation. This includes one's own styles, skills, preferences, and social capital. Also, the influence target (e.g., an employee or a unit such as a group or program that a change leader wants to influence) should be assessed to determine the tactics that are likely to work best, particularly considering the target's perspectives and preferences. Tactics will also vary based on the influencer's relationship with the target: upward (superiors), downward (subordinates), or lateral (coworkers, external community partners). Upward

Table 3.1 Influence Tactics for Organizations

- Articulate and build commitment to a desirable vision
- Behave in ways that are consistent with the organization's key values and culture
- Use rational persuasion: present facts, data, and a plan to support your proposal
- Use ingratiation: act in a friendly manner prior to making a request, sympathize about the hardships the request may cause, praise the person
- Use positive sanctions: promise desirable rewards
- Use reciprocity: offer something in exchange, remind of past favors, "chits" acquired
- Use coalitions to get others' support
- Use bridging: draw out the other person's needs or perspectives
- Seek participation and feedback from those you are trying to influence
- Get others involved and supportive regarding the idea, use their input and ideas
- Appeal to personal values
- Be assertive and explicit regarding what you want

tactics will receive more attention in Chapter 19 on staff-initiated organizational change.

Ethics in Change Leadership

I sometimes struggle with where ethics should be covered in teaching, writing, or training about administration and organizations. It deserves stand-alone attention, but it should also be something that a manager or leader will bring to awareness whenever needed. Here, ethics principles can be seen in terms of how they are manifested as leadership behaviors. Ethics issues sometimes emerge unexpectedly, such as when a complex problem occurs.

Yukl (2013), in his major survey of leadership, summarized ethical values derived from several current theories of leadership. The concepts in his list— integrity, altruism, humility, empathy and healing, personal growth, fairness and justice, and empowerment (p. 348)—should look very familiar to HSO administrators. They are also very consistent with the values of the human services professions. His guidelines for ethical behavior—set clear standards of ethical conduct, model ethical behavior in your own actions, help people find fair and ethical ways to resolve problems and conflicts, oppose unethical practices in the organization, and implement and support programs to promote ethical behavior (p. 355)—should also seem self-evident to HSO administrators. You can use these principles and guidelines as checklists in your daily work and as you lead organizational change.

Ethics regarding change leadership can be contextualized within several levels. First, a change leader is likely to be a member of a profession with a code of ethics, which should of course always be followed. Second, as a member of an organization, a change leader should be aware of official statements of the organization's principles regarding values and ethics and how these are reflected in policies and less formally in an organization's culture. A change leader in an administrative role should feel some responsibility for ensuring that ethics standards and systems are embedded and followed within the organization. Susan Manning has provided wide-ranging coverage of ethics as part of leadership (2003). She made some important, but not common, connections between ethics and organizational change, including issues such as organization design; organizational culture (e.g., collegiality, interdependence, and teamwork); learning organizations; and innovation. She noted that participation, by staff and potentially by community and other stakeholders, has an ethics dimension. I address that in the next chapter, regarding participative decision-making. She also covered organizational fundamentals that administrators should be aware of, including organizational codes of ethics, ethics committees, and ethics audits.

Ethics leadership regarding organizational change specifically has received less attention. One recent article (Sharif & Scandura, 2014) asserted that there had been "no studies investigating ethical leadership and organizational change" (p. 185). To introduce their study, they used this definition of ethical leadership: "the demonstration of normatively appropriate conduct through personal actions and interpersonal relationships and the promotion of such conduct to followers through two-way communication, reinforcement, and decision making" (M. Brown, Treviño, & Harrison, 2005, p. 120). In their study, they found that "employees who perceived their leaders to be ethical were more likely to be satisfied with their job, were better performers, and also engaged in citizenship behaviors in the organization" (p. 191). More specifically, regarding organizational change, they offered these recommendations:

> Given our finding that ethical leadership is important during organizational change, organizations should make particular efforts to develop ethical leaders. During change, it is even more crucial for organizations to insure ethical leadership. This may be accomplished through the development of training programs that focus on ethical behaviors during change. Additionally, it is important for ethical leaders to actively involve their subordinates in the change process. Employees who are directly involved in the change will outperform those individuals who did not have the opportunity to do so. Leader transparency and discussion with subordinates will reaffirm the leaders' ethical values, which contribute to the employees' dedication to the change process by increasing performance and citizenship behaviors. (p. 194)

Leader Development

After this discussion of competencies, traits, and skills, we spend some time looking at how you can draw on any of that material and your self-assessment to explicitly develop your leadership skills. Your own leadership skills in general will be very useful when you are in a change leader role. And, an important aspect of being a good leader is to be continually growing and developing. It will behoove any HSO administrator to engage in self-assessment and leader development on a regular basis.

A "strengths perspective" is now being used in a variety of ways and has direct relevance for leader development. Historically, development involved trying to "fix" weaknesses. Current thinking is that it is more effective to identify strengths of a manager, develop those, and put the manager in a role where the strengths can be best used. Buckingham and Clifton (2001) were early thought leaders on this. Their major point is that you should discover your strengths and apply them. They also add that, if you do have key weaknesses that get in the way of your performance, you should address those. They suggested several ways to do this, including getting better at your weakness and getting support from others. This thinking applies easily to the development of leadership skills or behaviors.

Leader development is getting increasing attention in HSOs. The Bay Area Network of Nonprofit Human Service Agencies (Austin, Regan, Samples, Schwartz, & Carnochan, 2011) has done leadership development in county human service agencies in the San Francisco Bay area. Some colleagues and I adapted their program for use in Southern California county HSOs (Coloma, Gibson, & Packard, 2012). The NCWWI, mentioned previously in this chapter, offers a range of excellent references for leadership development. Aarons, Ehrhart, Farahnak, & Hurlburt (2015) reported on the positive outcomes of the LOCI (leadership and organizational change for implementation) leadership and organization development intervention for evidence-based practice implementation

Common methods used in formal leadership development programs include training, coaching, mentoring, action learning (typically combining formal training with learning from experience; Yukl, 2013, p. 399), challenging work experiences (developmental and "stretch" assignments), and 360-degree feedback. The 360-degree feedback involves using standardized management style or behavior instruments that are filled out by the manager and their supervisor, subordinates, and peers. Results of instruments are typically collated by a consultant or training organization and fed back to the manager anonymously by the consultant, who then helps the manager process the results and decide on action steps to improve skills or adjust styles.

A survey of leadership development programs identified the following best practices: link to agency strategic objectives rather than just individual development; build on leadership competencies consistent with the organization's values; include action learning using real-life issues as the basis; encourage learners themselves to develop answers to tough questions; link to succession planning; provide top-level support; and include ongoing assessment of the effectiveness of the program (Fulmer & Wagner, 1999, cited in Bernotovics, Dutram, Kendall, & Lerman, 2014).

Other useful processes in leader development are coaching and mentoring. Coaching in particular is becoming increasingly specialized and popular. Essentially, coaching involves a consultant working with a manager to help improve the manager's effectiveness through helping a manager identify and build on strengths and work on identified goals for development. A coach can also "provide advice about how to handle specific challenges, such as implementing a major change, dealing with a difficult boss, or working with people from a different culture" (Yukl, 2013, p. 392). In contrast, mentoring typically involves a senior person in an organization working with a manager as mentee, focusing on career development, support, role modeling, and advising. Mentoring can be especially valuable for managers from groups that are underrepresented, particularly in the management ranks, in an organization (Ross-Sheriff & Orme, 2017).

If standardized instruments and a consultant or trainer are not easily available to you, you can still on your own create a list of some of the change leadership competencies covered in this chapter and ask your supervisor, board, peers, and/or staff members for feedback. Also, because "developmental opportunities to learn" (Woolever & Kelley, 2014), such as on-the-job experiences with challenging assignments, have been found to be important components of leader development, you can always work with your supervisor, coach, mentor, or board to create action learning projects or "stretch" assignments for yourself that will benefit the organization and advance your own development.

For staff new to an administrative role, another aspect of leader development is dealing with the changes in personal identity and new roles as one moves from a familiar role as a direct service practitioner to a supervisor or other type of manager. Austin, Regan, Gothard, and Carnochan (2013) developed a model to assist emerging leaders to manage role changes through their early management career. In the *emerging* phase, a new manager will be assessing their managerial potential, including their knowledge, skills, attitudes, and interests and how these fit with the new role. Asking a lot of questions and getting "stretch" assignments can help during this phase. Promotion typically leads to the phase of *becoming a manager*, in which the manager will be looking for role clarity and constructing a new "identity." For example, moving from clinical mastery to a generalist perspective and moving from an independent task focus to interdependence and team dynamics can be challenging. In the *acting* phase, managers often need to learn how to balance conflicting demands, such as between acknowledging their new managerial authority while trying to empower the autonomy of their work team and managing relationships up and down the hierarchy and in the community. In the *thriving* phase, they feel more competent in the new role of managing and leading. Support and guidance from a supervisor, coach, or mentor can clearly help throughout this process.

Appendix 1 includes a Leader Development Plan format that you can use to structure your leader development process.

If you have well-developed leadership skills, good relationships with members of your organization, and a reputation for competent job performance, you will be well equipped to take on a role as a change leader, but opportunities for growth will always be there.

Summary

I began this chapter by highlighting the role of leadership in organizational change, adding that change leaders can respond from many roles or positions, ranging from the CEO to line staff. Having and continuing to develop your leadership skills can make you particularly valuable in your organization when opportunities for change leadership present themselves. In fact, before beginning organizational change, it would be wise to assess yourself and consider what changes you should make in yourself.

I then reviewed some of the competencies that have been shown to be especially relevant for organizational change leaders and some of the general leadership theories that might be particularly useful in change leadership. Also included here was a quick review of task, relationship, and change behaviors and the use of influence tactics.

An irony regarding organizational change is that it seems that often people want organizational change in those above or below them, believing that either "my boss needs to change" or "staff below me need to change." This underscores the importance of assessing yourself as a change leader. Leader development, in general and for change leaders, requires a significant amount of self-assessment and work to increase your self-awareness of your basic philosophies and preferences as well as your strengths and areas that you may want to develop. All of these dynamics of change leadership will affect how a change leader will design and implement an organizational change intervention.

After reading this chapter and engaging in some self-assessment, perhaps also with someone who knows your work well, you may be wondering what actual leadership behaviors and activities can enhance your change leadership effectiveness. The next chapter offers you a "menu" of some theories of leadership that have particular relevance for change leadership and how they can be used to put your leadership skills into action. You'll be able to consider the extent to which any of them fit with your own development needs and goals so that you'll have a range of new leader behaviors available to you.

Reflection and Focusing Questions

1. What are the most important competencies for organizational change leaders? Which of these are strengths for me?
2. What are my goals for myself as a change leader?
3. What specific competencies or skills would I like to acquire or develop to make me more effective?
4. What am I willing to do to become a better (or excellent) change leader?
5. What would be the best ways for me to develop in these areas considering my preferred ways of learning?
6. Who can help me with my action plan?

4

Theories for Effective
Change Leadership

There is nothing so practical as a good theory.
—Kurt Lewin (*Field Theory in Social Science*, 1951, p. 169)

In this chapter, we look at some general leadership theories that have particular relevance for change leaders. One important principle that connects the previous chapter's discussion of competencies and ethics with leadership theories is the importance of role modeling. McKinsey & Company (2015), in their report of a survey regarding organizational transformation, noted the importance of role modeling this way:

> When company leaders walk the walk and role model desired mind-set and behavior shifts, it's more likely that employees will follow suit. Leaders can role model by setting examples of desired behaviors in their day-to-day interactions and by enlisting help from influential employees at all levels to champion the change. (p. 3)

Several of the leadership theories covered in this chapter pay particular attention to the importance of role modeling effective behaviors for organizational change.

Leadership Theories for Change Leadership

While leadership theories are usually considered to be relevant in any organizational setting, some theories have particular relevance for organizational change leaders. I discuss some of these here in terms of how the models can be specifically applied to facilitate organizational change. A general point, to state the obvious, is that an if an administrator has good leadership skills and applies these wisely in an organizational change process, things can be expected to go better than they would with no or ineffective leadership.

I begin with some classic theories from the human relations movement that have been very influential in the field of organization development and in

Organizational Change for the Human Services. Thomas Packard, Oxford University Press. © Oxford University Press 2021. DOI: 10.1093/oso/9780197549995.003.0005

organizational change in general. Considering the classic work of Likert (1967), I pay particular attention to the aspects of his model that emphasize employee participation in decision-making (hereafter referred to as PDM), which is a fundamental principle of organization development and of nearly all of the change models covered in this book.

If human service organization (HSO) professionals remember anything about leadership theory from their macro practice or organizational behavior class, it is probably McGregor's famous Theory X and Theory Y. I hope a brief restatement of his basic model suffices here. I then direct more attention to the less well-known but more useful model of Rensis Likert (yes, he is the one who developed the Likert scales to use for attitude surveys, a major development in the human relations movement and still a core technology of organization development). Theory X is actually a statement about one's views of people (in this case, staff in an organization). A theory X manager assumes that people dislike work and want to avoid responsibility. The natural result of this situation is that managers must base their organizations on the need to control; to supervise closely; and to use reward, punishment, and active persuasion to force employees to do their jobs. In contrast, theory Y assumes that people enjoy working, desire responsibility, have innate capacities for creativity, and have the potential to work toward organizational objectives with a minimum of direction. The implication for theory Y assumptions is that work can be organized in such a way that personnel at all levels have the opportunity to do creative, self-directed, and responsible jobs.

This thinking shows up in organizational change at primarily two levels. First, it may affect one's overall strategy of organizational change. Second, it can strongly affect one's preference of a leadership style. Contingency theory suggests that an effective leader will vary one's style basted on variables, including the followers, the task at hand, and the situation. In the context of HSOs, where the vast majority of staff are professionals, or even paraprofessionals with high levels of skills in their positions, and have strong commitments to very challenging human services work, a common approach will be to use styles that are more participative and less authoritarian. Of course, there will be situations where directive leadership would be appropriate, including a crisis, new employees who need a lot of direction, and cynical or negative employees for whom participative styles have not been effective.

Likert's Management Systems

Likert's classic work (1967) examined a number of specific organizational variables, including leadership, motivation, communication, decision-making, goal setting, and control. He divided organizations into four basic types, based on how they deal with these organizational variables. He described these as *organizational* types, suggesting an organization will have a culture that is dominated by one of these types, or systems; but, these can also be applied to the philosophy of an individual leader.

- **System 1 (exploitive authoritative)** organizations are characterized by leaders who distrust their subordinates, decision-making processes that are concentrated at the top of the organizational hierarchy, and communication that is almost exclusively downward, from supervisor to supervisees. Control and power are centralized in top management so that others feel little concern for the organization's overall goals.
- **System 2 (benevolent authoritative)** organizations also centralize power in the hands of the few at the top of the hierarchy but add an increased degree of communication. More trust is placed in subordinates, but it is condescending in nature.
- **System 3 (consultative)** organizations have more two-way communication than System 2, and employees have the opportunity to give input, although all major decisions are still made at the top of the management hierarchy.
- **System 4 (participative)** organizations are characterized by leaders who have complete confidence in workers, motivation that is based on responsibility and participation as well as on economic rewards, communication among all organization members, extensive interaction, decentralized decision-making, wide acceptance of organizational goals, and widespread responsibility for control.

Likert (1967, p. 46) said that most managers recognize System 4 as theoretically superior to the others. He pointed out that if clear plans, high goals, and technical competence are present in an organization, System 4 will be superior. The key to its value lies in its heavy use of PDM, including the *human resources* model discussed below.

Before discussing PDM, I need to note that System 4 or PDM might not be the appropriate style for all situations. Contingency theory suggests that there is no "one best way" to lead, that different behaviors are appropriate in different situations, and that the effectiveness of leadership styles depends to a great extent on how aspects of the situation, including staff characteristics and the nature of the task, fit together (Hersey, Blanchard, & Johnson, 2013). Participative approaches are more appropriate when the staff to be involved have the relevant knowledge and skills and motivational profiles that include preferences for self-direction and autonomy and commitment to the organization. Team or organizational cultural factors such as levels regarding teamwork, cooperation, and trust should also be considered. Decisions about a leadership style to use can be made at the level of the entire change process as well as at program or workgroup levels.

Participative Decision-Making

One very consistent theme regarding change leadership has been the value of using a participative leadership style. PDM and participative management have evolved as generic terms for involving employees in greater decision-making, based on the human resources theories of Likert, McGregor, and others. PDM is defined here as "actual staff involvement, whether formal or informal, direct or indirect, in decision processes regarding issues affecting the structure, funding, staffing, or programming" of the organization (Ramsdell, 1994, p. 58). PDM is not an either/or factor but is on a continuum from no involvement in the decision to "complete control or veto power over the decision" (Ramsdell, 1994, p. 58).

Participative decision-making can be seen as one practice, or type, of the broader category of empowerment (Spreitzer, 2008). Other empowerment practices mentioned by Spreitzer include skills or knowledge-based pay, an open flow of information, flat organizational structures, and training to build staff knowledge and skills (p. 58). In her review of over 20 years of research on empowerment, she concluded that "empowering systems and structures, while often more costly to implement, for the most part have positive outcomes for organizations in terms of firm, unit, and team performance" (p. 58). She also found that, at an individual employee level, empowerment has been associated with higher job satisfaction, higher levels of organizational commitment, a lower propensity to leave, and less job strain (p. 61).

In some of my own early research (Packard, 1989), I studied the use of PDM in a county child protective services division. I replicated some work by Raymond Miles (1965, 1975) in the business management sector, where he tested two different approaches to PDM. Miles contrasted two approaches. In one, which he called the *human relations* approach, which is probably quite common, leaders assume that if they give their subordinates participation in minor decisions that the workers will be more satisfied and therefore more compliant with their boss, who will still make the major decisions. In the other approach, which he called the *human resources* approach, supervisors allow PDM on major decisions, with the assumption that their staff has the commitment and knowledge to make better decisions than the boss could make alone, resulting in better performance, which then leads to higher satisfaction.

My study found that units whose supervisors were seen as more participative had higher performance (self-ratings, an admitted limitation) and job satisfaction than those with less PDM. I also found (Packard, 1993) that both the supervisors and their staff felt that workers were capable of much more PDM than they were currently allowed, suggesting that this is an underused approach.

Miles went further in his research, finding that at whatever level of management his survey respondents were located, they wished their boss would use the human resources approach with them because they saw themselves as capable of being involved in major decisions, while they preferred to use the human relations model with their subordinates, allowing their participation in only minor decisions. This dynamic is something for any manager to consider. For example, if you are a manager, do you think your boss should use more PDM with you? How much PDM do you use with your staff? Do you think they would like you to use more PDM with them?

This is relevant and potentially more complicated regarding organizational change leadership. In a large change initiative, there will be many ways in which staff at many levels could be involved, such as through problem-solving groups and quality improvement processes. Whereas an individual manager can thoughtfully assess a subordinate in terms of their ability and commitment when deciding how to use PDM or delegation, this is much more complex with large numbers of staff involved in different aspects of a change process. This receive attention later in this book, especially in Chapter 7.

Connecting PDM and organizational change, Burnes, Hughes, and By (2016) noted "the role of employee involvement and choice as key factors in change initiatives" (p. 4). On a broader and more impactful level of research, authors of a 60-year review of quantitative studies concluded that

> As a rule, change recipients who experienced high levels of participation tended to report higher readiness and acceptance of change, appraised change as less stressful and exhibited overall support for the change. . . . Participation during the change process was also linked with the experience of positive emotions, a greater understanding of the meaning of change, realizing possible gains associated with the change and greater involvement in implementing behavioral changes. . . . In addition, participation contributed to change recipients' sense of competence, improved interpersonal trust, and increased attachment to the organization. (Oreg, Vakola, & Armenakis, 2011, p. 491)

Notably, with reference to the previous discussion of ethics, they also found that "procedural justice was associated with higher acceptance, readiness, and commitment to organizational change" (Oreg et al., 2011, p. 492). Burnes et al. (2016), connected their work more directly with ethics: "Taken together, their findings can be seen to link successful change to the participative-democratic-ethical approach to change of Lewin" (p. 4). The reference is to Kurt Lewin, regarded as a founder of organization development, who was also influential in fields including social change.

Some of the conclusions of Oreg et al., 2011, are worth quoting at length:

> The consistent finding concerning the link between organizational trust and support for change highlights the special significance of trust in times of change. Furthermore, increasing change recipient involvement in the change

and setting change recipients at greater ease, by allowing participation and ensuring a just process, have been shown to go a long way in alleviating resistance. Therefore, beyond the overall importance of trust and commitment, managers should invest special attention in creating a supportive and trusting organizational culture if they expect change recipients' support and cooperation in times of change. (p. 516)

While the literature suggests that PDM is likely to be an effective approach in organizational change, a change leader will understandably feel nervous delegating a great number of decisions to those lower in the hierarchy, potentially including many employees who will be engaging in problem analysis and problem-solving and making recommendations for change that the change leader may never have thought of.

In a multiple case study of three agencies, Vito (2018b, citing O'Connor & Netting, 2009) noted some possible limitations of PDM: It can be time consuming and may present challenges for organizations with government contracts with expectations for efficiency and outcomes measurement. She added that "this approach does require clarity of roles and responsibilities and time to process decisions, . . . and it may not be appropriate for higher-level decisions" (p. 12). In one organization in the study that successfully used PDM, supportive conditions included "directors and supervisors both clearly understood this approach and endorsed it in practice; it was embedded into their agency culture and supported by a flatter matrix structure; and it included client involvement, which is ideal but rare" (p. 11).

Recognizing the challenges in shared decision-making, Shera and Page (1995) suggested strategies for employee empowerment that allow greater PDM: At the organizational level, this can happen through creating a culture of shared leadership and meeting chairing, team problem-solving and decision-making, and flexible job designs. Effective communication, rewarding employee initiative, mutual (two-way) feedback, and employee development can also enhance empowerment. They added that the agency's service delivery technology (e.g., focusing on client outcomes) and information sharing through computers can be empowering. Both of these are probably opportunities in many agencies for both increased PDM and organizational change.

Overall approaches to help structure your thinking regarding how much participation to allow in a given situation were articulated by Paul Gibbons, an iconoclastic writer on organizational change that I cite in several contexts. He referred back to the work of Peter Senge and colleagues regarding the implementation of his classic *Fifth Discipline* work (Smith, 1994). Gibbons adapted Smith's five degrees of involvement to consider as levels of PDM:

Telling is the lowest level of involvement: "This is what you are going to do."
Selling is: "This is what you are going to do, and here is why I think it is a good

idea." *Testing* allows still more involvement, challenge, and input, "Here is what I think we should do; how can we improve upon it?" *Consulting* provides even more involvement, "Here are some broad parameters; where do you think we should go?" Finally, *cocreating* starts with a blank canvas, "What basic principles should guide where we go, and how do we get there?" (Gibbons, 2015, p. 231)

A more detailed list of options uses this continuum from no to high participation of staff:

1. The leader makes the decision.
2. To help make the decision, the leader requests information from staff. The leader can explain the reason for the request or not.
3. The leader explains to staff the situation for information sharing purposes, but makes the decision.
4. The leader discusses the situation with the staff and entertains input, but still makes the decision.
5. The leader presents the situation to the staff who discuss alternatives and makes [*sic*] a decision through consensus. (Rofuth & Piepenbring, 2020, p. 129)

Another conceptualization of PDM, in a case study of three organizations (two of them in the public sector) (Clarke & Higgs, 2019), considered participation at different stages of the process (problem identification, creating solutions, and implementation); the breadth of participation (the range of activities that employees were involved in); and the depth of participation (the degree of employee involvement). These varied across the organizations, and the authors reported that employees and change agents saw greater project success, and employees felt less anxiety, when there was greater participation in all three types of participation. Information sharing was considered a form of participation, and this seemed to be particularly impactful. All projects had notable documented successes, including improved team functioning; cost reductions and improved efficiencies; improvements in business metrics, including growth and customer satisfaction; and employees releasing individual potentials that led to new career trajectories.

One concept that I have found to be particularly useful in this situation is the principle of *minimum critical specifications* from the sociotechnical systems model of organizational design (more on this in Chapter 14). The basic idea is, when delegating a decision, give to the group only the key factors that must be followed and allow them to be creative as long as they remain within those parameters. For example, there may be budget considerations or existing policies in areas such as human resources that can't be changed, at least for the time being. To some extent, this involves trusting a group to develop ideas that you may never have thought of, but that may be better than your own ideas in a particular situation.

Deciding how much participation to allow regarding what decisions, from forming a broad-based steering committee to guide the project to letting a problem-solving group analyze a problem and make recommendations for addressing it, can be stressful for a change leader or manager. The principles and findings in this section can help you reflect on your own philosophies regarding PDM and how you might use PDM in a particular organizational change process.

I recently found an excellent example of PDM in an unusual place. Many readers may know of Jackie Robinson as the first Black player to integrate major league baseball in the modern era. He had additional significant experiences both before and after his baseball career in the area of human rights. This example comes from his experience in the Army during World War II. He was assigned to an all-Black tank platoon and quickly admitted to his subordinates that he knew nothing about tanks. He developed a strong relationship with an experienced sergeant and explicitly learned what he needed to know. The men were impressed by his honesty and proceeded to do excellent work. When his lieutenant colonel commended him for his outfit having the best record of any at that camp, Robinson said it was due totally to the efforts of his men. For his work, he was promoted to morale officer for the whole unit (Abdul-Jabbar & Walton, 2004, p. 51). This story should have particular relevance for any manager taking a new position in an existing workgroup, who would be well served to explicitly state a lack of particular expertise and trust the group. Even for a manager who has been with a group for some time, this type of humility should facilitate greater PDM and probably better performance and commitment from staff.

In considering your own views on this, also bear in mind the notion of *pseudoparticipation*. Don't tell a group to come up with some ideas and make recommendations and then ignore them. This is actually worse than being directive, in which case you are at least being authentic and showing what is or is not acceptable in a particular situation. Make sure the parameters are clear before you begin.

The facts that human service workers are likely to want more PDM, that supervisors and managers believe they are capable of more PDM, and that there is growing evidence of the effectiveness of PDM with skilled and motivated workers (see also Pine & Healy, 2007) suggest that opportunities for PDM should be thoughtfully created throughout the organizational change process, as appropriate after assessing contingency factors such as the relevant knowledge, skills, and motivational profiles of employees to be involved. Manning (2003) has added another rationale: the "moral right to participate" (p. 244). Dignity, fairness, self-respect, and employee health are all rationales that should resonate in the HSO professions. The leadership models discussed next all allow for high levels of employee PDM.

Exemplary Leadership

Kouzes and Posner, in their modern classic *The Leadership Challenge* (2017) articulated a model of leadership that has several elements that could be fruitfully used by change leaders. Their model, exemplary leadership, has a broader empirical base than some other popular theories. Much of this research, which uses the Leadership Practices Inventory (LPI) instrument, is more likely to measure observations of leader behaviors and correlations with variables such as job satisfaction than to examine correlations with organizational performance. (See http://www.leadershipchallenge.com/Research.aspx for examples.) One study (Jaskyte, 2011) found relationships between the LPI and administrative and programmatic innovations.

Their model is structured around five "practices" of leadership:

- *Model the way* involves clarifying one's personal values and setting an example by aligning actions with values.
- *Inspire a shared vision* includes envisioning the future and enlisting others in a common vision.
- Exemplary leaders *challenge the process* by finding opportunities to innovate, change, and grow and by experimenting and taking risks.
- These leaders *enable others to act* by fostering collaboration through trust and cooperative goals and sharing power and discretion.
- Finally, such leaders *encourage the heart* by showing appreciation for individual excellence and celebrating values and victories through a spirit of community.

In their research, they found several characteristics that people look for and admire in a leader:

1. *Honest*: truthful, ethical, principled, worthy of trust
2. *Forward-looking*: articulating a vision and sense of direction for the organization; using strategic planning and forecasting
3. *Competent*: having a track record and the ability to get things done, understanding the fundamentals, having relevant experience
4. *Inspiring*: enthusiastic, energetic, positive about the future

Kouzes and Posner concluded that these four make up *source credibility*—people believe in and trust them; these people follow the acronym DWYSYWD: do what you say you will do. DWYSYWD requires that leaders practice what they preach, "walk the talk," and follow through.

Transformational and Transactional Leadership

Another theory, this one with even more evidence than exemplary leadership theory, could have useful applications in organizational change. With strong empirical support, it has been used in a variety of fields, including HSOs and substance use disorder treatment programs (Guerrero & Khachikian, 2020). The main proponents of the model, Bass and Avolio (2006), have contrasted *transformational leadership* with *transactional leadership*. They have found that the use of both styles can maximize leader effectiveness, but that transformational leadership is the one that results in the highest level of effectiveness. Transactional leadership is simply an exchange in which a leader and followers agree to do things that meet each others' needs. The first component of transactional leadership is *contingent rewards*, basically providing valued rewards for performing desired behaviors. A transactional leader provides basic support for an employee, including adequate working conditions, basic training and supervision, and adequate pay and benefits, to ensure at least adequate performance. The second factor, *management by exception*, assumes that under normal circumstances, little supervisory attention will be needed. When variations from routine activities occur, the supervisor intervenes.

In transformational leadership, in contrast,

the followers feel trust, admiration, loyalty, and respect toward the leader, and they are motivated to do more than they originally expected to do. The leader transforms and motivates followers by (1) making them more aware of the importance of task outcomes, (2) inducing them to transcend their own self-interest for the sake of the organization or team, and (3) activating their higher-order needs. (Yukl, 2013, p. 322)

I quickly suggest here how each of its four elements (idealized influence, inspirational motivation, intellectual stimulation, and individualized consideration) could be used by a change leader.

Idealized Influence. Leaders who are admired as role models, who display high moral and ethical standards, are trusted to do the right thing, and are emulated by followers are demonstrating idealized influence.

Inspirational Motivation. A key component of inspirational motivation is vision. The overuse of this concept in the popular press and misapplications in organizations has led to cynicism on the part of some employees. Nevertheless, when properly executed, visionary leadership can be a powerful tool for focusing and energizing staff. (However, one caveat was offered by Ates, Tarakci, Porck, van Knippenberg, and Groenen (2019). In their study, visionary leadership was *not* effective with middle managers unless those managers were already fully aligned with overall organizational strategy.) Another important aspect of this element is setting high expectations for the work unit or program. Enthusiasm and encouragement are then used by the leader to pull the team toward the vision and achievement of expected results.

Intellectual Stimulation. Intellectual stimulation involves encouraging innovation and creativity, questioning assumptions, and trying new ways of doing things. This principle is particularly important in the early stages of assessing the need for change.

Individualized Consideration. Individualized consideration involves coaching and mentoring workers as individuals and having ongoing personalized interactions with staff. Individual consideration involves finding ways for followers to identify growth goals and providing opportunities for them to achieve them. This can take the form of an explicit discussion with a follower, simply asking what is important to them and how these things can be achieved in a work setting.

Adaptive Leadership

Adaptive leadership offers another way to assess the scope of change that might be required. This theory, as developed by Heifetz and others and summarized here by Northouse (2019), makes a distinction between technical and adaptive challenges. *Technical challenges* are "problems in the workplace or community that are clearly defined with known solutions that can be implemented through existing organizational rules and procedures" (p. 260). Northouse suggested that these challenges can be addressed by the manager, but I would suggest that many such challenges can be handled by a workgroup, with perhaps only initial parameter setting and final approval by the manager. These challenges would correspond with developmental change as discussed in Chapter 2. *Adaptive challenges* "are not clear-cut or easy to identify" and "require that leaders encourage others, with their support, to define challenging situations and implement solutions" (p. 262). In other words, adaptive challenges do not have straightforward solutions.

An important aspect of the model is an intensive assessment to determine the level of challenge to be addressed.

Key leader behaviors in this model are the following:

- **Get on the Balcony**: Step away from the day-to-day activity and conflict to assess the big picture and identify dysfunctional dynamics.
- **Identify Adaptive Challenges**: Differentiate between technical challenges and adaptive challenges, so that the proper focus of leadership can be used.
- **Regulate Distress**: Help others recognize the need for change but not become overwhelmed; frame issues in a way that they can be addressed; create a "holding environment" (an atmosphere in which people feel safe in addressing the problem); provide direction; set "productive norms"; and explicitly address conflict,
- **Maintain Disciplined Attention**: Encourage people to focus on the "tough work" they need to do and address avoidance by encouraging people to confront the problems.
- **Give the Work Back to the People**: Know when to provide necessary structure and then empower others to be creative and solve problems.
- **Protect Leadership Voices From Below**: Be open to the ideas of others, especially people who may be "at the fringe" or in low-status positions.

Heifetz and Laurie (1999), major thought leaders regarding this model, provided a good example of how tensions among varied groups in an organization can be focused through disciplined attention. They used as an example Jan Timmer, former chair of Phillips Electronics, who said that top managers are either visionaries or engineers. According to Timmer, "Fire the engineers and you get harmony and daydreaming. . . . Every business needs the cold shower of the engineering type's numbers. Eliminate the visionaries and you have a business oriented to financial production controls, but without a clear purpose or meaningful work" (p. 74). HSOs can see this contradiction without engineers, but in the different perspectives of the "admin" or "data" staff and the "program" staff. Change leaders need to facilitate the difficult discussions between these groups and others to achieve common understandings of the challenge and the goal.

A key task for a change leader will be to correctly identify the scope of challenges that are being faced by the organization. There may be a tendency to underestimate the complexity or potency of a challenge and, related to that, assume that only minor changes will be necessary and that the change process will be easy, with lots of cooperation and positive energy on the part of staff. Some of these dynamics are addressed in the next two chapters, looking at how to best introduce the challenges that the organization is facing, creating an inspiring and energizing vision for improved functioning of the organization, and setting up systems to involve people and implement the change plan.

Compassionate Leadership

After this much theory, I think it might help to end this chapter with a more emotional tone. I again call on the practice wisdom of Jaiya John (2016, p. 67; italics in original):

> Compassionate leadership is not a style. It is a state of being. This means it is a state that can be arrived at by anyone. *Style* implies something you try on for fit and suitability. A *state* is a capacity arrived at through personal investment and practice. This is why a focus on leadership styles leads to inauthentic fads and flashes of impact. People can read authenticity, and its absence. With compassionate leadership, we have arrived at a place of wellness, having tapped our ability to engage with an open heart and mind. We have grown calm and centered enough for humility, and to learn, listen, intuit, and trust. Compassionate Leadership is not a form of being soft, easy, or laissez faire. It is entirely solid, fortified, and fierce. Its fierceness lies in its determination to be well in relationship to ourselves and others. To be aware, open, and available. For this way of being, we need to have faith in the power of caring. And if we do not, we may need to examine our choice to be part of the caring profession.

The next section of five chapters suggests processes to use for implementing the various steps of organizational change.

Summary

I included here a few leadership theories that I think have particular relevance for organizational change leadership. The classic model of Rensis Likert is especially useful in helping a leader consider the most appropriate leadership style for a situation, with particular attention to how one sees the capacities of staff of an organization or team and how they should best be involved in a change process. Likert's participative System 4 style seems especially well suited for HSOs, which are typically staffed by professionals with high skill levels and expectations of autonomy and empowerment.

Participative decision-making theory offers a good perspective from which to assess your own preferences and tendencies regarding organizational change strategies and leadership behaviors. I think the research of Miles is especially relevant here. His research showed that a managers, at any level, tend to think that their boss should allow for more participation in making decisions, especially major ones; that same manager believes that her/his subordinates are not capable of such high amounts of participation. It is a notable irony that at every level there is a tendency to want your boss to use a participative approach with you while you believe you would not use the same approach with your subordinates.

Exemplary leadership as articulated by Kouzes and Posner offers practice principles that are particularly relevant for leading at the level of a full organization. Transformational leadership can be applied broadly as well, but is particularly relevant for more hands-on leadership at a program or team level. Adaptive leadership is especially well suited for leadership of an organizational change initiative. Jaya John's articulation of compassionate leadership can be a reminder about how to treat the people you are working with, especially in situations of high pressure and work demands, which are inevitable in large-scale change.

Your own leadership styles and philosophies, such as preferences for participative or directive styles or preferences for a model such as transformational or transactional leadership, will be relevant to your performance and effectiveness as a change leader.

Reflection and Focusing Questions

1. Which leadership theories have particular resonance for me? How could I use those models in my own work?
2. What is my overall philosophy regarding employee PDM?
3. If I am a change leader, how much control am I willing to allow others in the organization to use, to suggest new ideas and changes that I may never have considered?
4. If I am at a lower level, how much PDM should my superiors allow me to use?
5. What do I have to offer as an organizational change leader?

SECTION 3
A CHANGE MODEL

5

Assessment and Goal Setting

> Good heavens! For more than forty years I have been speaking prose
> without knowing it.
> —Jourdain in *The Bourgeois Gentleman* by Molière

Much as Moliere's bourgeois gentleman had been speaking prose without knowing it, for as long as there have been formal organizations there have been leaders engaging in organizational change. An early example, reported in the book of Exodus, is the restructuring that Moses, with consulting advice from Jethro, did on the way to the Promised Land (Shafritz & Ott, 2001, p. 52). (Not to make too big a point of it, but the result was a great deal of delegated decision-making—perhaps the first recorded use of participative decision-making and a good use of bureaucratic theory.)

I readily acknowledge that many organizational change leaders have been successful, relying on some combination of their own practice experiences, good and bad examples of leaders and change efforts they have seen, mentoring, professional development experiences, and perhaps formal training or education. And, more specifically, three of the cases provided in this book represent successful organizational change by change leaders who apparently did not use an explicit change model such as the one presented here, but certainly used many of the tactics, probably not "knowing" that they were using research-based principles. In the fire department case, my colleagues and I did consciously use planned change technologies and processes that covered many but not all of the steps in this model. My hope is that you as a change leader will be even more effective to the extent that use of this formal model will add to your current skills, practice wisdom, education, and prior experiences when you have opportunities for change leadership.

The change model outlined in this book is presented as an "ideal," and perhaps comprehensive, approach. I recognize that it is not always possible to do things in the most ideal way, based on unique conditions in an organization and its environment. Nevertheless, my assumption is that the more an organizational change process uses the best available evidence and practice wisdom, the greater is the likelihood for successful outcomes.

Organizational Change for the Human Services. Thomas Packard, Oxford University Press. © Oxford University Press 2021. DOI: 10.1093/oso/9780197549995.003.0006

The steps in the model, covered in this and the next four chapters, are presented in the order that they should normally occur, but there may be times when the order may change or, more commonly, steps may need to be partly repeated based on new developments or on broadening the effort to new parts of the organization. For example, while this chapter emphasizes assessment, assessment can also occur in later steps, after the change initiative is announced to the rest of the organization. Additional assessment that includes input from other staff, particularly those at lower levels in the organization, should enrich the process and help lead to better outcomes.

This chapter addresses the first three steps: *Identify the problem, need, challenge, or opportunity; identify the desired future state, which is the change goal;* and *assess the present.*

Each step includes examples from the cases mentioned in the Introduction: Father Joe's Villages' homeless services program in San Diego, the San Mateo County Human Services Agency, San Diego Youth Services (SDYS), and the San Diego Fire Department (SDFD).

Step 1. Identify the Problem, Need, Challenge, or Opportunity

Sometimes the need for organizational change is very clear, such as when a funding organization requires that all funded programs must use an evidence-based practice model or when a funding organization switches from cost reimbursement to performance-based contracting. Loss of a major funding source can precipitate the urgent need for cost cutting or new revenue generation.

If the agency has a good strategic management process in place, it may be possible to identify at an early stage the need for organizational change to take advantage of a new opportunity in the environment or deal with a weakness, such as unsatisfactory performance in a program or poor morale as evidenced by high turnover or employee apathy.

Even if administrators are doing good analysis of external opportunities and threats and internal strengths and weaknesses, they may not be explicitly considering the perspectives of their key stakeholders. Austin and Vu (2012) developed a useful framework for assessing the multiple perspectives of clients, funders, workers, and managers. This can help ensure that administrators doing the planning are not missing anything important. For example, considering a client's perspective when assessing the need for organizational change might reveal excessive wait times, cultural insensitivity, or an overly complicated intake process. Client satisfaction surveys, or even outcome data that may show that clients are not seeing improved outcomes, can each indicate a need for organizational change. Workers' perspectives can be easily identified using staff surveys, which can obtain input on anything from working conditions and physical facilities to leadership and any aspects of organizational culture and climate. Funders are probably concerned with the organization's capacities at both program and administrative levels and with how the organization relates to the communities it serves. Management audits and stakeholder surveys, conducted by the organization or by a funder or consultant, can be very useful here.

In any case, staff and, most importantly, executive staff should be monitoring their external and internal environments regularly in a structured way so that they can proactively identify change opportunities.

Let's take a look at the cases that will show how the organizations I use as examples began the change process by identifying needs, problems, opportunities, or challenges that needed attention. I should add that none of these organizations used the structured process presented here. I retrospectively overlay concepts, principles, and tactics that this model and the literature suggest, showing how they used them even if, in the case of the three human service organizations (HSOs), they were not following a precise model. On the fire department case, my colleagues and I did recommend a structured change process, which the department pretty much totally followed. That was based on standard organization development theory and practices at the time (which, I must say, are still used today).

In the other cases, the executives brought to bear their own practice wisdom, including their own successes and failures, good and bad change processes they had seen earlier in their careers, and perhaps coursework, formal training, or mentoring, That's probably how most organizational change happens. I hope that through using methods such as those covered in this book that change leaders using tested planned change principles and processes will be more likely to be successful.

Here are the needs and opportunities for change that each of our organizations identified.

Father Joe's Villages

Julie DeDe and the managers in charge of case management saw some opportunities to make significant improvements to case conference meetings at Father Joe's Villages. Clients were being served by individual staff from various programs (e.g., career and education, case management, mental health, and addictions counseling), and there was ineffective coordination of client case plans and communication at team meetings. Additionally, clients in one of the major transitional housing programs had not been able to receive the full spectrum of case management and employment services due to funding limitations.

San Mateo County

In San Mateo County, agency director Maureen Borland agreed with her board member's concern that families coming to the agency did not have a single point of entry and contact, and that they should not have to deal with multiple, separate services and agencies and tell their story over and over to multiple people in order to receive services. The board member believed that the system was not customer friendly and was convinced that there needed to be a better way to serve clients in the community.

San Diego Youth Services

During the recent Great Recession, the SDYS chief executive officer (CEO), Walter Philips, saw the emerging downturn in the national economy, leading to the possibility of a decrease in funding. He had also noted within the agency some inefficiencies at the administrative level and some duplication of duties that, combined with a lack of coordination and integration among the programs within the agency, created conditions requiring significant change.

San Diego Fire Department

While the SDFD was not facing serious problems or challenges, the city manager and the new fire chief, Earle Roberts, nevertheless wanted to see enhanced management capacities of the department and the implementation of innovations that would improve services to the community and increase efficiencies. As Chief Roberts got familiar with the department, his initial assessments were consistent with those of the city manager. He saw a basically well-functioning department but did not see much staff interest in making improvements in operations.

Step 2. Identify the Desired Future State: The Change Goal

Goals are statements of broad outcomes and, as opposed to objectives, do not have to be strictly measurable. They should, however, describe a desired future state with enough clarity and specificity to guide all staff as they take steps toward goal accomplishment.

Just as goals are written for a new program or an administrative task such as the completion of a fundraising event, goals for an organizational change process can provide clarity to focus energy and can also aid in evaluating the extent to which the process, in this case a change initiative, was successful. But perhaps more than in the case of a program that is funded based on expectations of an external funding organization, goals for an organizational change initiative can easily be modified based on emerging developments in the process.

Beyond the technical aspects of developing goals, think strategically about the problem or challenge and what needs to happen in a broad, strategic sense. In addition to your own ideas for the change, consult with other stakeholders to get their analysis of the situation and what they would like to see happen. I talk later about developing support, from not only staff of the organization but also external stakeholders such as board members and perhaps outside organizations. It will be more time consuming at these early stages to talk to different people and groups and then try to incorporate their viable ideas into your plan, but if you do this, you are likely to get not only more buy-in but also additional ideas.

It should be helpful at this goal-setting change to consider the *level* of change anticipated. Small-scale, or developmental, change will not require an elaborate change process. Transitional change, such as implementing a new information system or evidence-based program, will require a fuller use of this change model; transformational change, such as a major strategy change or organizational redesign, will be even more intensive. Especially for the latter, bear in mind that

> the literature on organizational change consistently argues that for large-scale change to be successful the major components of an organization need to be changed. These are often identified as the business strategy, the formal organizational structure, the reward system, the people, and, finally, the information and decision processes. (Conger, Spreitzer, & Lawler, 2008, p. xli)

Don't underestimate the scope of a change. Even a new information system will go beyond technical changes to involve aspects of organizational culture and likely changes in human resource systems through revised job descriptions and perhaps changes to reward systems.

This will also be a good time to begin thinking about evaluation of the change initiative. This is covered in Chapter 9, but if attention is given to it now, evaluation will be a lot easier. Consider not only your goals and ideas for specific objectives, but also the possibility to build in objectives of others that will contribute to your vision of success. Then, make sure that the objectives are measurable, and that they will be easy to evaluate. Think also about what criteria stakeholders (maybe including funding organizations, staff, or community partners) would have for evaluating success and develop measures and objectives that will track them.

Begin at this stage to think ahead about how you will introduce this change goal to staff. As a change leader, it will be important for you to describe it in terms of a desirable and ideal future state: what the organization will look like when the change is successfully implemented. Staff will benefit from knowing at the beginning what the ultimate goal or outcome will be.

Here is how goal setting occurred in our case examples.

Father Joe's Villages

To address the challenges at Father Joe's Villages, Julie DeDe and the program managers concluded that a major redesign of their case management system, based on the principle that every client would be assigned to work with a specific case management team rather than just individual staff members, would improve service quality and client outcomes. This change was also intended to increase the number of clients receiving comprehensive case management and employment services.

San Mateo County

In San Mateo County, Maureen Borland wanted to see the system changed so that it would be easier for clients and the community to understand. The goal was to reduce the need to shop around or call multiple locations to address the needs of residents and to ensure coordination of services and communication among the multiple county staff who would be working on a case. She concluded that creating such a systems change would require strategic planning.

San Diego Youth Services

At SDYS, to address the challenges they were facing, the agency launched a formal organizational change process to streamline management and decrease administrative costs, clarify the management structure and philosophy with respect to management of budgets and staff, and consolidate programs under divisions to increase integration and accountability.

San Diego Fire Department

We began our work with SDFD initially with Chief Roberts and his senior staff. This group set the following goals for the change initiative:

- Increase accountability and measurability
- Improve management skills
- Implement team development
- Implement a performance appraisal system
- Delegate authority and responsibility to the lowest possible level
- Develop and implement a reward system
- Improve department morale and attitude
- Improve information flow
- Implement group problem-solving
- Improve internal development capability
- Enhance department image

Step 3. Assess the Present

Assessing the present state of the organization involves three dimensions of the anticipated change initiative: *process*, *content*, and *context*. Assessment regarding the *process* of change looks at preconditions, including the organization's readiness and capacity for change. Assessment regarding *content* includes identification of problems, issues, or conditions in the organization that may benefit from or require organizational change. While most attention will be paid to the content and process of change, it is important to initially consider important contextual factors, outside and within the organization, which may be important in designing a change process. After looking at the context, we move to content—what needs to be changed—and then to the change process dynamics.

Assessing Context: The Big Picture

Organizational change is often precipitated by changes in the organization's environment. Common factors, described by Aarons et al. (2011) as the "outer context," include legislation, court decisions, and other policies affecting the organization; funding and funder expectations such as contracting and relationships with other provider organizations; communities being served; client advocacy organizations; and interorganizational networks with which the organization interacts. Ideally, an organization's executive leadership would be monitoring all these outside forces that are relevant to the organization and in fact be trying to impact them for advocacy, collaborations, and other external activities.

It may help to first look at the agency's strategic plan to contextualize the problem you are focusing on. One recent theory of organizational change uses strategic planning principles that are familiar to many HSO administrators: SWOT (strengths, weaknesses, opportunities, threats); PESTL (political, economic, social, technological, legal) factors; and also ACCRE (assets, capabilities, competencies, resources, evaluation) to assess the organization's context and also to help identify needs or opportunities for change (Jacobs, van Wittleloostuijn, & Christe-Zeyse, 2013). A particularly valuable technique to identify organizational change opportunities is a stakeholder analysis. Bryson (2018) has made the important point that an organization needs to be paying particular attention to how the organization is performing *from the perspectives of key stakeholders*, using *their* criteria for effective performance.

Internal context issues such as leadership effectiveness; management systems such as human resources and finance, organizational culture and climate; and staff factors such as work attitudes may need to be addressed when assessing, planning, and implementing change. As with external monitoring, a proactive organization will have mechanisms for monitoring internal organizational dynamics to be alert to emerging concerns, such as lowering morale or increasing stress among employees.

A broader internal context factor is *change turbulence* (Herold, Fedor, & Caldwell, 2007). The work of Herold et al. suggests some questions to consider:

- Is it a turbulent time for the organization overall?
- Are there other current distractions or demands impacting work units?
- Have there been other recent changes that have caused unusual pressure or stress on staff?
- Are there other change initiatives going on at this time?

Sometimes there is no choice but to embark on a significant change; but as much as possible, administrators should consider what possible delays or workarounds might make the proposed change seem more manageable to staff.

Dean Anderson and Linda Ackerman Anderson (n.d.), two highly regarded organizational change consultants, have offered these suggestions to executives considering embarking on a major organizational change.

A candid look at capacity requires a real partnership between your executives, mid-managers, supervisors, and employees. Trust issues across your organization's hierarchy, as well as people's fears of admitting to being overly stretched, will negatively impact the accuracy of your organizational and change capacity assessment. Do your best to invite and respect an honest review.

Do take things "off the plate!" Your capacity review is not a lip-service exercise. Make the tough decisions to ease the strain—at least to what is humanly possible under the best of circumstances. Show your workforce that you can and do see the true workload reality of your organization. You will send a visceral message, a truly bold action, by taking work "off the plate" to accomplish higher gain work and organizational change.

Cases: The Contexts

There were several common external contextual factors facing our four case organizations. The three HSOs were operating in environments of decreasing resources and funding challenges as well as increasing demands for service effectiveness. Internally, notable problems did not exist with either staff morale or general operations processes. The SDFD was different in the sense that it was seen by all stakeholders as a highly regarded public service, second only to the police department in priorities for funding support. While the department was seen as performing adequately, the new fire chief was thinking ahead to possible funding cuts in the future to which the department would need to respond, through advocacy for continued support and efficiency improvements or new revenue sources. More importantly, he saw opportunities to actually increase the quality of existing services and management operations.

Assessing Content: What Needs to Be Changed

A change leader, especially at or near the executive level, must always be monitoring and assessing the organization's environment and internal functioning; there will be times when it seems that transitional or transformational change is called for. Some assessment will have occurred at the first stage as part of identifying the problem, need, or change opportunity.

If there is a clearly defined goal, such as implementing an evidence-based practice, the only assessment needed may be regarding the process of change discussed below. However, if an administrator does not have a clearly focused change goal but thinks that change is needed because of factors such as poor service quality or low morale, a full assessment may be needed to identify factors contributing to organizational problems: the *content* of change.

Assessing at the content level involves examining the current functioning of the organization: how well it is doing with respect to factors such as leadership, management processes and systems, program quality, mission and strategy, organizational structure, the transformation processes (e.g., service delivery), and employee perspectives (e.g., satisfaction, organizational climate), considering how each of these affect desired outputs or outcomes.

Another very useful method for assessing an organization's functioning—the use of action research in organization development—may also be part of the change process itself and is covered in more detail in Chapter 11. Organization development, perhaps the most common method of organizational change, uses action research, which usually includes not only administrators but also many other levels of staff, in gathering data on organizational functioning using tools such as employee surveys (particularly useful in identifying job satisfaction and climate issues) and organizational performance data. Data gathered are then analyzed, and action plans are developed. The management audit is another useful tool for such an assessment. In the nonprofit arena, management capacity (the effectiveness of management processes) and program capacity (effectiveness of programs) (Sowa, Selden, & Sandfort, 2004) can be assessed with a management audit. These tools and others are covered in detail in the chapter on data collection and assessment.

Also important are organizational system dynamics and alignment or fit across these factors. Diagnostic models (see, e.g., Palmer et al., 2017, and Burke, 2018, and, in the human services field, Aarons et al., 2011) provide conceptual frameworks for assessing these and other factors.

This assessment guides the selection of the change goal. Anticipating two of the next steps, *create a sense of urgency* and *communicate the change vision*, you should already have some preliminary data or indicators of the problem or need. Pull together additional data that may be relevant to identifying and addressing the problem and goals as you will present these to staff to launch the change process.

At this point, you should also determine the level of change that will be needed. Will this change be developmental, transitional, or transformational? Developmental change will not require all of the following steps, whereas transformational change will, and transitional change may.

Additional assessment can occur at a later stage, when change structures, including a steering committee and action teams, have been formed. At that point, these groups can conduct additional assessments regarding what factors need to be addressed as part of implementation of the change process.

Before we move on to a discussion of assessing the change process, we now look at how the change initiatives began in our four cases. In each of our cases, the change leaders spent some time with their teams doing an initial assessment of the conditions they were facing and how they could achieve their identified change goal.

Father Joe's Villages

The initiative in Father Joe's Villages began with the managers in charge of case management assessing the current functioning of their case conferencing and case coordination. The content of the change had to do with the fact that clients were being served by individual staff from various programs (e.g., career and education, addictions counseling), and there was ineffective coordination of client case plans and communication at team meetings. After the goal of improving case management and case conferencing was set, the program managers asked agency executive staff to join these discussions to include analysis of how such a change would affect current funding and related grant compliance requirements. A great deal of analysis was done regarding numbers of clients, staff roles and allocations, service delivery processes, and physical facilities in all the programs. A series of meetings led to the idea of creating a new system of multidisciplinary teams to address their issue and achieve their change goals. They concluded that this would also require related organizational restructuring and office relocations, including a "rapid rehousing team" to extend case management and employment services into two of the agency's main programs and shift the focus more firmly to moving clients to permanent housing.

San Mateo County

The content of the change in San Mateo County initially emerged when a member of the board of supervisors (elected officials for the county) shared her concern with the director of the Human Services Agency about the number of families who had complained about the fact that there didn't seem to be a single point of contact for somebody who had any kind of a social service need. She felt that clients should not have to deal with multiple, separate services and agencies and tell their story over and over to multiple people in order to receive the services they need. The supervisor wanted to see the system changed so that it would be easier for clients and the community to understand.

In assessing all the programs administered by the agency, staff found that services for children and families had deteriorated and that people did not have information about how clients were doing or not doing. They looked for ways that they could serve clients across multiple problem areas and began to look at the issues from the client or customer service perspective.

San Diego Youth Services

The initial assessment at SDYS began, as noted in Step 1, with CEO Walter Philips reflecting on the downturn in the national economy, leading to the possibility of a decrease in funding. He had also noted within the agency some inefficiencies at the administrative level and some duplication of duties that, combined with a lack of coordination and integration between the programs within the agency, created conditions requiring significant change. He also noted the recent prominence of trauma-informed care, and concluded that this was a model that would greatly benefit all of the agency's programs. He had long used a participative leadership style, so he soon communicated his assessment of the needs for change to the Board of Directors and the Executive Leadership Team.

San Diego Fire Department

The change process in the SDFD began shortly after Earle Roberts was hired as the San Diego fire chief. He was brought in partly because of his reputation as assistant fire chief in Phoenix as a competent and innovative leader. He assessed the senior staff of the SDFD and concluded that this was a competent and committed group of managers who would be willing to support his vision of making the department more progressive and innovative. By reviewing existing data and reports and visiting fire stations, he saw a department that was technically competent in basic firefighting and fire prevention but had little apparent interest in growing or developing in new ways to respond to a changing world of local government and public service. He saw himself as a leader who would help transform the department, getting battalion chiefs to see themselves as managers and empowering all employees to use their creativity to improve department operations. Chief Roberts believed there would be some resistance to change from "old-line" firefighters and battalion chiefs and began efforts to educate them about his vision and the need for change, showing how it would benefit them.

Assessing Process Aspects of the Change: Readiness and Capacity

Years ago when I was involved with the local chapter of the Organization Development Network, a professional organization for consultants, a consultant told the story of a preliminary meeting with a prospective client organization. After the executive explained the situation, the consultant said, "You could have used me 2 years ago, but now you need a bankruptcy attorney." As I thought about when an HSO executive should start getting familiar with organizational change, I reflected on how sometimes books on management or self-help tell the reader to either read the chapters in order or read selectively based on your current situation. For this book, it occurred to me that the promotional materials for the book could say, "Buy this book a year before you need to do organizational change and immediately read the sections on readiness and capacity for change."

Since that is not likely to happen, I still think you as a change leader can now assess your organization's readiness and capacity for change, and as needed address these factors to enhance readiness and capacity before beginning a change process, or if necessary, simultaneously with the process.

Early work on assessing the process of change focused on *resistance* to change. While resistance has received considerable attention, it has recently been reexamined (Ford & Ford, 2009). It was historically seen as a problem of individual employees reacting to a proposed change, but is now seen more from an employee's point of view and how the proposed change would impact the employee's working life. This offers broader possibilities for how it can be addressed, primarily by supporting staff as they go through the change process. Resistance is also now seen in a broader context that includes *readiness* for change (Rafferty, Jimmieson, & Armenakis, 2013).

Assessing the process aspects of change involves looking at the organization's *readiness* for change and its *capacity* for change. Readiness for change includes "the extent to which an individual or individuals are cognitively and emotionally inclined to accept, embrace, and adopt a particular plan to purposefully alter the status quo" (Holt, Armenakis, Feild, & Harris, 2007, p. 235). Change capacity can be defined as "a combination of managerial and organizational capabilities that allows an enterprise to adapt more quickly and effectively than its competition to changing situations" (Judge & Douglas, 2009, pp. 635–636). Buono and Kerber (2010, p. 10) made this distinction: "Differentiate change readiness in respect to the ability to implement a specific change, from *change capacity*—the ability of an organization to change not just once, but as a normal course of events in response to and in anticipation of internal and external shifts, constantly adapting to and anticipating changes in its environment."

We consider both staff and organizational readiness and then organizational and leader capacity.

Several instruments are available to assess readiness and capacity for change. If an agency cannot or does not want to use a formal instrument, informal assessments of readiness and capacity can be done by change leaders (e.g., the agency's executive team), possibly including other key stakeholders, such as informal leaders, using criteria covered here.

Staff Readiness and Capacity
Some research has examined individual employee factors that are relevant in organizational change implementation. I mention them here as questions to ask when considering a change process.

- How well will staff see this change as fitting with the vision and mission of the organization?

- How committed will staff be to the purpose, value, and necessity of the change?
- Will staff feel that they have to go along with the change or that it would be too costly for them to resist it or speak out about it?
- What is the nature of employees' felt relationships with the organization in terms of their job satisfaction, commitment to the organization, and trust in other staff and managers?
- What level of role autonomy do staff have? Staff who feel more autonomous or empowered typically have higher readiness or capacity for change.
- What level of tolerance do staff have for ambiguity, which is likely to increase in times of change?
- What level of self-efficacy do staff have? Self-efficacy and self-confidence are especially important factors, so I provide some additional detail here.

If you believe that any of these raise concerns about launching a change initiative, you can prepare answers to address them and share these when you officially roll out the change plan, particularly when you share the problem or need and the change goal, create a sense of urgency, and communicate the change vision. Later, and throughout the initiative, you can do a lot to develop and maintain support for staff and the change process.

Holt et al. (2007) grouped individual readiness into three factors:

- Change *self-efficacy*, or *change self-confidence*, "refers to the extent to which one feels that he or she has or does not have the skills and is or is not able to execute the tasks and activities that are associated with the implementation of the prospective change" (p. 238).
- *Discrepancy*, or the *perceived need for change*, "refers to the extent to which one feels that there are or are not legitimate reasons and needs for the prospective change" (p. 238).
- *Personal valence*, or *feeling that the change will be personally beneficial*, "refers to the extent to which one feels that he or she will or will not benefit from the implementation of the prospective change" (p. 238). Examples of potential benefits include a more manageable or meaningful job or new career opportunities.

It is important for change leaders to consider these concerns from the points of view of the involved staff members. This involves serious empathy: looking at the change not from your vantage point of one who is likely to benefit, but from the vantage point of employees who may have just had this change idea sprung on them. Staff are likely to be thinking, "What's in it for me?"—a legitimate question that should be fully addressed.

Information on how the organization stands with reference to these questions and issues regarding staff readiness should be clearly noted at this point, specifying areas that should be addressed before full implementation of the change process. Addressing the perceived need for change and staff feelings that the change will benefit them personally will be particularly important. This amounts to improving the preconditions for implementation, which should enhance prospects for success. To the extent that staff do not feel they have the skills or confidence to play their roles in implementing the change process, training and support can be provided before the initiative fully begins. Strategies to address these concerns are covered in Chapter 7 regarding developing support for the change initiative and addressing resistance.

Organizational Readiness

There are also tools for assessing *organizational* readiness for change. Here we look specifically at an instrument designed for HSOs (more specifically, addiction treatment). The Organizational Readiness for Change (Lehman et al., 2002) measures four major areas:

- *motivation for change* assesses program needs for improvement (strengths and weaknesses of the program), the extent of immediate training needs in that program, and pressures for change felt by staff or coming from external sources
- *adequacy of resources* includes offices, staffing, training, computer access, and e-communications
- *staff attributes* focus more on individual staff members rather than the organizational level and includes staff perceptions of their interest in professional growth, feelings of self-efficacy, their ability to influence colleagues, and their adaptability
- *organizational climate* includes staff awareness of the organization's mission and goals, staff cohesiveness and trust, staff feelings of autonomy, management openness to suggestions from staff, levels of stress, and perceptions that management is open to change

Even though this focuses on a program level, rather than an entire organization, it assesses conditions that could be applied on a change initiative affecting an entire organization. The extent to which these factors (except stress) are seen in the organization suggests a higher level of readiness for change.

The factors in that instrument are similar to those in other instruments, but one instrument (Bouckenooghe, Devos, & Van den Broeck, 2009) includes an important factor not covered by others: politicking. This dimension includes power games between departments, favoritism, and staff members being taken advantage of (p. 567). The authors noted, perhaps stating the obvious to those who have worked in a dysfunctional bureaucracy, that "a high degree of politicking leads to unnecessary expense, considerable delays, and unwillingness to share knowledge" (p. 598). Organizational change is clearly subject to the effects of organizational politics. Dealing with these dynamics may require attention beyond regular organizational change activities. Ideally, in advance of any other change process, administrators as change leaders would have implemented a culture change process to move the organization toward a more positive, humanistic, and results-oriented culture. Organizational culture change is discussed in more detail in Chapter 15.

The questionnaire mentioned above regarding staff readiness (Holt et al., 2007) also listed two factors regarding organizational readiness:

- *Organizational valence* [termed *organizationally beneficial* on the questionnaires] refers to the extent to which one feels that the organization will or will not benefit from the implementation of the prospective change. (p. 239)
- *Senior leadership support* refers to the extent to which one feels that the organization's leadership and management are or are not committed to and support or do not support implementation of the prospective change. (p. 239)

Readiness and change capacity should look the styles and philosophies of the change leaders, such as participative or directive styles, or preferences for a model such as transformational or transactional leadership (Bass & Avolio, 2006). Burke (2018) suggested that a change leader should begin a major organizational change initiative with self-examination, focusing on one's self-awareness, motives, and values, and then use insights from this assessment when leading the change process.

Organizational Capacity

Based on a literature review, Judge and Douglas (2009, p. 638) developed an instrument to measure change capacity that includes these factors:

- *Trustworthy leaders*: the ability of senior executives to earn the trust of the rest of the organization and to show organizational members the way to meet its collective goals
- *Trusting followers*: the ability of the nonexecutive employees to constructively dissent with and/or willingly follow a new path advocated by its senior executives

- *Capable champions*: the ability of an organization to attract, retain, and empower change leaders to evolve and emerge
- *Involved midmanagement*: the ability of middle managers to effectively link senior executives with the rest of the organization
- *Innovative culture*: the ability of the organization to establish norms of innovation and encourage innovative activity
- *Accountable culture*: the ability of the organization to carefully steward resources and successfully meet predetermined deadlines
- *Effective communication*: the ability of the organization to communicate vertically, horizontally, and with customers
- *Systems thinking*: the ability of the organization to focus on root causes and recognize the interdependencies within and outside the organizational boundaries

You can use these factors to stimulate thoughtful discussions with key stakeholders about the extent to which these conditions exist in your organization. If some are not apparent and are likely to be essential factors in the success of the initiative, see what can be done to work on them to create a higher level of readiness or capacity.

Change Leader Capacity

At this initial stage, an essential aspect of the assessment process is to determine your role as a change leader in the process. Will you be in charge of this or working for or with someone who will be the change leader? Specific change agent roles are discussed in Chapter 7 regarding development of the action system. Given your role, what characteristics and competencies of your own will be relevant during this process?

If you are, or are ready to become, a change leader, you may be feeling that Chapter 3 covered all that needs to be said or looked at about you: your capacities, your values and priorities, and your possible limitations or development needs. This is especially important if you are at a high management level, where your role and power can help isolate you from outside perspectives and can give you a false sense of your capacities and your self-assurance. Therefore, a good place to start the assessment of your organization as you begin a change process would be for you to assess yourself.

As noted in Chapter 3, there are key success factors related to characteristics and skills of the change leader. Your level of self-awareness, your tolerance for ambiguity, your energy level and ability to work long hours when needed, your skills in interacting with and energizing others, your task orientation and goal focus, your leadership philosophy, and your team-building skills will be very important success factors. This might be a good time to take another look at those factors and assess yourself with reference to the criteria or skills covered there.

As part of this assessment, ask trusted colleagues and yourself about your capacities in these areas:

- What are your assumptions about how people are motivated and how they should be led?
- Is your general management style more participative or directive?
- What is your level of trust that others will make decisions that are well thought out and are for the good of the organization, even if you may disagree with some of them?
- Does your leadership style fit with the characteristics and needs of the organization and the employees?
- Do you have realistic expectations about the pace of change that will inevitably place additional demands on the time and feelings of comfort and safety of the staff?
- Will you be comfortable seeing the culture of your organization change if that will be needed to achieve the desired outcomes and performance improvements?
- What is your basic philosophy regarding change strategy?
- Can you effectively use the task, relationship, and change behaviors such as those listed in Chapter 3?
- Do you have the influence skills listed in Chapter 3, and can you use these effectively?

Some of these questions were raised at the end of Chapter 4, but you and other key change leaders may now benefit from a more introspective discussion about them. In addition to asking these questions about yourself, encourage key members of your team to ask these questions of themselves. It may be helpful to take the time in a team-building session to discuss these, frankly and deeply, and to identify any changes you might want to make to better position yourselves to be effective change leaders.

Taken together, assessing staff, organizational, and leader readiness and capacity for change and then planning ways to enhance them can help you create preconditions that can help the change initiative be successful. A classic organization development tool, the *force field analysis*, can be very useful in laying out the key factors that could support or resist the change so they can be addressed. Resistance is addressed more fully in Chapter 7 as part of developing and maintaining support for staff and the change process.

Force Field Analysis

A force field analysis explicitly identifies driving forces, which aid the change or make it more likely to occur, and restraining forces, which are points of resistance or things that get in the way of change (see Cohen & Hyde, 2014a, for some human services applications). The current state of the organization is represented by a line down the middle of a piece of paper. The change goal, or desired future state, is slightly to the right of that line (see Figure 5.1).

The change process involves moving from the current state to the ideal future state. To the left of the second line (the current state) are listed all driving forces (individuals, key groups, or conditions) that may assist in the implementation of the change. On the other side are listed restraining forces that will make the change more difficult to implement. The example in Figure 5.1 is a force field analysis of a change goal to implement a program evaluation system (Linn, 2000).

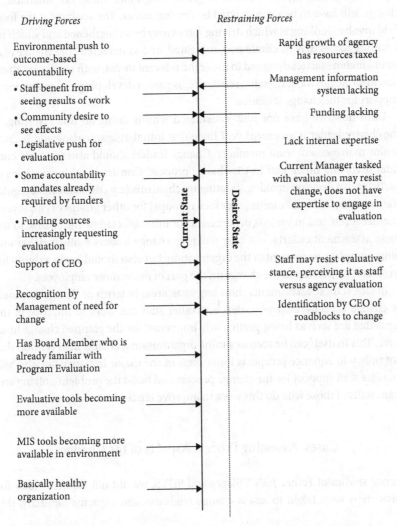

Figure 5.1 Force field analysis: implementing a program evaluation system.

Key stakeholders should also be listed here. Particularly important to consider will be powerful or influential managers who will be needed to support the change, bureaucratically oriented staff or others likely to prefer the status quo, and outside forces such as governing boards or community stakeholders. In a large organization such as a county HSO, other departments (finance, human resources, etc.) may need attention. In an organization with unions or other employee organizations, these groups should be seriously considered. Working with employee organizations is briefly addressed in later chapters.

Arrows from both sides of the force field touch the "current state" line, representing the constellation of forces. Each force is then assessed in two ways: its potency or strength and its amenability to change. More potent forces, especially restraining ones, will need greater attention. Those not amenable to change will have to be counteracted by driving forces. The analysis of the force field involves looking at which driving forces may be strengthened and which restraining forces may be eliminated, mitigated, or counteracted. The change plan would include tactics designed to move the relevant forces, with particular attention to strategies for addressing resistance, as part of developing and maintaining support for the change initiative.

Until now, we have not fully considered who is doing all this assessing. If the change leader is an executive, I hope that initial assessments would include senior management team members. Change leaders should also seriously consider involving other staff in the change process. Consistent with principles of participative decision-making, creating mechanisms (e.g., discussions at regular staff meetings, all-staff meetings, or focus groups) for other groups of employees, at other levels and in various departments or units affected by the change to use these assessment criteria, not only will give change leaders a much richer and more complete assessment of the organization, but also should begin to build interest and ownership in the change on the part of many more employees.

In fact, if these assessments show any weak areas in terms of change readiness or change capacity, change leaders and other staff can work to improve in the areas that are seen as being particularly important for the planned change initiative. This in itself can be seen as a mini-organizational change intervention that not only will enhance prospects for success of the major initiative but also will increase staff support for the change process and build the problem-solving and team skills of those who do this work to improve readiness and capacity.

Cases: Assessing Process Aspects of the Change

In our studies of Father Joe's Villages and SDYS, we did not explicitly look for what steps were taken to assess change readiness and capacity. Similarly, this assessment was not documented in the San Mateo County case. The SDFD case was assigned to the consulting unit where I worked, and my colleagues and I did not give formal attention to readiness and capacity. These terms were not common in the organization development field, and it didn't occur to us that we needed to pay explicit attention to these considerations beyond doing a force field analysis—a common organization development technology at that time.

Summary

While organizational change typically starts with an agency's executive identifying a need or challenge that is often, in HSOs, precipitated by outside forces, the process should soon become participative. Discussions at the agency executive team level can begin analysis of the current situation: both the pressures for change and internal organizational conditions. Assessment of an organization's readiness and capacity for change can point to preliminary changes, perhaps in organizational culture, that can create conditions to enable the change effort to be launched successfully.

Reflection and Focusing Questions

1. What problems, needs, challenges, or opportunities are facing your organization? Pick one that is large enough to be addressed with this planned change process.
2. What would be the desired future state for your organization after a successful change process has been completed? What would be the overriding change goal?
3. How would you assess staff and organizational readiness and capacity for this change?
4. What aspects of staff and organizational readiness and capacity should be worked on before a change initiative begins?

6

Launching the Change Initiative

> Vision without action is a daydream. Action without vision is a nightmare.
>
> —Japanese proverb

As noted in the previous chapter, steps in this process are presented in the order that they should normally occur, but there may be times when the order may change or, more commonly, steps may need to be partly repeated based on new developments or on broadening the effort to new parts of the organization. One "step" in particular, *develop and maintain support*, is covered in the next chapter but should be happening pretty much throughout the initiative. Change leaders should always be alert to human factors, including staff concerns and perspectives and their need to be informed of activities. Involving staff in the process should have a significant effect on creating staff commitment, as well as leading to better ideas and outcomes.

After the needs and opportunities for change are identified and the initial change leaders have done an assessment of the organization's readiness and capacities for change, a change strategy can be developed to guide the overall initiative. The initiative can then be introduced widely throughout the organization or at least the parts of the organization that will be involved. This chapter addresses the initial implementation steps of determining an overall change strategy, communicating the need for and desirability of the change, creating a sense of urgency and communicating the change vision.

Step 4. Determine the Overall Change Strategy

First, as a point of clarification, change strategy here means the *process* aspect of change. Sometimes changing organizational strategy can actually be an organizational change *content* goal. For example, if the updated strategic plan has major new initiatives, any of those could be the content of a change initiative. And, if an organization will be engaging in a major strategic planning process, that in itself may be a bit of a culture change or a change in planning processes. This section

Organizational Change for the Human Services. Thomas Packard, Oxford University Press. © Oxford University Press 2021. DOI: 10.1093/oso/9780197549995.003.0007

addresses only the process aspects: the strategies for implementing a change initiative.

As noted in Chapter 2, there are three overall change strategy options to consider: empirical–rational, normative–reeducative, and power–coercive strategies (Burke, 2018, pp. 195–199). *Empirical–rational* strategies use research findings and analysis of organizational conditions to show the need for change. *Normative–reeducative* strategies use extensive employee participation in the change process to involve staff in problem analysis and problem-solving and to build commitment for change. *Power–coercive* strategies may be needed if there are external forces such as legislative or policy changes that require change.

The leadership models covered in Chapter 4 are most aligned with normative–reeducative strategies, so these receive particular attention here. Power–coercive strategies are not much advocated in the leadership literature, but their use as a leadership style in organizational change might be appropriate when a change mandate comes from the outside, such as implementation of a new policy. In this case, the change leader can state the goal as a given and then use other leadership behaviors to facilitate implementation.

Empirical–Rational Strategies

Empirical–rational strategies would seem to follow from external forces such as expectations that evidence-based practices be used and that there are expectations for documented changes in client outcomes. Especially with professional staff who have been educated about the importance of the scientific method, it is reasonable to expect that such professionals can understand the importance of data and new knowledge in guiding change. Agency or program performance data can be very helpful in showing the need for change. Sometimes an agency can compare its data on outcomes with other agencies or with industry standards, such as foster home placements or time to complete an adoption. If a program is performing at levels below those established in a grant or contract, data can be a powerful motivating force for staff.

Empirical–rational strategies can be used to tap the legitimate self-interest of employees, such as their concerns about job stability and meaningful work.

Normative–Reeducative Strategies

Normative–reeducative strategies are reflected in the use of extensive employee participation in the change process through techniques such as group problem-solving and participative management styles. Much of the literature and practice wisdom suggests that this overall approach is the most appropriate for organizations such as human service organization (HSOs).

Within normative–reeducative (e.g., participative) leadership, the change process may also include analytical tasks such as gathering and analyzing data (e.g., types and amounts of services delivered, client outcomes, client satisfaction, and agency process workflows such as the process for applying for Food Stamps/SNAP [Supplemental Nutrition Assistance Program]). Quality management techniques such as Total Quality Management and Continuous Quality Improvement use both: precise analysis of data for process and quality improvement and employee participation in the analysis and problem-solving process.

Burke (2018) suggested that within a normative–reeducative approach there are two main thrusts: "improving the problem-solving capabilities of a system" and "releasing and fostering growth in the persons who make up the system to be changes" (p. 199). These approaches suggest that the "client system" (i.e., people in the organization) should be heavily involved in the change process, and that the change should not be imposed on them. Several leadership styles covered in Chapter 4 align directly with this approach.

Power–Coercive Strategies

Organizational power and politics have, mostly deservedly, a reputation as "bad" aspects of organizational behavior. Nevertheless, there will clearly be political dynamics in major organizational change (Price, 2019), so these dynamics should be explicitly considered when planning and implementing a change initiative. In fact, these can sometimes be used in a positive way. For example, most discussions of organizational politics (e.g., Buchanan & Badham, 2008; Price, 2019) emphasize self-interest on the part of an employee—not generally seen as a desirable perspective in HSOs, but one that should legitimately be considered. It is addressed in some detail in the next chapter as an aspect of addressing resistance and developing support for the change. One aspect of this that is worth mentioning here, regarding strategy selection, is the notion that, when a power–coercive strategy is used, some staff may act as if they are going along with the change to "fit in" (Price, 2019). Change leaders should be alert to this dynamic and try to establish a climate in which staff resistance and concerns can be raised and addressed without fear of reprisals. This, of course, enters the realm of normative–reeducative strategy.

An early article (Hasenfeld, 1980) using a political economy perspective on organizational change suggested that a change agent should be able to

a) Mobilize external resources and legitimation to counteract internal and external resistance to the change;

b) Possess sufficient technical expertise and knowledge to operationalize the proposed change; and

c) Occupy a position of functional centrality in the organizational division of labor and offer sufficient inducements to overcome internal resistance (p. 512).

These guidelines seem sensible and relevant regardless of the overall change strategy to be used.

Another perspective on power in organizations that can be useful here is critical theory, more specifically feminist theory (Netting et al., 2017, pp. 214–216). Some HSOs might be seen as reflecting the theory of organizations as instruments of domination or exploitation (mentioned in the Introduction). There are clearly elements of this perspective in the history of HSOs and other formal organizations regarding various aspects of marginalization, discrimination, and power imbalances affecting underrepresented populations in a workforce. This perspective has shown up more often in the literature on staff-initiated organizational change (covered in another chapter), but it can also be useful to change agents in a power position in the organization. In fact, it may be even more important for an executive-level change leader, particularly white males, who still are overrepresented at this level, to use this perspective to guide change initiatives, particularly in areas that include changing organizational culture to make it more inclusive, advancing social justice within the organization, and changing human resources practice to address systemic mistreatment of women and underrepresented segments of the workforce.

A final important distinction can be made here, based on McClelland's classic motivation theory, contrasting personalized power—traditional self-interest—and socialized power, which involves a change leader using power or influence for larger organizational interests or goals. One definition that touches on this distinction is by Ferris et al. (2005, p. 127): "the ability to effectively understand others at work, and to use such knowledge to influence others to act in ways that enhance one's personal and/or organizational objectives." If we can focus only on organizational objectives, the use of power can be seen as potentially a positive force in organizational change. In fact, Buchanan and Badham (2008, p. 22) listed a few common tactics in this spirit: building a network of useful contacts, using "key players" to support initiatives, and making friends with power brokers.

In a less positive vein, a change leader operating in a particularly political environment may use the "backstage" political skills of "(i) constantly analyzing and monitoring the situational politics, and (ii) countering the political moves of others with their own developed political strategies in order to gain support for the change" (Hamlin & Russ-Eft, 2019, p. 39, citing Buchanan & Boddy, 1992).

Even this strategy may be done from a positive perspective using the influence tactics in Chapter 3.

Strategy Selection

It is clearly possible to use more than one strategy on a change initiative. Empirical–rational strategies can sometimes be used to provide a rationale for an externally mandated change, along with the normative–reeducative approaches of providing leadership. For example, Gibbons (2015, pp. 239–240) offered several principles for influencing with facts in organizational change. First, perhaps obviously, facts do matter and should be used. For example, if a court decision now requires a child welfare agency to add mental health services for all cases, agency change leaders can provide data showing where the lack of mental health services negatively impacted cases and where mental health services have made a positive difference.

Gibbons also added that change leaders should not unnecessarily overload staff with facts, and that visuals, such as graphs, should help. Finally, he suggested paying attention to staff self-esteem, such as how their identity may be threatened by a change. This might be especially salient when a county policy change requires the merger of mental health and substance abuse services into a new behavioral health department. Each of those professions may feel threatened by possible challenges to their expertise, and such concerns should be thoughtfully addressed. This actually gets into the realm of normative–reeducative strategies, which are likely to be the most effective for change leaders.

The literature on organizational change seems to tend toward a use of a normative–reeducative strategy, sometimes augmented by the use of analytical techniques such as Total Quality Management. Choi and Ruona (2011) suggested that individuals are more likely to have higher levels of readiness for organizational change when they experience normative–reeducative change strategies.

In the human services field, staff typically have professional values regarding the primacy of human relationships, including positive treatment of clients and colleagues. Their professional education also leads to expectations that they be involved in decisions that affect them since, as professionals, they have skills that would warrant their involvement in decision-making. These factors suggest the use of normative–reeducative strategies. Overall, a normative–reeducative strategy and elements of an empirical–rational strategy using organizational performance data and analytical techniques such as Total Quality Management are likely to be especially appropriate for HSOs.

Power–coercive strategies might sometimes be dictated by the environment, in the form of a new policy directive (e.g., all child welfare families must have mental health assessments, there must be time limits on the use of Temporary Assistance for Needy Families [TANF]). The organization's change leaders can then use some combination of empirical–rational, normative–reeducative, and power–coercive strategies to implement policy directives. In the case of such an externally required change, a change leader could say that "we have to make this change because of a required new policy [power-coercive and empirical-rational], and we will ensure that we implement this in a way that will enable us to provide the best possible services for clients [normative-reeducative]."

Case Examples

In studying our four case examples, I didn't find much explicit attention to overall change strategy with reference to the approaches just explained. My sense is that in the three HSO cases empirical–rational strategies were the most common. Needs for change were identified with reference to data, mostly starting with anecdotal assessments of service delivery processes that could be improved, later moving to more detailed analysis of processes, programs, and structures. As those projects unfolded, normative–reeducative strategies were used in getting staff involved in the process and focusing on the importance of providing high-quality services to clients. The fire department used more of a normative–reeducative strategy through Chief Roberts using a participative leadership style, supported by our organization development model, which is inherently participative. The department solicited employee involvement through a staff survey and many team-building sessions, and the later formation of problem-solving groups, all of which helped evolve the organizational culture to a more participative and improvement-oriented one.

Step 5. Communicate the Need for and the Desirability of the Change

Up to this point, most of the change-related activity will have been conducted by a relatively small group, typically at the organization's executive and/or management levels. This chapter started by discussing the development of an overall change strategy. This flows from the processes in the previous chapter, including the initial analysis of external and internal forces suggesting the need for major change, the change goal, and assessing the process aspects of change, including the preconditions of readiness and change capacity to move forward. All these factors are used to develop an overall change strategy to guide how people will behave during the change process.

After a core leadership group has done this initial work, it will be time to introduce the change initiative to all involved staff. The following steps in the change process refer to all aspects of the people and systems that will be engaged in the process. This step and the next two, creating a sense of urgency and communicating the change vision, will essentially be occurring simultaneously.

Data gathered and analyzed earlier can be shared with staff to show the need for the change. If the change is expected to impact client outcomes or other performance measures, change leaders can share existing data and, aligned with the communication of the change vision, suggest changes in the data that can be expected. They can also refer staff to the agency's statements of mission, visions, and values and to the current strategic plan, showing how these will guide the change process and how the results will be consistent with them. Change leaders can also refer to the codes of ethics and practice principles of their profession and other professions represented in the organization to show how the change initiative is in alignment with those principles.

In addition to using what organizational change thought leader John Kotter called "business case for change," Kotter has asserted that "people also need to feel the need and urgency for change through tactics aimed at the heart" (2008, p. 40). He suggested that changing both hearts and minds can be aided by delivering the message with confidence, credibility, passion, and conviction and addressing multiple senses using visuals, stories, and sharing of feelings. If it can be said without seeming contrived, a change leader can suggest that the crisis may be a blessing, or maybe reassurances can be given to "change-weary" staff that this effort will be more thoughtfully done and will not repeat ineffective processes used in past change efforts that failed.

Kotter also emphasized (1996) that change leaders cannot "overcommunicate" the need and urgency for change. It is easy for change leaders and managers involved in a change process to assume that everyone else knows as much as they do about the process and therefore not communicate as much to or not involve more fully and broadly other staff members in the process. He also suggested that members of the organization should be encouraged to talk directly with stakeholders, especially those who may be dissatisfied with the organization's current performance. Employee surveys or focus group results can be used to convince staff that there are things that need to be changed.

Here are some examples of how the change leaders in our cases introduced the need for and the desirability of the change.

Father Joe's Villages

Managers of St. Joe's Villages communicated the need for the change at many staff meetings, describing why the changes would be good for the agency. Similar meetings were held with clients, who were told about the need for the change and how it would improve services. Extensive written materials covering the current limitations in case management and service delivery and staffing concerns were shared at a number of meetings.

San Mateo County

As an outcome of a strategic planning process, the San Mateo County agency created an advisory council to oversee the efforts to improve the system. It comprised staff from public and community-based organizations, former clients, political representatives, and a board member from a local foundation. A new mission statement was developed, and principles and values for the process were rolled out to staff for discussion and input. They conducted client satisfaction surveys to determine both satisfaction and dissatisfaction with all services.

San Diego Youth Services

For restructuring at San Diego Youth Services (SDYS), two key factors regarding the need to address the problem were presented to the management team and later to staff: (1) the economic downturn and how other nonprofits and businesses overall were being negatively impacted and (2) projections of specific program losses and the negative impact on the entire agency's financial performance. To set the stage for implementing trauma-informed care in all their programs, Chief executive officer (CEO) Walter Philips emphasized the agency's commitment to providing the best possible services.

San Diego Fire Department

The change process in the San Diego Fire Department began with the senior staff (the chief, assistant chief, deputy chiefs, and the director of administrative services) holding a 3-day team-building session. They then did some planning regarding next steps. They invited the president of the firefighter's union, who was himself very change oriented, to some of these meetings. They had the training unit prepare a video to introduce the change process. The video featured segments from the chief and from the union president stating their support for the process. This was shared at all fire stations and work areas. The department also started a newsletter on what was known as "the organization development project" and set up a hotline to chief's secretary where questions could be asked to be forwarded to the senior staff for answers.

Step 6. Create a Sense of Urgency

The sixth step, creating a sense of urgency, may be done at least partly in conjunction with the two previous steps: communicating the need and communicating the change vision. Initially, people will need to be convinced as to the urgency of a change in order for them to become open to change happening. Often, environmental developments such as funding cutbacks, healthcare reform, and privatization create obvious pressure for change. Internal conditions such as quality, efficiency, program effectiveness, or morale may also need attention and would benefit from the use of an organizational change process.

Whatever conditions can be identified to show the urgency of change, the change leader will need to fully communicate these pressures and the need for change. Such communication should accent the importance of the crisis, using any available data or examples, and give staff a picture of what will happen if the problem is not addressed.

Staff may be comfortable and happy with the status quo and feel overworked enough as it is and therefore may be disinclined to take on a significant change in the way they or their programs operate. The change formula referred to in Chapter 8 can be useful here, accenting dissatisfaction with the current state, conveying a clear and compelling vision of an ideal future state of the organization, and describing a clear and feasible process for reaching the desired state that minimizes the "costs" to participants.

As much as possible, take the perspective of staff who will be affected and how *they* can be helped to see and feel the urgency for change. The change leader can use data to show that if a change is not made, the organization and staff will suffer undesirable consequences, such as loss of clients, loss of funding, a decrease in service quality or productivity, or a serious morale problem. Problems can range from new directives from funders, funding cutbacks, or expectations for improved services to low staff morale, burnout, or inadequate management systems. As much as possible, existing data should be used to demonstrate the urgency for change.

John Kotter was the first to popularize the notion of the importance of creating urgency for change. It was a step in his model that many, including yours truly, have incorporated into their models. He thought it was so important that he wrote a separate book (Kotter, 2008) about creating urgency. He first made the point that organizations can experience not only complacency but also a false sense of urgency: "frenetic activity which exhausts and stresses people," which is often due to intense pressure from an external source (p. 3).

Another caveat about overusing urgency to motivate staff to change was seen in a study of federal executives who had recently been involved with major organizational transformations. Using the modern classic "burning platform" metaphor (think of a fire on an oil rig at sea, presenting employees with the option of acting [jumping] or dying), they noted two dynamics to be alert to: first, if an organization overuses burning platform messages, staff may become numb to them, and, second, in their words:

> If you choose to seek to achieve transformation initiatives based on the urgency of a burning platform, you must recognize that you are likely to be sacrificing some analytic precision and deep understanding of the forces surrounding your action, and it will be difficult to sustain the response among large cross-boundary groups over time. (Reisner, 2011, p. 13)

This suggests that combining all three of the steps we are looking at—persuasively show the need for change, especially using data; appealing to organizational norms such as customer service, professional standards, or organizational excellence; and conveying urgency—may be the most impactful.

Kotter added that change leaders must "behave with true urgency themselves *every single day*" (2008, p. 58; italics in original), creating a culture of urgency in which people are always looking for new opportunities for improvement. Jumping ahead briefly to the implementation stage, he suggested that as possible, early in the change process, you should take on some "quick-and-easy" activities that contribute to the overall effort, resulting in some quick, short-term successes. He added, however, that urgency must be kept up after these successes.

This section ends with some examples from our cases.

Father Joe's Villages

Because the need for change at Father Joe's Villages was not driven by external forces but mainly by administrators who saw the need for improving services to clients and better using staff resources, managers needed to convey urgency without a "threat" from the outside, such as a requirement from funding organizations. One aspect of urgency was the feeling that client outcomes needed to improve in a major residential program that at that point had limited case management services. After initiation of the process, urgency was demonstrated through timelines and dates for action plan implementation. Ultimately, the need was understood, with a later focus group participant reporting hearing, "This is a best practice and here's why this is the best way to go."

San Mateo County

In San Mateo County, urgency was reflected in the concern from the board mentioned in the previous step about the number of families who had complained about the fact that there didn't seem to be a single point of contact for somebody who had any kind of a social service need. Also, the Human Services Agency (HSA) conducted client satisfaction surveys to determine both satisfaction and dissatisfaction with all of their services. This enabled them to identify what they could improve and monitor over time. Management also shared with staff the findings regarding declines in social indicators. Management also reinforced the data through continual messages that "we are here to serve the community and to serve the customers more effectively."

San Diego Youth Services

At SDYS, Walter Philips attended many meetings, from those of the board to those of program staff, to articulate the need for the change. Regarding trauma-informed care, the agency showed urgency by quickly forming a workgroup to address this issue.

San Diego Fire Department

The San Diego Fire Department was by no means in crisis, but in the antigovernment and low-tax climate of the 1980s, Chief Roberts knew that the department would need to become more efficient and take on new roles beyond just responding to fires. In his meetings with staff and managers, he showed them how tax revenues would be decreasing, and that the mayor and council would be expecting them to operate more efficiently, broaden the services that they provided to the community, and show greater accountability.

The chief made it clear that the department could not operate as usual, and that in order to continue to be seen as valuable and worthy of increased city support, it would need to become more innovative, with higher levels of management competence. He immediately made some changes in his senior staff operations, arranging an off-site team-building workshop and implementing new processes, including management by objectives.

Step 7. Communicate the Change Vision

Thus far I have addressed three specific change tactics in this model: *communicate the need for and the desirability of the change* and *communicate the urgency for the change*. After staff learn about the current needs, problems, and challenges that the organization is facing, and understand the change goal and the urgency with which it should be approached, they will understandably want to know how in the world the organization can deal with all that and accomplish the desired goal.

So, at the same meeting or in other communications with staff, they should hear at least the basics about what the next steps will be to get the change initiative launched and what activities will be occurring to implement it. This will require that the change leaders will have already done a good deal of planning for the next major steps, covered in detail in Chapter 7: the action system that will be used and some basics of the change activities. The overall message may be something like the following:

> This will require a good deal of time and effort on the part of many staff because we will need your expertise to come up with the best solutions and ideas for change. We will have a well-structured process, with a committee that includes staff representation to guide the initiative, a staff member designated to provide support and training, and some processes for problem analysis and problem-solving.

Communicating the change vision actually addresses two of the key tactics in this change model: *clearly communicate the vision and outcomes for the change* and *clarify the plan for how the change process will be implemented (including basic activities and who would be involved)*. One aspect of this is conveying the vision for success: the change goal that reflects the desired future state of the organization. The other aspect of the change vision is a clear and specific plan for how the change initiative will be implemented, including people and groups to be involved and planned activities and persons accountable for them. These plans are covered in more detail in Chapter 7, but the basics should be shared with employees at this stage. The plan should also describe how any additional data will be collected and analyzed and the use of task forces and other change processes. The time frame for the project and available resources (especially staff time and any necessary financial support) should be noted. Connecting the change outcome with the plan for how to get there can be a good reminder to staff, especially at difficult times during the process, that all the hard work will pay off. This should be communicated clearly, enthusiastically, and regularly as needed during implementation.

Leaders can provide staff some general information regarding who will be in charge of and supporting the effort and the activities that will be part of the change process. This often involves plans for more detailed data collection and analysis regarding the problem, formation of problem-solving task forces, use of change processes that will be described at a later step, and clarification of the staff time and resources that will be committed to the project.

In addition to covering these more technical aspects of the change, some McKinsey consultants (Bucy, Hall, & Yakola, 2016) suggested that to help articulate a compelling vision of the desired future—what the organization will look like and how it will be operating after successful change—change leaders should tell a "compelling story" to more fully engage staff:

> Most companies underestimate the importance of communicating the "why" of a transformation; too often, they assume that a letter from the CEO and a corporate slide pack will secure organizational engagement. But it's not enough to say "we aren't making our budget plan" or "we must be more competitive." Engagement with employees and managers needs to have a context, a vision, and a call to action that will resonate with each person individually. This kind of personalization is what motivates a workforce. (p. 7)

Consistent with the spirit of engaging staff through participative decision-making, Jaiya John offered some additional thoughts on going beyond simply stating your own vision by creating dialogue with employees to get their visions for what the organization will be after the change process and how the change process could occur.

> Leaders often focus more on a vision than on tapping into their [staff's] streams of inspiration, passion, and purpose. These streams soak the words and tone of leaders with sincerity and belief. This is what stirs a work tribe into courageous change. (John, 2016, p. 64)

Next are some examples of how change leaders in our cases developed and communicated their visions for change.

Father Joe's Villages

Visions for the new system at Father Joe's Villages, including detail on the new case management system, were communicated at meetings with staff and clients. Documents explaining the new model were prepared for review and approval by the agency's central administrative office, and briefings were held with staff, clients, and outside stakeholders (including grant partners on two federal grants). Documents that were shared included briefing sheets describing the need, components of the new model, and benefits expected; PowerPoint presentations; detail on changes in programs, including new service delivery processes and current versus proposed staffing; spreadsheets with client and staffing data; flow charts showing how clients would move through the system; organizational charts; and office space layouts. Documents with commonly asked questions and answers were also used at meetings with staff and clients. At a later focus group, respondents reported hearing the following from the change leaders: "You'll be able to help more people in less time and with less work."

San Mateo County

In San Mateo County, the HSA decided to work together with the community to form a network of services that provided a continuum of services that improved the lives of children and families. The overall goal was to reduce the need to shop around or call multiple locations to address the needs of residents. Ultimate goals were to promote economic self-sufficiency, strengthen family functioning, and build community capacity for prevention and early intervention. Creating a customer service focus required identification of client outcomes, requiring a new automated information system.

They began their planning by assessing all the programs administered by the HSA. Most of the programs were mandated by the federal and state governments and included different populations, policies, forms, and eligibility requirements. They looked for ways to serve clients across multiple problem areas, looking at the issues from the client or customer service perspective. They undertook a review of the many different processes utilized in the different programs to determine how much of it was federally or state imposed versus locally designed and how much flexibility there was to change those processes within the confines of federal and state laws or regulations. The executive team completed a strategic planning process that led to the development of an operational plan that could guide the change initiative.

San Diego Youth Services

At SDYS, Walter Philips used meetings with many staff groups to clarify the change vision for restructuring: to reduce administrative overhead, consolidate administrative and management positions, and reorganize programs into more appropriate bundles of services. Much of this communication occurred along with the descriptions of need and urgency. One later focus group participant reported that after restructuring implementation, "It was clear to me; my supervisor was a champion of it." Regarding trauma-informed care, there was ongoing discussion at program manager meetings. One focus group member reported being very clear on the vision, but not as much on the outcomes. Regarding rebranding, executive staff shared at program manager meetings the new logos and colors for letterhead and the rationale for why this would be good for the agency, and program managers were asked to communicate this information to their staff.

San Diego Fire Department

Chief Roberts of the San Diego Fire Department had several clear visions for the department that he began sharing, first with his senior staff and then with battalion chiefs and the rest of the staff. In addition to specific program initiatives such as having fire companies do inspections of buildings in their districts, he wanted to improve management and accountability and empower staff to share ideas for improving operations.

He requested consulting assistance from the city's Organization Effectiveness Program. Shortly after the launch of the project, I joined another consultant who had been working with the fire department for a few months.

We recommended a change process that would include collection of data to identify problems, using an employee attitude survey and surveys of outside stakeholders, including the Civil Service Commission, town councils, the city council, and recent victims of fires. Results of these surveys would be fed back to employees, setting the stage for formation of problem-solving groups to address identified problems.

The senior staff also identified the need for workshops in key areas needing change, including the Fire Prevention Bureau. Chief Roberts made it clear that the department would provide adequate resources in the form of consultation support and release time for employees to attend necessary meetings.

Summary

Quickly after the assessment process in the previous chapter, change leaders can develop an overall strategy for implementing the change and begin communicating both the urgency of the change and the change vision. This should result in staff throughout the organization having clarity on current challenges and problems, the change goal, the urgency for addressing the problems, and the vision of how the change process will unfold. The next chapter discusses in detail the formation of an action system and an overall implementation plan for the change initiative.

Reflection and Focusing Questions

Regarding the change initiative that you identified in the Reflection and Focusing Questions in the previous chapter,

1. Given characteristics of the organization, what overall change strategy would be the most appropriate? Or would there be elements of more than one? Why would this one or this combination be the best?
2. How would you create a sense of urgency for the change?
3. How would you articulate your change vision? How would you incorporate visions from staff?

7

Implementation Systems and Processes

I love it when a plan comes together.
— "Hannibal" Smith, *The A-Team*

This chapter covers the key structures and processes that will guide the change initiative. Structural aspects include the action system and roles of change participants. Key implementation processes include action teams and tactics such as communication processes, training staff regarding change skills, and providing opportunities for team building and conflict management.

Step 8. Develop the Action System

Large-scale change cannot be accomplished by only the executive or top management team. An organizational change initiative will be more successful if a diverse and skilled set of staff and managers is recruited for participation. Building a broad-based action system with designated responsibilities for implementing and overseeing the change initiative serves several functions. If many staff members are involved, then multiple talents can be brought to bear to address the challenges and tasks ahead. Tapping the knowledge and expertise of a wider group of people will result in more creative ideas and solutions. Spreading the workload can help ensure that the additional demands of change do not significantly disrupt ongoing work. Additionally, getting staff members involved can increase their sense of ownership of the results.

Formal Roles

There are a number of formal roles that have been found to be useful in large-scale organizational change. All of these may not be needed, especially for some transitional change efforts or in smaller organizations. Key roles, which are reviewed here, include a change sponsor, a change champion, a supportive executive team, a number of smaller teams, and perhaps facilitators and/or

Organizational Change for the Human Services. Thomas Packard, Oxford University Press. © Oxford University Press 2021. DOI: 10.1093/oso/9780197549995.003.0008

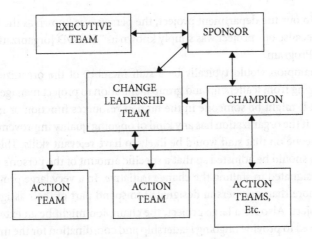

Figure 7.1 The action system: key change initiative roles.

consultants. These roles are represented in Figure 7.1. The lines represent communication relationships.

Sponsor: The change initiative should include a designated sponsor, typically the chief executive involved, such as a department or division head. This person must demonstrate, on an ongoing basis, organizational commitment to the process and assurance that necessary resources (especially including staff time) are allocated.

Ackerman Anderson (2020, p. 9) listed the following "deliverables" for a sponsor:

- Achievement of the organization's business strategy through the creation and oversight of the change strategy, initiatives, and conditions required to produce the necessary business outcomes
- Mobilization and alignment of the entire organization undergoing the change
- Clear direction and path for the change
- Sustained well-being in the organization during and after the change
- Being a model of the mindset, behavior, and cultural changes required for a successful change

Champion: A person with a designated staff assignment, including time and other necessary resources, should be designated as a champion: the person with day-to-day responsibility for implementing the change effort and providing ongoing energy and focus for staff. The position can have any title that describes the role. In our fire department project, the person was known as the OD coordinator because our project was simply known as "The OD [organization development] Program."

The champion would typically be a staff member of the organization with skills ranging from leadership and group facilitation to project management and planning. It might be someone in the human resources function or in another staff unit. If the organization has any kind of ongoing quality improvement function, someone on that staff would be likely to have relevant skills. This person's job duties should be adjusted so that a specific amount of the person's workload can be designated to staffing the change initiative. In a very large project, there may be more than one person designated to spend part of their assigned tasks to the project. Also for a large project, the champion might be an external consultant hired to provide ongoing leadership and coordination for the initiative.

Regardless of this person's role, the person should be recognized as having significant influence, authority, and responsibility, reflected in support from senior management. The consultant and project management aspects of the role are covered in more detail in the next section—implementing the plan for change. For now, it is worth noting that the champion role operates on a fine line: not fully a line manager with the authority to delegate work, but not necessarily a person in a staff function who has advisory authority only. In group process terms, there are *task* functions, including keeping track of all activities and action plans and implementing directives from the leadership team (e.g., setting up an action team to address a problem), and *maintenance* functions, including group facilitation and providing socioemotional support to other staff who are involved, such as chairs of action teams.

Executive Team: Regardless of the scope of the change initiative, it will help if the organization's executive team plays an active role in supporting and overseeing the change process. They will not need to have involvement on a daily basis, but they should regularly review the progress on the change initiative as they would monitor progress on other important initiatives and strategic priorities of the organization. Ackerman Anderson and Anderson offered these suggestions for the role of the executive team:

- Clear expectations for the changes required within the organization
- Effective operations of the business while the change is taking place
- Being a model of the mindset, behavior, and cultural changes required for a successful change

Change Leadership Team: One of the specific tactics in this model is to *select a cross section of employees for a team to guide the change.* This can be seen as an organization-wide steering committee or, using Ackerman Anderson and

Anderson's term, a change leadership team, or another common term: a guiding coalition. Kotter (1996) referred to this group as a "change coalition." This group should have representatives from all key stakeholder groups in the organization, including different levels of the hierarchy (from executives to line staff), different program and administrative areas, and labor organization representation if appropriate. If the organization has formal labor/employee organizations, official involvement of representatives of these groups should help and might even be required by a collective bargaining agreement. The change leadership team should provide oversight, coordination, communication, and guidance on the project. The group must be seen as legitimate by most members of the organization.

Employees from various management and staff levels should be invited to participate based on their relevant knowledge and skills. People with credibility in the organization and formal or informal power and particular interest in the problem should be especially considered. People who are directly affected by the problem are especially important for inclusion.

According to Ackerman Anderson and Anderson, the responsibilities for this group include

- A change strategy and change process plan that will produce the desired outcomes of the change effort
- Continuous oversight and realignment of the change strategy, initiatives, and process to meet the emerging needs of the change effort during the continued successful operation of the business
- Successful integration and alignment of all change initiatives
- Being a model of the mindset, behavior, and cultural changes required for a successful change

Other Change Agents: Depending on the size and scope of the initiative, there may be many other change agents who are responsible for implementation at the unit or team level. They may be action teams or task force or problem-solving group members and chairs, facilitators, or external consultants. Action teams or problem-solving groups are commonly used to analyze specific problems and recommend solutions. These groups may be involved with additional data collection and analysis and the design and implementation of new systems or processes. Because action teams are so essential to the change process, they are discussed in more detail in the next section regarding implementing the plan for change.

As is the case for the change leadership team, employees from various management and staff levels should be invited to participate based on their relevant knowledge and skills. People with credibility in the organization, formal or informal power, and particular interest in the problem should be especially considered. People who are directly affected by the problem are particularly important for inclusion. Facilitators may be used to assist groups in problem analysis, meetings management, or action planning. These facilitators may be staff from the organization if they have proper training or may be external consultants. Consultants may also be involved to lend needed expertise in areas such as OD or quality improvement methods. Potentially, many staff will play change agent roles as chairs and members of problem-solving groups

Other Stakeholders: Two sources of support, referred to previously—political overseers such as board members and collaborating organization and community partners—can be considered as part of the action system. For a major change initiative in a nonprofit human service organization, the agency's board of directors should at least be informed of the initiative. Depending on the goals and nature of the problem, challenge, or opportunity, the board may also be useful in helping in ways such as analysis, brainstorming, and showing support in meetings with staff. In a government department or agency, the executive should ensure that her/his supervisor is involved in the process, from the initial discussions through project completion and evaluation. Sometimes outside stakeholders such as community partners or clients can be involved, based on the specifics of the situation.

Other sources of support can include staff with credibility and formal or informal power within the organization, any staff with interest in the problem, staff who will be affected by the process in significant ways, and staff with relevant knowledge and skills regarding the goals of the initiative. These people should be given opportunities to become involved. Their involvement could be in an official role such as a member of a change team or through informal contacts to receive input and hear concerns.

The following are some of the things that the leaders in our cases did to form the action system and create change agent roles.

Father Joe's Villages

Julie DeDe, the director of programs for Father Joe's Villages, served as the change champion on this project. Key change leaders included not only upper managers but also case managers. The program managers in charge of case management were actively consulted and involved, but there was not a formally designated team. At a later stage, team leads for the new teams led the detailing of implementation such as office moves.

Board of directors' support was arranged at the beginning. Because of staffing changes at the executive level, two board members began to play direct hands-on roles as agency managers, making it clear to staff that the board supported this change.

Detailed action plans were shared with staff on a regular basis, with weekly reports at program manager meetings. In my research after the project, focus group respondents noted that there was very clear documentation on what was to be done, and that change leaders gave unit staff a lot of flexibility on how to implement within timelines (e.g., team formation, office moves).

San Mateo County

The director of San Mateo County was clearly the sponsor, restating her support throughout the process. The county supervisors continued to demonstrate support. The Human Services Agency executive team served as a steering committee for this initiative. The team comprised the regional directors and the directors of the key support services.

The HSA created a position for an internal OD specialist to fill the role of champion, the OD specialist worked with each of the regional directors to build their policy teams. She also worked with each director (team leader) to help team members understand their roles in sharing information and leading action planning in their regions.

In their own regions, the regional directors and their management teams were key change agents. The OD specialist spent a good deal of time helping these multidisciplinary teams understand their role, operate and make decisions as a team, and hold productive case-planning discussions as equals.

A human services advisory council was created to oversee the efforts to improve the system. It comprised staff from public and community-based organizations, former clients, political representatives, and a board member from a local foundation.

San Diego Youth Services

The San Diego Youth Services change team for the restructuring initiative primarily consisted of the upper management team, where most of the changes would need to take place. Other staff were sought for feedback and input. Middle managers such as program directors were talked with on numerous occasions.

The staff most affected were directors and above, with center directors being the most impacted. Each director was talked with on numerous occasions individually and in groups. They were involved to some degree, but the bulk of the planning, development, and implementation of the change was led by upper management. Program staff were more involved in the activities to implement trauma-informed care.

San Diego Fire Department

On the San Diego Fire Department project, the chief and his senior staff, with guidance from the consultants, discussed which key individuals and groups should be formally involved in the change process. They knew that all levels and divisions in the department should be involved and recognized that the firefighters' union was a clear stakeholder that would need to be involved. Fortunately, the union president was himself an intelligent, energetic, and innovation-oriented leader, much like the chief. A steering committee and task forces, described later in the chapter, were formed.

Chief Roberts was clearly the sponsor, restating his support throughout the process. He maintained a standing offer to have lunch in fire stations to discuss the project.

An OD Newsletter was used regularly to communicate progress throughout the department, and the regular weekly department newsletter added a column on the OD project. A video prepared by the department's training unit was shown in all fire stations and work areas to announce plans for the project. A hot line to the chief's secretary was available for any employee to ask questions and offer suggestions, with results shared in the newsletter.

For a change leadership team, the department formed an OD steering committee to guide the project and review recommendations for change. They also served informally as champions. All key department stakeholders were represented. Members included Chief Roberts, the director of administration, two battalion chiefs, the firefighters' union president, and the department affirmative action officer. Other change agent roles included the city's consultants and several department employees, noted in the previous chapter as sources of support for the project: an OD coordinator who served as project champion and seven staff who had been trained as problem-solving group facilitators.

Step 9. Implement the Plan for Change

After the situation is analyzed, people are involved, and change management processes are in place, strategies and processes can be initiated to implement the change. Some generic change management processes are covered here, and more specific change methods are treated in more detail in Section 4. For now, some common OD processes that would be of use in any change initiative are mentioned here. These include basic action planning and project management processes, action research, and problem-solving groups.

First, it should be noted that significant change activity will obviously require resources, particularly staff time. The major staff resource commitment will be to free staff to attend meetings as part of problem analysis, problem-solving, review, and decision-making. Financial resources may be needed if consultants need to be hired or other expenses are incurred. Technological support in the form of, for example, new software or information technology or research staff to analyze data, may be needed.

Implementation Processes

Overall implementation will receive strategic direction and oversight from the organization's executive team and the change leadership team. These groups are responsible for setting overall strategy, developing specific goals and objectives processes and outcomes, allocating resources, and setting overall direction. After these groups have completed the analysis and planning that is needed to launch the operation, they would typically set up various problem-solving groups or action teams to analyze specific aspects of the change process and make recommendations for action. Strategies and processes to implement the change should begin by providing necessary information and training to give staff the capacities to complete assigned change activities. Eventually, the groups may use some of the change methods discussed in Section 4.

An action planning process, typically including tasks to be completed, due dates, and responsible people, will be necessary. Action plans can be used to monitor progress and to ensure that stated goals and objectives are being met and planned activities are occurring.

Monitoring tools should be created to track progress and results and to allow for the revising of project activities as appropriate based on new information or changing conditions. An action planning and monitoring system can be useful for this.

For the project as a whole, timelines such as Gantt charts, familiar to anyone with project management experience, can be useful to track major processes of the change initiative. Columns indicate each key activity, persons or groups responsible, beginning and end dates, and a column for current status.

At the level of a team or group, a simple action plan format that includes required tasks, persons responsible, and timelines should be used to track progress. Action plan reviews should be an agenda item at every meeting. Monitoring systems should also be able to identify staff concerns, so that these can be addressed. Progress on the change process should be regularly and fully communicated to all staff. Proposals for change are commonly submitted to the change leadership team and then forwarded to executive management for final approval.

Action Teams

Action teams, going by various names such as task forces or problem-solving groups, are always needed in planned organizational change. Such groups, consisting of members of an organization and sometimes others, including clients, board members, or community members, are a powerful mechanism for assessing an organizational issue or situation needing attention and developing ideas and proposals for change. Sometimes problem-solving groups use Total Quality Management (TQM) techniques such as workflow or process analysis and cause-and-effect diagrams. Change efforts should usually include the analysis of existing organizational performance data to identify where quality, efficiency, and effectiveness improvements need to be made. Additional data may be gathered as needed. Following are some typical processes for using problem-solving groups or action teams in an organizational change initiative.

A problem-solving group or action team would receive sanction or a mandate from the change leadership team to work on a problem or issue. This should include any guidelines regarding the scope of the group's work, membership requirements, parameters (e.g., cost considerations for recommendations), or deadlines. It should also include the provision of necessary resources (e.g., making scheduling or workload adjustments for participants, meeting rooms, materials, clerical support). The organization design principle of *minimum critical specifications* can be useful here. Specifications for an acceptable solution should be provided by the change leadership team. These should be only the required specifications, with the assumption that within those specifications the group can be as creative as they like in coming up with solutions that solve the problem or fulfill the mandate, as long as the specifications are met. Typical specifications may set parameters on budgetary expenditures or, of course, compliance with existing governmental policies or directives.

The change leadership team should designate appropriate membership, including those who are affected by the problem or have an interest in it and any individuals with necessary specialized knowledge (e.g., financial management, human resources). They should ensure that members have the necessary sanction and support to make decisions and commitments. If the workplace is unionized, it is often wise to include official union representation and support. Optimal size for a working problem-solving group is generally five to seven members, and groups of over 10 members may become inefficient. Membership should be voluntary.

The formation of a group should be announced to other staff, and the group's work should be reported to others on a regular basis (e.g., sharing or posting meeting minutes).

Groups should have designated roles, including a chair, someone to take notes, and perhaps a facilitator. The group should set norms and develop ground rules at its first meeting.

A simple problem-solving process can use these steps:

1. Gather information on the current state, using as data sources any staff involved or affected, relevant organizational performance data, and perhaps additional interviews or surveys.
2. Develop a clear problem statement: its effects, who and what are affected, and so on; describe a vision, ideal state, or end result.
3. Develop criteria for a successful solution:
    a. What conditions need to be satisfied?
    b. What budgetary constraints need to be addressed?
    c. What policies or regulations need to be complied with?
    d. What do the key stakeholders and decision-makers need?
4. Analyze potential causes, determine the root cause(s). TQM techniques, (e.g., cause-and-effect diagrams, flow charts, Pareto charts, histograms, or control charts) may be useful. (There are some examples in Chapter 14.)
5. Identify possible solutions, using brainstorming:
    a. No evaluation of ideas
    b. Wild ideas are encouraged
    c. Quantity, not quality, of ideas is encouraged
    d. Piggyback on others' ideas
    e. Clarification questions only
6. Refine the brainstorming list and select the best solutions(s)
    a. Adapt, modify, or combine ideas
    b. Now is the time to evaluate ideas, using the criteria from Step 3
    c. Choose the best solutions(s)
7. Develop an action plan for implementation:
    a. Write a detailed plan with action steps, responsible persons or groups, resources needed, cost, and deadlines
    b. Consider possible barriers or challenges to implementation and develop plans for addressing them (e.g., use a force field analysis)
    c. Prepare the plan for review by decision-makers and others whose support will be needed
8. Present the plan to decision-makers (probably the change leadership team) for approval or adjustments as needed.
9. After approval by decision-makers, modify implementation plans as needed and implement. As part of implementation, prepare a process for monitoring progress and evaluating results after implementation.

10. Monitor and evaluate, plan, and take additional actions as needed. Celebrate accomplishments.

Several more detailed problem-solving and decision-making processes, including the nominal group technique, in which each group member is encouraged to share ideas or concerns orally or in writing; and adaptations of Kepner-Tregoe's (https://www.kepner-tregoe.com) classic stages of situational appraisal, problem analysis, decision analysis, and potential problem analysis are available in the work of Rofuth and Piepenbring (2020).

Additional Aspects of Change Process Implementation

There are several additional tactics that are key to successful implementation of the change initiative but have not yet been explicitly stated. Some of these are addressed in the formation of the action system and performed by the key roles discussed in the previous section. The remaining tactics follow.

Provide Staff the Information and Training Needed to Implement the Change

In addition to providing necessary information on the content of the change, change leaders should ensure that staff receive any additional training they will need to be involved in the change process. This might include training in problem analysis and problem-solving or specific quality improvement methods, some of which are mentioned in Chapter 14, or team-building and conflict management skills. It will likely eventually include training for staff regarding the content of the change, such as a new evidence-based practice, a new information system, or cultural competence training.

Provide Adequate Opportunities for Team Building and Conflict Management

Staff reactions to change have been mentioned several times, most recently regarding dealing with resistance. Depending on the scope and scale of the change initiative, it may help to provide formal team-building opportunities or conflict resolution processes, using consultant facilitators, as discussed in Chapter 10. Even if these dynamics are not addressed through formal processes, key change agents from the sponsor and champion to other change agents should have enough training and interpersonal skills to identify problems or concerns of staff and ensure that these are addressed.

Clearly Communicate Progress on the Change Process Throughout the Organization

Communication systems need to be set up to ensure effective functioning of the process. This includes communication processes to ensure that all staff members are aware of what is happening. Newsletters, email bulletins, all-staff meetings, and reports at regular unit meetings should all be used on an ongoing basis. Communication systems for all the involved groups to coordinate with each other and several mechanisms for communicating progress on the initiative should be developed. Kotter (1996) has said that when it comes to organizational change, "you cannot overcommunicate." Messages about the need for change and what is being done need to be ongoing and frequent.

Updates on activities to date should include, as possible, information on actual accomplishments of the process, in John Kotter's term, "short-term wins." He saw this as so important that he made it one of his eight key steps. He suggested that getting some quick wins builds momentum and credibility of the change process and can diffuse cynicism, pessimism, and skepticism. It is important that these early accomplishments are seen by staff as substantive and not trivial and contributing to actual organizational improvement and concerns of staff.

Here are some examples of how our cases implemented their change management processes.

Father Joe's Villages

Managers at Father Joe's Villages prepared preliminary plans for program restructuring, revised staff allocations and office locations, and new service delivery processes, including team meetings. While the change plan was created mainly by management, staff and supervisors were involved with, in the words of a focus group member, "tweaking," such as configuring the new teams and staff hiring.

The overall plan for the change was that program locations would remain the same, while additional clients would be able to access available services. All clients were to be supported by a multidisciplinary team and case management within 20 days of program entry. Each client would be assigned to not only a team but also an individual case manager. The types of services provided didn't change, but the delivery method did. Expected benefits highlighted at these meetings included more individualized services and quicker movement through the system toward self-sufficiency.

Weekly meetings were held with program managers to monitor implementation and conduct necessary problem-solving. Implementation was continuously monitored with spreadsheets indicating tasks, responsible people, beginning and ending dates, and status reports.

This change process overlapped with the opening of a new building for the agency, which made many office moves easier to manage. After the change, all service delivery staff had new office space, with each staff person in a family, veterans, career, benefits, rapid rehousing, or co-occurring disorders team.

Regular attempts were made to address staff concerns. Some teams were very cohesive, and this change resulted in the disbanding of many such teams. Some departments had difficulty getting used to the new model, such as mental health clinicians, who were now administratively supervised by nonlicensed clinicians. This culture change took persistence and consistency, allowing people to share their feelings and deal with the stress, with people adjusting in their own time. Change leaders paid special attention to taking the time to answer questions and address the impacts on staff that would be affected.

To monitor progress, spreadsheets including timelines as described above were seen as useful. The change leader held weekly meetings with program managers to monitor progress. One focus group respondent said, "I felt they were willing to tweak plans, not having meetings to just get people to feel good."

San Mateo County

An early activity in San Mateo County was the creation of a community strategic planning process that included 600 people representing different segments of the community. Three major directions to work on together were identified: (1) monitoring client outcomes, (2) building community partnerships, and (3) creating responsive customer services.

An outcome of the strategic planning process was the creation of a human services advisory council to oversee the efforts to improve the system. It comprised staff from public and community-based organizations, former clients, political representatives, and a board member from a local foundation. This community group met monthly to oversee the implementation of our plan.

As another part of the process, dialogue among the top managers critically assessed how they needed to structure themselves and operate differently. A new mission statement was written, and principles and values were identified. All were shared with all staff for discussion and input. An agency-wide newsletter designed to keep staff abreast of important changes was distributed on a regular basis.

A consultant was used to conduct an "assessment/service survey" to learn more about the impact of changes on staff, with specific attention to effectiveness and quality of the work environment, staff perceptions of customer service, and opportunities for improving decision-making in the organization. After data analysis, the consultant identified broad issues needing attention. The consultant prepared recommendations based on the key findings.

A consultant team conducted focus groups and interviews with select staff and worked with an internal team to construct a report for management on how change was progressing and where there were problems that needed intervention. The report was rather candid and laid out many areas that needed additional attention.

The survey results were distributed to the entire agency staff with an accompanying report indicating that the executive team was in the process of crafting a plan of action to deal with the survey recommendations. The survey findings provided a new "shared sense of reality" that needed to be taken into account so that staff could work together toward a set of agreed on goals. The executive team action plan was distributed to staff 8 weeks later.

After the consultants' report was shared at a meeting with the County Board of Supervisors, the organizational self-assessment process was adopted by several other county department directors after they heard the consultant's presentation. One limitation of the project was that there was no formal feedback mechanism for staff, especially front-line staff, to share their experience and reactions to implementing the organizational changes.

San Diego Youth Services

The restructuring at San Diego Youth Services started with chief executive officer (CEO) Walter Philips, the chief financial officer (CFO), and associate executive directors. The CEO and CFO did an analysis of the fiscal performance of each of the programs over a 5-year period and shared findings with the executive leadership team, which then developed several options and models for the reorganization of programs into divisions. This included analysis of program services, contracts, and budgets to determine what made the most sense programmatically and fiscally. Models included ideas for the number of divisions and what programs fit best under each division. The ideas were brought to the center directors. This was met with some anxiety, as this is where people saw possible impacts on their jobs.

The change was not communicated to lower level line staff until plans were finalized and implementation plans were developed, approximately 6 months later. When possible, staff changes were made through attrition to try to minimize the impact on individuals. However, some staff did lose their jobs, and some staff were demoted to lower level positions. Salary reductions were implemented for high-level (director and above) staff, with the CEO taking the largest percentage reduction.

Regular updates were provided to management staff and directors, but these were inconsistently communicated to other levels in the agency, depending on the individual manager.

Several tools were developed to monitor progress. A performance-based contract fiscal report was developed, specifically designed to track programs' fiscal performance under the new type of contract. A special residential fiscal report was developed to track revenue based on occupancy. This allowed the agency to monitor revenue generated compared to expected revenue based on bed availability. They brought in a quality assurance coordinator, who developed new tools for monitoring and tracking program performance to ensure that the agency was in compliance with contracts and providing quality services.

San Diego Fire Department

The San Diego Fire Department made a strong resource commitment to this project, arranging for the city's Organization Effectiveness Program to commit consultants for three full years. Two of us worked on the project at nearly a full-time basis for 2 years, and another consultant, from the analysis and productivity improvement side of our Organization Effectiveness Program, was added to help with analytical projects, such as an employee survey.

The OD steering committee met regularly to set priorities for OD activities, provide guidance to the change agent, and review proposals from problem-solving groups. After problem-solving groups presented their findings and recommendations to the steering committee, these were sent to the department senior staff for final decisions. Approved recommendations were implemented through normal department processes, with consultant assistance as needed.

A data collection task force and the consultants developed an employee survey and surveys for stakeholder groups. Results were fed back to staff to guide formation of problem-solving groups.

Two hundred employees volunteered to participate in group problem-solving and many did, with over 20 problem-solving groups formed in the first 2 years of the project.

To ensure quick results, one of the first problem areas to be addressed was training. This offered many opportunities for quick and low- or no-cost improvements in training systems that showed quick and appreciated changes.

As consultants, we facilitated many team-building and role clarification workshops as well as data collection task force meetings and senior staff weekly meetings and daily briefings. Action planning and management by objectives were used to monitor progress.

Summary

An action system will include a change sponsor and a change champion, support and involvement from the organization's executive team, and other groups such as problem-solving groups to implement the change. Processes and systems need to be developed to provide guidance on specific activities of action teams and methods of communication and decision-making. The use of a formal problem-solving process will be a core activity of most change initiatives. Action plans and timelines can be very useful for monitoring progress.

The next chapter covers key processes for generating support for the initiative and providing support to staff and also addressing resistance.

Reflection and Focusing Questions

1. Which individuals and groups will fulfill the various roles (sponsor, champion, teams, etc.)?
2. What implementation structures and processes will be set up?

8

Support and Resistance

> Many dolts will impede your brilliant plans. You can minimize their
> collective resistance though a process called "getting buy-in." This
> involves collecting the opinions of people who care about a decision,
> acting interested, then pretending that your plan is a direct reflec-
> tion of what the majority of people want.
> —Scott Adams (*The Dilbert Principle*, 1996, p. 82)

For those who know of the hapless software engineer in the comics, please note
that the above quotation is not from Dilbert himself, but rather from Dogbert,
the cynical dog who usually comes from the dark side when giving Dilbert advice. I see it as a humorous reminder to be self-aware of how you are using your
leadership styles and can avoid using the pseudoparticipation that I mentioned
in Chapter 4. Staff will likely see through inauthentic behavior of a leader and
will follow under those conditions only out of a sense of grudging compliance
rather than a strong commitment. These relationship dynamics between a
change leader and staff are key factors in the success of organizational change.

This chapter covers various aspects of gaining and maintaining support, with
a particular emphasis on supporting staff who are involved in a change initiative
and, as part of that, dealing with any of their concerns about or resistance to the
change process.

Step 10. Develop and Maintain Support

There are several dimensions of support. The change leader must

- show support for the change process, especially through a personal investment of time and energy and allocation of needed resources such as staff
  time to participate in change activities,
- identify relevant stakeholder groups within and outside the organization
  whose support will be needed for success, and then do what is needed to
  ensure their support,

Organizational Change for the Human Services. Thomas Packard, Oxford University Press. © Oxford University Press
2021. DOI: 10.1093/oso/9780197549995.003.0009

- support staff by acknowledging the demands they are facing and showing that they are appreciated, providing necessary resources, and
- by showing support for staff, enhance their support for the change process.

One of the 21 tactics, *provide top management support and commitment*, should actually occur throughout the change process. Developing support should begin *before* the process, when the person who is now a change leader should have been personally developing and using their leadership skills and building positive relationships and social capital throughout out the organization. In fact, effective management and leadership are valuable and may be essential preconditions for successful large-scale organizational change. If an organization has leadership or management weaknesses, particularly in higher management positions, it would be ideal to work on those weaknesses before embarking on a major change initiative. I assume here that you as a change leader have gone through the self-assessment, self-reflection, and development processes that were discussed in Chapter 3. With a history of your own competent management and leadership performance and good relationships with staff in areas of the organization that will be affected by the change, you will be in a good place to begin.

Developing support can occur during the early steps in Chapters 5 and 6, as you as a change leader use both head and heart to share with staff the importance of and urgency for the change and engage in collaborative, participative assessments of the external conditions (e.g., forces for change) and the organization's current readiness and capacity for change. You and other members of the organization can then continue to build stronger working relationships as you all use results of the assessments of the present state of the organization to improve readiness and capacity.

Sources of Support

Four of the 21 change tactics in this model are concerned with support for the change initiative (support from top management, political overseers [e.g., board members], and collaborating organizations and community partners) and provision of resources such as staff time and funding. The specifics and mixes of resources will, of course, vary based on specifics of the setting, but top management support will be hugely important, and in a sense will support or facilitate development of the other sources.

Top Management
Change leaders will need to continuously show support for the process and anticipate and address resistance. Top management, such as the organization's

executive, and, in some cases the agency's board, should formally show support for the process. As noted in the previous chapter, a senior executive may take the role of sponsor of the change, and an assigned manager can become the champion for the initiative through frequent communication with employees.

In a governmental organization, top management support, beyond the director of the department or agency, may involve the chief executive officer (CEO; e.g., in local government, a county chief executive or a city manager). Some change initiatives may in fact be initiated by the CEO.

Additional Management Support

Top management support must be filtered down within the organization. In their extensive study of the organizational change literature, ten Have, ten Have, Huijsmans, and Otto (2017) emphasized the importance of middle management. Middle managers are often neglected in organizational change, with upper management reaching out to line workers without attending to middle managers, who play key roles in implementing change by showing support for upper management and also supporting their own subordinates. On our fire department project, we quickly learned the importance of the battalion chiefs (BCs) as middle managers. They supervised captains in the stations and ensured coordination and information sharing up and down the chain of command and across stations and battalions. We made sure that they were represented by two BCs on the organization development (OD) steering committee; and before that, we had done extensive role clarification workshops with all of them, helping them see more clearly their roles as not only firefighting leaders but also managers of the organization and letting them suggest changes in their roles.

Below middle management, first-line supervisors are at least equally important. ten Have et al. (2017) concluded that supervisory support is, indeed, critical to the success of change. They added that "especially in times of organizational change, when employees are often affected by uncertainty, senior management would do well to ensure that supervisors are suitably trained and attuned to be able to provide support to their subordinates" (p. 107).

Political Overseers

Sometimes the local elected officials, such as a county board of supervisors or a city council may have particular interest in a project. This was very relevant in the San Mateo County case.

In the case of a nonprofit agency, a major change initiative should be an item that the CEO regularly discusses with the board, for the same reasons that a public sector chief executive would do so with their local elected officials.

Below the top governance level, any change leader who is not the chief executive should at least get the support from their direct superior, even if the superiors don't show such interest. This will be important to validate the change process as supporting some overall strategy, priority, or key result area for the organization as a whole. Keeping one's superiors informed gives the change initiative status as an important accountability area for the change leader. It will also be important when extra or reallocated resources are needed for the project.

Collaborating Organizations and Community Partners

Either a public or a private agency may also have community advisory boards. If so, the change leader should consider involving them, at least by sharing information with them, and quite possibly involving them as stakeholders who provide input and advice. The same holds true for any other collaborating organizations or community partners. With interagency collaborations becoming increasingly common, change leaders should carefully consider which of their collaborating agencies and community groups might have an interest in the change process so that they can offer input that might be helpful. In some cases, especially if an organization has a client advisory board or committee, it might be useful to get them involved. Traditional Total Quality Management processes (discussed in Chapter 14) often had direct involvement of customers—those who bought the products being made.

The local situation will help determine which other stakeholders need to be involved. Involvement of stakeholders, at least through being informed, may be important to the extent that their support will be needed to ensure implementation. They can also be valuable sources of input, suggesting organizational improvements that could enhance program performance and client outcomes. If key stakeholders have any specific interests, needs, or agendas, these should be known and addressed by the change leaders.

Supporting Staff

Supporting staff during the change initiative can happen on a regular basis and can occur in several ways. Leadership styles covered in Chapter 4, and particularly transformational leadership and exemplary leadership, suggest a number of ways for change leaders to show support. Participative decision-making supports staff to the extent that it can empower them to make suggestions and decisions that can improve their quality of working life. Enhancing staff and organizational capacity for change, not only at the beginning of the process but also during as needed and possible can support staff in their work on the change initiative. Change leaders can also support staff by building into the change process mechanisms for team building and conflict management. Ongoing communication to staff regarding how change activities are progressing and mechanisms for staff to communicate upward regarding questions, suggestions, or concerns also show support.

Marshall and Nielsen (2020) have creatively applied motivational interviewing (MI) to organizational changes such as implementing a quality improvement program, focusing on leaders as supervisors and leaders of work teams—essential arenas for a change leader to show support for staff. As with traditional MI, there is a strong emphasis on being a good listener. Rather than having a leader try to persuade or pressure staff to "get with" the change, this model suggests that the change leader should seek to understand staff perspectives and concerns, act with compassion and empathy, and help show how staff interests can be met through the change initiative. These principles are especially important at the first stage: *engaging.* Staff ambivalence about the change should be recognized and accepted. As covered in Chapter 6, helping staff understand the vision for the change and how it will be implemented, including how they will be involved in the process, can help put them at ease and build their commitment. This fits with the *focusing* stage of MI. The *evoking* stage of MI can include asking staff about their dissatisfactions about the current state of the organization and their own views and hopes regarding the proposed change. Building trust and staff confidence about their abilities to implement the change are also important. The *planning* stage essentially involves reviewing the action system and specific implementation activities, grounded in goals and specific objectives.

A national study of the implementation of a new child welfare practices model (National Child Welfare Workforce Institute, n.d.) noted implementation challenges that included resistance to change, workload concerns, and competing priorities. The study identified several mechanisms to get "buy-in" from front-line staff:

- build a shared understanding of a vision for change
- make staff part of the solution
- conduct training to support change
- introduce tangible aids to support change
- engage supervisors and middle managers
- recognize successes

All of these guidelines except the final one have been covered here, so recognizing successes deserves additional attention. The study found that

buy-in increased gradually as initial successes took hold and were celebrated. [Project] stakeholders underscored the importance of recognizing successes during meetings and group communications and acknowledging staff who contributed to and supported the initiative. One leader consistently ended meetings with a success story. Such recognition can help keep staff motivated, particularly when roadblocks and challenges arise.

The study also found that sharing data on how the change initiative was improving organizational outcomes supported buy-in. Tracking data to demonstrate the initiative's impact on outcomes is another powerful tool in gaining stakeholder buy-in.

Damschroder et al. (2009), in their presentation of an implementation science model, succinctly outlined needed resources for a change initiative: "money, training, education, physical space, and time" (p. 9). New funding may be needed for consultants or trainers or for new equipment, such as software or physical changes to facilities. As suggested in the following discussion of resistance, the process could include providing training for staff in areas ranging from skills in problem analysis and problem-solving to a new evidence-based program model or information system that may be part of the content of the change. The most relevant resources may be staff time to attend meetings to work on change implementation and time required for communications (giving and receiving information) on the change process.

Staff who have active social networks through professional associations, work teams, or employee organizations can be tapped as advocates to influence others to support and get involved with the change process. These people and others, as active or potential informal leaders, can be offered training, development, and support to take more active roles as leaders on the change initiative.

Another way to show support to staff is to understand and address the feelings they have as they go through the change process. The classic work of Bridges and Bridges (2016) about understanding the transitions that staff go through is covered in Chapter 16 regarding culture change. Any major organizational change is likely to involve culture change to at least some extent, so their guidelines are relevant here as well.

Jaiya John (2016, p. 9) has offered a more feeling-oriented, but no less important, perspective on demonstrating support:

> And if you are an administrator, an executive, then you, my friend, should care about agency, worker, and leader wellness because this wellness absolutely determines the bottom line (fiscal), the top line (political), and the real line (social, generational outcomes).

Here are some other pieces of his practice wisdom (2016, pp. 64, 65, italics in original) that are worth mentioning here:

> Work together to create conditions in which each person feels she or he has equal social power within the change process . . . Compassion is not kindness, sweetness, softness. It is a professional capacity arrived at through daily hard work. A determination to *feel* another's life, and out of that feeling to harvest

understanding, perspective, insight, and something world changing that we might call . . . *relationship*. Filling out forms and completing tasks is not the work. Staying vulnerable, humble, open, attentive, curious, caring, and present *despite* the conditions . . . this is the work.

Here are some examples of how support was developed and provided in our case organizations.

Father Joe's Villages

The initiative at Father Joe's Villages started with the managers in charge of case management considering how to improve case conference meetings. At that time, clients were served by individual staff from various programs (e.g., career and education, addictions counseling), and there was ineffective coordination of client case plans and communication at team meetings.

It was clear from ongoing support from the agency executive and the change leadership by the director of social services that this was an important priority for the agency. Focus group respondents noted that management scheduled, as needed, meetings with staff to do nothing but address feelings of negativity and discomfort, and that it was very important to hear this "support from the top." A focus group respondent added that management motivation and excitement were clear:

> They hyped it up. . . . Communication of benefits took a long time but was ef-
> fective. . . . They got people to embrace it, share the benefits of the change to
> staff, such as serving more clients but in less time, deciding your own session
> schedule, etc. . . . I have more control.

A large number of meetings were held with all staff and client groups to explain the change and the effects of the budget cuts under the theme of "enhancing the continuum of care." Presentations began by highlighting the agency's notable strengths and accomplishments and moved into discussions about ways to address the growing need for services. Strategies included incorporating some nationally recognized homeless prevention models, such as shelter diversion and rapid rehousing, into the continuum of care.

San Mateo County

Since this project in San Mateo County began with discussions between the county board of supervisors and the agency director, executive and board support for the change initiative was clear. The fact that the director brought in an OD consultant and devoted large amounts of time for the formation and development of the teams to work on the project, was also an important sign of support.

San Diego Youth Services

In the San Diego Youth Services, CEO Walter Philips and his management team clearly and regularly showed their support for this process. He personally spent time meeting with each of these individuals as well as with staff throughout the organization to discuss the changes to go over the reasons why the changes were necessary, and he was very clear about his expectations for them as they went through the change process.

To show commitment for restructuring, over a 3- to 4-month period, Walter Philips attended staff meetings with all the programs and administrative departments to outline the needed change, the reasons for the change, and the plan for implementation. One thing that brought credibility for the change was that salary reductions were implemented only for high-level staff, with the CEO taking the greatest cut.

San Diego Fire Department

City manager support for the San Diego Fire Department change project was clear. The manager's office assigned the consultants; the city manager and the deputy city manager in charge of personnel were regularly briefed on the project; and the deputy city manager overseeing the fire department participated in some senior staff workshops and meetings.

The senior staff showed support by having at least one of their group attend each employee survey feedback session. They were available at the sessions to hear concerns and answer questions. Notably, in order to have meetings by battalion, the department arranged complex "move ups" of fire companies to cover stations while those crews were at feedback sessions—another sign of senior staff support for the project.

Support for staff came through the resources the department provided. In addition to our work as consultants, a fire captain was appointed "OD coordinator," receiving release time to handle internal coordination of OD activities. (This role, a "champion," was covered in the previous chapter.) The department arranged for seven department employees (firefighters, captains, and a civilian analyst) to be trained as group facilitators and then paid them to serve as problem-solving group facilitators. Other support activities included a newsletter and a hot line to the chief's office.

One "early win" (Kotter's concept) was the formation of problem-solving groups to address problems of staff training that were highlighted in a department-wide employee survey. We thought problem-solving to improve aspects of the department's training program would be relatively easy. In fact, early recommendations to change aspects of training were approved and implemented, which seemed to give the change process some momentum

Resistance

Next, we'll specifically consider the historically important notion of staff resistance to change and how resistance can be converted to staff support for the process.

While resistance has traditionally been seen as a problem of individual employees, it is now more commonly seen as something that can be tapped as a positive source of change. Mathews and Linski (2016), referencing earlier work, put this eloquently:

> Dent and Galloway Goldberg (1999) argue that this view of resistance to change is flawed in that individuals do not actually "resist" change, rather they do not fully embrace change due to a variety of barriers and impediments. They include organizational structures, such as poor reward mechanisms, personal investments in the existing status quo, and of course internal ability challenges that make adopting the change individually difficult. It is important to understand that these impediments to embracing change are not the manifestations of resistance; rather they are the reason for so called "resistance." Thus, Dent and Galloway Goldberg (1999) posit that resistance to change is better described in terms of the specific impediments that are encountered rather than as an overarching phenomenon that management must defeat. (p. 964)

Ford, Ford, and D'Amelio (2008) presented resistance as a resource in several ways. If conversation is allowed, dialogue can help keep people engaged in the process, and engagement through dialogue might in fact lead to a higher level of commitment on the part of staff. Staff who are, in fact, committed to the organization may raise concerns because they care about the future of the organization. Listening to and addressing legitimate concerns can further enhance staff commitment to the organization. These authors supported several of the tactics in our model, including extensive communication, allowing staff participation, and providing needed resources.

The mere threat or anticipation of resistance can encourage change agents to adopt some of the management practices known to reduce resistance and strengthen change. These practices include communicating extensively, inviting people to participate, providing people with needed resources, and developing strong working relationships. (p. 370)

Jaiya John has suggested using empathy when having discussions with staff regarding their concerns:

Think about how you would want someone to tell you that you need to change. Whatever you come up with can be your template for nurturing others through their fear. Also, the more groups talk supportively about their various fears, while exploring actionable resolutions and supports, the more that fear evaporates. Fear really only lives inside humans and in the atmosphere of fearful groups. Once it has been released into a strong, faithful environment, it fades away. (p. 61)

In the spirit of using dialogue to address staff concerns, he suggested that a leader should

allow safe space for expression of change-related questions and stresses. Invite and welcome feedback in an inclusive fashion. Regularly status-check on both the personal and group level, and course, correct when necessary. . . . Allow for healthy grieving of lost habits, processes, and traditions. Celebrate the birth of new habits, processes, and traditions. (p. 64)

Regardless of how resistance is framed, it will need to be thoughtfully addressed. According to Galpin (1996), people resist for three possible reasons: not knowing about the change, not being able to change, or not being willing to change. Imagine a pyramid with the largest section at the bottom representing *not knowing* about the change, a smaller middle level of *not able* to help implement the change, and a small top level of staff *not willing* to support the change process. Each level of resistance requires different strategies.

Not Knowing: Those who don't know about the change can be influenced by change leaders communicating the who, what, when, why, and how of the change and by getting them involved in the process.

Not Able: Those who feel not able to change can be educated regarding the new knowledge and skills that will be needed during and after the change. This might involve training and problem-solving methods, new management skills, team building, or conflict management.

Not Willing: A small number of staff may be unwilling to change. Their concerns should be recognized through active listening to understand their objections and an attempt to show how these concerns will be addressed by the change. If possible, it should help to show how they may benefit, or at least how concerns could be minimized. Feedback and coaching, and perhaps use of rewards and performance management, may be used as needed. While I suggested previously that power–coercive strategies are not likely to have long-term positive outcomes, this may be necessary with some who continue to resist after all attempts using rational persuasion.

Mathews and Linski (2016) offered a new way to look at resistance that focuses on more deeply understanding staff perspectives about the impending change. They use the term primary human goods (PHG), defined by Ward (2002) as "actions or states of affairs that are viewed as intrinsically beneficial to human beings and are therefore sought for their own sake rather than as means to some more fundamental ends" (p. 515). Examples include healthy living, mastery of occupational skills, and quality relationships. According to this model, an organizational change may be seen by staff as something that could disrupt some aspects of their PHG. Notably, they suggested that a significant disruption can be to staff capacity, such as expecting them to perform their work with skills that they don't yet have, which might then affect their self-esteem. They suggest the use of principles of dialogic OD (a change technology covered in another chapter), that uses principles of social construction and storytelling to help bring to the surface the varying perspectives of the change process as seen by different staff. The key activity is to create forums for dialogue, with groups or individuals, to share perspectives on the change process and develop common understandings. Change leaders can use what they hear from their staff to adjust change activities or reframe them to show benefits to staff.

These employee perspectives can be summarized in a change formula that has been used by Beckhard and Pritchard (1992, p. 75) and others: Change can occur when

(Dissatisfaction + Vision + Process) > Cost of changing.

In other words, if an employee

- perceives a high level if dissatisfaction with the current state,
- sees the desirability of a better future state, and
- sees a change process that will not require excessive time and energy, then the perceived benefits factored together may be greater than the perceived costs of the change, and the employee will have high enough readiness.

Clearly, the costs of change can be significant. In addition to the time demands for participating in a change process, pulling a worker from the ongoing demands of a large caseload or managerial projects can easily lead to some confusion and uncertainty. Proehl (2001, p. 72) identified several specific potential costs to staff. First, power dynamics may change: Those who have power may have less after the change. Also, an employee's sense of competence may change, to the extent that new competencies will be required after the change. Related to this, one's personal identity may even change, perhaps from being a highly autonomous therapist to an equal member of an interdisciplinary team. Relationships with other staff members may also change if people will need to move to different work units or teams. Proehl noted that even rewards, from titles and job perquisites such as private offices to pay levels, may change.

Oreg et al. (2011, p. 517) offered these suggestions for addressing issues of resistance:

> Change recipients will understandably tend to resist change. This may seem obvious, but findings demonstrate that managers are often oblivious to how change recipients will respond to the change and do not give enough thought to change recipients' perspectives. As a start, global and local change agents need to be clear, early on, about the precise ramifications the change program will have for change recipients. More importantly, however, change agents must give special consideration to these ramifications and aim to understand and incorporate change recipients' perspectives in the design of the change.
>
> Practically, they should carefully plan the change effort and make every effort to explain how any threat can be dealt with, and at the same time introduce and highlight the personal benefits change could have for employees, beyond its importance for the organization.

By seriously considering employee perspectives and concerns, the change leaders can better design ways to introduce the change and create conditions that will deal with them. Referring back to the change formula, here are some suggested action steps:

- Address the perceived costs
  - Assess likely realities; provide safeguards, reassurance, and information on what will be involved in the change process (meetings, time to read announcements, etc.)
- Create dissatisfaction
  - Provide information from the environment (e.g., client or funder expectations) pointing to the need for change
  - Use employee surveys to identify possible dissatisfaction among staff
- Develop a compelling shared vision for the future of the organization
  - Set high but realistic standards and expect them to be met
  - Build commitment to the change by showing its benefits to the organization
  - Demonstrate leadership/management support for the change

- Create an effective and efficient change process
  - Develop change leadership skills
  - Use relevant and evidence-based change strategies and tactics
  - Use relevant and evidence-based change technologies such as OD or quality improvement processes

Mathews and Linski (2016) gave an example of the use of these principles in a change initiative in a nonprofit human service organization that radically altered the way case managers delivered services to clients. When change leaders perceived resistance, they used dialogic OD (Bushe & Marshak, 2015) and aspects of implementation science (covered in Chapter 16), holding individual and group sessions with staff. They learned that

> the change restricted [staff] ability to make decisions about case plans and limited their ability to be creative in their development. These negative experiences of the change and the subsequent interactions among the case managers cultivated foundational narratives that became their social reality... leaders were better able to understand the behaviors they were encountering and... this affirmation cultivated new narratives of collaboration, support, and acknowledgment within the organization that acted as the foundation for a new social reality. (p. 969)

Another creative angle for dealing with resistance is to present organizational change as a way to maintain the status quo. Dryburgh (2016) suggested that keeping the organization going or growing, and maintaining staff employment, are more positive ways to frame the need for change. He gave one example in which the change leader introduced the need or change by asking, "What do we need to do to ensure the longevity of the organisation, and the longevity of the careers of the people working there?" leading to "huge change with minimal resistance." In our field, framing a need for change in terms of "What do we need to be doing to ensure that we can keep providing high-quality services, increase staff morale, and use our resources in the most efficient ways?" may help staff feel more proactive about engaging in change.

Staff may also have feelings of concern based on their past experiences with change projects that were presented as ways to improve things but may have ended with disappointment and little change. If change leaders allow time to debrief such past experiences, they can learn from staff what went well and did not go well, so that those learnings can be used to design a better process for the current initiative.

Finally, I once again mention the value of participative decision-making. This principle and other aspects of support are embedded in the previous steps: development of the action system and actually implementing the change process.

Here are some of the activities used in our cases to address resistance.

Father Joe's Villages

Areas of resistance in Father Joe's Villages were recognized and addressed at meetings in the programs. The main concern of staff was that their workload would increase. Managers responded by noting, with reference to their analysis of the new staff roles and team structures, that increased efficiency would be a net benefit, enabling staff to spend more time with client services.

San Mateo County

Getting staff "buy-in" was a struggle in San Mateo County. There was initially a lot of pushback and negativity from staff members, who were more comfortable with the concept of "client" than the concept of "customer."

Regarding resistance, "not knowing" was the biggest problem, and this was addressed by ongoing communication with employees about the project. "Not able" concerns were addressed through workshops and the training of agency staff in areas including the new customer service culture, training for managers and supervisors on new competencies, training for new staff job roles, facilitative leadership, managing with data, and project management.

Continual dialogue with staff at all levels about agency values, which included treating customers with dignity and respect and a commitment to excellence in delivering customer services, was necessary to get them focused on what they could do differently. Since the word *customer* seemed to be more an issue than the concept of improving service, they decided to use *customer* and *client* interchangeably. This concession reduced the resistance considerably. The shift to a customer service approach to service delivery involved constantly pointing out where comments or actions diverged from the values identified in the strategic plan.

San Diego Youth Services

Resistance in San Diego Youth Services was an especially difficult area, particularly for several middle managers, whose positions were being considered for elimination or consolidations. Walter Philips personally spent time meeting with each of these individuals to discuss the changes and the reasons that the changes were necessary. He was very clear about his expectations for them as they went through the change process.

He also made sure to meet with most of the staff throughout the agency at staff meetings to ensure that they heard directly from him about the changes that were going to be made and the rationales for them.

San Diego Fire Department

The union president of the San Diego Fire Department was involved partly to help address possible resistance from the firefighter ranks. And one particular "old line" BC was recruited for the steering committee to show that traditional views would be represented in the process. Chief Roberts encouraged his staff to get as many people involved with the process as possible. He said he wanted to "get everyone's fingerprints on the knife"[1]—his vivid way of saying he wanted buy-in and commitment from all key stakeholders.

In the fire department case, "not knowing" was the biggest problem, and this was addressed by ongoing communication with employees about the project. "Not able" concerns were addressed through workshops with BCs in areas such as role clarification and through the training of department staff in areas, including group facilitation, creative problem-solving, effective meetings, and conflict management.

Summary

After the organization's change leaders have identified the change goal, demonstrated its urgency and importance, and suggested how the initiative will proceed, a great deal of attention needs to be paid to developing, and then maintaining, support from staff and other stakeholders and providing ongoing support to staff. This includes identifying and dealing with resistance, especially by understanding the sources of resistance and proactively addressing them, for example, by providing training and other necessary resources.

It is important that adequate resources in terms of staff time and any necessary financial and technological support are made available. Of course, widespread participation of staff in the change process will be a potent source of support. However, care should be taken to not "overtax" staff by requiring too much of their time for change activities.

Regarding time and resource challenges, a summary from the National Child Welfare Workforce Institute study mentioned previously is worth sharing here:

> Because systems change takes a long time and considerable effort to achieve, initiative leaders need to exercise patience, continually return to and communicate their overall vision and strategic plan, align the Systems of Care initiative with other ongoing efforts, reengage stakeholders on an ongoing basis, coordinate with partners to identify efficient use of available resources, and work methodically toward the ultimate goals of improving outcomes for children and families. (National Child Welfare Workforce Institute, 2010, p. 69)

---

[1] If you'd like a less violent metaphor than *Murder on the Orient Express*, think of everyone at the wedding carving the cake.

Finally, as suggested by Kotter (1996), it will be important for the change process to show some quick results so that staff can see clear evidence of progress.

The next chapter covers the final stages of the change process: institutionalizing the changes by building them into organizational systems, such as policies and procedures as well as in the organization's culture, and evaluating the change in terms of the change process itself and the ultimate outcomes and goal accomplishment

Reflection and Focusing Questions

1. Who are the key stakeholders, external and internal to the organization, whose support you will need? How will you get the needed support from each?
2. What resources (e.g., staff time, financial support) will the project need, and how will you ensure that resources will be adequate?
3. What will you do to support staff and the change process?
4. How will you address concerns that manifest as resistance?

9

Institutionalization and Evaluation

What gets measured gets done.

—Anonymous

In one sense, a change initiative has a final ending, but in the spirit of action research and organizational learning, an evaluation of the initiative can be treated not only as a summative report of results but also as a data collection process that can suggest lessons learned for future initiatives, and perhaps additional steps, if there were disappointing results that should still be addressed. When all activities have been completed, steps must be taken to create mechanisms that will institutionalize the changes to ensure that they become part of the normal culture and operating systems of the agency. Also, a formal evaluation should be completed, and monitoring systems should be set up to track activities into the future to make adjustments with additional changes as needed. These processes should not be seen as static but should be monitored and assessed for adjustments and continuous improvement.

In fact, institutionalizing and evaluating the change are closely intertwined. Both involve looking at data, which can include managerial aspects such as implementation of new procedures or programs; "softer" factors such as organizational culture, leadership style, and the functioning of teams; and, of course, results regarding desired outcomes. At the formative level, findings are used to make adjustments, and at the summative level, findings are used to assess success. Both of these should be part of a highly performing organization where staff always want to learn and improve.

This chapter covers the last two steps of the change model: institutionalizing changes within the organization and evaluating the initiative.

Step 11. Institutionalize the Change

I begin this section with some more practice wisdom from Jaiya John (2016, pp. 191–192). He has a unique way of looking at formal or technical processes and humanizing them, giving them another dimension.

Organizational Change for the Human Services. Thomas Packard, Oxford University Press. © Oxford University Press 2021. DOI: 10.1093/oso/9780197549995.003.0010

It is always a challenge to sustain and perpetuate any change once the initial process or initiative has been completed. Sustainability comes from shared accountability. The more mutuality there is in your culture of care, the more sustainable the culture. We look too often for technical strategies to create sustainability. But this particular creature lives inside of relationships. . . . Build the identified change principles onto your personal and group traditions, habits, and processes that will internalize the changes and help the changes withstand personnel and leadership turnover and other unpredictable variables. Continuously promote and celebrate the values relevant to your change initiative. Create sustaining processes to ensure the incorporation, integration, and perpetuation of your change principles. This involves processes such as recruitment, hiring, orientation, ongoing development, and cultural maintenance. Identify torch-bearers (role models or exemplars) for the change principles. Have these torch-bearers regularly mentor promising new torch-bearers. Create and preserve storytelling modes and traditions that will promote, celebrate, and generationally extend change-related practices, values, and visions. . . . Change is not sustained magically. It survives and thrives where language, process, structure, story, and celebration are in place to carry it forward until it is considered normal.

Changes need to be institutionalized. For example, when a new system is designed, procedures will need to be written and staff will need to be retrained to reflect the new system. Training for new staff should also reflect the new system. Job descriptions and performance appraisal systems may need to be modified to support the new systems. Perhaps new funding will need to be secured, or dialogue with current funders can be used to make necessary modifications to existing contracts and grants.

A report by McKinsey and Company (Basford, Schaninger, & Viruleg, 2015, p. 3) identified four components of an "influence model," concluding that transformation initiatives "are most successful at shifting mind-sets and behaviors when they draw upon all four components of this model." One of these, *reinforcing change through formal mechanisms*, is concerned with institutionalizing change. They asserted that

structures, systems, and processes are all formal mechanisms that can support employees' efforts to adopt new mind-sets and behaviors. Organizations can reinforce desired changes by adjusting these mechanisms—for example, setting individual and organizational performance goals and motivating people through both financial and nonfinancial incentives—so they align with the changes.

Whelan-Berry and Somerville (2010) reviewed the literature to find common organizational "change drivers" and accented institutionalizing the change as a key element. They concluded that aligning organizational structure and control processes (outcome measures, planning processes, budgeting, and information systems) with the change results can help ensure that groups and individuals do not "revert to the pre-change state, process, or approach" (p. 182). They paid special attention to aligning human resources (HR) practices with the new state. Staff training, recruitment, selection and socialization of new employees, performance appraisal criteria, and formal and informal incentives and rewards could all be reconfigured in ways to support continuation of the new state.

I found HR practices to be a notable factor in institutionalizing changes in an organizational change initiative that I had been involved with. I have been using Father Joe's Villages organizational change to a new case management system as an example of the use of change tactics. I now use that agency with a different example. In 1992, I was asked by an executive at the agency if I would consult with them on the development of a set of organizational values. She believed that the agency had a mission statement that was well understood and supported by employees, but wanted an additional way to help ensure that the mission was operationalized in the day-to-day work of staff. She thought that a formal statement of organizational values that aligned with the mission would be a good way to guide staff behavior. Another consultant and I facilitated a half-day workshop that was open to all staff at which we took them through some processes that led to the creation of a statement of organizational values. The result was a set of core values of compassion, respect, empathy, empowerment, and dignity, creating an acronym of "CREED," which had additional resonance in this religious organization.

Five years later, I did a follow-up study (Packard, 2001) to look at the effects of the CREED. At least 69% of employees surveyed said they were made aware of the CREED through each of several methods (new employee orientation, documents posted on the wall, supervisors mentioning it, administrators mentioning it, other employees mentioning it, staff retreats, and in-service training). Each method had a positive effect on at least 73% of staff. I was told that the CREED had been widely circulated, most prominently in the new employee orientation, in agency documents, and on walls. At staff meetings it typically came up in the context of staff sharing frustrations related to the difficult work of the agency. Staff, including the HR director, reported that several years prior, a representative group of employees assisted in the revision of the agency's performance appraisal system, and based on employee input, the CREED became a significant element of the performance criteria. The CREED was also part of the 360-degree feedback process used for all management employees. They added that when staff discipline concerns are brought to the agency's HR, the CREED was used to focus the discussion regarding how the situation should be handled. (While I have not systematically followed up on this since then, I can say that up until this writing, I have been asking students who have worked or interned at there about the CREED, and they always say that is still prominent in the work of the agency.)

Implementation of new systems should be monitored, with further adjustments made as needed. If goals and objectives of the change initiative are not being met, conditions can be reassessed and new plans made and implemented.

During the next step, evaluation, there will of course be close attention paid to what actually happened as a result of the change initiative, with particular attention to how the process worked and what goals and objectives were accomplished. Goals and objectives can be used during the institutionalization stage as well, just as they can be used in a formative evaluation of a program, to see what progress is being made. This is actually a form of action research, an organizational change method that is covered in Chapter 11. Basically, action research is an ongoing process of gathering and analyzing data, taking necessary actions, and again gathering data to observe progress or results. This can be used to assist institutionalization by using progress on goals and objectives as a monitoring activity. If inadequate progress is being made in locking the changes into the management systems of the organization, adjustments can be made. This might involve reconvening problem-solving groups or other teams to analyze barriers to full implementation and institutionalization and developing other ideas and mechanisms to ensure that the changes are locked in to ongoing operations.

If culture change was a goal, this also will need to be built into daily operations through mechanisms that are often associated with organizational culture. Culture change is harder to institutionalize than a new information system, but change leaders can continually reinforce the new ways of operating. Culture can also be reflected in basic management processes, such as modified job designs, job descriptions, and performance appraisal systems. These can help support the use of new behaviors, such as treating clients or colleagues in different ways or something as technical as the use of a new information system. Leaders can use transformational, exemplary, or other leadership styles in their daily behavior to help support a new culture.

Mechanisms such as follow-up staff surveys or focus groups, and perhaps even surveys or interviews with clients and other stakeholders, can be used to monitor culture changes.

Remembering Kotter's (1996) emphasis on communicating multiple times using multiple methods, special attention should be paid to making staff aware of the results of the change process. Reminding staff of what has been accomplished will help keep the changes on their mind, perhaps helping them pay more attention to ongoing support of the new systems and processes that are being institutionalized.

Changes and successes should be celebrated in ways consistent with the organization's culture. Proehl (2001, pp. 178–179) suggested the following as ways to celebrate the change:

- Post results of the change, or its evaluation on bulletin boards or in newsletters
- Host events such as receptions or parties for members who contributed to the effort
- Present to those who participated token gifts such as coffee mugs or mouse pads
- Send thank you letters, with copies to the staff member's personnel file
- Have a retreat to review the project and provide closure

Successes can also be rewarded and celebrated more informally in staff meetings and other arenas.

Ideally, an outcome of the process would be the creation of organizational systems and an organizational culture committed to ongoing change and improvement.

Here are some examples of how change leaders in our cases helped institutionalize their changes.

Father Joe's Villages

New office arrangements and rewritten policies ensured institutionalization of the change in Father Joe's Villages. Changes were made to the procedure for billing case manager time for different grants. Some programs moved to a paperless information system that saved time for team members.

San Mateo County

For San Mateo County, the previous data focus in the Human Services Agency had been on tracking task completion and not on client outcomes. As a result, information on community needs and agency-based decisions on resource allocations were being made on anecdotal information. Creating a customer service focus required focusing on identification of client and community outcomes agency-wide and for each program. It also required developing a plan for information systems that served the agency and its contract agencies. This involved a multiyear plan to implement a new information system.

The training course on core competencies for managers and supervisors remained in existence as a valued program within the organization.

The planning and evaluation unit had taken the lead in coordinating the Continual Quality Improvement efforts of the agency. This unit was responsible for researching evidence-based and best practices and working with the service programs to review their outcomes and promote dialogue and decision-making on what needed to be changed.

Because organizational change is dependent on leadership setting behavioral examples, executive team meetings were seen as opportunities for team building and open dialogue on issues leading to consensus decisions and set an example for how other teams in the agency could work. Seeing things change for the better created hope among staff and unleashed their ability to be creative, think, and develop the community relationships necessary to generate innovation.

A range of other significant improvements in outcomes of various programs were noted 5 years later (Borland, 2019).

The organizational change process itself became institutionalized when the organization development consultant was given ongoing responsibility for staff development in the agency. New change leadership systems included these:

> OD [organization development] tools and techniques were introduced to the staff development trainers. Staff development trainers became comfortable with utilizing team-building and visioning exercises, cross-Agency strategies for consensus building, and working with managers and supervisors to develop enhanced leadership training and coaching. The OD approach has become institutionalized in HSA and has contributed to the development of a "learning organization" culture. (Borland, 2019, p. 166)

San Diego Youth Services

At San Diego Youth Services (SDYS), the results of the change were institutionalized through incorporation into agency policies and procedures. These included a new organizational structure, new team meeting processes, new job titles and descriptions, new supervision lines of authority, and new fiscal reports and procedures. Staff were trained on their new model of trauma-informed care.

San Diego Fire Department

Senior staff members in the San Diego Fire Department had organization development responsibilities as part of their ongoing management by objectives and performance management processes. Action planning also became part of the culture for battalion chiefs, who increasingly adopted a "manager" role as part of their identity, which had previously been seen as basically directing firefighting operations and ensuring that fire companies were trained and ready for fire-fighting duties.

Changes were made in department policies and procedures as needed regarding changed functions in areas ranging from training to equipment maintenance and repair.

Changes and accomplishments were widely publicized in city reports, and the chief and other staff presented results of the project at professional conferences.

Nine years after the project started, the OD steering committee, OD coordinator role, and problem-solving groups were still functioning.

Step 12. Evaluate the Change

Just as program evaluation in HSOs often gets a lot less attention than it deserves, I expect that evaluation is the aspect of organizational change that gets the least attention. Also similar to HSO programs, an evaluation of an organizational change initiative can serve multiple purposes. Formative evaluations can assess the extent to which the planned processes are being implemented as designed (e.g., having roles such as sponsor and champion adequately filled, how action teams operate, what action teams actually accomplished, how well staff are supported and trained). Such a review can enable timely changes and adjustments to be made. Outcome evaluations can examine the extent to which desired impacts (improved services to clients, better operating systems, lower turnover, satisfaction of external stakeholders, etc.) were achieved.

In a special issue of *Training and Development in Human Services*, C. Parry (2011) noted some of the challenges in evaluating organizational change interventions, including

- Attribution of responsibility for outcomes: can one change initiative, such as implementing an evidence-based practice, be shown to impact client outcomes?
- Resource limits: comprehensive evaluations including, for example, randomized control trials, are not likely to be funded for individual agency initiatives
- A likely time lag between the intervention ending and results in improved program or client outcomes.

C. Parry (2011) concluded that "making appropriate attributions of positive outcomes to a specific intervention can be a formidable technical problem for evaluators and involve a substantial commitment of time and resources for an agency" (p. 39). She created 10 recommendations for those evaluating change initiatives in HSOs:

1. *Adopt a systems perspective*, considering contextual factors that may affect the change process and its outcomes.
2. *Gear the evaluation to the intervention's level of development* (formative evaluation during the initiative, outcome evaluation later, when effects can be expected).
3. *Think of evaluation in cycles*, starting with a pilot study, and building on evaluations of similar initiatives.
4. *Treat evaluation as a part of program development*: Don't wait until the end of the initiative to evaluate; get stakeholder buy-in and input early.
5. *Develop a shared understanding of the boundaries of the intervention*: Will it impact other organizational systems such as HR and information systems?
6. *Work with the program to articulate and map a theory of change.* Colleagues and I did this for an evaluation of a county initiative to provide behavioral health services to child welfare client families. A logic model and client flow chart provided clarity on what staff expected to happen and would need to be measured.
7. *Take a participatory approach*—one more example of the value of participatory decision-making to use staff expertise and enhance buy-in.
8. *Use multiple methods*: My research typically includes surveys of staff, focus groups, interviews with change leaders, and document analysis.
9. *Measure implementation*: As I note in Chapter 16 regarding implementation of evidence-based practices, a program model that has a strong evidence base cannot be expected to be effective if it is not fully implemented with fidelity to the model.
10. *Build a case for impact*: Be clear on the extent to which one organizational change can be expected to have broad impacts, such as on client outcomes.

Schalock and colleagues (2014) developed an evidence-based approach for evaluating HSOs that can also be used to evaluate an organizational change process. Their principles have several elements in alignment with Parry's (2011) recommendations:

- Use best practice indicators: "objective measures of organization processes and performance" (p. 111).
- Use multiple performance-based perspectives, such as in the balanced scorecard (see Niven, 2008).

- "The customer perspective focuses on personal goals, assessed support needs, individualized supports, and personal outcomes.
- The growth perspective focuses on program options, high performance teams, direct support staff involvement, and networks, consortia, and partnerships.
- The financial perspective focuses on a standardized approach to calculating unit costs, cost accounting, cost allocation, social capital, fixed and variable costs, overhead rate, and resource allocation models.
- The internal processes perspective focuses on horizontal and vertical alignment of program components, mapping system(s), research and evaluation capacity, data sets, data collection systems, and quality improvement activities" (Schalock et al., 2014, p. 111).
- Use a collaborative approach to evaluation, such as participatory evaluation, utilization-focused evaluation, and empowerment evaluation. These are all very consistent with leadership principles of participative decision-making.
- Use continuous quality improvement methods. They gave us an example the Plan, Do, Evaluate (or Study), Act model of Continuous Quality Improvement. (This is discussed as a change technology in Chapter 13).

While their model applies more directly to general program evaluation, their four principles can be adapted for the evaluation of an organizational change initiative.

Also from the perspective of general evaluations of HSOs, the challenges of validly measuring organizational performance, in terms of both outcomes and organizational processes, are well known (Yoo, Brooks, & Patti, 2007) but not insurmountable. All the dilemmas of regular program evaluation are present in the evaluation of a change initiative. If the original goals and objectives were clear, relevant, and measurable, evaluation will be much easier and more useful.

Many of the processes used in traditional program evaluation can be directly applied to an organizational change intervention. Clear, measurable objectives can provide clarity to focus staff energy and can also aid in evaluating the extent to which the process, in this case a change initiative, was implemented as designed and was successful.

The outcomes of an organizational change effort can be evaluated in terms of both process and content. Evaluation of the change *process* typically assesses the extent of implementation of the change process as designed (e.g., the extent to which the change process plan was followed). If a specific change model, such as ARC (availability, responsiveness, and continuity), was used, then the change process can be evaluated in terms of model fidelity: the extent to which the model was implemented according to defined standards. Also, building on the previous section, evaluation can include assessing the extent to which the results are institutionalized through formal changes in policies, procedures, staffing structures, culture change, or other changes in organizational operations.

A useful way to evaluate the change *process* is a method adapted from the US Army's After Action Review. This was used to assess processes used in a research project in the San Francisco Bay area (Hengeveld-Bidmon, 2015) and can be easily used to evaluate the processes used in a change initiative. The following questions can be asked in group settings with key participants in the change process (here, referred to as the "project"). Collated results can be shared throughout the organization to enhance prospects for success on future change initiatives.

1. What did we set out to do?
2. What were the key events, meetings, and the like that occurred during the project?
3. What were the roles of the various participants?
4. Was the project successful? Did we achieve what we set out to achieve?
5. What challenges did we face—individually? As a group?
6. What worked well—For you? For the group? To achieve the end product?
7. What, if anything, could have been done differently to achieve a better outcome?
8. What are our "takeaways" or recommendations?

This shorter list of questions (Akingbola et al., 2019, p. 232) was developed for nonprofit organizations, but would also apply to a change initiative in a government organization:

- Did the change implementation proceed as planned? If not, why [not]?
- What problems were encountered during implementation? How were they resolved?
- Was the change implemented on budget and on time?

Evaluating the *content* of an organizational change examines its impact in terms of some important aspect of performance, such as improved outcomes for consumers, client, and/or stakeholder satisfaction; improved efficiency or cost savings; a better service delivery model; a more appropriate culture and climate; lower turnover; new staff knowledge and skills; increased organizational learning capacity; enhanced management capacity; or improved employee quality of working life. Factors such as these can often be evaluated in a simple Management by Objectives format: Were the goals and objectives accomplished?

Akingbola et al. (2019, p. 232) also developed what they called *product* evaluation questions that can also be seen as outcome evaluation questions regarding the content of the change initiative:

- Is the target of the change (a process, a program, a service, etc.) running better as a result of the change?
- What are the positive and negative results of the intervention?
- How sustainable are the improvements that are the result of change?
- Can the results of this change be applied to other organizational efforts?

Depending on the change goals, fiscal audits or management audits can be useful evaluation tools. Pre–post employee surveys can be useful to assess changes in employee quality of working life aspects such as job satisfaction, morale, organizational culture, or organizational commitment. Employee attitude surveys are covered in more detail in Chapter 11. Surveys of clients can also be useful. If change goals envisioned changes in program outcomes, program data can be used to assess changes.

Akingbola et al. (2019, p. 248) also raised some excellent questions that can be used as a "meta-evaluation," essentially evaluating the evaluation process:

- What was the initial purpose of the evaluation? Did the evaluation as conducted serve that purpose?
- Did all the appropriate individuals and organizational stakeholders provide input during the evaluation process?
- Was the selected evaluation design appropriate for the phenomenon being studied?
- How well did the data collection approach selected assist with gathering necessary information?
- Were the data analyzed correctly, whether via quantitative or qualitative analysis? Did the individuals performing data analysis have the requisite skills to conduct analysis properly?
- Was the chosen presentation method the most appropriate and effective for communicating results to various stakeholders?
- Which activities done and decisions made along the entire course of evaluation could have been improved?

This is an excellent example of organizational learning (covered here in Chapter 17): to help the organization do something better in the future. Some of these questions also illustrate the importance of designing the evaluation process at the beginning of the change initiative so that data needed to assess completion of activities and accomplishment of objectives are built into the plan. As one example, the second question suggests that provisions should be made in advance to ensure that appropriate individuals and organizational stakeholders do, in fact, have opportunities for input during the evaluation process.

Such an evaluation process also helps support institutionalization of the initiative. As Van Eron and Burke (2016) noted, building in time for reflection on what happened, where everything from disappointments to excitement can be shared, can provide opportunities for closure as well as for organizational learning for the future.

The last of the 21 change tactics introduced in Chapter 2—*making staff aware of the results of the change initiative*—was briefly mentioned in the previous section on institutionalizing the change. It is worth mentioning again, partly because this feedback to staff is important in terms of showing that organizational leadership is committed to learning from experiences, in this case a major change initiative, and both building on successes and identifying other aspects of organizational functioning that may need additional attention. Seeing the results of all the work they put into an organizational change initiative may also enhance staff commitment and motivation. To the extent that it was seen as a positive and successful process, staff may be more committed to implementing future organizational change initiatives.

Here are some examples of evaluation processes and results from our cases.

Father Joe's Villages

In our research on the Father Joe's Villages change process (Packard, 2019), we gathered data on perceptions of goal accomplishment of the change process through a department-wide survey, an interview with director Julie DeDe, and a focus group.

One question on the survey asked respondents to assess the extent of goal achievement. Twelve percent indicated that goals for the change initiative were fully achieved, with 48% believing goals were mostly achieved, and 40% believing that goals were partly achieved. No respondents indicated that goals were minimally or not at all achieved. Respondents were also asked an open-ended question regarding the results. Examples of the ways in which goal accomplishment was described are listed here. These generally suggest positive results, and some also reflect the complexities of measuring such outcomes.

- Multidisciplinary teams have provided clients with a more structured curriculum, but I do not see a big difference as far as an increase in client successful exits.
- Residents getting on a case plan sooner.
- More effective delivery of services.
- Short-term residents now receive case management.

- Going to teams has helped clients hold themselves accountable for their stay here.
- We are serving more clients from various backgrounds.
- Rapid rehousing program, case management, new housing.
- Improved communication helps clients move through the program faster.
- The integration of the teams would probably have worked better if we had the financial resources (staff). Currently, we still have a wait list.
- I liked the teams approach for sure—but . . . I was not affected greatly by the changes.
- Unable to tell; most heard observation is that everyone has more work and no recognition.

Many improvements in services were noted in the program director interview. Case managers became more nimble through the merger of case manager and career counselor positions into case managers who also conducted career counseling. Improved outcomes (e.g., permanent housing) were apparent through program data tracking in the major program that did not have the case management system before the change. Time on the wait list decreased. In addition to increased numbers of clients receiving case management services, the MDT meetings resulted in improved communication. Team leaders had more accountability for client outcomes (in contrast to program supervisors before). The status of team leaders was elevated through their monthly attendance at program manager meetings, where they could share their input and expertise.

The program director later reported that in the 16 months before implementation of the team model, the average percentage of people in one program who exited to permanent housing was 17%. In the 16 months after implementation, 62% of clients assigned to a team exited to permanent housing. In two other programs, for the 16 months before implementation, the average percentage of people who exited with employment income was 51%. In the 16 months after the team implementation, the average percentage of people who exited with employment income was 70%. Of course, this design did not allow us to presume causality.

San Mateo County

In San Mateo County's Human Services Agency, outcomes were tracked. This helped create a culture committed to improvement. Information on outcomes was regularly discussed for quality improvement purposes.

The planning and evaluation unit analyzed administrative data for the programs to help them with their decision-making.

Staff did struggle with the fact that they did not have the resources to evaluate all their programs and their impact on client outcomes.

San Diego Youth Services

Key outcomes from SDYS's restructuring initiative included major structural changes, elimination of some management positions, and a range of fiscal and service improvements. A very visible result of the restructuring was a new structure with a new leadership team. Nine center directors were reduced to three new division directors, who, along with the heads of HR, information technology, marketing, and development departments, formed the new team. Other results included

- new job titles, job descriptions, salary scales, supervision lines of authority; and technical changes to the data systems
- improvements in the fiscal bottom line for the agency
- administrative overhead reduced by 2%
- programs that had traditionally operated with financial losses either reduced their losses, were breaking even, or were in the black
- programs worked more closely together
- better coordination through weekly leadership team meetings to improve integration, coordination, and communication within and among the divisions
- new fiscal reports and procedures to track performance

In my research (Packard, 2017) conducted after completion of the initiative, several survey responses to the open-ended question asking for examples of results corroborated the results noted by the chief executive officer and focus group respondents:

- a more harmonious leadership team
- information is better communicated
- more consistency throughout the agency
- the agency continued to provide services throughout the financial crisis
- significantly reduced the number of management positions in the agency
- more streamlined way of doing business, more integration of like services among the agency, saved money
- development of a clearer agency structure; more universal job descriptions across programs that enabled us to better define positions
- more equitable salary scale and process for determining wage increases

- stronger quality improvement/quality assurance system
- development of agency workgroups
- shift of management roles and lowered payroll costs strengthened our bottom line
- keeping the agency more stable as it was being hit with funding decreases
- streamlining and financial stability to the overall agency

San Diego Fire Department

The San Diego Fire Department project included the most complete evaluation I have ever done on an organizational change initiative. The fact that the project had a clear logic model that included goals and objectives helped. Our consulting unit, the Organization Effectiveness Program, routinely did reports for the city manager on our major projects, and in this one we were able to provide some good documentation of results. We repeated the employee survey after 15 months and found statistically significant improvements on 36 of 52 questions in categories including leadership and decision-making, goals and workload, cooperation and communication, immediate supervision, rewards and promotions, work assignments, job satisfaction and training, repairs and maintenance, and union/chief cooperation. Of course, direct causality can't be shown. We also documented cost savings of over $365,000, which was relevant to city administration. After the third year of the project, 60 of 71 project objectives had been completed, with 9 still in progress (Packard & Reid, 1990).

Through ongoing monitoring and feedback, adaptations were made as needed, including the formation of new problem-solving groups, conflict management sessions, and training of more staff as facilitators.

Summary

Just as evaluation is very commonly a weak or neglected aspect of a program, so it is with organizational change initiatives. A good evaluation of a change process can be useful to show improvements to stakeholders such as boards, policymakers, community members, funding organizations, and others. Having staff see vivid examples of the success of something that was probably very demanding on their time and maybe their psyches should give them some satisfaction as well as more optimism about their future in the organization.

Institutionalization of the results of the change process may actually be even more important than evaluation because the evaluation will probably consider the extent to which the change outcomes endured. Bureaucratic inertia can easily creep in if the organization does not give sufficient attention to making sure that the changes become part of normal, everyday life in the organization. And, consistent with principles of action research, Continuous Quality Improvement, and learning organizations, continuous change should become the normal state of affairs for the organization.

This completes coverage of the 12 main steps of an organizational change process. The next two sections provide detail on some of the concepts and processes that were briefly mentioned in discussions of the change process.

Reflection and Focusing Questions

1. What formal and informal mechanisms should you put in place to ensure that the effects of the change will become part of normal operations? What management systems need to be changed or set up to ensure that the results of the change will be maintained? What do you need to do regarding people dynamics and organizational culture to sustain the change?
2. What systems will you set up to track results of the change to see if adjustments need to be made or additional change measures need to be taken?
3. How will you evaluate the change, both how the implementation went and what was actually accomplished?
4. Who are the key stakeholders who will be interested in the results of this change? What criteria and standards will they use to evaluate the success of the initiative? How can you address these in your evaluation?

SECTION 4

GENERIC CHANGE METHODS

10

Using Consultants

Consultant: "So, are you planning to change anything?"
Manager: "Well . . . yeah, I suppose."
Consultant: "Do you have a change management plan in place?"
Manager: "What's that?"
Consultant: "*You're doomed!!!* Give me money, quick!"
                                       —Scott Adams (Dilbert, 1996, p. 197)

In situations in which an administrator or the agency does not have the knowledge or skills to respond to a particular need for change or for the use of a very specialized change method or model, consultants can be an appropriate, effective, efficient, or even necessary alternative. Just as experts in management information systems are used to aid in automation or fundraising specialists assist with development of a fundraising strategy, organizational change consultants provide expertise in specific organizational change methods. The model for organizational change that I presented Section 3 is designed to be implemented without necessarily using consultants. However, there are a number of organizational change activities, variously called methods, interventions, or processes, that will almost certainly require expertise beyond what a typical human service organization (HSO) would have on staff.

In this chapter, I describe two fundamental types of consultants. First, *process* consultants offer a structured method but rely on the client organization to decide how to use the method, including making the decisions on what to actually do. These consultants are inherently more participative, expecting people within the organization to be making most of the decisions regarding what to do. Organization development (OD) consultation, a method that I discuss in some detail later in this chapter, and many quality improvement processes are examples.

The more well-known type is referred to as *expert* consultation. These consultants are contracted to fully complete a project or set of tasks. Setting up a new software system or set of human resources (HR) processes or perhaps doing fundraising or developing a marketing plan might be examples. There are no pure types: process consultants do tell the client organization what to do, in some respects, and expert consultants often spend a lot of time gathering input

Organizational Change for the Human Services. Thomas Packard, Oxford University Press. © Oxford University Press 2021. DOI: 10.1093/oso/9780197549995.003.0011

from people in the client organization before they prepare a product or set of recommendations. For example, a marketing consultant will want a lot of input from the client organization on what their core competencies are, what they want their niche to be, and how they want to represent themselves.

I also contrast the common role of *external* consultants, who work with an organization on a contract basis, and *internal* consultants, who are employees of an (often large) organization to be available to provide consulting services to departments or divisions as needed and requested. Staff who manage an organization's Continuous Quality Improvement program might be seen as internal consultants: They offer technical expertise, but rely on managers and other staff in a program to be heavily involved in the change tasks and make the actual decisions about using consultant expertise or recommendations.

Next, I offer some suggestions for selecting and working with consultants. The chapter closes with a discussion of the most common type of process consultation: OD. I hope that discussion will give you a fuller understanding of how process consultation can work.

Types of Consultants: Expert and Process

Yankey and Willen (2006) described two broad types of consultation. The *expert model* involves a content expert, such as a specialist in program evaluation or information systems design, who applies specific expertise to address a goal that the organization identifies. Organizational change typically involves the other type, a *process model*, in which the consultant is in more of a facilitator role, using expertise in change management processes but not giving expert advice on what an organization should do to solve its problem, except by suggesting change technologies to use. Activities such as team building, role clarification, and conflict management would use a process model, with the consultant not providing "expert" advice on what decisions a team should make, but rather providing expertise in setting up and facilitating the events and using interpersonal and facilitation skills. Employee surveys are an example: A process consultant has expertise in conducting surveys and survey feedback but would not tell what the client organization should do in response to survey results.

A type that is somewhat in between the two is an organizational consultant, who uses a particular change model that requires a great deal of expertise. Some of the models to be covered in Chapter 17, such as the ARC (availability, responsiveness, and continuity) or sanctuary models, may require such specialized knowledge that only a trained expert can provide the service. Even within that expert context, a consultant facilitating the implementation of a change model would also be a process consultant in terms of not telling staff of the client organization exactly what to do. The consultant would give advice on the change steps to take, but leave open to staff the details of how they would implement the model. This role relationship should be clarified through contacting, which I address later in the chapter.

Types of Consultants: Internal and External

Another distinction in types of consultants is *external* or *internal*. Most people are familiar with the idea of external consultants, who work on their own or as part of a consulting, technical assistance, or training firm or occasionally as faculty or staff at a university. These consultants or their organizations contract with an organization to provide designated services. Alternatively, consultants are sometimes employed by the organization where they are delivering services.

Internal Consultants

Large governmental organizations and also large nonprofit or for-profit HSOs may employ internal consultants. Bernotavicz, Dutram, Kendall, and Lerman (2011) listed the following roles that might be seen as either internal consultants or basic staff support functions for an organization:

- Administrative support
- Communications specialist
- Evaluator/researcher
- Human resource planner
- Instructional media specialist
- Instructor/trainer
- Organization development specialist
- Training program and curriculum designer

To use an internal consultant, an executive or manager would contact the head of the consulting unit and arrange a meeting to go over the department's or division's situation, needs, and requests for assistance. Staff in the consulting unit would assess the situation, and, if they had the expertise and time to be allocated for a project, a consulting agreement would be reached.

I was an internal consultant when I worked for the city of San Diego's Organization Effectiveness Program. We had a staff of about 13 people (half OD consultants and half productivity analysts) who were available to respond to requests from city departments for consulting services. We were located in the

Financial Management Department, reporting directly to the city manager, but it may be more common that an internal consultant would be a member of the HR department or perhaps a quality improvement unit. The location does not matter as much as the relationships with client departments or programs.

I noted in a book chapter (Packard, 2012) that the role of HR professionals has broadened in recent decades, from an initial focus on strictly personnel functions such as recruiting, hiring, training, performance appraisal, and discipline to now a conceptualization of *strategic human resource management* (SHRM). According to Pynes (2009), SHRM "refers to the implementation of human resources activities, policies, and practices to make the necessary ongoing changes to support or improve the agency's operational and strategic objectives" (p. 31). Facilitating organizational change has been identified as one SHRM function in this new conceptualization. Jamieson and Rothwell (2016) have noted the increasing convergence of HR and OD in recent years.

Contemporary HR staff who in the past were heavily involved with overseeing and conducting staff training are now in many cases also fulfilling roles as internal organizational consultants or change agents who advise managers or play a lead role in initiating and managing processes for improving the internal functioning of the organization. These can range from management development and leadership training to facilitation of problem-solving groups or providing expertise, as one's training allows, in processes such as Total Quality Management and OD consulting.

For example, Balogun and Hope Hailey (2004) suggested that the HR system can function as a "change lever" (p. 91), filling traditional HR functions and also providing OD consulting, discussed later in the chapter. In a similar vein, Alfes, Truss, and Gill (2010) have described the current HR manager as a change agent, facilitating organizational change processes through activities such as staff surveys and organization-wide communication processes regarding organizational change. Many useful guidelines and tools that an HR professional can use to lead or facilitate organizational change are detailed in *The Essentials of Managing Change and Transition* (Harvard Business School, 2005).

Hamlin (2016) has studied the benefits and challenges regarding using HR staff as organizational change consultants. He suggested that they could

> engage in a change management process by: (i) conducting organization wide "health" checks to identify required changes and the associated learning and development needs of managers and non managerial employees at the organizational, group, and individual level; (ii) providing "expert" advice on how best to meet these needs; (iii) recommending or taking the requisite action, and/or responding to needs resulting from "top down" OC initiatives; and (iv) developing the skills and abilities of managers to manage change effectively and

to cope effectively with any unintended consequences of the planned changes. However, much depends on the extent to which they can improve their "credibility" in the eyes of line managers. Hence, HRD [human resource development] practitioners need to "sell" their potential as valued strategic business partners of managers and in particular the distinctive contribution they can make in formulating and implementing organizational change programmes. (pp. 9–10)

Jamieson and Rothwell (2016) described the ways HR management and OD are converging and highlighted the needs for both professions to clarify their roles and unique skills as strategic partners with each other and the organization's leaders.

An advantage of having an internal consultant resource, an HR specialist or otherwise, is that the consultant and the client organization are part of the same system, and the consultant can more easily get up to speed with the client's situation. An internal consultant is likely to be aware of existing organizational norms and culture issues, including any political dynamics. Also, there may already be a trusting relationship that had been built through past work. These services are usually less expensive to the organization, with staff on salary having a lower hourly rate.

A possible disadvantage, or at least an issue to be addressed, involves independence and confidentiality. An external consultant can say yes or no to any work, while an internal consultant may have to take a less-than-ideal assignment when ordered to do so by a higher level executive. Confidentiality may also be a concern, with clients worrying about the consultant sharing confidential information, such as conflict within a management team, with someone at the executive level. This can definitely be avoided by having clear ethics standards and procedures that clients know that a consultant will be following.

External Consultants

External consultants are the ones that people typically think of when the term *consultant* is used. An organization may realize that it needs to change or implement something for which it does not have the technical expertise, such as implementing a new information system or developing a marketing plan. The next section offers details on how to go about finding an appropriate consultant and developing a viable working relationship and a plan for the process. There are individuals and consulting firms large and small that operate in particular niches, such as the fields of child welfare, behavioral health, or core social services. Some firms also specialize in particular methods, such as quality improvement, implementing evidence-based practices, or enhancing cultural competence.

Another variation on this in the nonprofit world would be the use of consultants who are employed by a funding organization that can require that an agency that it funds use a particular consultant to deliver a service that the funder thinks the agency needs. This is typically presented as a form of capacity building, which I cover in Chapter 17. There need not be conflict or disagreement in a relationship between a funding organization and the organization receiving funds, but the fact remains that a funding organization may be able to dictate consultation that the agency may feel is unnecessary or inappropriate.

Selecting and Using Consultants

At the risk of stating the obvious, if you are considering using a consultant, make sure you follow any policies or procedures that your organization has established for acquiring and using consultants. Government organizations in particular will have very precisely defined procedures to follow in preparing a scope of service and budget for a consulting project, requesting and evaluating proposals, selecting a consultant, and signing a contract. Large nonprofit and for-profit organizations may also have formal policies and procedures regarding consultants. In any case, an organization's legal staff may need to be involved in preparing, reviewing, and/or approving a contract.

Consultants and clients should thoughtfully consider the needs of the situation and arrange for the best approach. The expert model can be used, for example, if a program has identified a specialized need, such as training on working with incest victims. The agency can then solicit consultants with this expertise. For complicated situations ranging from poor morale to funding crises, process skills will likely be needed because there will be no easy "right" answer. Ideally, a consultant would have both process skills and expertise in selected areas. For example, in a funding crisis, process skills would be needed to help the client organization sort things out, identify issues, and consider actions; expertise skills in areas such as strategic planning, budgeting, cutback management, and fund development would be valuable as well. In any case, a consultant should keep the client's needs paramount and, if lacking needed expertise, suggest the use of other consultants.

Yankey and Willen (2006) provided useful guidelines for selecting and using consultants as well as guidelines for making the consultation useful. To find a consultant, managers can ask managers in other agencies about consultants they have used or can contact relevant foundations, funding organizations, or professional organizations. Internet searches can be especially useful here. A consultant being considered based on such a search should be asked to provide references from former clients.

Yankey and Willen (2006, p. 414) suggested that consultant interviews should cover not only consultant expertise and prior work but also these characteristics:

- Honesty about his or her capabilities,
- Compatibility with the organization,
- Beliefs and values regarding organizational development,
- Personality fit,
- Motivations,
- Ethics, and
- Appreciation for confidentiality.

There should be clarity regarding the consultation itself, reflected both in the request for proposals, if one is used, and in the contract with the consultant chosen. A contract should outline responsible parties and their roles, the problem and goal, individuals and/or units or programs to be involved, consultant "deliverables" (e.g., a report, recommendations, services provided), ground rules, fees, and a schedule.

Here are some considerations from an OD perspective, adapted from Weisbord (1978), that might be relevant for your consultation. Review this list with your consultant and reach clear agreements on how any of these would be addressed.

- Be clear on how decisions will be made regarding goals and planned activities. Will it be a mutual process, involving both you the client and the consultant?
- Clarify exactly what the consultant and your organization will do. For example, in process consultation such as OD, the consultant will typically provide methods, techniques, and a conceptual framework to help you and involved staff to understand and work more effectively on your issues. You and your staff would provide energy and commitment, including ultimate responsibility for success.
- A process consultant will typically not recommend expert solutions, but will help staff in the organization to develop solutions that would work in your setting.
- An OD consultant will probably want to feel free to raise "sticky issues" related to identified problems. After you and the consultant discuss the issue and possible scenarios or likely outcomes based on acting on or ignoring issues, you would reserve the right to choose not to deal with those issues. Ichak Adizes, one of my professors in the Graduate School of Management

at UCLA, said that he sometimes operated as an "insultant," to bring a difficult issue to the surface to have it confronted directly. Sometimes an outside
voice can help challenge you.

- An OD consultant will typically help raise group members' awareness of
  what they do and the possible consequences of their actions, and, as just
  noted, group members will then choose what to do or not to do.
- An OD consultant will expect you to raise any questions or concerns that
  you have about consulting activities (ideally as soon as you feel the concern)
  so that they can be directly addressed.
- Confidentiality agreements should be very clear. If a consultant is doing individual process consultation with you, anything you say must remain between the two of you unless you both agree to share something with others.
  This can create a dilemma for an internal consultant, who, as a member
  of the organization, has accountabilities through a chain of command.
  General guidelines on this should be articulated by the consulting unit, so
  that any other unit of the organization that engages an internal consultant
  will be clear on what can and cannot be shared. When I was working in the
  Organization Effectiveness Program with the city of San Diego, one manager with whom I was consulting told me that I was like the chaplain he
  talked to in the Army: He could say whatever he wanted with knowledge
  that it would not be shared with others, and also that he would not feel
  judged or told what to do.
- Confidentiality also applies in the case of data collection from any individuals or groups in the organization. A core technology of OD, action research, is discussed in detail in the next chapter. Basically, this involves the
  consultant gathering data, sorting the data into themes or categories, and
  presenting the results anonymously to those who provided the data for action. This is common in team building (discussed in Chapter12): The consultant will interview team members, compile the data, share the data with
  the team leader, and then share the data with the whole team at an off-site
  team-building session for action planning. The same principle applies to
  staff surveys, also covered in the next chapter.
- While a scope of services and timeline will be agreed on early in the process, an OD consultant may also want to debrief with you after a consulting
  activity to see if modifications to the plan seem appropriate. Whereas expert consultation, such as installing a new information system and training
  staff, can be very structured, process consultation such as OD often reveals
  new information and issues as it is implemented, so not everything can be
  planned in advance.
- A consultant will typically want to be able to identify your organization as a client (e.g., to professional associates and perhaps in

marketing materials), with no sharing of details about consulting activities. Agreement should be made regarding what can be shared, if anything, outside the organization.

Another important consideration to raise with your consultant is the extent to which you would like to have built into the contract the consultant training you or your staff on any of the consulting activities. For example, if a consultant is helping your organization implement a quality improvement process, you may be able to arrange to have some of your staff trained in the method so that you will have staff (who essentially become internal consultants) who can facilitate other staff on quality improvement processes in the future. Some models have a built-in structure for this, such as Six Sigma (mentioned in Chapter 14), which uses colored belts (e.g., green belt, black belt) as in martial arts to designate a person's skill in using the method. This can be a valuable form of capacity building for the organization, making it less reliant on consultants in the future.

Consider how responsibilities for change management and change leadership will be divided between executives or managers and consultants, whether internal or external. One consultant (Ashkenas, 2013) described a case in which a major change management approach was implemented in a large organization, with managers being trained in the concepts but the work being done by consultants and HR staff. He said that "eventually, change management just became one more work-stream for every project, instead of a new way of thinking about how to get something accomplished," suggesting that things could have gone better. He suggested that the organization's executives or managers ask the following three questions:

1. Do you have a common framework, language, and set of tools for managing significant change? There are plenty to choose from, and many of them have the same set of ingredients, just explained and parsed differently. The key is to have a common set of definitions, approaches, and simple checklists that everyone is familiar with.
2. To what extent are your plans for change integrated into your overall project plans, and not put together separately or in parallel? The challenge is to make change management part and parcel of the business plan, and not an add-on that is managed independently.
3. Finally, who is accountable for effective change management in your organization: Managers or "experts" (whether from staff groups or outside the company)? Unless your managers are accountable for making sure that change happens systematically and rigorously—and certain behaviors are rewarded or punished accordingly—they won't develop their skills.

As I noted in a previous chapter, a major change management initiative should be framed within the organization's overall strategies so that it clearly contributes to strategic goals. And, related to strategic priorities, and bearing in mind the change roles of sponsor and champion in Chapter 7, line managers (and probably executives) need to be directly involved with the change process so that it is not seen as just one more "project" to be implemented. Internal consultants may have an advantage here, depending on their placement and overall role in the organization. I remember complaints from internal consultants about feeling left out of the "big issues" and major decision-making in the organization, wishing that they could be directly involved in strategy implementation. Relationships and roles between consultants and client managers should be clearly defined in the contracting process, even though internal consultants don't have contracts in the traditional sense.

Next, I discuss OD, seen as both a change method and a profession. This is one type of consultation that definitely requires a consultant. In addition to giving you some information on OD specifically, I hope this section can give you more insights regarding the dynamics of process consultation.

Organization Development

The terms *organization development* and *organizational development* have been used in general management practice and in HSOs with varying meanings, ranging from referring to developing a new program to improving operations or resource development. OD has a specific meaning as a professional practice field. The term *organizational development* is sometimes used to refer to such organizational change consulting, but OD professionals prefer the term without the "al." Furthermore, *organizational* development is often used in HSOs, especially nonprofits, to refer to activities related to developing funds for the organization or developing new programs. Here, OD refers specifically to activities of planned organizational change.

Organization development can be defined as a

> long-term effort, led and supported by top management, to improve an organization's visioning, empowerment, and learning, and problem-solving processes through an ongoing, collaborative management of organizational culture—with special emphasis on the culture of intact work teams and other team configurations—using the consultant-facilitator role and the theory and technology of applied behavioral science, including action research. (French & Bell, 1999, pp. 25–26)

This obviously implies a lot of things. "Long term" can be broadly construed to mean at least a year, although many system change processes such as organizational culture change take much longer. Top management support and a collaborative or participative management philosophy are expected, even essential. OD by definition does require the use of a consultant. There are degree programs in OD, but many who identify as OD consultants have other professional backgrounds, in fields including industrial/organizational psychology, leadership, business administration, and, yes, social work.

A notable difference between OD consulting and some forms of "expert" consulting regarding finances or information systems is the explicit attention to organizational culture. If an organization's executive approached an OD consultant to see about fixing a specific problem, the consultant would be likely to take the discussion to possible problems at a larger or deeper systems level. That might then point to organizational leadership as something that needs attention. However, many OD consultants might take assignments without insisting on a system-wide focus, and many of them would probably be happy to engage in more limited interventions, such as team building or management coaching. I note in later chapters where a consultant would be needed or advisable for a change technology being described.

Organization development is a values-based approach to systems change in organizations and communities. Its values are very consistent with principles of the human relations movement in the management literature and related participative styles such as those described by Likert and McGregor. These values are also very well aligned with the values of the human service professions. Values such as respect for human dignity, justice, compassion, authenticity, collaboration, learning, growth, and empowerment (Organization Development Network, n.d.) are characteristic of OD practice and should resonate easily with human services professionals. Learning and growth are very compatible with principles of lifelong learning and the creation and nurturing of learning organizations. The study of learning organizations and organizational learning has had significant impacts on many organizations, including HSOs. This is touched on in Chapter 16.

Organization development strives to build organizational capacity to achieve and sustain a new desired state that benefits the organization or a community. It involves an OD consultant working collaboratively with an organization or community to jointly identify problems, goals, and visions and develop and implement plans for improved functioning.

Any change leader who is considering hiring an OD consultant should expect to be told by a prospective consultant that a full OD process is likely to take at least a year, to look broadly at systems change, and to have at least some involvement of all or nearly all staff in the organization or unit (e.g., a division, region, or bureau). A participative leadership style will probably be expected. An OD consultant may be willing to engage in a more narrow scope of work but will still want to serve as a process, rather than expert, consultant, not giving much direct advice except on change methods, and asking penetrating questions.

Finally, more broadly, if you are considering using a consultant for OD methods, Curran and Bonilla (2010) suggested that you consider these questions:

- How willing are you to shift your thinking to include group dynamics (i.e., power and control, teamwork, building leadership qualities, etc.) in your survival strategies?
- Can you, as a leader, accept responsibility for these less obvious but still pivotal challenges you are facing?
- How comfortable are you with feedback that addresses both the organizational strengths and areas to be improved, and your own?
- Are you willing to re-examine, and possibly let go of, the habits and strategies that made you, as a leader, and your organization, so successful—in order to get to a new level of success?
- How will you prioritize an organization development intervention as an investment of time and/or money?
- If you have decided to invest in OD, how will you communicate this need to your funders? (p. 6)

Summary

This chapter started with discussions of types of consultation (expert and process) and types of consultants (external and internal). I covered some ideas on how to assess and select a consultant and considerations in developing clear plans regarding roles and change activities. Issues including confidentiality, how "deep" the consultation will potentially go into systems issues in the organization, and how much the consultation will include developing internal skills and knowledge of staff are especially important. We ended with an overview of a major process consultation method and field of practice: OD, including large group interventions.

Reflection and Focusing Questions

1. Given the goals and plans for a change initiative, what capacities does the organization have to have in order to fully implement the plan? What expertise is the organization missing that would require use of a consultant?

2. What criteria for consultant expertise, style or philosophy, and "fit" with the organization will be important?
3. What explicit agreements should be made with a consultant regarding respective roles for decision-making and responsibility for project success?
4. How open will you be to having a consultant raise sticky issues or challenge you to look deeper at underlying problems or issues?
5. How will adjustments be made regarding plans based on new developments during the process?
6. How will success of the consultation and the change initiative be assessed?

11
Data Collection and Assessment

No action without research, no research without action.
— Kurt Lewin (*Field Theory in Science:*
Selected theoretical papers, 1951)

Kurt Lewin, one of the founders of the organization development (OD) profession, used the above principles to guide organizational change initiatives. These principles can be represented more crudely by variations on the "ready, aim, fire" metaphor: Cynics describe the practitioner perspective as "ready, fire" and the academic perspective as "ready, aim, aim . . ." Clearly, planned change, to be successful, needs to be based on some amount of thoughtful analysis of relevant data to guide goal setting, planning, and implementation.

And, more precise distinctions should be made between, *data* (facts, typically represented in numbers, but also observable behaviors, e.g., staff complaining about management); to *information*, which attributes meanings to data (e.g., program performance, staff turnover rates); to *knowledge*, which uses information to draw conclusions such as correlations among variables. For now, we focus mostly on information. The increasing attention to knowledge is discussed a later chapter, regarding creating and nurturing learning organizations and the newer field of *knowledge management*. Notably, while CEO (chief executive officer), COO (chief operating officer, often the second-in-charge person), and CFO (chief financial officer) are fairly common terms in large human service organizations (HSOs), chief information officer and even chief knowledge officer are becoming more common, recognizing the increasing importance of these functions. (*Wisdom* is sometimes listed as the top level in this hierarchy. In organizations, that can be seen in the ways that very experienced staff are able to draw on years of experience to put their knowledge to effective, creative, and innovative use.)

This chapter provides some detail on methods for gathering data and turning data into information to help identify problems, needs, or opportunities for change that were covered in Chapter 5. In that chapter, regarding the assessment and goal-setting stage, assessing the context, content, and process for a particular change, the focus was mostly on change process assessment—factors including

Organizational Change for the Human Services. Thomas Packard, Oxford University Press. © Oxford University Press 2021. DOI: 10.1093/oso/9780197549995.003.0012

readiness and capacity for change on the part of staff and the organization as a whole. The tools here would be useful in assessing the content of the change: what issues, problems, or other concerns need to be addressed.

Specifically, the action research process is offered here as an overall process of gathering data, analyzing data, developing action plans, implementing plans, and then gathering data again to assess results and identify new opportunities for change and improvement. Employee surveys, customer surveys, stakeholder surveys, and management audits are covered as tools to gather data in a structured way. Existing organizational performance data and "unobtrusive" measures such as absentee and turnover rates can also be used to identify areas needing attention. Finally, appreciative inquiry is discussed as a more strengths-based perspective for looking at the organization, as opposed to action research, which historically has had more of a problem-oriented focus. Actually, a combination of both perspectives could be used in a given change process.

A few words of warning are relevant here. First, be prepared to be surprised to some extent by the results of any data gathered, especially not only from employees, stakeholders, or a management audit, but also potentially from taking a close look at any organizational performance data. Administrators may think they are fully aware of what employees or outside stakeholders think of their organization, but in my experience they are sometimes surprised to learn that others do not see things in the organization to be going as well as the administrators think they are. An example might help here. Our neighbors recently found water dripping from the ceiling of a room in their house. Plumbers later found that there had been a small leak in a water pipe, which finally let out enough water to show up in the ceiling. Before the damage was visible, they of course assumed that everything was fine. In an organization, administrators may assume things are "fine" if there are no obvious signs of problems such as complaints from staff, excessive absenteeism or turnover, or even job actions by employee organizations. As management guru Tom Peters was quoted in Chapter 1, "If it ain't broken, you just haven't looked hard enough" (1988, p. 3). Some proactive administrators do employee surveys regularly just to have a pulse on how things are going to enable quick action before small problems become larger.

Employees and maybe even outside stakeholders such as clients or others that the agency interacts with may be guarded or concerned about saying what they really think on a survey, fearing negative repercussions if management does not like the results. Therefore, climate setting from the change leaders will be essential. This should involve communicating clearly and honestly that the change leaders want respondents to be as honest as they can, and there will be no repercussions for "bad news." Of course, anonymity should be ensured to protect individuals (a consultant can help with this). Also, you should communicate clearly in advance how all data will be used, including sharing as much of the results (typically compiled and summarized by a consultant) as possible, with opportunities for discussing the findings at feedback sessions, and what the processes will be for addressing issues that showed up in the data. And finally, of course, when you do share your reactions to the data, do so in a nondefensive way, thanking people for providing useful information, admitting that there are things to work on, and supporting follow-up actions.

Action Research

Action research is a core OD technology that can also be very useful in any organizational change process. It is essentially a straightforward, if not necessarily simple, process to assist an organization and groups working within it to gather relevant data, analyze the data, develop a plan, implement the plan, and examine the results. It involves iterative cycles of data collection (research), data analysis and planning, implementation (action), further data collection to assess accomplishment of goals and plan further action, and implementation of additional change activities. The cycle can be continuous, as in the case of a learning organization that is gathering and analyzing data on a regular basis.

Some in the human services field are familiar with the related term *participatory action research*, which has been used in organizational and community settings. From an OD perspective, action research is inherently participative, with the consultant acting as a facilitator, and participants, in this case members of an organization, taking the lead in deciding what data to collect, analyzing data, and developing action plans. Through a process of gathering data (research), assessing the data and implementing plans (action), and continuing the cycle with more data collection to assess results and then implement new plans, the organization can engage in ongoing learning and change. Sometimes data collection (e.g., employee surveys and focus groups) requires anonymity, which would require the use of consultants.

Action research is sometimes contrasted with appreciative inquiry (discussed later in this chapter), with action research being seen as too "problem oriented," while appreciative inquiry uses a strengths perspective. I don't see these perspectives as incompatible with each other.

The executive team and change leadership team can use action research by simply gathering data to assess progress on plans, analyze the current state, make adjustments to the plans as needed, implement new activities, and gather data to assess progress. Action teams or problem-solving groups typically use the same process at a micro level, gathering data on the problem area they are attempting to solve, developing and implementing a plan, and gathering data to assess the results.

Because of the emphasis on participation, a consultant takes on more of a facilitator role than an "expert" role, although the role can also be a blend between these two. In most cases, the client group is involved in every aspect of the action research aspect of a change project, including

- Establishing change priorities
- Collecting and interpreting data
- Disseminating and making sense of the results
- Creating action plans based on the results
- Implementing the action plans
- Assessing results and taking additional action steps as needed

For any data gathered for a change project, using any of the methods described next, it is essential that there is a clear process for compiling data (often done by consultants to ensure anonymity and the use of good summarizing of themes) and sharing data with employees, followed by some action. Many employees are understandably cynical about the prospect of administrators wanting their input on something, especially if in the past they have been surveyed with no follow-through on the sharing of findings or commitments to action. At the same time, it is important that change leaders and other administrators are clear on the parameters for change so that staff do not have unrealistic expectations. For example, in our survey of the San Diego Fire Department, frustrations with the promotions process were common. The department had to make it clear which aspects of promotion processes were in fact open for employee input and which aspects were essentially unchangeable as part of existing city regulations and policies.

Employee Surveys

A very common use of action research and a popular method for assessing the internal climate of an organization is the *employee survey*, sometimes known as an *attitude survey* or *organizational survey*. On an organizational change process, surveys can be used to enable employees to identify particular areas of concern or, more broadly, provide a picture of organizational culture and climate and views on issues from overall leadership to having necessary equipment and supplies that can guide change leaders in their planning. A survey can also be used as a pre–post measure of an organizational change activity. Kraut (2009) noted a "fundamental shift" over the last 50 years, asserting that "more organizations than ever are using surveys as strategic tools to drive and measure organizational change" (p. 308).

A survey can be broad in scope, with questions on many aspects of an organization's management and leadership systems and processes, or can be very focused. On the fire department project that I discussed in previous chapters, the new fire chief wanted to get a comprehensive picture of how all employees saw operations in the department, so our survey covered everything from leadership to training systems and the promotion process. In the past, I had students who told me that the Navy did routine employee surveys on ships to get a general impression of sailor morale. The Academy for Professional Excellence (https://theacademy.sdsu.edu/resources-and-tools/), a major program in our School of Social Work that provides a wide range of training, consultation, and research services for county HSOs, does annual staff surveys to check the pulse of the organization and identify opportunities for continuous improvement. I expect that most change initiatives are more specific, in which a need or opportunity has already been identified. In such a case, an employee survey would probably ask only questions that would provide useful data in accomplishing the change goal. For example, there are survey instruments to assess staff attitudes and readiness regarding implementing evidence-based programs, which would be useful prior to starting an evidence-based practice implementation.

As is the case with other OD activities such as team building, this is best conducted with the assistance of an experienced consultant and should at least ensure anonymity for all respondents regarding data input, analysis, and feedback. It should begin with a serious discussion within the organization, ideally at all levels, about the organization's need to learn about its functioning and the level of commitment to making change. Top management support (the sponsors of the organizational change process being initiated) will be needed, and there will need to be champions in the form of staff assigned to fill leadership roles in the design and implementation of the survey. An organization-wide steering committee may be formed to provide overall policy and direction and guidance. A survey team is often responsible for the design of the survey and its implementation.

The survey team begins by determining the factors to be measured on a survey. An employee survey may have questions that solicit employees' opinions on any aspect of organization's functioning, including views on the mission; leadership behavior; processes such as hiring and promotions, facilities, and equipment; supervisory styles; workgroup climate; and quality of working life factors, ranging from pay to the job itself. Usually questions should only be asked regarding areas in which the organization can implement change and is willing to consider changing. This helps avoid respondents developing unrealistic expectations (e.g., major salary increases or new staff positions) that things will change based on the survey.

After determining a survey's purpose and focus, a survey that addresses identified areas must be found or created by the organization. There are "off-the-shelf," standardized attitude surveys that can be purchased by an agency or provided by consultants, or the agency could develop a "home-grown" survey of items specifically addressing the focus of the survey. For a home-grown survey, consultation from an expert from a local university or consulting firm would ensure good psychometric properties of the items.

The advantages of a standardized survey are known validity and reliability of the instrument, perhaps industry-wide norms that may be available for comparison, and data compilation and analysis software. Validity and reliability may be disadvantages of a home-grown survey, which has the advantages of being uniquely tailored to the needs of the organization and a greater sense of staff ownership over the process. We collaborated with fire department OD participants to create a home-grown survey on that project. Our program also did this on projects with other departments and divisions, with good results.

Here are some examples of survey questions:

- The jobs in this organization are clearly defined and logically structured.
- This organization is characterized by a relaxed, easygoing working climate.
- I understand the policies and practices for getting promoted to better jobs.
- Where I work, policies are administered fairly and consistently.

Questions are written so that they may be answered on a Likert-type response scale, usually ranging from four to seven responses, with low and high responses such as "strongly disagree" to "strongly agree." Usually, a question is worded as a statement of high-level or desired functioning, so that a "strongly agree" response suggests a positive rating on the question. Questions should be worded in a neutral way, not "loaded" to encourage a positive or negative response.

There is typically a space at the end with open-ended prompts, such as "Please comment on any other areas of concern that were not included in the survey" or "Please note things in the organization that are going particularly well that should continue." Surveys should be anonymous, but respondents may be asked to indicate demographics such as their program or work unit, their job title, and how long they have worked for the organization for aid in collating and analyzing trends and themes.

Implementation of a survey should be preceded by announcements from the organization's chief executive and the survey team outlining the purpose of the survey, how it will be implemented, the uses of the data, and expected follow-through. It is essential that anonymity of all respondents can be ensured.

Surveys are completed anonymously and returned to a consultant for data collation and analysis. Typically, frequencies or mean scores for each question are presented, and the themes from the open-ended questions are summarized. Collated data are fed back to the organization by consultants for discussion and action planning. Data feedback begins with the executive management team, the steering committee, and the survey team. Data are then fed back to all workgroups in the organization. Members of a workgroup normally receive data for the organization as a whole and for their own work group. In order to protect anonymity, work units with fewer than five staff should not receive data for their work unit only.

After results are reviewed at a feedback session, participants may discuss the findings and develop recommendations for further action, both within their work unit or program and the organization as a whole. Notes from all feedback sessions should be collated and presented to the executive management team, the steering committee, the survey team, and at least in a summarized form to all staff.

Following up on survey results is crucial: If no actions result from the survey, employees are likely to become disillusioned. After survey data feedback and analysis, the change process would typically include the formation of problem-solving groups or action teams to address key issues identified in the survey. Their recommendations are presented to the executive management team and the steering committee for action. Staff, especially those who have experienced prior surveys that raised expectations but led to no change, will be following this process closely to see if the employee input is actually used to guide change.

The survey should ideally be repeated after an appropriate interval (e.g., 12–18 months) to assess changes and newer change opportunities. If this is used as an evaluation tool, mean scores on the same questions are compared for the two periods to identify the extent of change. Tests of statistical significance can be valuable for adding credibility of the data for staff and strengthening the use of findings for an evaluation of the change initiative. A consultant with statistics expertise may be needed to ensure that this is properly done to ensure statistical appropriateness and respondent anonymity.

The Management Audit

An employee survey gathers data from an employee perspective, typically emphasizing organizational culture and climate issues, but such surveys also often gather employee perceptions of core management processes such as planning, information systems, human resources, and program evaluation. The management audit focuses specifically on management and sometimes leadership processes, with reference to best practices or some other standard.

Consulting organizations specializing in nonprofit capacity building often have standard instruments that can be used to identify opportunities to improve management processes in an organization. Allison and Kaye (2005) included a management audit form in their book on strategic planning.

Traditionally, management audits are conducted by consultants who examine agency documents, observe agency processes, and interview staff. (This is the "expert" consultation mode described by Yankey and Willen in Chapter 10.) Consultants then prepare a report for management outlining findings and recommendations. They may use a standardized form or checklist.

An alternative is to have a management audit done participatively, with staff that have knowledge of the management functions being considered for involvement with its design and implementation, much as an employee survey is conducted. The key factors are that the method used and the criteria being assessed need to be seen as valid and appropriate by members of the organization, so that the findings will be seen as relevant and legitimate. A management audit format that has been used in HSOs appears in Appendix 2. Such a form may be filled out by any members of the organization who have knowledge of the factors under consideration. Some items on the form may also be appropriate for inclusion on an employee survey. As in the case of an employee survey, results can be collated by a consultant for feedback to staff. Of course, any staff members that have provided data for a management audit will expect to see the findings and will expect to see action taken. Action teams or problem-solving groups can be formed to address weak areas in the agency's management systems.

Client Surveys

Specifics on client surveys are not covered here, with my expectation that a well-functioning HSO will already be gathering customer survey data for regular use. If an organization is not currently gathering data from clients, such as at program completion and, ideally, on a follow-up basis, this would be an opportunity for an organizational change initiative.

I would also add here that client survey data can be used just as employee survey data are used: to identify opportunities for improvements in organizational performance. Such data should obviously be used in program planning and perhaps strategic planning. In the context here, such data may also suggest opportunities for organizational change. The same can be said for gathering and analyzing broader data on the clients, communities, and geographic areas served by a program as well as data from an organization's key stakeholders.

Stakeholder Surveys

Stakeholder surveys are a relatively common tool used in strategic planning. A stakeholder is an individual, role, group, or organization with a stake in what the agency does. Usually, a stakeholder has specific expectations of an organization and standards, at least implied, about how it judges how well the organization is doing. Some stakeholders are very powerful, such as funding sources and regulators, while others such as clients and community groups may be important but lacking in formal power. Identifying every stakeholder is neither possible nor necessary, but key stakeholders need to be identified so that their interests and concerns can be addressed by the strategic plan.

The criteria by which each stakeholder assesses the agency should be identified and viewed *from the point of view of the stakeholder, not the agency*. Once the criteria are clear, assess how well the organization is currently meeting them. Typical data collection methods of surveys, interviews, and focus groups may be used, appropriate to the situation.

Findings may result in sobering insights, especially if it is determined that the organization is not doing well at meeting the needs of particular stakeholders. This is nevertheless a solid place to begin because it allows strategies to be developed to improve stakeholder relations, and it ensures that the agency is under no illusions regarding how well it is doing.

John Bryson (2018), in his important book on strategic planning, discussed a number of techniques for identifying stakeholders and their interests and then gathering and analyzing stakeholder data. One of his additions to the process discussed above is that the organization's staff can "guess" what a stakeholder's criteria are and how the organization is performing with reference to those criteria. This can not only save time but also address the possibility that some stakeholders (e.g., politicians) may not be fully honest about what they expect from the organization.

Organizational Performance Data

Ideally, your organization would have comprehensive information and knowledge management systems to enable the tracking of key performance metrics. If a management audit, for example, shows weak areas and opportunities for the improvement of an organization's information systems, that in itself can be the subject of a change initiative. An information system would obviously include performance data on all service delivery systems. The use of such data should of course already be established in an organization. If good data are gathered but not used for performance improvement, this is another opportunity for organizational change. That would likely involve some amount of organizational culture change to build a performance orientation philosophy and spirit among staff. Enhancing organizational learning capacity and quality improvement processes are covered in Chapters 13 and 16.

Other data sources might include unobtrusive data, such as staff turnover and sick leave usage.

In some cases, focus groups can be used to identify current conditions and opportunities for change. When I worked in the city of San Diego's Organization Effectiveness Program, the city manager had taken the lead in launching a diversity initiative for all departments. A consulting firm was used to hold focus groups with a wide number of employee groups, such as female police officers and race or ethnic groups in particular departments. Anonymous summarized data were shared with executive staff to aid in problem identification to guide the diversity initiative.

Organizational performance data can be assessed by looking at program data trends over time or comparing the organization's results with best practices or other industry standards (e.g., in child welfare, data on child permanence, safety, and well-being).

San Diego Fire Department

Our San Diego Fire Department project used a fairly elaborate process for an employee survey and feedback sessions to all staff. Existing department performance data that were identified for analysis included sick leave, equipment breakdowns, employee grievances, fire company performance standards (e.g., response time), accidents, and injuries. To gather customer and stakeholder perspectives, we also sent mailed questionnaires to recent fire victims, senior citizen groups, town councils, the city council, and staff in the city manager's office. The results from these surveys were generally so positive that they were not useful for problem identification.

Over 50 feedback sessions were held, offering all staff in the department an opportunity to attend. Sessions lasted 3 hours, with representatives from department senior staff attending for a half hour to listen and offer support. At the sessions, participants analyzed the data and made recommendations for topics for problem-solving groups to take action. The employee survey was repeated 15 months later. Results showed statistically significant improvements on 36 of the 523 questions (Packard & Reid, 1990).

Appreciative Inquiry

Appreciative inquiry is a relatively new process for gathering data on an organization's functioning and processes. It is a strengths approach that focuses and builds on the strengths and potentials of an organization to help develop an image of a positive future and mobilize staff energy to pursue that vision. From a strengths perspective, it "invites people to appreciate and ask about the best of what exists within their systems, envision what might become in the future, dialogue about what should evolve, and innovate together to make their highest hopes become reality" (Stavros, Godwin, & Cooperrider, 2016, p. 123). The focus is on what is going well, rather than on problems. It involves the following:

- *Discovery* (appreciating what is; what gives life to the organization). As Cooperrider, Whitney, and Stavros put it, this is "the discovery of what gives 'life' to a living system when it is most effective, alive, and constructively capable in ecological, economic, and human terms" (2003, p. 3). This is often done by listening to "stories" from staff and other stakeholders about their best experiences with the organization (Bushe & Kassam, 2005).
- *Dream* (imagining what could be: the ideal organization): "Past achievements and successes identified in the discovery phase [are used] to imagine new possibilities and envisage a preferred future" (AI Commons, n.d.) for the organization.
- *Design* (determining what should be): This "brings together the stories from discovery with the imagination and creativity from dream. We call it bringing the 'best of what is' together with 'what might be', to create 'what should be—the ideal'" (AI Commons, n.d.).
- *Destiny* (creating what will be): As opposed to the OD model of action planning, appreciative inquiry "creates plans and processes that encourage and nurture improvised action by system members" (Bushe & Kassam, 2005, p. 168).

Staff are encouraged to create a picture of the organization at its best and then take steps to create this organization and ensure that the desired positive characteristics are always present. This innovative approach emphasizes asking positive questions to reveal the positive elements of an organization to help achieve its ideal future. Destiny also includes creating appreciative learning cultures and empowering staff for sustained change. This change method would probably require a consultant who is very familiar with appreciative inquiry principles and practices.

A meta-analysis of the appreciative inquiry literature (Bushe & Kassam, 2005) found positive, though not always transformational, outcomes from this model.

Summary

While Chapter 5 covered the assessment and goal-setting stage of the change process, this chapter elaborated on some of the data collection methods used in organizational change to assess organizational conditions and identify opportunities for change. In addition to traditional OD technologies of action research and employee surveys, surveys of clients and other stakeholders of the organization can be valuable in showing opportunities for change. Existing organizational performance data can be used not only to track performance and evaluate programs but also to identify opportunities for change. If, on examination, existing performance data systems are not adequate to provide needed information for the organization to assess ongoing performance, improving these systems can be an important change goal. Appreciative inquiry is becoming more common as a method for identifying opportunities for change from a strengths perspective, as opposed to action research, which traditionally has been problem focused. Ensure that any data gathered from staff are fed back for analysis, and that there is an implementation plan.

And remember, when an organization takes a hard look at relevant data and engages in a change process, things can get worse (discovering the extent of problems to be addressed and the resulting stress and confusion) before they get better (through a change process such as the one covered in previous chapters). Don't be surprised or discouraged by "negative" data and, as suggested earlier regarding launching and supporting a change process, show support for staff as everyone works toward improvement.

Reflection and Focusing Questions

1. What data do we need to give us valid, useful, and complete information to guide our planning of a change process?
2. Are our existing information systems capable of providing needed data? If not, what do we need to do to improve those systems?
3. Do we have internal capacity, through staff consultants or human resources staff, to manage an action research process? If not, how can we acquire the needed consultant help?
4. Which processes (e.g., an employee survey) will definitely need consultants to ensure anonymity and confidentiality of data?

12
Change Interventions

"Change management" does not refer to a prescription for getting rid of the people who run the organization. Rather it is a menu of management strategies to change the philosophy of management to accomplish an objective or set of objectives such as, for example, improving efficiency and competitiveness, motivating employees and increasing their job satisfaction, or reducing absenteeism.

—Gary Grobman, nonprofit author
(*The Nonprofit Handbook*, 2008, p. 295)

Organizational change activities are variously described as techniques, technologies, methods, or interventions. In the field of organization development (OD), the main profession providing planned organizational change consultation, such activities are typically called *interventions*. An OD intervention is defined as "a sequence of activities, actions, and events intended to help an organization improve its performance and effectiveness" (Cummings & Worley, 2015, p. 157).

This chapter covers some of the generic organizational change interventions that are most likely to be used in human service organizations (HSOs). Some, including team building, will require a consultant because they are likely to raise potentially very difficult issues and have anonymity and confidentiality aspects. Large group interventions will require consultants with even more specific expertise. A large organization may have staff who are internal consultants capable of doing such work. These are presented as a "menu" of possible interventions to be used on a change process, depending on particular goals and organizational conditions. A comprehensive change process could easily include several of them.

Methods to be covered here include

- Team building
- Conflict management
- Role clarification
- Image exchange
- Transition management
- Large group interventions

Organizational Change for the Human Services. Thomas Packard, Oxford University Press. © Oxford University Press 2021. DOI: 10.1093/oso/9780197549995.003.0013

Based on the change goals and an assessment of problems, needs, change readiness, and change capacity covered previously, these methods can be used as specific change process activities, mainly at the implementation step.

Team Building

An astute reader may remember that one of the change tactics mentioned in a previous chapter suggested that provisions must be made to address opportunities or needs for team building and conflict management. Both of these are common methods in OD. We discuss here how these can be applied during organizational change.

For organizational change to be successful, having highly functioning teams is important in two ways. First, the organization's executive team needs to be highly functioning in order to be able to demonstrate a clear strategic direction for the organization and vividly and regularly show support for the change initiative. Teams at lower levels (departments, divisions, programs, etc.) should similarly be functioning well so that they can manage and support the change process in their areas.

Also, new teams, such as a steering committee and various task forces or problem-solving groups, will be formed as part of the change process. Special attention should be paid to team development as these teams are formed. Such groups, being newly formed, will not have histories of conflict or dysfunction as existing teams may, so their main team-building tasks will be related to group formation. This will include standard processes in group dynamics, including clarifying the team's purpose and mandate; having members get acquainted in terms of their interests, strengths, and personal style preferences; developing operating norms; and assigning roles, including chair and recorder, to ensure effective functioning.

Team building is referenced in a wide range of ways in organizations, ranging from ropes courses for a work team to having drinks after work. In an organizational change framework, and in OD specifically, it has a more precise conceptualization.

"Team," as suggested above, pertains to various kinds of groups. Most typically, it refers to intact, relatively permanent workgroups, comprising peers and their immediate supervisor. But there are other kinds of teams, which may be more temporary in nature, whose charter is to come together for the purpose of accomplishing a particular task. Committees, task forces, and, of course, problem-solving groups set up as part of a change initiative may all be seen as teams.

For a group to function effectively as a team, several important elements must be present. First, the group must have a charter or reason for working together. The members of the group must be interdependent: They need each other's experience, abilities, and commitment in order to arrive at mutual goals. Group members must be committed to the idea that working together as a group leads to more effective decisions than working in isolation. Finally, the group must be accountable as a functioning unit within a larger organizational context.

In this light, team building is seen as a vital part of many organizational change processes. It affords a work-group the opportunity to assess its strengths, as well as those areas that need improvement and growth. A group's team-building effort has definite implications for the total effectiveness of the entire organization. This is a change method that will require the involvement of a trained outside consultant.

Usually, a team-building intervention will begin when the manager becomes aware of a certain concern, problem, issue, or set of symptoms that suggests that the effectiveness of the staff or work unit is not at an appropriate level. Below is a list of major symptoms or conditions that usually would bring a manager to the point of seriously thinking about some remedial actions.

For an existing team, symptoms that might signal the need for team building include

- loss of production or team output
- increases of grievances or complaints from the team
- complaints from users or customers about quality of service
- evidence of conflicts or hostility among staff members
- confusion about assignments, missed signals, and unclear relationships
- misunderstood decisions or decisions not carried out properly
- apathy and general lack of interest or involvement of team members
- lack of initiation, imagination, or innovation
- ineffective meetings, low participation, or poor decision-making
- start up of a new group that needs to develop quickly into a working team
- high dependence on or negative reactions to the team leader (Dyer, Dyer, & Gibb, 2013, pp. 85–86)

Dyer et al. referred to these as "consequence symptoms" (p. 86), which are often caused by other factors, such as ineffective leadership or conflict among team members.

Goals for a team-building intervention will be based on the specifics of the situation, but they generally address task and interpersonal issues that impede a team's functioning. Team building aims at improving the problem-solving ability among team members by working through these issues. This major goal could include a number of subgoals:

1. A better understanding of each team member's role in the work group;
2. A better understanding of the team's charter—its purpose and role in the total functioning of the organization;
3. Increased communication among team members about issues that affect the efficiency of the group;
4. Greater support among group members;
5. A clearer understanding of group process—the behavior and dynamics of any group that works closely together;
6. More effective ways of working through problems inherent to the team— at both task and interpersonal levels;
7. The ability to use conflict in a positive rather than a destructive way;
8. Greater collaboration among team members and the reduction of competition that is costly to the individual, group, and organization;
9. A group's increased ability to work with other workgroups in the organization;
10. A sense of interdependence among group members. (Dyer, 1995)

The final aim of team building, then, is a more cohesive, mutually supportive, and trusting group that will have high expectations for task accomplishment and will, at the same time, respect individual differences in values, personalities, skills, and idiosyncratic behavior. Successful team building should nurture individual potential.

After determining the need for team building, the willingness of the leader and team members to have team building should be assessed. Dialogue may be needed to get clarification on the need and staff commitment to the activity. A consultant will meet with the team and explain the process and answer questions. Next, the consultant will interview team members individually to identify problems and issues for the workshop. After analyzing and compiling the data, the consultant will present compiled data (anonymously) to the team leader. The consultant and team leader will plan the specifics for the workshop, typically with at least some team member involvement.

A team-building workshop should be done at some off-site location and may take 1 to 3 days. A typical workshop agenda would include the following:

- Opening comments by the leader
- Review of goals, agenda, and roles
- Set norms for the session

- Review of data, organization, and setting priorities for discussion and action
- Problem-solving and discussion
- Training activities as needed
- An action plan
- Decisions and agreements
- Critique of the session

The workshop may include, in addition to data feedback, discussion, and problem-solving regarding identified issues, structured experiences such as problem-solving activities or style instruments as needed. During the session, any decisions or agreements reached and any action plan items should be noted on chart paper. Action plans typically list action steps and for each item the main responsible person (sometimes known as the "most responsible person," who will be the champion for that item, and a completion or review date. The chart notes should be transcribed and shared at a subsequent regular meeting of the team. Follow-up on these should be regular items for the team's meetings as long as they are current and relevant. A critique or debrief of the session typically involves participants sharing thoughts on what went well that the team should continue and what did not go well. Discussion can identify things to do at future sessions to address what did not go well. Participants may also be asked what they learned about themselves and about the team that can inform future practice.

Conflict Management

Conflict is inevitable in organizations, at the level of two individuals as well as within teams and between different units, such as programs or divisions in the organization. One of the tactics listed in Chapter 8 identified the need for conflict management mechanisms during organizational change. This tactic came from the ARC (availability, responsiveness, continuity) model (Glisson, 2012). According to the ARC model, change management must include mechanisms to

> resolve conflicts at the interpersonal, intra-organizational, and interorganizational levels to mediate differences in opinions and competing interests that threaten service effectiveness. Use information sharing, clarification of issues, prioritizing, and established procedures for identifying implicit schema that drive behavior in the newly formed OAT [organization action team] and ARC teams to moderate or resolve conflicts. (Glisson, 2012, p. 178)

The framework presented here offers a conceptual model and some practice skills that can be used to augment the techniques suggested by Glisson.

First, it may help to consider how an existing climate for managing conflict can be assessed. Two OD practitioners, Crosby and Scherer (1981), developed a tool for diagnosing an organization's conflict management climate. There is not a strong evidence base for this, but it nevertheless may be useful to change leaders as part of a preliminary readiness and capacity assessment or at any time in the process when conflict seems to be emerging. Figure 12.1 identifies the factors in their model and how they can be assessed. The right column indicates conditions that are better suited to effective conflict management. These two columns represent extremes. Any organization may be at different points on the continuum for each factor.

Assessing the organization's conflict management climate at the beginning of a change initiative can provide data that change leaders and others can use to improve the climate for resolution of conflicts that will inevitably occur. After assessing conditions, steps can be taken to establish a climate, with training and related procedures, that more closely corresponds to conditions in the right column.

In addition to conflict management climate, conflict management styles for individuals and an organization can be assessed. A classic model (Ruble & Thomas, 1976) presented styles in a matrix that was based on amounts of assertive behavior and cooperative behavior. These styles can be seen in Figure 12.2.

Compromising is a style that falls in the middle of each continuum: moderately assertive and moderately cooperative, which looks for a mutually acceptable middle ground that partly satisfies both parties. You can probably imagine situations in which each approach may be the most appropriate. Nevertheless, in an organization, it would probably be best to try to establish collaborating as the preferred style.

Ross (1982) has offered these things to keep in mind when working on a conflictual issue:

- Be prepared to work toward a mutually agreeable solution, not just toward "winning."
- Remember that it is all right to disagree and that the other person is not "bad" if they disagree with you.
- Keep some perspective. Relationships are not destroyed but can even be enhanced by working toward a mutually satisfactory solution to a conflict.
- Do your best to put yourself in the other person's shoes.
- Establish a common goal and stay focused on it.
- Be persistent in coming to a satisfactory solution if the issue is really important to you.
- At the end of the discussion, summarize what has been decided and who will take any next steps.

Very risky without commitment to work on climate issues	Ready to work on conflict with little to no work on climate
Power is massed either at the top or at the bottom of the organization	Power is distributed evenly and appropriately throughout the organization.
Expressing strong feelings is costly and not appreciated.	Expressing strong feelings is valued and easy to do.
There are no clear conflict resolution procedures that many people can use.	Everyone knows about and many people use a conflict resolution procedure.
People do not openly disagree very much; "going along to get along" is the motto.	People feel free to disagree openly on important issues without fear of consequences.
No one uses third parties [e.g. consultants, other staff] to help resolve conflicts.	Third parties [e.g., consultants, other staff] are used frequently to help resolve conflicts.
Third parties are usually superiors in the organization.	Third parties are people of equal or lower rank, or are external consultants.
Third parties are never neutral, but serve as advocates for a certain outcome.	Third parties are always neutral as to substantive issues and conflict resolution methods used.
Leaders do not deal openly with conflict but work behind the scenes to resolve it.	Leaders confront conflict directly and work openly with those involved to resolve it.
Leaders are defensive and/or closed and seek vengeance on those who criticize her/him.	Leaders receive criticism easily and even seek it as an opportunity to grow and learn.
Agreements always fall through the cracks; the same problems must be solved again and again.	Accountability is built into every conflict resolution agreement.
No effort is made to solicit and understand reactions to decisions.	Feedback channels for soliciting reactions to all major decisions are known and used.
Few, if any, people possess basic communication skills or at least do not practice them.	Everyone in the organization possesses and uses good communication skills.
Very few, if any, successful conflict resolution experiences have occurred in the recent past.	Many stories are available of successful conflict resolution experiences in the recent past.

Figure 12.1 Conflict management climate. Based on Crosby & Sherer, 1981.

Assertive	Competing: Pursuit of one's own concerns at another's expense	Collaborating: Work with the other to find a "win-win" solution that satisfies both parties
Unassertive	Avoiding: Sidesteps or postpones an issue or withdraws from a conflict situation	Accommodating: Neglects one's own concerns to satisfy the needs of others
	Uncooperative	Cooperative

Figure 12.2 Conflict management styles.

Of course, any two individuals or groups could simply get together and try to work things out by themselves, using guidance such as just offered by Ross. Greater success can be expected if a third party, especially a consultant or human resources professional with appropriate training, is involved as a facilitator.

A conflict management intervention can use a process similar to team building, with a consultant meeting with the involved parties to get a common understanding of the issues, set goals for a session, and perhaps discuss ground rules that participants will follow. This would typically include norms that are often generated by a team before a team-building session, such as mutual respect, commitment to listening and understanding the other person, focus on behaviors, no personal attacks, and more.

French and Bell (1999, p. 184) summarized the classic work by Walton, who used the term *third-party peacemaking* for this intervention, listing these ingredients for productive confrontation:

1. mutual positive motivation to resolve the conflict
2. a balance of power of those involved
3. allowing time to work through negative feelings and clarification of comments
4. norms of openness
5. effective communication
6. optimum tension (moderate, not severe, stress)

The consultant–facilitator's job at the session is to ensure that norms are followed and that the parties are effectively listening to each other, keeping the focus on key issues, facilitating a process for making agreements for behavior changes, and planning for follow-up. Follow-up sessions would enable participants to see if agreements made were being followed and doing what else is necessary to maintain an effective working relationship.

Role Clarification

Early in my consulting career, it used to surprise me to learn that in so many work units or management teams there was a lack of clarity and mutual understanding of exactly what role functions were being filled by members of the unit or team. Role clarification can be helpful for an existing team who has experienced some role confusion or disagreement and can be especially helpful for a newly formed group, such as a task force, interdisciplinary team, or interagency collaborative.

A good piece of evidence for the importance of role clarity comes from the highly influential research by the Gallup organization, which used their data from over a million employees to identify characteristics of the most effective workplace (Buckingham & Coffman, 1999). They came up with 12 questions that reflected the core elements of an effective workplace. The first is, "Do I know what's expected of me at work?"

Another research study (Hassan, 2013, p. 216) found that

offices with a high level of role clarification had significantly higher levels of work satisfaction and lower rates of turnover. Additionally, the effects of role clarification on work satisfaction and turnover behavior were mediated by overall role clarity perceived in these offices.

Jaiya John (2016, p. 178) developed some useful insights about filling roles by studying several indigenous cultures:

When someone in a particular role passes away or is otherwise lost to the community, that role is filled not just to fill the space. The role is filled only when a person with the right nature and giftedness is identified. Role assignment is not a bureaucratic procedural. It is a spiritual and social practice of preservation. . . . Role assignment in our organizations can be facilitated in a similar fashion. Create graphic representations of the web of relationships and roles that make up your team, unit, or tribe. Have conversation, regularly, about each person's nature. This is honoring, affirming conversation, even if the subject is traits that may not be socially desirable in the broader world. Take the conversation along its course until each person is able to get her or his story out into the atmosphere.

Role clarification (Jones, 1978) is often done in a workshop setting with assistance from a consultant, but can also be handled by an administrator or other change leader with good facilitation skills. The word *staff* is used here, but this may also include board members or sometimes (e.g., in the case of an interagency collaboration or multidisciplinary team) people from outside the organization. The outcome of the process is typically clear, agreed on roles and functions for all involved staff.

Before beginning role clarification, existing agency plans (strategies, goals and objectives, action plans) should be up to date and commonly understood and agreed to by all. These should be amended as needed before role clarification or as a result of it.

Goals for a role clarification workshop could include ensuring that all team members

- have a clear understanding of the major requirements of their own job
- feel that the others at the team-building meeting also clearly understand everyone's position and duties
- know what others expect of them in their working relationships
- feel that all know what others need from them in their working relationships (Dyer et al., 2013, p. 137)

After the administrator introduces the need for role clarification and gets all relevant staff to agree to work on this, involved individuals review existing agency plans and responsibilities, including goals and objectives and job descriptions, and note changes they would like to see in their role (e.g., the functions they want to continue as is, add, drop/reassign, do more of, or do less of). The Role Functions Worksheet in Appendix 3 may be used for this.

Then, at a meeting or workshop, each team member presents (ideally written on chart paper) their prework from the Role Function Worksheet. Clarification questions are asked and answered. All roles are reviewed to note overlap, gaps, and disagreements. Negotiation about who should be responsible for functions can occur, ending when all functions are clearly assigned and each member is comfortable with their role.

If this is being used on a particular project, a Responsibility Chart (Appendix 4) may be completed by all involved to ensure that specific tasks are all assigned and agreed to. Each function or task on the project is listed, and each involved person is listed by role. Under each role, that person's involvement for each task is indicated using the key (e.g., director, supervisor, worker, should be consulted, etc.). Boxes are filled only when that role has a responsibility on a particular task.

After the session, necessary changes should be made in job descriptions and any personnel or program manuals. Changed roles should then be announced to staff. The effects of the changes should be monitored and assessed, with adjustments made as needed.

Image Exchange/Intergroup Design

The image exchange (Pfeffer & Jones, 1974), an *intergroup design*, is a useful activity when two or more distinct groups are working together and there may be some unease, suspicion, or mistrust between them. I used this occasionally when I was an OD consultant with the city of San Diego. This could be done if two separate programs or units, or staff from two different departments, need to work together on a common task. Colleagues and I also used it with good success with colleagues on a grant to provide training on interdisciplinary collaboration for community service providers (Packard, Jones, & Nahrstedt, 2006). In that case, we had a session with county child protective services workers, domestic violence workers, substance abuse workers, mental health professionals, law enforcement, staff from generalist community-based organizations, and client parents.

In a workshop setting, participants are grouped by their profession, field of service, or role. Each group goes to a different part of the room to answer (and write on chart paper) the following questions:

1. How do we (as a team/group) see ourselves?
2. How do we see each of the other teams/groups?
3. How do we think other team(s)/group(s) see us?

The following questions could be added as appropriate for the small groups:

1. What actions do other groups engage in that create problems for us?
2. What actions do we engage in that we think may create problems for them?
3. What recommendations would we make to improve the situation? (Dyer et al., 2013, p. 172)

For example, child welfare staff would describe themselves and then create separate lists to describe each of the other participating groups. They would also create a list of what they thought the other groups thought of them. Answers to any other questions would also be answered and put on chart paper.

The facilitators then sort the groups' charts to look at one field of service at a time; that is, one set would include (a) how child welfare workers see themselves, (b) how others see child welfare workers, and (c) how child welfare workers think they are seen by the other groups. The facilitators allow time for all to read the charts on the wall from all the groups and then facilitate a discussion based on the following questions:

1. Did they find anything surprising?
2. Did they learn anything about their own or other's professions?
3. What are the implications for collaborative practice?

The facilitators probe for insights and record major themes on chart paper. The facilitators then lead a discussion to elicit ideas from participants regarding how they want to work together in the future. Ideally, the group would, at future meetings, allow time to discuss how they are working together, especially with reference to agreements they made at the original session.

I've found that this activity can give team members new insights about the perspectives, worldviews, and norms of the other professions and about the challenges that the different professions are facing, which can deepen their professional relationships and enable them to work more effectively together.

Transition Management

When a new manager joins a team, or when a new team forms, the getting acquainted process may be expedited by these transition management activities. This situation could occur when a new team is formed to oversee a new program, when a new manager is hired to come in to lead an existing team, or when someone is promoted from team member to leader/manager. When I was a consultant with the city of San Diego, one manager who was new to a team told me that this process expedited their getting acquainted and becoming a team by 6 months.

This was originally designed to be facilitated by an OD consultant, but can usually be done by a competent manager without consultation. If notable difficulty or conflict may be expected, the use of an OD consultant is strongly recommended.

This process should ideally begin within the first week or two that a new manager is on the job or a team forms. The key event is a transition meeting, often held for a day or more in an off-site setting. That session is preceded by some prework, detailed below.

This process is designed to

- Provide the new manager with information needed to make sound decisions in establishing priorities and implementing change
- Build trust and respect by allowing participants and the new manager to get to know each other better
- Establish updated organizational goals and action plans that are consistent with existing strategic and operational plans
- Allow participants to address their expectations of the new manager

The process begins with some prework, starting with the new manager introducing the idea with the team. Prior to this, there may need to be some thought and discussion devoted to who are the members of the "team" to be included. This transition process would of course involve all the direct reports of the manager, but may be broadened to include others, such as subordinates of team members, whose involvement would be valuable to expediting this transition. Commitments are made to engage in this process. The manager outlines the steps: Each participant, including the new manager, will complete some prework in the form of answering a set of questions. Then, a session will be held to review and discuss the data, make decisions regarding how the members will function and work together, and make plans for moving the organization forward.

The manager should of course be familiar with the current state of the organization by having reviewed key documents, including existing plans; program activities and performance (e.g., program data, grants, and contracts); governance documents (e.g., bylaws); annual reports; most recent audit results; and policies and procedures.

The items in the Transition Management: Team Leader document in Appendix 6 can be used as a menu for the new manager and/or the team to select the ones that are most relevant. The manager should prepare responses to the items chosen, adapted and augmented as appropriate. If information such as the manager's prior history and experience has not already been answered, this can be included as the final item.

Similarly, each team member should answer the items in the Transition Management: Team Member document in Appendix 5 (again, the ones chosen because of their relevance, adapted and augmented as appropriate). The items may be addressed at a group meeting or individually in writing or in an interview with a consultant.

Data from the questions are normally shared at an off-site workshop in a team-building format. At least a full day should be allocated. Depending on the number of team members and questions, this may take up to 3 days. A suggested agenda follows. The agenda should be shared with participants in advance of the session.

- Welcome by the manager
- Appoint a recorder to chart necessary items for discussion on chart paper
- Review of session goals
- Review of session agenda
- Development of norms/ground rules for the session
- Data sharing by the manager (answers to questions, clarification questions by team members)
- Data sharing by team members (answers to questions, clarification questions by the manager) (these may be clustered, e.g., each person answers a set of questions in order, or grouped so that each member answers the same question before moving on to the next question)
- Discussion: areas needing clarification, resolution, problem-solving, or action planning

- Review decisions and agreements made
- Review action plans
- Critique of the session
- Final comments by the manager

At subsequent team meetings, there should be time to review status on action items and to discuss implementation of decisions and agreements and to make any adjustments necessary for improving team and program performance.

Large Group Interventions

Large group, sometimes called *whole system*, *interventions* (Anderson, 2017; Grobman, 1999c) are OD methods that have applications not only for whole organizations but also potentially for HSOs to engage with related stakeholders, to address community-wide issues. They are touched on here mainly to offer a menu for change leaders to consider if they are addressing very large-scope issues that might involve people outside the organization. These interventions can sometimes involve hundreds of people. They have been done not only within an organization but also with multiple organizations, community groups, or other stakeholders to address broad issues from interagency collaboration to local environmental issues.

Search conferences and *future search conferences* (Anderson, 2017; Bunker & Alban, 2014) typically occur over 2 to 3 days, involving multiple stakeholder groups and up to 150 or more participants. They are designed to "get the whole system in the room." These processes require highly trained facilitators, who allow participants to "hold a broad dialogue about their shared past and present before attempting to plan a future" (Anderson, 2017, p. 306). Comments are noted on chart paper for later review and discussion. Finally, agreements and action plans are developed.

The *World Café* is a similar process, with participants typically seated at tables. With facilitation, participants discuss an important question, with ideas shared as people rotate among tables (Anderson, 2017; J. Brown, 2005; http://www.theworldcafe.com/).

These seven design principles guide the process:

1. **Set the Context:** Use the purpose and goals of the session to determine who should be involved and what themes should be addressed.
2. **Create Hospitable Space:** Create an environment that is welcoming, comfortable, safe, and inviting.
3. **Explore Questions That Matter:** Develop questions that are of real concern to participants.

4. **Encourage Everyone's Contribution**: Make sure that all can contribute and that their ideas make a difference at the session.
5. **Connect Diverse Perspectives**: Create opportunities for participants to interact with new people and share diverse perspectives.
6. **Listen Together for Patterns and Insights**: Be alert to themes, patterns, and insights and work to connect these in a larger whole.
7. **Share Collective Discoveries**: Have participants share what is learned at their tables. Sessions often end with a "harvest," which helps create an overall sense of wholeness (J. Brown, 2005; World Café, n.d.).

Open space technology (Anderson, 2017; Owen, 2008) is a less structured method. It operates with four principles:

1. Whoever comes is the right people.
2. Whatever happens is the only thing that could have.
3. Whenever it starts is the right time.
4. When it's over, it's over (Anderson, 2017, p. 326).

The model also uses the "law of two feet": people are free to move from one discussion to another based on their interests.

Grobman (1999c) offered some "key considerations" before an organization decides to use a large group intervention:

1. Take the time and care to achieve clarity of purpose: What does the organization want to be different as a result of this undertaking? Invest a lot of conversation to get the issue framed well and stated well.
2. Be willing to step into some anxiety and unknown waters in order to achieve something extraordinary.
3. Involve the whole system, or at least a critical mass that is truly representative of the whole. Use a steering group that cuts a diagonal slice through all the organization's layers and across all its functions.
4. Create conditions for effective dialogue among people with different perspectives. Use experienced resources to guide the design and to facilitate the large group events. Interactive meetings of 80–100 people (or more) are not the place for untrained facilitators.

All these change technologies are complex and large in scope and require a consultant (or more than one consultant) who is well trained in the specific method to be used. As a single event, the intervention should be framed by at least some of the steps in the change model in Section 3, starting with an assessment that identifies issues that would be best addressed by a large group intervention through announcing this to staff, getting participation in the design of the event, and follow-through.

Summary

This chapter examined some common organizational change interventions that can be used as parts of a change initiative, mainly at the implementation step. We covered several major methods used in OD, such as team building, and some more specialized methods, including role clarification, transition management, and conflict management.

Depending on the assessment of conditions in the organization experiencing a change process, any of these may be used, either on an organization-wide basis or as needed within particular programs or work teams.

Some of these, and quite likely all of them, would require a trained consultant who could address issues such as anonymity and confidentiality as well as provide expertise that a typical HSO would not have on staff.

Reflection and Focusing Questions

1. Which of these interventions might be useful in a current or planned change initiative in your organization?
2. For each, what problems do you expect it to solve, or what goal do you expect to accomplish?
3. For each, does your organization have the capacity (i.e., with qualified consultants) to implement the intervention? If not, do you know how you could find a qualified consultant to help?

13

Advancing Diversity, Equity, Inclusion, and Social Justice

> Antiracist policies and procedures benefit every staff member and
> client within an organization.
>
> —Mary Pender Greene and Paul Levine ("Promoting
> Organizational and Systemic Change," 2016, p. 3)

While the material here focuses specifically on human service organizations
(HSOs), this subject is an essential one for virtually all formal organizations—
nonprofit, governmental, and for profit. I include this chapter in the section
on generic change methods for that reason. While the next section, on change
methods for HSOs specifically, can be looked at as a menu of intervention ideas
to consider and use as needed, I believe any formal organization should pay particular attention to this constellation of issues to consider what it needs to do to
advance diversity, equity, inclusion, and even social justice with reference to its
staff and internal organizational conditions as well as to the people, institutions,
and communities in its environment.

This chapter reviews some of the literature that describes organizational
change activities to specifically address one or more of these issues. As is the case
for other chapters in Sections 4 and 5, this chapter provides an overview of activities or interventions as a menu of items for you to consider and perhaps probe
more deeply as you plan your own organizational change activities. One difference between this chapter and the others in these sections is that this chapter
addresses both the *content* and the *process* of change, with more focus here on
the content. There is a growing literature on the content of change to increase
diversity, equity, inclusion, and social justice in HSOs. An excellent example is
Carten, Siskind, and Greene's (2016b) book on deconstructing racism in the
health and human services. I have cited several of the chapters here, and the book
has a wealth of additional useful information on organizational change activities
regarding racism that can also be applied to other areas of discrimination and
oppression.

Because these issues are relevant in virtually any HSO, I think it is important
to describe the specifics of some of the work in these areas. Some of this also

Organizational Change for the Human Services. Thomas Packard, Oxford University Press. © Oxford University Press
2021. DOI: 10.1093/oso/9780197549995.003.0014

addresses the *process* of change as applied specifically to diversity and social justice work within organizations. The material here can be used in conjunction with the generic organizational change process model in Section 3. Actually, any content change ideas such as those in this chapter can be augmented by the use of specific change tactics. For example, implementing a process to increase cultural competence and/or humility of staff could be undergirded with tactics such as clearly articulating the need and supporting it with data, conveying the urgency for change, showing top management support, using processes to build teams and deal with conflict, and institutionalizing the changes within organizational policies and procedures. An organizational change agent can use elements of any of these change processes to support implementation of change activities regarding this issue, adapted as needed to a particular organization and change goal.

Background

Advancing diversity, equity, inclusion, and social justice in HSOs is a growing and extremely important content area for organizational change. While diversity issues regarding demographic characteristics of staff have existed for decades, more attention is now being paid to equity (treating people fairly in a social justice framework) and inclusion ("the extent to which employees feel valued for their unique characteristics and have a sense of belonging, thus feeling comfortable about sharing their 'true selves' within the work organization". Brimhall & Mor Barak, 2018, p. 475). Araque and Weiss (2019) devoted a full section of their recent book on HSO leadership to diversity issues, with chapters on race and ethnicity, cultural proficiency, equity, and women in leadership. Briggs, Briggs, and Briggs (2019), in their book *Integrative Practice in and for Larger* Systems, included material on enhancing organizational and managerial cultural responsiveness, integrating evidence-based practices and cultural competence, and ensuring that these practices are implemented. Akingbola et al. (2019, p. 210) highlighted challenges faced by nonprofit trade and professional organizations implementing diversity initiatives, including perceived threats such as changes in power, control, and professional identity, adding that leaders can respond by legitimizing the initiative, changing organizational culture to value diversity, and embedding new practices through agency structures and policies. There's growing evidence that enhancing diversity and inclusion can impact not only staff factors such as job satisfaction but also client outcomes (Armstrong et al., 2010; Brimhall & Mor Barak, 2018).

A recent report by McKinsey & Company (Dixon-Fyle, Hunt, Dolan, & Prince, 2020), that focused on "diversity of gender and of ethnicity and culture in executive teams—the leadership groups that drive company strategy and organizational transformation" (p. 10), added to the growing evidence of the "business case" for diversity. In a study of over 1,000 for-profit organizations, they found that more diverse and inclusive organizations outperformed their industry peers in profitability. At the same time, while they found notable, but slow, progress in organizations regarding diversity, there was less progress in creating inclusive work cultures.

There are essentially two areas of focus for change in these areas. Most well known are efforts by organizations to improve the cultural competence of programs and staff members and, more recently, to enhance staff cultural humility, with a specific focus on improving services. Another area of interest is implementing organizational changes with the organization itself as a target. Examples can range from building a more diverse workforce and ensuring equity and representativeness, particularly at management and executive levels, where nondominant groups and women are typically still underrepresented, to deeper levels of addressing racism and other forms of oppression within the organization. I start with cultural competence change goals and then cover efforts to make deeper changes in organizational culture and operations.

Cultural Competence

There is a clear and growing demand for evidence-based practices to advance cultural competence in HSOs (Zeitlin, Altschulb, & Samuels, 2016). Also growing is the list of resources to help organizations with such change efforts. The National Center for Cultural Competence at Georgetown University offers extensive resources regarding advancing cultural competence, particularly regarding promising practices and assessment instruments (https://nccc.georgetown.edu/resources/type.php#promising).

The Agency for Healthcare Research and Quality in the Department of Health and Human Services lists several resources for enhancing cultural competence (https://www.ahrq.gov/topics/cultural-competence.html). The Department of Health and Human Services Administration for Children and Families lists several resources (https://www.childwelfare.gov/topics/systemwide/cultural/agencypractice/).

The Toolkit for Modifying Evidence-Based Practices to Increase Cultural Competence (Samuels, Schudrich, & Altschul, 2009) focuses mostly on the content of the change, but does include some change process aspects (e.g., assessing readiness and change capacity, forming a team, identifying project champions, and establishing communication processes) that fit with the change model in this book and evidence-based practice implementation processes in Chapter 17.

Other examples include the Toolkit for Applying the Cultural Enhancement Model to Evidence-Based Practice (Walker, Trupin, & Hansen, 2013) and Improving Cultural Competence: Quick Guide for Clinicians (Substance Abuse and Mental Health Services Administration, 2016). A guide for community-based organizations (Lopez, Hofer, Bumgarner, & Taylor, 2017) includes detail on choosing interventions for diverse populations, conducting a needs assessment, designing measurements for the intervention, and budgeting, as well as lists of other resources.

One cultural competence change model (the Cultural Competence Organizational Review; Truong et al., 2017) includes assessment, intervention, and evaluation elements. A study of the implementation of this model in three community-based health care settings found that sustainability of new strategies occurred when they were embedded within broader agency plans. The authors added that, "It is important that cultural competence is viewed as a fundamental part of an organization's core business, and not just an add-on or accommodation to certain groups" (p. 7).

A model by Calzada and Suarez-Balcazar (2014) provides useful detail on the levels at which cultural competence needs to be addressed, from the organizational level (including organizational climate) to staff and service providers, leading to "culturally adapted/responsive programs and evaluation" (p. 3).

Regarding organizational change specifically, Guerrero et al. (2019) found that the implementation of cultural competence in several community-based substance use disorder treatment was enhanced by transformational leadership, and programs with Latino directors tended to have higher knowledge of ethnic minority communities.

An evaluation by the Colorado Trust (Woods & Lee, 2012) assessed the extent of improvements in cultural competency in 13 health-related organizations. Success factors included committed leadership, a climate in which staff feel free to state and discuss issues, implementation structures such as workgroups, clear and measurable expected outcomes for cultural competency, and community support. Some success factors were noted by their absence, including inadequate financial resources and support, such as technical assistance and trainings. Organizational structure and climate were factors to the extent that in some cases staff were not able to candidly discuss cultural competency, and other staff were resistant to the initiative. Lack of clear direction and information about the change effort was also cited as barriers.

One underresearched area in cultural competency is organizational change to impact lesbian, gay, bisexual, and transgender (LGBT) inclusion, access, and health disparities. Eckstrand, Lunn, and Yehia (2017) searched the literature regarding racial/ethnic and sex-based disparities in healthcare and identified 10 relevant reports. They found change content factors such as "knowledge of best practices for sex diversity" and "recognize disparities and commit to reducing them" (p. 176) and some change processes that are consistent with the model in this book. Examples included top leader support, thorough ongoing communication about the change process, empowerment of staff, adequate resources, gathering data to monitor implementation and assess outcomes, and institutionalizing the changes so that they are " 'hard-wired' into institutional policies, performance metrics, and training" (p. 178).

The National Council of Nonprofits (n.d.-b) has developed materials that pay particular attention to the organization's board of directors. Also included are questions to ask in an assessment format to identify opportunities for change and "practice pointers," beginning with discussions of implicit bias, leading to broader discussions of diversity, inclusion, and equity.

One model that addresses increasing cultural competence, *multicultural organizational development* (MCOD), goes beyond staff skill development to address underlying issues of racism and sexism in organizations (Hyde, 2018). As is typical with generic organization development, the process begins with an assessment, in this case, of development on a continuum from monocultural to multicultural. Interventions can include

> legal compliance (e.g., affirmative action), prejudice reduction, intercultural
> awareness and education, cultural competency-skill building, managing diver-
> sity, valuing differences, diversity audits, antiracism practice, and community
> partnerships. (Hyde, 2018, p. 54)

As is the case with the change model in Section 3, key success factors include strong support from organizational leadership and a lot of attention to organizational culture and climate (Cohen & Hyde, 2014a). One difference from traditional organization development is that MCOD has a greater emphasis on low-power staff (consistent with the *staff-initiated organizational change* model covered in Chapter 19).

More recently, the term *cultural humility* (Foronda, Baptiste, Reinholdt, & Ousman, 2016; Ortega & Coulborn Faller, 2011) has been used to enrich efforts to improve cultural competency. Ortega and Coulborn Faller asserted that "cultural competence training has been argued to not go far enough in holding workers accountable for the privileged and power position their role entails" (p. 30). These authors listed several aspects of cultural humility that might require notable organizational change to "build organizational support that demonstrates cultural humility as an important and ongoing aspect of the work itself" (p. 44):

- an assessment of the organizational environment, policies, procedures, knowledge, and skills connected to worker practices

- identify ways in which a cultural humility perspective can be embraced and promoted
- uncover barriers and obstacles within the organization that inhibit a cultural humility approach
- written plans, training, and organizational support are called on that hold the organization accountable to the diverse make up and needs of the community being served (Ortega & Coulborn Faller, 2011, p. 35)

Other experts have asserted that cultural competence is necessary but not sufficient. For example, Abrams and Moio (2009) noted, from a social work education perspective, that

> critics charge that the cultural competence model is largely ineffective and that its tendency to equalize oppressions under a "multicultural umbrella" unintentionally promotes a color-blind mentality that eclipses the significance of institutionalized racism. (p. 245)

They suggested the use of critical race theory to address some of the limitations of the cultural competence model. For example, *antioppression practice* can include a "structural analysis of oppression; how it is created, sustained, and justified" (p. 253). Beyond an academic setting, more recent work uses an *antiracism* perspective, discussed just below.

A related point was made by Mor Barak et al. (2016), who concluded after an analysis of the literature that

> it is important to develop organizational policies and practices that move beyond simply promoting diversity representation to creating policies that actively and effectively manage diversity and engender an inclusive work climate. (p. 327)

They added that increasing inclusion involves not only recruiting and hiring to create a more diverse workforce but also "instituting policies and procedures that give every member of the workforce a sense of being valued for who they are and engenders a sense of belonging" (p. 327). Developing a "climate of inclusion" can start with an assessment of existing conditions. An instrument for this is available in Mor Barak's (2017) work.

Katz and Miller (2016) developed a model for leveraging diversity that includes "a mindset of joining rather than judging others" and four "keys": leaning into discomfort, listening as allies, stating one's intent and intensity, and sharing your "street corner" (i.e., one's point of view). Their specific strategies include "Executive Feedback Pods" (essentially honest feedback from colleagues), internal change agents who have completed an education program and can model new behaviors and an "embedded" consultant.

To summarize so far, HSO leaders not only need to ensure up-to-date and relevant cultural competence capacities in their staff and programs, but also need to look deeper into other aspects of the organization that need to change. Briggs et al. (2019) built on this concern, noting "a dearth of research on culture-specific interventions" and "miniscule attention to structural determinants of culture" (p. 17), suggesting, among other things, that agency leaders should

> partner with the research faculty of schools of social work to explicate and study the direct and indirect relationships between the manifestations of the culture of white privilege in larger systems as moderators and mediators of the relationship between the social determinants of well-being and key factors such as race, cultural diversity, social justice, civil and human rights, discrimination, and oppression. (p. 43)

Equity and Social Justice

Addressing racism and other forms of oppression within the organization is likely to be more challenging than building cultural competence capacity with reference to clients and communities since it requires a deep examination of existing organizational practices, values, and culture. The following paragraphs offer examples of some of the work being done in this area. These can be blended as appropriate with change processes covered elsewhere in this book.

One resource that should be useful to identify current conditions and needs regarding racial inequity in an organization is an organizational assessment tool developed by the Annie E. Casey Foundation (n.d.). It enables staff to rate the organization in terms of staff competencies and organizational operations. Based on scores, next steps with action tools are offered.

Another tool, a Continuum on Becoming an Anti-Racist Multicultural Organization (Crossroads Ministry, n.d.), describes organizations ranging from *monocultural* to *antiracist multicultural*, with a related continuum that describes in detail organizations at various stages, leading toward a "Fully Inclusive Anti-Racist Multicultural Organization in a Transformed Society," with detail on conditions at each stage.

More broadly, the National Child Welfare Workforce Institute (2019) has developed a Racial Equity Discussion Guide that applies a "racial equity lens" for assessing and changing organizations. While focusing on child welfare, the principles are broadly applicable for other HSOs.

An excellent work edited by Carten, Siskind, and Greene (2016b) offers a range of intervention technologies for deconstructing racism in HSOs. These "antiracism models encourage an examination of the implications of racism for society as a whole" asserting that

it is the responsibility of every individual to engage in planned and sustained actions in an effort to dismantle the legacy of racism and white supremacy that pervades all institutional and organizational structures in American society. (Carten, 2016, p. xli)

They added that "antiracist policies and procedures benefit every staff member and client within an organization" (Greene & Levine, 2016, p. 3) and then presented a model used to transform a large community agency using anti-racist principles. Activities featured workshops including a 2½-day "undoing Racism" workshop developed by the People's Institute for Survival and Beyond (see Billings, 2016) for mid to senior managers; chief executive officer commit-ment and support, including placing a person of color in a top executive posi-tion; diversifying staff; creating "affinity groups" for staff of color and White staff; articulating new role expectations for managers and supervisors regarding cul-tural competency and addressing oppression and privilege. They concluded that sustained commitment to this process required

1. leadership from the top;
2. a cadre of knowledgeable and articulate supporters on different levels of the agency;
3. structures such as committees and regularly scheduled events; and
4. written policies to make something important a sustainable component of a human service organization. (p. 12)

As is common in major organizational change initiatives, the agency had to bal-ance competing time demands from external policy changes with the commit-ment to the change initiative.

Other change technologies covered in that book include conveying urgency for the change; using employee surveys to identify dynamics of White privilege; applying the change process at the board level (e.g., with board diversification) (Siskind &Schenk, 2016); and using critical race theory (establishing a critical perspective, recognizing dynamics of intersectionality, using storytelling to ad-vance discourse, and supporting egalitarian empowerment approaches (Finch, 2016). The PAST (privilege and subjugated task) model (Hardy, 2016) was shared as a useful tool to guide conversations about race. Other chapters provided detail for work in specific populations, including child welfare (Mallon & McRoy, 2016), older adults (Huggins, 2016), and mental health (Lindsey & Watson, 2016).

One chapter (Best-Giacomini, Howard, & Ilian, 2016) described a staff development strategy in a public child welfare agency that began with the formation of a task force on racial disproportionality and disparity, which then implemented Undoing Racism training sessions. A subsequent series of four workshops covering self-care and internalized oppression, use of the cultural genogram, skills for facilitating challenging discussions, and unpacking discussions of race at family team conferences was offered to master's of social work students who were child welfare workers. An evaluation offered lessons learned regarding the value of experiential learning and addressing internalized racial oppression, implications of group identity, and the value of allowing organizational "space" for discussions of racial oppression.

The editors concluded with implications that executive staff and boards must facilitate the development of antiracist visions to help meet an organization's program goals, and that these executives need to be accountable for addressing oppressive practices and to devote resources to supporting antiracist practices (Carten, Siskind, & Greene, 2016a).

In another intervention using the Undoing Racism workshop, Blitz and Kohl (2012) described a process in a large nonprofit organization (over 1,500 staff) to implement an "antiracist multicultural model," noting that "racial affinity group meetings, or caucuses, can be effective tools for human service agencies to address cultural responsiveness or shift their organizational paradigm toward antiracism." The agency had a goal to "increase its ability to hire, retain, and promote staff of color" (p. 487). A diversity task force had met for several years, but progress had not kept up with service demands for cultural competence. After task force members attended an Undoing Racism workshop, staff became committed to undoing institutional racism in the agency. Antiracism activities included "implementing a training series for program managers; overseeing the dissemination of antiracism information; sustaining an antiracism training project for social work interns; and benchmarking and tracking staff and client demographics within various service delivery systems" (p. 488). With top management support, a new antiracism task force "facilitated the development of three separate race-based caucuses: men of color, women of color, and White allies." Consultants were hired to assist with staff training and organizational culture change. An antiracist strategic plan was developed. Caucuses were involved in deep discussions of issues, including privilege and accountability for antiracism work.

They eventually identified three benefits of White antiracism caucusing: "Members increased their understanding of hidden and unconscious organizational racism and privilege and learned to use this understanding to inform their practice and managerial skills"; a list of "observable behaviors and practices illustrating White privilege" was developed and shared; and "cross-racial relationships within the organization were reinforced, impacting workplace culture in a way that supported the goals of increased hiring, retention, and promotion of people of color" (pp. 494–495). Twelve recommendations for White antiracist caucus work ranged from clarifying systems of accountability and coordinating with other organizational initiatives for an inclusive workplace to using dialogue regarding power, race, and marginalization to enhance movement to more fairness, equity, and inclusion.

Closely related to race and ethnicity issues in organizations, gender equality remains an issue still in need of a great deal of organizational change. After a comprehensive review of the literature, Benschop and Van Den Brink (2018), asserted that there are "three core issues that feature most prominently in current writings about organizational change toward gender equality": the change of organizational cultures and structures (rather than focusing on individuals), the commitment of top management, and the engagement of men in change efforts (p. 194). They found little empirical work on the effectiveness of efforts using consultants to "change gendered structures and cultures," adding that the limited research that does exist "mainly highlights the reasons for the limited success of change initiatives" (p. 196). Related work in the area of "critical diversity studies" focuses on increasing inclusiveness of women in workplace processes (e.g., Catalyst, n.d.; Mor Barak, 2017) that "encompasses involvement, engagement, and the integration of diversity into organizational processes" (Roberson, 2006, p. 228, cited in Benschop & Van Den Brink, 2018) and supports an inclusive culture that values individual employee uniquenesses, enhances feelings of belonging, involves staff in processes such as decision-making, and supports equal treatment while also acknowledging individual differences.

Their second core issue, support from the top, also includes making the issue a priority, creating a sense of urgency, and providing necessary resources, all of which are part of the model covered Section 3. Benschop and Van Den Brink added another aspect of top leader support: "display gender-aware leadership" (2018, p. 199). Their third core issue, engaging men in the change effort, is unique to this content area. This involves explicitly addressing power relations; developing men's competence and commitment as change leaders on this issue (without marginalizing the roles of women as change leaders); using male change champions as role models; noting that this can lead to a win–win, rather than a zero sum, outcome; and perhaps strategic alliances between women and men. They concluded that the "politics of knowledge" needs to be addressed by both academics and consultants, with academics engaging with consultants regarding complexities of change implementation through, for example, collaborative action research projects.

Gillberg and Jones (2019), in discussing feminism and healthcare, asserted that "gender equality and gender equity are . . . insufficient tools for organizational change." Another application of feminist theory in organizational change comes from case studies of a "small wins approach to organizational change" (Correll, 2017).

Summary

Initiatives to improve cultural competence in HSOs have a strong recent history and are commonly accepted as important in improving services to diverse clients. In addition to working to create more culturally competent workforces and programs, some organizations are working at deeper levels to explicitly challenge racism, sexism, and other forms of discrimination, and even oppression, in HSOs. Such change initiatives are likely to be more challenging, with greater potential for staff and administrator discomfort and even conflict. Such change initiatives have the potential for being hugely impactful in improving the quality of working life for staff, but especially for diverse staff, as well as improving services for clients.

An organization's leaders will need to maintain a strong commitment to doing this difficult work and must serve as role models, focusing first on themselves as targets of change, as I suggested in Chapter 3. As transformational change, this work is challenging and requires not only content knowledge about dynamics of discrimination and oppression but also strong commitments from organizational leadership and other staff to do the necessary work. This tactic—top management commitment—is one of several in the generic change model in Section 3. Other tactics that have been used in diversity and antiracism initiatives include an assessment of the problem, data collection to document the problem, conveying urgency, an action system including knowledgeable staff from multiple levels and action teams, extensive staff participation, and providing necessary resources. Transformational change interventions such as these are also likely to require strong process consultation to facilitate interpersonal and intergroup dynamics and expert consultation from those with specific training and expertise in this area.

Reflection and Focusing Questions

1. What issues of cultural competence, diversity, equity, inclusion, and social justice might exist in our organization?

2. How can our organization develop a deeper understanding of these issues and their effects on staff and clients?
3. What expertise regarding these issues exists in our organization?
4. What is our level of commitment to truly identifying and addressing any of these issues?
5. What should our organization do to address the identified issues?

14
Quality and Efficiency
Improvement Processes

> The aim of leadership should be to improve the performance of man
> [*sic*] and machine, to improve quality, to increase output, and simul-
> taneously to bring pride of workmanship to people. Put in a negative
> way, the aim of leadership is not merely to find and record failures of
> men, but to remove the causes of failure: to help people to do a better
> job with less effort.
>
> —W. E. Deming (*Out of the Crisis*, 1982)

W. E. Deming, known as the founder of the quality movement, had a background
in electrical engineering and statistics and developed detailed analytical methods
to improve the quality of manufactured goods. In addition to an engineering and
analytical mindset, he recognized the importance of people in improving work
processes.

Many, if not all, structured processes to improve quality or efficiency in an
organization originated in manufacturing settings. These are now being used in
human service organization (HSOs) to analyze work processes and determine
ways to improve quality and efficiency. These processes can be used for relatively
routine tasks not only in programs such as Food Stamp/SNAP (Supplemental
Nutrition Assistance Program), Medicaid, or welfare-to-work applications but
also in more complex programs such as child welfare.

While some of these methods can be used by existing staff in a unit or program without consultation, more specific quality improvement methods are
quite technical and should use a qualified facilitator.

I start with the classic Total Quality Management (TQM) process and its evolution into the more commonly used term *Continuous Quality Improvement*
(CQI). I present an example of a CQI model for child welfare, followed by brief
discussions of some more recent and popular quality improvement methods.
I briefly mention a contrasting efficiency improvement method: industrial engineering. All of these include intensive use of data analysis procedures, and
all but industrial engineering are very participative, involving some or all
members of the work unit using the process and sometimes other staff who

Organizational Change for the Human Services. Thomas Packard, Oxford University Press. © Oxford University Press
2021. DOI: 10.1093/oso/9780197549995.003.0015

have some interest in the process and even occasionally clients or community members.

Total Quality Management

Most current quality improvement models are very similar to the earliest version of quality improvement in the United Sates: *Total Quality Management*, or TQM. It has been defined simply as an organization-wide philosophy and process of continuous improvements in quality by focusing on the control of variation to satisfy customer requirements, including top management support and employee participation and teamwork. TQM typically occurs at a workgroup level, involving people in the same unit who are jointly engaged in a work process. Members of the unit become a team that identifies a work process that could be improved and systematically analyzes it to identify areas where quality needs to be improved or steps that could be eliminated or combined to increase efficiency.

A more recent version of TQM, *Continuous Quality Improvement*, is increasingly being used in HSOs. CQI and one of its subsets—Plan, Do, Study, Act (PDSA), also addressed below—have been noted as examples of evidence-based management practices "that could improve the effective implementation of EBPs [evidence-based practices] in SUD [substance use disorders] treatment"; (Frimpong & Guerrero, 2020). I believe they have similar potential in other HSO programs.

Change agents wanting to use any of these models should get more detail on the specific model to ensure that key steps are used. In some fields, such as public child welfare, there may be technical assistance available from federal or state government sources. For example, the Federal Administration for Children and Families (US Department of Health and Human Services, 2014) has developed guidelines for the use of CQI in child welfare organizations.

Continuous Quality Improvement

Continuous Quality Improvement is one of the most current versions of quality improvement methods and is being used extensively across the country in public child welfare programs (Administration for Children and Families, 2012). It typically incorporates in some ways the PDSA process.

One definition of CQI is that it is

the complete process of identifying, describing, and analyzing strengths and problems and then testing, implementing, learning from, and revising solutions.

It relies on an organizational culture that is proactive and supports continuous learning. CQI is firmly grounded in the overall mission, vision, and values of the agency. Perhaps most importantly, it is dependent upon the active inclusion and participation of staff at all levels of the agency, children, youth, families, and stakeholders throughout the process. (Casey Family Programs and the National Child Welfare Resource Center for Organizational Improvement, 2005, p. 1)

After a meeting with CQI experts in the child welfare field, the Casey Family Programs and the National Child Welfare Resource Center for Organizational Improvement (2005) developed these six key components:

1. Organizational culture supports and actively promotes CQI.
2. The agency adopts specific outcomes, indicators, and practice standards that are grounded in the agency's values and principles.
3. Agency leaders, staff, children, youth, families, and stakeholders receive training in the specific skills and abilities needed to participate actively in CQI.
4. Agencies collect qualitative and quantitative data and information from and about children, youth, families, and staff.
5. Staff, children, youth, families, and stakeholders review, analyze, and interpret qualitative and quantitative data to inform agency practices, policies, and programs.
6. Agencies use CQI results to improve policies, practices, and programs.

Plan, Do, Study, Act

Wulczyn, Alpert, Orlebeke, and Haight (2014) have developed a CQI process, represented in Figure 14.1. This uses a classic model that evolved out of early quality improvement models, with the assistance of the godfather of the quality movement, W. E. Deming, quoted above: PDSA. Sometimes "Check" is used instead of "Study," resulting in PDCA. As its title suggests, it has four basic steps (Wayne, et al., 2011):

1. Plan—develop a plan for improvement
2. Do—implement the plan
3. Study—get feedback on the results of the plan and
4. Act—make improvements to the process based on the feedback.

This process is increasingly being used in healthcare organizations (Agency for Healthcare Research and Quality, n.d.).

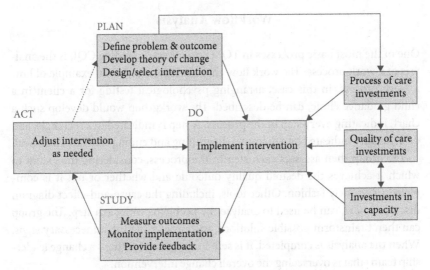

Figure 14.1 The cycle of CQI. From Wulczyn et al., 2014, p. 3.

The Plan step begins when the agency "defines the problem it wishes to solve by observing baseline performance on an outcome of interest. Next, the agency identifies an intervention that is expected to improve that outcome and sets targets for improvement" (p. 3). The intervention model chosen should be one with evidence to support it. It should also have an explicit "theory of change" that shows how the causes of the client problem are addressed by the model. The Do step involves implementing a new intervention, that "requires the agency to invest in three major areas: the quality of services to be delivered, the processes by which they are delivered, and the capacity of the agency to deliver them with fidelity." During the Study step, the agency conducts a process evaluation "to monitor the extent to which the intervention is being implemented with fidelity to its design." It also measures client outcomes to see if the model as implemented was effective. At the Act step, the agency uses the findings from the process and outcome evaluations to assess the extent to which the original problems were addressed and if the intervention should be continued, modified, or discontinued. The cycle then repeats.

Consistent with other quality improvement models, the analysis of performance data (in this case, within the child welfare process) are analyzed to identify "variations," where there is a problem with the quality of the activity (e.g., the number of days in foster care) and then make corrections in the process. The theory of change for the intervention can point to possible problem areas.

This CQI process is continuous and should be built into the organization's culture.

Workflow Analysis

One of the most basic processes in TQM and others, including CQI, is the analysis of a work process. The work flow chart in Figure 14.2 is an example of how a work process, in this case, arranging psychological testing for a client in a child guidance clinic, can be described. The workgroup would develop such a chart, indicating every step in the process. A step is indicated in a rectangle, and decisions are indicated by a diamond. Beginning and ending steps are in an oval.

The group then assesses each step in the process, considering the extent to which it achieves the desired quality outcome and whether or not it is completed in a timely fashion. Other tools, including the cause-and-effect diagram discussed next, can be used to analyze the problems with each step. The group can then brainstorm possible solutions, such as eliminating unnecessary steps. When the analysis is completed, it is sent to the group (perhaps a change leadership team) that is overseeing the overall change intervention.

Cause-and-Effect Diagram

Another TQM tool is the cause-and-effect diagram; sometimes, for obvious reasons, it is known as a fishbone diagram. The team doing the analysis creates lines in a fishbone format and then inserts possible causes for the quality problem that is being analyzed. Causes can be grouped along one diagonal line to aid in the analysis.

The example in Figure 14.3 is from an analysis of no-shows at a clinic.

Lean Transformation

Lean transformation is another quality improvement technique that began in manufacturing and has increasingly been applied in service organizations such as HSOs. According to Miller, Bogatova, and Carnohan (2011), "The essence of lean philosophy is to deliver the most value to customers while consuming the fewest resources" (p. 7). Value is defined by the customer. After value has been determined, the process focuses on identifying *wasteful activities* that "use up resources in a nonproductive way" (Miller et al., 2011, p. 4). These authors identified three important principles for applying lean to service organizations:

1. Focus on the value stream: The value stream includes all the steps of a process such as, in child welfare, from a child abuse hotline call to a final outcome of a safe return home for a child or a placement such as adoption. Workers and managers look for ways to eliminate non-value creating steps.

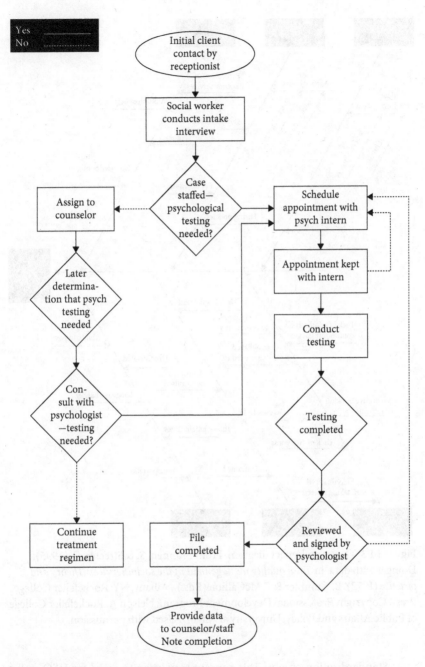

Figure 14.2 Workflow analysis. From Brannen, S. & Streeter, C. (1995). Doing it with data. in *Total quality management in the social services: Theory and practice* (P. 74). B. Gummer & P. McCallion (Eds.)., Albany, NY: Rockefeller College Press. Copyright Professional Development Program, Nelson A. Rockefeller College of Public Affairs and Policy, University at Albany. Used with permission.

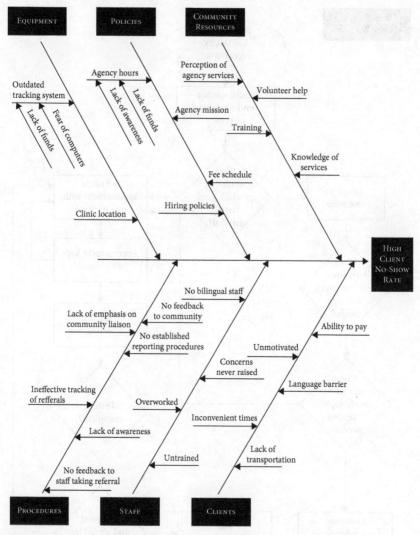

Figure 14.3 Cause-and-effect diagram. From Brannen, S. & Streeter, C. (1995). Doing it with data. in *Total quality management in the social services: Theory and practice* (P. 72). B. Gummer & P. McCallion (Eds.)., Albany, NY: Rockefeller College Press. Copyright Professional Development Program, Nelson A. Rockefeller College of Public Affairs and Policy, University at Albany. Used with permission.

2. Standardization of jobs: This concept may bring to mind for HSO staff a boring assembly line. In service organizations, attempts are made to, in fact, standardize jobs, from Medicaid eligibility determination to child abuse risk assessments, so that variation and chance are eliminated. This

may go against the grain of some HSO professionals, who prefer to make decisions based on client uniquenesses, and not treat every client in the same way.

3. Worker empowerment: This principle will be more familiar and appealing to most HSO workers. Empowerment here applies to training workers on work process analysis and problem solving so that they can improve a work process. (pp. 8–9)

There are obvious challenges here for HSOs, starting with determining who the client is. In child welfare, an abused or neglected infant is a client, but there are other stakeholders, including biological parents, and perhaps the Juvenile Court, other agencies, and community members. Defining "value" for each stakeholder may also be difficult, and there may be conflicting values of all involved with a case.

In spite of these limitations, Lean transformation techniques can be effectively adapted to HSOs. As is the case for other quality improvement models, Lean involves forming a group to "map" a work process by defining each step, perhaps using a logic model or a theory of helping; gathering data on a process; determining performance measures; and identifying ways of streamlining the process and improving quality. Also as is true for other models, there is an intention of creating an organizational culture that supports continuous improvement and innovation.

Six Sigma

Another quality improvement model that is increasingly being used in HSOs is Six Sigma. This method uses statistical methods to identify "defects" in a process. It was originally used in manufacturing settings. The Six Sigma refers to six standard deviations, which represents the point at which over 99.9% of items do not have a defect. It uses an analysis process similar to TQM and CQI processes: assigning a work unit to examine a process to identify areas for improvement, using participative methods.

Lean Six Sigma

The two previous models have been combined to create yet another model. The variation that added "Lean" to Six Sigma adds the dimension of waste elimination to the analytical process.

A workgroup using Lean Six Sigma may be assigned full time to work on a problem for a week, with the expectation that problems will be solved and new methods proposed within that time frame.

One county HSO has applied Lean Six Sigma using these principles:

1. Directly observe work as activities, connections, and flows
2. Systematically eliminate waste
3. Establish high agreement of both what and how
4. Systematically solve problems
5. Create a learning organization (Flinchbaugh, 2007).

Here are some examples of projects on which this county used Lean Six Sigma for quality improvement in their income maintenance programs:

- Online client access to pre-eligibility and online applications
- Interactive voice response systems
- Call centers/virtual call centers for clients to inquire about benefits
- Electronic case management/document imaging

Industrial Engineering

Partly for historical context, and also to alert you to this as an alternative to more participative methods such as CQI and organization development problem-solving, I touch on a less participative approach that some consultants may still use. These analytical methods were first used in factory settings, using a nonparticipative approach to efficiency and quality improvements. Grounded in Frederick Taylor's scientific management, the field of industrial engineering best exemplifies this approach. (Shortly after Taylor's early work, researchers began studies at the Hawthorne plant of the Western Electric Company near Chicago. This was the beginning of the human relations movement and, yes, the origin of the Hawthorne effect.)

Industrial engineering and other analytical methods were commonly used by major consulting firms (often initially with groundings in accounting as well as work process analysis) later in the twentieth century. In industrial engineering, experts do analysis and audits of management structures, goals and objectives, and processes, including organization charts, staff utilization, coordination mechanisms, roles and responsibilities, and work methods, in order to improve efficiency and reduce costs. Recommendations often include efficiency improvements, reorganization, consolidation, downsizing (discussed later in the chapter on organization redesign), and, in government settings, sometimes privatization.

Methods of analysis of work processes include techniques such as work measurement studies, work standard setting, work simplification, and work unit and job-task analysis to recommend the most efficient methods of accomplishing tasks.

This is an example of the *expert* consulting model, where the consultant, historically an industrial engineer, did the analysis and made the recommendations. Employee involvement typically included, at the most, being interviewed by the experts, who then suggested changes to management. In the late twentieth century, the national and international consulting firms, which historically paid major attention to auditing processes, began to adopt many of the philosophies and methods of the more participative organization development field and the earlier human relations movement. Often these analytical methods evolved into TQM and other CQI models that use analytical tools with a great deal of employee participation in decision-making regarding the analysis of problems and development of solutions.

Summary

Quality improvement processes such as TQM and CQI are organizational change models that are increasingly being used in HSOs. I also touched on industrial engineering methods that have mainly been replaced by more participative approaches. They were mentioned here mainly so that if you find such methods being suggested in a change initiative, you can suggest alternative approaches that are more participative and are likely to be more effective.

Depending on the assessment of conditions in the organization experiencing a change process, any of these may be used, either on an organization-wide basis or as needed within particular programs or work teams.

Reflection and Focusing Questions

1. Which of these interventions might be useful in a current or planned change initiative in your organization?
2. What problems do you expect this intervention to solve, or what goals do you expect to accomplish?
3. Is this problem actually part of a larger issue, organizational process, or system? If so, what other activities would need to be used to maximize the benefit of a CQI process?
4. Does your organization have the capacity (i.e., with qualified consultants) to implement the intervention? If not, do you know how you could find a qualified consultant to help?

15

Organization Redesign

> We trained hard, but it seemed that every time we were beginning
> to form up into teams we would be reorganized. Presumably the
> plans for our employment were being changed. I was to learn later in
> life that, perhaps because we are so good at organizing, we tend as a
> nation to meet any new situation by reorganizing; and a wonderful
> method it can be for creating the illusion of progress while produ-
> cing confusion, inefficiency and demoralization.
>
> Charlton Ogburn Jr., "Merrill's Marauders"
> (*Harper's Magazine*, 1957)

While most of this book looks at the *process* of change, this chapter focuses to
some extent on change *content* as well: what is being changed, in this case the
structure (or, more accurately, the design, as I clarify in this chapter) of the organization. Actually, the change model in Section 3 can be applied regardless of
the change content, from implementing an evidence-based practice, a cultural
competence program, or an automated information system to, as in this chapter,
redesigning the organization.

After some introductory comments, this chapter looks at the dimensions of
organization design, using particular types of structures and noting that design
also includes attention to organizational processes. We look at criteria for a good
design of an organization, process criteria for a redesign process, and then a redesign model. Organizational culture change, which usually also includes attention
to other organizational processes, including coordination, decision-making, and
communications processes, receives a bit of attention here, but because it is such
a common issue in organizational change, it is covered in more detail in the next
chapter. I cover business process reengineering as a change technology that not
only has had some controversial results but also can offer some useful design principles. This chapter includes some lessons learned on a research project I did with
some colleagues; the project examined several organizational redesigns in county
agencies.

Organizational Change for the Human Services. Thomas Packard, Oxford University Press. © Oxford University Press
2021. DOI: 10.1093/oso/9780197549995.003.0016

Background and Definitions

Arguably the most common type of organizational change is *restructuring*. This is often seen as a desirable change, especially in the public sector, because its results are visibly different from the previous state. There is a new organizational chart, with new departments, divisions, and staff roles. The change leader, often a new executive, or one who has felt pressure to "do something" about large-scale organizational problems, can show a relatively quick success: Things are different now, at least on paper.

A study by the consulting firm McKinsey & Company (Carucci, 2017) found that fewer than 25% of redesign efforts were successful. We should therefore be alert, thoughtful, and maybe even cautious when considering "restructuring" as the solution to the organization's current problems.

If you as an administrator feel such pressure for change, I would suggest that you first do a comprehensive assessment of your organization to review your current strategic plan so that you and your team fully understand the challenges, problems, strengths, and opportunities that can open your thinking to other change possibilities. Maybe restructuring is not the best or only solution to the organization's problems and challenges. What are your goals for a redesign? Better services for clients, more efficient operations, improved morale, improved communication and collaboration across program or agency functions? If you stay focused on goals—a more ideal future state—and strategy, and at least initially not on how to get there, you and your employees will be open to a wider range of possible solutions.

My second suggestion is to reframe: Instead of merely *restructuring*, envision *redesigning*. As I discus in this chapter, *design* includes not only structure but also processes. The structure shows reporting relationships and program and unit arrangements, but says nothing about how people will work in such a system. Organizational *processes*, including decision-making, communication and co-ordination mechanisms, and more broadly organizational culture, are probably more important than structure, even though they are less visible.

Restructuring is often not very successful because little attention is paid to these organizational processes. McKinsey & Company, in a report (2001) on capacity building for nonprofit organizations, put it this way:

> Structural "fixes" have to be taken with a grain of salt, however. A nonprofit can keep changing its organization chart every 3 months if it wants, but it will never achieve institutional alignment unless its organizational design supports not only systems and human resources, but also its aspirations, strategies, and skills. (p. 59)

Another McKinsey study, this one of for-profit organizations, found that "less than a quarter of organizational-redesign efforts succeed. Forty-four percent run out of steam after getting under way, while a third fail to meet objectives or improve performance after implementation" (Aronowitz, De Smet, & McGinty, 2015, pp. 1–2).

This finding might be partly explained by their definition of this broader framing of organization redesign, suggesting elements that might be missed by traditional restructuring:

> Organizational redesign involves the integration of structure, processes, and people to support the implementation of strategy and therefore goes beyond the traditional tinkering with "lines and boxes." Today, it comprises the processes that people follow, the management of individual performance, the recruitment of talent, and the development of employees' skills. When the organizational redesign of a company matches its strategic intentions, everyone will be primed to execute and deliver them. The company's structure, processes, and people will all support the most important outcomes and channel the organization's efforts into achieving them. (p. 2)

Their research led them to present nine "golden rules" for redesign, which I cover later as design process criteria.

Dimensions of Organization Design

One additional conceptual distinction needs to be made before we get to organization design criteria and redesign processes. Organization design is both a noun and a verb. As a noun, it describes the structure (e.g., the organization of programs and functions and reporting relationships) and key processes (e.g., organizational culture, communication, and decision-making) of the organization. As a verb, it is the process used to select the most appropriate structures and processes for the organization, given its environment, size, programs, and strategies.

As another contextual factor, I reinforce here the point that design should be driven by strategy, so redesign should not be considered without first having an up-to-date and relevant strategic plan for the organization.

Galbraith et al. (in Anderson, 2015) made this point in an even broader context. They included the following elements of design:

- *Strategy*: the organization's direction and long-term vision
- *Structure*: roles, responsibilities, and relationships among functions

- *Processes and lateral capability*: decision-making processes, integrative roles, and cross-functional collaboration mechanisms
- *Reward systems*: compensation and recognition, goals and measurement systems
- *People practices*: hiring and performance reviews, training and development

Misalignment in any of these factors can lead to further problems:

- Missing or unclear *strategy* causes confusion, with a lack of common direction or criteria for decision-making.
- *Structure* misaligned with strategy causes friction and ineffective execution.
- If *processes and lateral capacity* do not provide adequate coordination, gridlock, poor information sharing, and ineffective decision-making can result.
- If *reward systems* do not support goals, inadequate performance, frustration, and turnover can result.
- If *people* are not supported and empowered, inadequate performance and low job satisfaction can result. (Adapted from Galbraith, Downey, & Kates, 2002, p. 5)

This conceptualization reinforces the importance of not only structure but also design processes: Five of these six elements go beyond the more common focus on structure.

Organization Design as a Noun

Organizational Structure

Organizational structure is what people usually think of when describing an organization: how departments and other functions are organized and who reports to whom. A thorough discussion of structure is beyond our scope, so I provide only some basics here.[1]

Organizational structures can range from a simple structure in a very small agency in that one supervisor can oversee all activities to complex forms such as a matrix in which workers may have more than one supervisor. Decisions regarding how the parts of the organization are grouped and located with reference to each other are often called *departmentation*. Departments, or units, can be defined in different ways, which, in human service organizations (HSOs), can

---

[1] Some of this material is adapted from Lewis, Packard, and Lewis (2012).

sometimes overlap. Common ways of defining these are by function, program, process, client, and geographic area.

Functional structures are very common, particularly in bureaucratic agencies. Functional departmentation involves grouping together all personnel who share common functions or areas of technical expertise, such as human resources, finance, information systems, or administrative support. Service delivery units may also be structured by function. For example, a welfare-to-work program might have units for skills training, child care, and job placement. Sometimes divisions are made based on funding requirements that originate in the laws or regulations that created the programs.

This type of departmentation is usually considered efficient because functions are routinized, and duplication of effort is minimized. A weakness of the functional structure is that individuals tend to be so aware of their own departments that they lose sight of the common purpose of the organization as a whole. This model might treat clients in a fragmented way: Client needs may span multiple programs, requiring a transfer of a client to a new worker at each stage in the service delivery process. This structure often works well for organization-wide functions such as financial management and human resource management because these are often standard throughout the organization.

Program departmentation involves organizing by a particular client problem or population, such as teen pregnancy or drug counseling. This is appropriate when services require staff with specialized knowledge or skill.

Process departmentation can be used when different skills are needed at different points in service delivery. For example, a child protective services division may have units for intake, court intervention, permanency planning, and adoptions.

Customer or client departmentation involves all the workers dealing with a specific category or segment of the public being grouped together, such as children and adult units in a psychiatric hospital or in a homeless shelter.

Geographic departmentation involves decentralizing operations of a large agency so that smaller organizations are duplicated in several geographic areas. This model, using community-based sites rather than centralized offices, can be more convenient for clients in terms of travel time and access, both getting to the site and navigating different programs that are co-located there rather than spread out geographically.

Matrix designs are rare and more complex, blending functional and other forms. Organizations using this structure are functionally divided but use teams or task forces for projects that require the work of several specialists. Each project has its own manager, and personnel receive temporary assignments to work with special projects. The strength of this structure is that it uses the positive aspects of both of the other types of departmentation. It tends to be complex and require strong human relations skills on the part of managers, who must share authority with others, but it allows for rapid reorganization in response to immediate needs for change. Historically such structures have been most common in medical centers, which have very high needs for coordination across and among functions.

There is no one "best" structure. Varying environmental and organizational conditions suggest the use of a contingency approach: creating a design that fits the needs of the situation. Even when conditions are thoroughly assessed, there may be more than one solution that would work well. In a later section regarding criteria for a good design, I mention the findings of a study that colleagues and I did of seven county human services systems to examine the best designs for agencies that had clients served by more than one program. Based on recommendations from the county directors who had commissioned the study, we studied four counties that had structurally integrated to improve services to multiproblem clients and three counties that had separate free-standing agencies with elaborate coordination mechanisms. While it was not a purpose of our study, I was curious about whether structural integration was more successful in terms of client outcomes than was the service integration in the other three counties, and it seemed to me that good results were possible either with or without structural integration.

Organizational Processes

An organizational chart cannot show how decisions are made, how communications occur, or how organizational culture affects organizational performance. These factors deserve at least as much attention as do structural considerations, which often dominate discussions of "reorganization."

Organizational processes are key activities that occur within the structure, including coordination among functions, organizational communication processes, decision-making, and organizational culture. Organizational culture change is such an important factor in organizational functioning and such an important consideration in organizational change, including redesign, that it is covered in detail in the next chapter. Here, we first review some other important organizational processes: linking (also known as integrating) and coordinating mechanisms, decision-making, and communication processes.

The HSOs typically have multiple functions that, because of their unique activities, are differentiated from each other. In child welfare, different units or programs have staff using different skills and methods, ranging from the child abuse hotline to investigation and assessment, court intervention, case management, foster care, and adoptions. In any HSO, such specialized functions need to be integrated so that clients receive coordinated services and the organization as a whole can function well.

The simplest integrating mechanisms are bureaucratic, including a hierarchical command and communication system (direct supervision) and the use of rules, regulations, plans, and schedules. Other formal integrating mechanisms include staff meetings, task forces, and organization-wide communications through mechanisms that include email blasts, websites, and videos. A valuable integrating mechanism is an *integrator role*, which may be formal, such as a liaison position, or informal, in which an individual can serve as an internal boundary spanner, communicating with different groups in the organization to ensure that they work well together. Organizations with multiple programs serving the same clients can use multidisciplinary teams to coordinate services. The matrix is the most complex and formal way to ensure high levels of integration.

Managers also need to ensure that the organization has mechanisms for coordinating with its environment. Networking and linkages are especially useful as coordination functions. Networking involves a recognition that human services are part of a helping network that includes a range of HSOs, including a wide variety of specialized agencies as well as educational institutions and sometimes law enforcement agencies and faith-based and other community organizations. Agency involvement in community collaboratives and other community planning processes can be essential aspects of ensuring the most impactful service delivery and community support systems.

Decision-making processes at the broadest level can be described using theories of leadership. Leadership models covered in Chapter 4 and other less participative models have a huge impact on how decisions are made and by whom. Of course, contingency theory suggests that there is no one best way to lead and have decisions made, but managers as leaders should be thoughtful about which decisions should be made by which roles in the organization.

Perhaps the most commonly cited problem in organizations is "poor communication." Because communication is so fundamental, communication processes and mechanisms in organizations, paradoxically, are often neglected. Communication mechanisms that should receive specific attention when redesigning an organization include in-person processes such as staff meetings and the organization's electronic systems, from email to websites, videos, and newsletters. The use of more informal mechanisms such as rituals and ceremonies is discussed in the context of organizational culture in the next chapter.

An untapped resource for communication is the use of staff in communication roles. Liaisons were mentioned briefly as integrating functions in the organization. Their main responsibility is to serve as links between different groups and coordinate their joint work. Liaisons need to be able to generate respect and trust from the different groups they are working with. The linking pin role identified by Likert is an example of a formal liaison: an individual who has membership in two or more groups and serves as a communication link between them. Boundary spanners are liaisons who interact with the environment. They may be upper level managers who meet with external groups as part of their jobs, intake workers or others who interact with other agencies as part of their job, or employees who serve as members of external task forces or coalitions. Liaisons and boundary spanners are key roles, and individuals who can fill them should be identified and sanctioned by the organization.

Informal communication roles such as gatekeepers and opinion leaders should also be acknowledged when assessing organizational communication patterns. Gatekeepers are individuals who control the flow of information as part of their job (Bowditch, Buono, & Stewart, 2008, p. 133). They are often administrative assistants who have access to large amounts of information and can decide what information to pass on to whom. An effective gatekeeper needs to be aware of managers' information needs, know when information is needed, and assess the quality of information being shared. Opinion leaders are able to informally influence other members of the organization. They are usually influential only in specified areas. Managers can share information with opinion leaders to get initial feedback and reactions before making formal announcements and can attempt to influence opinion leaders to share particular information or preferences with others in the organization.

In addition to linking and coordinating mechanisms, decision-making, and communication processes, organizational culture is another key aspect of organization design because it helps shape how programs, subsystems, and people in the organization operate and behave. Since organizational culture change is now seen as hugely important, and improving an organization's culture is now a common change goal, this receives more detailed attention in the next chapter.

Criteria for an Effective Design of an Organization

Again, looking at design as a noun, we can consider criteria to be used to assess an existing design to see if it could be improved. The following design criteria (O'Looney, 1996), specific to HSOs, can be used as standards when you are first assessing your existing design to see how it could be improved, and then using these as criteria that should be adequately addressed in a redesign (organization design as a verb, discussed next).

1. Ensure that the design is in alignment with the strategic plan. Structures and processes should facilitate implementation of strategies, programs, and action plans.

2. Organize around outcomes, not tasks. Have one person perform as many steps in a process as possible or have this done by a team who works closely together.

3. Keep in mind the client's perspective. How will the client experience the organization? Clients should have as simple an experience as possible. If a client needs multiple services within the agency, have a case manager who can coordinate the work of different staff who will be involved and be certain that the client does not "fall between the cracks."

4. Ensure clarity of individual roles and reporting relationships. It is important that individuals have a clear idea of expectations and know to whom they are accountable. This does not mean that a bureaucratic structure must be followed. Even in a strongly decentralized decision-making structure such as Likert's System 4, participants do know what role they can expect to play, what kind of decision-making power they have, and how subsystems interact within the organization.

5. Maximize the ability of staff to act autonomously, within broad policy guidelines. If agency staff are trained professionals, they will not normally need close supervision and should be able to operate with a minimum amount of bureaucratic oversight.

6. Minimize the number of layers in the hierarchy and the number of support staff so that several managers will not need to get involved in decisions that line staff can make. Keep the structure as simple as possible.

7. Ensure that the various functions coordinate and communicate well with each other and outside agencies. The effective HSO needs to emphasize coordination, both within the agency and between the agency and its environment. All employees need ready access to information that is necessary for them to do their jobs.

8. Build a structure that allows for responsiveness to the need for change. Human service agencies need to combine some degree of clarity of structure, communication, and decision-making with the kind of flexibility that can bring needed adaptations to changing client needs. One key to dealing with this issue is the management philosophy used by leaders. Participative styles such as System 4 enable an organization to respond quickly to new needs and situations.

9. Create a culture of teamwork, trust, and support. In such a climate, communication can be open and effective, and workers will be able to do their work in state of high morale.

Design criteria such as these will ultimately result in organizational structures of units, roles, and responsibilities as well as decision-making and communication processes.

Organization Design as a Verb

While organization design as a noun looks at the content of change—what the organization looks like now and how it will look after a change initiative—organization design (actually, *redesign*, unless this is a new organization) as a verb addresses the *process* of change. After staff have done a thorough assessment of the organization's current state, and it is determined that an organization redesign will be part of a good solution, a redesign process can begin. This involves seeking the best answers to the following questions, which actually include elements of not only organization design but also program design and individual job design:

- What activities need to be performed to implement the organization's mission and strategies?
- How can the necessary activities be divided so that individuals or groups can be assigned responsibility for performing them?
- How should the different programs and units of the agency be organized with reference to each other and to client services?
- How and by whom should decisions be made?
- How can communication and coordination among members of the organization be optimized?
- How can coordination and communication with the external social environment be optimized?
- How specialized should roles and jobs be?
- Who should control the nature and quality of the work being performed?
- Once activities have been grouped into specific jobs, what kind of authority and responsibility should be assigned to each position? (Lewis et al., 2012, p. 103)

The answers to these questions will help guide the redesign of an organization or subunits of it in terms of both structure and processes. The nature of the design that is finally chosen will vary tremendously, based on the strategies, goals, needs, size, environment, technology, age, and resources of the organization, as well as on leadership styles and the organizational culture of the people engaged in the design process.

Criteria for an Effective Redesign Process

Organization redesign involves significant decisions about both structure and processes: how to divide activities among groups or departments and how people should behave in coordinating efforts both within the organization and at interfaces with the environment.

In many HSOs, organization redesign is approached simply as restructuring: moving around boxes on the organizational chart without thoughtful consideration of strategy, technology parameters and options, and effects on processes such as decision-making. This restructuring is typically done by the agency's top managers, occasionally with consultant help and more rarely with the input of other managers. According to Mohr (1989), traditional approaches to organization redesign rarely deliver promised improvements because they

- are not based on a detailed operational analysis of actual, current work practices,
- have not meaningfully involved those persons closest to the operational process (i.e., workers and line managers),
- focus on solving only today's—or even yesterday's—problems rather than creating an organization capable of flexibly responding to tomorrow's challenges,
- do not have the necessary commitment and support of those at lower levels, that are required for successful implementation,
- are based on the false assumption that modifying only authority/reporting relationships will be sufficient for obtaining intended results,
- use analytic perspectives that make the "designers" prisoners of their own histories, cultures, and traditions, and
- stem from a constraint orientation emphasizing all that cannot be changed, rather than from an inventive/creative orientation central to effective organizational change. (p. 208)

One additional contextual factor regarding redesign is worth mentioning: its scope. Often the whole organization is the target for redesign. In very large organizations, redesign may be done for smaller groups of programs or units. Redesigns are often initiated, appropriately, for client service reasons. For example, in a large governmental agency or large nonprofit agency, clients may be seen by staff in more than one program. In order to deliver more coordinated services with less confusion and "bureaucratic runaround," an HSO may redesign both how its programs operate in order to provide better services and also how administrative functions such as financial management and human resources management should be redesigned to support service delivery.

A Redesign Model

I now offer a model that can be used if you do need to redesign your organization or parts of it. Depending on the scope, a consultant could be very helpful in guiding you and other staff through the process. This model is loosely based on a model that I was exposed to in the Graduate School of Management while I was at UCLA, and that was very popular and well researched from the 1950s through the 1980s, with some current work being done today: *sociotechnical systems* (STS) (Cummings & Worley, 2015; Taylor & Felten, 1993). The term *sociotechnical* is still often used by writers to remind readers that the social systems in an organization should not be ignored when technical changes are being planned. The usage I describe here is quite specific and is based on a long history of research on STS that has been used in countries, including not only the United States but also England, India, and Sweden. While its most famous applications were in manufacturing settings, its principles have wide relevance for HSOs. The model is complicated and has elements that would probably not be relevant for HSOs, so only key principles are covered here.

A basic premise of STS thinking is that the success of an organization is dependent on alignment of the organization's core technological processes and the organization's social system. In human service settings, examples of core technology include practice/treatment models, assessment tools, case/care planning approaches, and case review processes. While manufacturing organizations transform raw materials into products such as cars and smartphones, and banks transform people who can't afford to buy a home into people who have funds to buy a house, HSOs transform people facing serious challenges in living into people who have a higher degree of functioning and quality of life. The social system includes factors such as organizational culture, management processes, leadership styles, and communication processes.

To achieve alignment of social and technological processes, STS asserts that these systems should be *jointly optimized*. Rather than trying to get the "best" technology and the "best" social system, they need to be looked at together: how service delivery systems, organizational structure, and processes such as decision-making, coordination, communication, and organizational culture are best aligned.

The design guidelines suggested here can be used to implement an organizational redesign process that uses an explicit analysis and design process and that suggests high involvement of workers from all levels of the hierarchy. Any design or redesign process needs top-level sanction and support, known as sponsorship, and a champion responsible for making things happen on a daily basis. The process will also be guided by the leadership philosophies, including preferences for an overall change strategy. For a typical HSO, a combination of normative–reeducative and empirical–rational approaches would probably be best. Of course, I would suggest the use of a participative approach.

In this model, two groups are set up to do the redesign. A steering committee, consisting of representatives of key stakeholder groups, including executive and middle management, supervisors and line staff from different programs, support staff, and representatives from employee organizations, provides overall guidance and policy direction for the effort. A design team, similarly constituted as a representative group, focusing more on the lower levels of the organization, will do the detailed analysis and make recommendations for a new design to the steering committee. The design proposal should include not only the flow and processing of clients but also necessary changes to support systems (functions such as the information system and human resources aspects such as job descriptions).

Final decisions are usually made by the organization's executive management and governing board, although if the process is well done, recommendations should be mostly approved as submitted. After implementation, the new design should be evaluated, with adjustments, continual change, and improvement (Cummings & Worley, 2015).

The steps are highly participative. After the executive level gives sanction to the redesign initiative, action teams are formed to "diagnose" the work system (e.g., the ways clients move through the agency's service delivery system) and then suggest appropriate designs in terms of structures, workflows, and administrative support systems. A key principle from STS, *minimum critical specifications*, suggests that redesign work teams are given only the required parameters for a solution. For example, a team could be told that as long as their redesign meets with organizational policies, is compliant with any funder guidelines or outside regulations, and is within a budget limit, it will be considered viable. Leaders are taking a risk here, of course. The team may come up with ideas that leadership had not thought about, but if the proposal meets stated requirements, it should be seriously considered for adoption. I share two personal examples here.

When I was the manager of a runaway center long ago, our paid staff were routinely working over 50 hours a week just to meet basic program demands. At that time, I didn't know about minimum critical specifications, but I did know about participative decision-making. I gave them the basic parameters: a staffing model that ensured no one working over 40 hours per week, all 24-hour shifts covered, no budget increase, and paid staff having time to do their counseling sessions and supervision of volunteers. A task force came up with a creative staffing design that met the criteria and worked for all.

Much later in my career, as part of a federal grant, a team I led acted as consultants to a public child welfare bureau that was redesigning itself from a functionally based structure (e.g., initial services, court intervention, family maintenance, adoptions) to a more regionalized, geographic, model with better integration of the various program components. After the major program relocation decisions were made by the bureau's middle managers, the bureau executive staff sanctioned a sociotechnical systems redesign process to detail out design elements for the new system. They formed a steering committee and a design team, both with members from different levels and programs. The steering committee provided minimum critical specifications for the work of the design team, which then formed three subcommittees: technical and social systems analysis, stakeholder analysis, and a subcommittee to plan the physical moves of people and equipment. The technical and social systems subcommittee then worked with staff in the programs to identify opportunities for improvement. Recommendations in areas including clerical processes for cases, forms redesign, placement of specific programs such as guardianship and specialty units, and case assignment processes were submitted to the steering committee and bureau executive staff, which approved many of them.

For other design process considerations, Aronowitz et al. (2015) offered several "rules" to consider. Based on their research and their own work with "multiple companies" (p. 3), they asserted that "73% of the executives whose companies followed more than six of them felt that the organizational redesign had succeeded" (p. 3). Their rules are as follows:

1. Focus first on the longer term strategic aspirations . . .
2. Take time to survey the scene [i.e., do a thorough assessment of current conditions] . . .
3. Be structured about selecting the right blueprint [e.g., the design criteria for your situation] . . .
4. Go beyond lines and boxes [to include people and processes] . . .
5. Be rigorous about drafting in talent [design the roles first; don't design based on which people should be where] . . .
6. Identify the necessary mindset shifts—and change those mindsets [the culture] . . .
7. Establish metrics that measure short- and long-term success [organizational performance indicators] . . .
8. Make sure business [division, program, or unit] leaders communicate . . .
9. Manage the transitional risks [in HSOs, this could include timing, such as where the organization is in its fiscal year, upcoming policy or budget changes, etc.] (pp. 5-10)

Within the STS framework and the design suggestions just listed, here are some steps for the redesign of an organization:

1. Review the organization's purpose and strategic directions. Consult the agency's strategic plan for guidance in terms of the way services should be delivered and the way staff should communicate and coordinate their work.

2. Determine the best, evidence-based service delivery technologies for each program area.
3. Examine in detail the processes through which clients travel during service delivery. Note the ways in which clients encounter staff from multiple programs and as needed devise coordination mechanisms to minimize steps that clients need to take and maximize efficiencies and quality.
4. Assess the organization's social system, including organizational culture, decision-making and communication processes, coordination across functions or departments, and employee quality of working life considerations and use these factors when considering structures.
5. Determine the most appropriate organizational structure, with supporting social systems. Actually, Steps 3 and 4 might best be addressed simultaneously to ensure joint optimization.
6. Ensure that the entire system, including service delivery programs, structure, staff roles, and organizational processes are all aligned, or "fit" together.

This organization redesign model fits with the generic change model covered in Section 3. Change methods such as action teams and processes such as work process analysis and other quality improvement methods are likely to be used in analyzing workflows, job roles, and other aspects of a redesign. Other tactics in the model (e.g., conveying urgency, building support) might also be useful here.

These guidelines cover both the content and the process of a redesign effort. In addition to those, I can offer here some findings from some research on organizational redesign that I was involved with. These can be seen as *process* guidelines—things to build into the design steps. Some years ago, my colleagues and I in the Academy for Professional Excellence in our School of Social Work were asked by the executives of nine counties in Southern California (the Academy's Southern Area Consortium of Human Services program) to find California counties that had reported successes in organizational redesigns through structural changes or cross-department collaborations and to learn about their processes and success factors.

We found four counties that had reported successful structural integrations and three in which county departments remained separate but developed strong collaborative relationships. We summarized our findings (Packard, Patti, Daly, & Tucker-Tatlow, 2012, 2013; Patti, Packard, Daly, Tucker-Tatlow, & Farrell, 2003) into the following major themes, some of which align directly with steps in the change model in Section 3:

- *Ensure and Communicate the Need*: Persuasively communicate the need for change (in our study, by emphasizing the importance of improving services through coordination) and project a vision for how that might happen.

- *Mobilizing the Executive Team*: Build an executive-level core action system committed to the changes sought and willing to spend personal energy and professional capital to achieve them.
- *Leadership: Articulating the Vision*: Executives or other change sponsors need to project a vision and expectation for results (e.g., improved interagency coordination).
- *Marketing Change Goals*: A committed executive team should convey a constant and consistent message out to employees and community stakeholders and solicit feedback that could be helpful in implementing plans.
- *Involving Stakeholders*: Explain the rationale for change and the benefits that might accrue, involving staff and community constituents in planning for implementation and involving them in change processes such as assessments and problem-solving groups.
- *Provide a Plan*: Ensure that all employees, with particular attention to middle managers and front-line staff, are aware of the plan.
- *Build Internal Support and Overcome Resistance*: Involve staff and community constituents in planning for implementation to help build acceptance of the change and enthusiasm for implementation.
- *Long-Term Vision and Incremental Change*: Maintain marketing efforts, information dissemination, and involvement in planning to address staff concerns on an ongoing basis. As possible, spread change incrementally out over time to reduce work overloads for staff.
- *Developing Teamwork Across Professional and Program Cultures*: Structural changes need to be supplemented with training and team development to help build understanding and trust across program and professional cultures.
- *Institutionalize Changes*: Institutionalization of the new structures through not only formal organizational chart and reporting relationships but also culture change through staff development and team building.

Business Process Reengineering: A Cautionary Tale

Before ending this discussion of organization redesign, one famous redesign model—*business process reengineering* (BPR)—warrants some attention mainly as a warning of things to be very alert to when embarking upon a redesign process. BPR became hugely popular in the 1990s. It was defined by its initial developers as "a fundamental rethinking and radical redesign of business processes to achieve dramatic improvements in critical contemporary measures of performance such as cost, quality service, and speed" (Hammer & Champy, 1993, p. 32). BPR reached fad status in the business and government sectors in the United States, in spite of evidence that many such efforts fail (Hammer

& Champy, 1993). Because reengineering often resulted in the elimination of positions (often in middle management), the term *downsizing* was often used, particularly in government organizations. This later evolved into the euphemistic *right-sizing*; and cynics suggested that the final result for the organization may be *capsizing*.

More seriously, and more broadly, one researcher (Freeman, 1999) studied the ways that downsizing and redesign played out in 30 subunits of two large corporations. She found that when redesign drove downsizing (rather than the reverse), there was more attention to change tactics, including staff participation; systematic analysis (e.g., of structure, processes, and staff positions); and attention to interorganizational relationships, suggesting that downsizing in the context of thoughtful redesign is likely to lead to broader, and more impactful, change. Regardless of how it is done, downsizing clearly causes trauma, not only for those who lose employment but also for colleagues. This issue, including its ethics aspects, receives more attention in a discussion of cutback management in Chapter 18. I also touch on the ethics issue in the last chapter.

An experienced HSO administrator has probably at some point faced a challenging ethical dilemma. Such dilemmas can occur with reference to client issues, but administrative or organizational dynamics can sometimes raise an ethical issue. Reengineering is an area where this might occur. Reengineering's reputation as a downsizing tool is probably deserved and can bring up ethical concerns about conditions under which administrators make layoff decisions.

Business process reengineering is mentioned here more as a cautionary tale than a promising example. If it is used, it should be undertaken only after very thoughtful analysis and will probably involve the use of outside consultants. Without a full-blown use of the model, administrators as change leaders may be able to use specific principles and processes within their own redesign processes.

It typically involves a thorough examination of the whole organization, focusing on structures and processes. The current organization is assessed, and a new, ideal organization is proposed that eliminates all processes that do not add value for customers. Since it typically requires the use of an outside consultant who can suggest a complete process, I provide only a brief outline here.

The reengineering process typically begins with the organization developing a vision of a preferred future, identifying change opportunities, forming reengineering teams, and focusing resources. At the next stage, the current processes are assessed, often known as defining the current business model: the way the process identified for reengineering is done at present. After choosing processes that seem to be good opportunities for reengineering, benchmarking and identifying best practices can locate organizations whose practices can be used as standards and goals. Sometimes the organization conducts a gap analysis to show the differences between the current state and the ideal state (sometimes known as the future business model), which is based on benchmarks and the organization's vision. Next, reengineering teams solicit input from customers and employees and redesign existing processes by eliminating steps that do not add value to the product or service.

This stage usually includes getting rid of the "silo mentality" of many organizations, in which staff from different functions or units do not communicate or work well together. Often management positions are seen as not adding value but rather slowing things down, and positions can be eliminated. Here is where reengineering got its reputation as a euphemism for downsizing. When positions are eliminated, an organization should do everything possible to retain employees in still-needed positions. After viable proposals for change are approved, the organization needs to transition to the new designs and systems. Monitoring continues to see whether changes are having the intended effects and to identify other change opportunities.

If you want to consider using reengineering methods, social work writer Gary Grobman (1999a), in an excellent book on quality and performance in nonprofit organizations, offered this summary of steps that can be taken in a reengineering effort:

1. articulating the organization's goals and vision for the future, and quantifying objectives
2. identifying all business processes
3. benchmarking all of those processes
4. performing an environmental analysis to identify economic, legal, political, technical, social, and other external forces
5. reviewing customer needs, complaints, and suggestions and using surveys and focus groups to collect more customer input
6. brainstorming by senior staff on how to improve business processes and meet customer needs regardless of the constraints of current design
7. developing a consensus among management on a plan to redesign business processes
8. developing a timetable for redesign
9. designating a management team responsible for implementing the redesign, and motivating that team
10. designing a pilot for each redesigned business process and testing that pilot
11. conducting staff training to implement the redesign
12. communicating to all employees the goals and status of the project
13. implementing the redesign
14. evaluating the redesign

15. minimizing the collateral damage to employees who are no longer needed as a result of the redesign
16. implementing continuous improvement to capitalize on the benefits of the BPR intervention

Even if an agency does not conduct a formal reengineering process, some of these techniques may be used to good effect in a regular redesign process.

Summary

While organizational restructuring, or, more fully, organizational redesign, is a commonly proposed solution for major organizational problems, it should only be considered after a thorough analysis of existing conditions and desired outcomes. If, in fact, redesign is an appropriate change technology, it should be approached thoughtfully and comprehensively, with attention to both structure and organizational processes. This chapter listed a range of criteria to consider in planning a redesign effort and suggested a broad, participative process for engaging many of the staff affected through structures such as a steering committee and design teams. BPR was mentioned as a redesign strategy that has a very mixed, and probably overall negative, reputation. While some of its techniques can be used positively and ethically, applications of BPR principles should be considered very thoughtfully. The ethics issues that I mentioned in that section can also be applied to any type of organization redesign. Manning (2003, pp. 34–38) listed several dilemmas of organization design (or redesign), including managing conflicting expectations from funders and clients and general tensions between organizational/bureaucratic pressures and client needs. She asserted that HSOs need to have social responsibility to clients, communities, and employees as a top consideration when making design decisions.

I also noted how some of the principles from the generic change model in Section 3 can be applied in organizational redesign.

Reflection and Focusing Questions

1. Given our assessment of the organization's current state and needs for change, is organizational restructuring or redesign the answer?
2. If redesign is the solution, or part of the solution, what problems or new strategies would be adequately addressed by an organizational redesign?
3. What processes should be set up as part of the design process (e.g., design teams, other aspects of the organizational change process covered in Section 3?

16

Changing Organizational Culture

Question: Which comes first—strategy or culture? Answer: Neither. What always comes first is, "What's our problem? Why are we even worrying about this?" The problem will often tell you whether it's a strategic problem or a culture problem or a mixture or something different altogether.

—Edgar Schein ("A Conversation With Edgar Schein," 2017a, pp. 64–65)

While "restructuring" is a common change goal, "changing our culture" is also often identified by administrators as a need. Neither restructuring nor culture change should be a free-standing change goal. If a consultant is told that the change goal is to change the culture, Edgar Schein, the most prominent scholar of organizational culture change, suggested probing, to see what the underlying issues or agendas are, to define the actual "business problem" that needs to be addressed, and how that will help create the desired "new way of working" and new behaviors (Schein, 2014). An implementation of a new evidence-based practice (EBP) or information system may indeed involve changing some aspects of the culture, but culture change should be a secondary or supportive objective in service of the ultimate goal.

This chapter examines organizational culture change as a specific intervention, while recognizing that it is very often an important part of a change initiative with a larger goal. After some definitions, we consider characteristics of effective cultures and then cover some models for culture change.

Culture and Climate Defined

Organizational culture and organizational climate are related terms that are very important for an organization's functioning and its amenability to change. Simply put, organizational culture takes a sociological perspective, looking at dynamics of organizational norms and behavior expectations, while organizational

Organizational Change for the Human Services. Thomas Packard, Oxford University Press. © Oxford University Press 2021. DOI: 10.1093/oso/9780197549995.003.0017

climate uses a psychological perspective to examine individual staff perceptions of their work environment.

Organizational culture can be seen as

the *shared pattern* of beliefs, assumptions, and expectations held by organizational members, and their characteristic way of perceiving the organization's artifacts and environment, and its norms, roles, and values as they exist outside the individual. (Bowditch, Buono, & Stewart, 2008, p. 320; italics in original)

These elements are reflected in several "dimensions" of culture described by Bowditch, Buono, and Stewart (2008, pp. 326–328). Cultural artifacts reflected in the organization's physical layout, furniture, and logos provide clues regarding values of the organization. Organizational heroes "represent what the company stands for and reinforce the values of the culture by underscoring that success is attainable, acting as a role model for others." (pp. 326-327) Organizational myths and stories are very useful for passing on belief systems. Behavioral norms including organizational taboos, rites, and rituals such as awards ceremonies guide organizational behavior. Organizational values also provide guidelines for how people should behave in the organization.

Organizational culture expert Edgar Schein has defined the culture of a group as

"a pattern or system of beliefs, values , and behavioral norms that come to be taken for granted as basic assumptions and eventually drop out of awareness" that are "taught to new members as the correct way to perceive, think, and feel behave. (Schein, 2017b, p. 6) He (2017b, p. 18) defined these three levels of culture:

1. Artifacts
   - Visible and "feelable" structures and processes
   - Observed behavior
     - Difficult to decipher

2. Espoused Beliefs and Values
   - Ideals, goals, values, aspirations
   - Ideologies
   - Rationalizations
     - May or may not be congruent with behavior and other artifacts

3. Basic Underlying Assumptions
   - Unconscious, taken-for-granted beliefs and values
     - Determine behavior, perceptions, thought, and feeling

In contrast to culture, organizational climate is created by employees' shared perceptions of the psychological impact of their work environment on their own personal well-being and functioning. The perceptions that are shared by employees in a given work environment represent an agreement in their personal appraisals of the meaning and significance of their work (Glisson, 2015, p. 246).

Organizational culture and climate also have value dimensions. In a human service organization (HSO) context, Manning (2003) noted that leaders "assert the moral code" of the organization, adding that "organizational culture is the context for ethics" (p. 197) and "ethical organizations institutionalize important values" (p. 198). Climate is important as well because it "informs the leaders and constituents about what they can do or ought to do regarding particular ethical situations, according to organizational norms" (2003, p. 191). In Chapter 9, as an example of institutionalizing an organizational change, I described how Father Joe's Villages developed a set of organizational values to guide the behavior of staff. This can be seen as a culture change with reference to articulating specific organizational values as guides for behavior.

Schein (2017b, p. 183) identified six "primary embedding mechanisms" of culture:

- What leaders pay attention to, measure, and control on a regular basis
- How leaders react to critical incidents and organizational crises
- How leaders allocate resources
- Deliberate role modeling, teaching, and coaching
- How leaders allocate and reward status
- How leaders recruit, select, promote, and excommunicate [i.e., remove]

Schein also identified six "secondary reinforcement and stabilizing mechanisms" that a leader can use to shape culture:

- Organizational design and structure
- Organizational systems and procedures
- Rites and rituals of the organization
- Design of physical space, facades, and buildings including symbols
- Stories about important events and people
- Formal statements of organizational philosophy, creeds, and charters.

Administrative mechanisms such as these can help shape a culture as humanistic or bureaucratic, performance or process focused, and team or individualistically oriented.

Administrators are seen as leaders who play an important role in "embedding" and transmitting the culture that they believe will most enhance organizational functioning (Schein, 2017b). Leaders represent and can describe an organization's existing culture and, in the case of organizational redesign, can help change an organization's culture, to align it with the structural changes, to better adapt to new conditions in the environment. These leaders have a particular responsibility in creating a culture that is consistent with the agency's strategic plan and facilitates accomplishment of goals and effective organizational functioning. They give staff important clues based on the aspects of the organization they pay attention to. For example, if leaders focus on agency outcome data and the functioning of teams, they are likely to get different results than if they focused on following procedures and power struggles for resources. If leaders allocate resources for diversity initiatives and allocate rewards based on improved client outcomes through EBPs and collaboration, employees will get clues regarding what is seen as important. Employees know to look beyond merely what a leader says in meetings or newsletters to see what behaviors the leader models on a daily basis.

Some aspects of culture (e.g., employee styles of dress, office layouts, structure of meetings) are relatively easy to change, while deeply held beliefs, unstated assumptions and values, and underlying philosophies of employees are much more difficult to change (Anderson, 2015).

Organizational cultures are difficult to define precisely. Anderson (2015, p. 281; italics in original) summarized these four idealized culture types:

- *Clan.* People strongly identify with the group, as in a family, placing a strong emphasis on the team and teamwork...
- *Adhocracy.* Innovation is prized, with organizational members having a large amount of independence and autonomy...
- *Hierarchy.* Tradition and formality are dominant values....
- *Market.* Organizational members are competitive, hardworking, and demanding.

An instrument, the Organizational Culture Assessment Instrument (Cameron & Quinn, 2011; Heritage, Pollock, & Roberts, 2014) is available to assess an organization's culture using the *competing values* framework, which uses variables of flexibility versus stability and internal versus external focus to define *clan, adhocracy, market,* or *hierarchy* cultures.

Of course, any organization will not closely resemble any specific type, and any culture may be effective or ineffective based on local conditions and priorities.

Characteristics of Effective Cultures

It would be impossible to define a "best" culture because, to be effective, any organization's culture must be well aligned with other aspects of the organization, especially with reference to factors including strategy, mission, values, structure, leadership styles, and desired outcomes of the organization and its subunits. In that sense, an organization's executive staff would be well advised to design some activities to explicitly consider what the characteristics of their ideal culture would be.

Here, I present one set of criteria based on the ARC (availability, responsiveness, and continuity) model (covered in Chapter 18 and later in this chapter). Hemmelgarn and Glisson have combined culture and climate and added work attitudes (morale as reflected in job satisfaction and organizational commitment) to create a key variable regarding organizational effectiveness: *organizational social context* (OSC). In their comprehensive book (Hemmelgarn & Glisson, 2018), they discussed OSC as a major element in their ARC organizational change model. They have a well-developed instrument to measure all the dimensions of OSC.

The three dimensions of culture assessed by the OSC are *proficiency*, *rigidity*, and *resistance*. Service providers in *proficient* organizational cultures report that they are expected to be responsive to the unique needs of the clients they serve and have up-to-date knowledge and practice skills. In such cultures, staff also have positive attitudes regarding the use of EBPs. In contrast, *rigid* cultures expect staff to follow bureaucratic rules and regulations and give staff less discretion and flexibility in staff decision-making. *Resistant* cultures have little interest in change or innovation.

The climate aspects of the OSC are *engagement, functionality*, and *stress*. In *engaged* organizational climates, service providers see their work as personally meaningful and feel personally involved with their work. In *functional* climates, service providers believe they are accomplishing worthwhile goals, receive support and cooperation from other staff, and have clear roles and opportunities for growth and development. In *stressful* climates, service providers have high levels of role overload, role conflict, and emotional exhaustion.

Many of these characteristics will be seen as desirable or, in the cases of resistance and stress, undesirable in many HSOs. Here, treat these as examples of things to consider when developing an ideal culture for your organization.

Culture Assessment

Before trying to change an organization's culture you should assess it. Schein (2014, p. 354) suggested this process for assessing an organization's culture:

1. Obtain Leadership Commitment
2. Select Groups for Interviews
3. Select an Appropriate Setting for the Group Interviews

4. Explain the Purpose of the Meeting
5. Explain the Culture Model
6. Elicit Descriptions of Artifacts
7. Identify Espoused Values
8. Identify Shared Tacit Assumptions
9. Identify Cultural Aids and Hindrances
10. Joint Analysis and Next Steps

Structured questions for group or individual interviews in this process could include the following:

1. Describe the organization's existing culture, including specific examples of artifacts, rituals, and language.
2. Define the organization's explicitly stated values.
3. Analyze whether the values fully explain the existence of artifacts or whether there are underlying assumptions that amount to hidden cultural values.
4. Describe how the explicit or hidden values inhibit or strengthen how the organization achieves its goals.
5. Share any subcultural differences among the teams.
6. Discuss and come to agreement on action plans to change the negative cultural values (Anderson, 2015, pp. 281–282).

For example, the organization may have an espoused value of cooperation, but people's assumptions are that competition is the way to get things done. The discussion can lead to suggesting a "new way of working" for the organization: a newer and more appropriate culture.

A culture change process could begin with such group interviews and/or the use of the OSC or another instrument, followed by dialogue to reach consensus among staff about the existing culture and what an ideal culture would look like.

Culture Change

Organizational culture is hugely difficult to change, most likely requiring *transformational* change in the way the organization operates. Such a change requires totally new thinking and perspectives on the part of employees, and thus is extremely challenging and complicated, and typically occurs over a period of years. According to studies by Hemmelgarn and Glisson (2018, p. 80) of their ARC model, changing climate can take a year, and culture change can take 3 years. One reason for the difficulty of culture change is that the culture of an organization, reflected in its behavior patterns, has evolved to the present state because "it worked" (Ehrhart, Schneider, & Macey, 2014). A current culture may now seem to be ineffective, and maybe it is, because conditions affecting the organization have changed faster than the culture changed. Therefore, just as "poor communication" is often seen as the major problem of an organization, "change the culture" is often seen as a way to improve the organization.

Changing a culture might be a good thing to do, but I suggest that a change goal should be extended a bit further: What are the outcomes you want for the organization? What is the ideal future for how things should be operating to ensure excellent services, a high quality of working life, and efficient stewardship of organizational resources? Quite possibly, changing the culture will be part of the solution, but the focus should remain on ultimate organizational performance. In other words, culture change is not an end in itself, but a process in service of the larger goal of improving operations and outcomes of the organization.

Consistent with the sociotechnical systems principles in Chapter 15, restructuring and culture change should be done simultaneously to jointly optimize aspects of each, even though I cover them separately in this book. One good reason for discussing culture change separately is that it can happen with any other type of major organizational change besides restructuring. For example, all four of the cases I used in previous chapters involved culture change to some extent. Three—San Mateo County, San Diego Youth Services, and Father Joe's Villages—involved changing the culture regarding customer service. The example I gave in Chapter 9 when discussing institutionalization of an organizational change, Father Joe's Villages implementing a set of organizational values, was in fact a culture change regarding how staff would work with clients.

The San Diego Fire Department project created culture change through new managerial roles for battalion chiefs and a commitment to ongoing participative decision-making to identify and solve organizational problems.

So, for any organizational change, consider how changes in the organization's culture may support implementation of the change goal, which should in any case be focused on some aspect of improving the organization's performance. Consciously attend to these dynamics, such as how leadership style, norms, or communication processes should change. Implementing a new EBP, a new information system, or a new performance appraisal process would involve changing some aspects of an organization's culture.

Employee Perspectives

From an individual employee's perspective, Schein used Lewin's classic concepts of unfreezing, changing, and refreezing to illustrate how employees experience the culture change. Unfreezing creates disequilibrium in employees' cognitive structure by presenting *disconfirming data* that lead an employee to believe that current conditions are no longer comfortable. This, of course, creates psychological anxiety, which must be addressed by the leader creating *psychological safety*, so that staff will feel safe in trying out new ways of operating. These new behaviors and attitudes are then reinforced and rewarded by leadership, thus refreezing a new or modified organizational culture.

Schein (2017b) suggested several tactics to create psychological safety for staff. First, as mentioned previously, a compelling vision for a new future can show how the organization can look when improved. Formal and informal training, with active involvement of staff in the learning process, can be supported by "practice fields" where it is safe to try new behaviors, supported by coaches and useful feedback. Leaders can act as role models for the new ways of thinking, and support groups can aid staff in the learning process. Finally, management systems including structures and rewards need to be changed to be in alignment with the new thinking.

The classic work on organizational transitions (Bridges & Bridges, 2016) can be especially helpful in examining employees' perspectives on a significant organizational change such as a culture change. In fact, many organizational changes are likely to have at least some level of change to organizational culture and climate. This transition model is also relevant to developing and maintaining support as covered in Chapter 8. I include this material here because it relates closely to the need to create the psychological safety that Schein saw as important.

Getting employees to "let go" of an old culture involves, first, identifying "who's losing what" (Bridges & Bridges, 2016, p. 29). In Chapter 8, I noted that employees might feel losses of power, a sense of competence, personal identity, and relationships with colleagues. Change leaders need to accept the realities of these losses from the perspectives of the staff affected and not be surprised if staff "overreact" (p. 31) to the change. Rather, change leaders should acknowledge the perceived losses, react with empathy, and help staff go through the classic grieving process of anger, bargaining, sadness, anxiety, disorientation, and even depression. Bridges and Bridges suggested that, as possible, the administrators should figure out ways to compensate staff for the losses, such as through training and as possible enhancing staff feelings of control over the situation. Endings should be acknowledged, and where possible the good aspects of the past should be recognized and validated. Change leaders also need to regularly and fully share information on the change process and show continuity with important organizational aspects such as mission and positive aspects of the former culture.

The next step in the Bridges model is going through the "neutral zone" when old "ways" have ended but new systems are not yet in place. Validate and explain this time as a normal stage in a process and create "temporary systems" (pp. 51–52), such as clear (if temporary) policies, procedures, and roles. Ask other managers and supervisors what additional supports they could use to help manage the transitions. The change management team for the overall change process should play an active role in managing transition dynamics. The typical problem-solving and action research processes discussed in Chapters 8 and 11 can help here.

Finally, launching a "new beginning" includes the regular change leadership tasks of clarifying the entire change process and showing how current activities will help achieve the original change goals. Bridges and Bridges particularly noted the importance of reiterating, through regular communications, the *purpose* of the whole change process, including the vision of the new state for the organization. They also suggested getting some quick successes and celebrating them, as I suggested in Chapter 8.

Tactics for Culture Change

Schein asserted that creating a new culture requires of leaders that they have persistence and patience as well as flexibility and readiness regarding change (2017b, p. 351).

Some specific activities that change leaders can use to create culture change include hiring and promoting managers who model the new culture's values and behaviors; changing artifacts, rituals and ceremonies to reflect the new culture; regularly discussing the new values in meetings and other settings; and modeling the new culture through their daily behaviors.

Heckelman, Garofano, and Unger (2013) suggested that culture change needs to be addressed at three levels. At the organizational level, change leaders need to "define and prioritize the desired culture (vision, values, and core belief [and] build commitment to purpose, mission, and values" (p. 31). At the team level, change leaders need to "translate strategic goals to team responsibilities [and] address the impact of the changes to work and the team" (p. 31). At the individual level, change leaders need to "clarify roles, responsibilities and desired behaviors [and] reward and reinforce intended desired behaviors" (p. 31).

Consistent with other writers, Cummings and Worley (2015) suggested formulating a clear strategic vision for the organization (including updating current strategies as needed), displaying top-management commitment, modeling change behaviors, and modifying organizational systems and processes (e.g., structures, human resource systems, job designs, and other management processes) to align with the new culture.

An impressive review of the literature on culture and climate change in youth-serving organizations (Ouellette et al., 2020) found interventions that clustered into four areas: skill development (e.g., training on EBP implementation), continuous quality improvement, restructuring, and provision of social and emotional support (e.g., mindfulness). Measurements of organizational culture and climate outcomes were similarly clustered, into five categories:

(1) Organizational values and norms;
(2) Interactions between people in the workplace;
(3) Collective perceptions of job demands;
(4) Perceptions of collective emotional healthiness of organization, and;
(5) Global metrics of an organization's perceived readiness for change and/or effectiveness. (p. 8)

There was great variation in how the results of interventions were documented and evaluated, with many mixed results and some findings of positive change. They did find that, consistent with the traditional literature, changes required a period of time—up to several years—to be evident. Findings related to client outcomes were similarly mixed. The authors offered recommendations for future research that might better describe interventions and outcomes, which ranged from better specification of interventions and factors that might affect outcome to more rigorous evaluation designs. Practitioners as action researchers on a culture change project may use these findings by being as precise as possible in clearly describing the change goals, assessing organizational readiness and capacity, using evidence-based change methods, and clearly articulating an evaluation plan.

The Gallup organization, famous for their opinion surveys, has done a lot of excellent work on what makes some organizations so effective, starting with the popularization of a strengths perspective in management and organizations (Buckingham, 2007; Buckingham & Clifton, 2001). Their recent book , *It's the Manager* (Clifton & Harter, 2019), not only addresses culture change in the context of organizational strategy and branding, but also focuses culture change on the role of managers working with employees, from attracting talent and hiring and onboarding staff to engaging and developing them, especially through coaching. Those processes and systems are essential and are part of the focus in this chapter on changing culture as a whole.

Their culture change model has three elements:

1. *Identify your organization's purpose and brand.* For HSOs, this involves examining and reaffirming or updating the organization's mission, vision, values, and strategies.
2. *Audit all programs and communications.* This involves assessing all the organization's performance measures and management processes. The

latter can include tools such as an employee survey and a management audit, covered in Chapter 11.

3. *Shift your managers' mindsets from being a boss to being a coach.* In the change model in this book, this new mindset of employee engagement is represented by employee participative leadership models and providing support for staff through the change process.

You can use these tactics as a menu of activities to consider as you embark on a culture change.

Summary

Because organizational culture is such a popular term, it is important to discuss exactly what it is and also consider the related concept of organizational climate. Organizational culture is sometimes hard to describe, or even "see," beyond physical representations such as posters, artwork, and other characteristics of physical facilities. We reviewed some dimensions of culture that should help you as you look at your own organization to assess what is working well and what could be improved in terms of the existing culture and how that affects organizational performance and staff morale. It is essential not to look at culture change in isolation. Any change initiative should first look broadly at organizational conditions that need to be changed to ensure that the new culture is aligned with organizational systems, strategies, and goals. This chapter has focused on organizational culture as the *content* of change. The change model covered in Section 3 can be used for the *process* of change to change the culture, probably as part of a larger change initiative to improve organizational effectiveness overall.

Reflection and Focusing Questions

1. How do people in your organization see its culture and climate? Are there aspects of culture or climate that should be changed to enhance the effectiveness of the organization?
2. To what extent are the organization's strategies, goals and objectives, program models, administrative systems, culture, and leadership philosophies in alignment? Where are there misalignments that need attention?
3. If culture change is indeed a relevant change goal, how can it be done to ensure alignment with other systems to enhance organizational effectiveness?

SECTION 5

CHANGE METHODS FOR HUMAN SERVICE ORGANIZATIONS

17

Improvement Methods for Human Service Organizations

Why is it that no one has time to do it right, but everyone has time to do it over?

—John Wedemeyer, MSW, founding executive director,
San Diego Youth Services

Chapter 14 covered generic change processes that originated in for-profit organizations but that have obvious uses in nonprofit and governmental human service organizations (HSOs). This chapter addresses processes and models that have unique relevance for HSOs. I start with a strengths-based, proactive approach: *capacity building*, which is used to enhance management systems capacity in areas such as strategic planning, information systems, and fund development. I briefly discuss the generic methods of *benchmarking* and *best practices* research as they apply to HSOs. This is followed by discussions of some other change processes that are unique to HSOs. Implementing evidence-based practices (EBPs), known broadly as *implementation science* (IS), is a very common organizational change challenge for HSOs these days. I mention four common EBP implementation models. Related to this, *organizational learning* and *learning organizations* are receiving increasing attention in HSOs. I touch briefly on each of these.

Capacity Building

In a sense, almost anything that happens in an organization can involve capacity building. Small-scale, developmental changes are happening on a regular basis, leading to an improvement in some aspect of capacity and performance. Someone on a treatment team can come up with an idea to improve team meetings, or minor changes can be made to an intake process. Even at an individual worker level, a counselor using a new practice model could be getting better with it every day, building their capacity. Transitional or transformation change processes, to the extent that they are successful, inherently involve a good

Organizational Change for the Human Services. Thomas Packard, Oxford University Press. © Oxford University Press 2021. DOI: 10.1093/oso/9780197549995.003.0018

amount of capacity building. An agency whose staff become competent using a new treatment model has enhanced capacity, as does an agency that has a new automated information system that tracks client outcomes, or an agency that has implemented a new strategic planning process that results in new funds.

A more formal definition for capacity building for nonprofit organizations is

the funding and technical assistance to help nonprofits increase specific capacities to deliver stronger programs, take risks, build connections, innovate, and iterate. *Technical assistance* is the process by which organizations obtain the necessary knowledge, tools and other resources to develop, implement and assess targeted improvements in their work; this process is often supported by a consultant or expert. Technical assistance is a term sometimes used interchangeably with capacity building. (Grantmakers for Effective Organizations, 2015, p. 3; italics in original)

Areas for capacity building include

- organizational development (e.g., governance, finances, information systems)
- program development (e.g., program enhancement or evaluation)
- revenue development (e.g., diversifying funding sources, financial sustainability)
- leadership development (e.g., training, career development)
- community engagement (e.g., asset mapping, needs assessments) (Minzer, Klerman, & Spreitzer, 2014)

While the discussion here focuses on nonprofits, capacity building can also happen in government organizations.

Treating a capacity building initiative as organizational change implies the use of any of the generic tactics and methods that I covered as you introduce the need for capacity building and then launch the initiative. For example, a funder may conduct a capacity assessment (discussed in the next section) with an organization it is funding. If it finds, for example, weaknesses in the organization's information systems or program evaluation capacities, it may suggest or require that the organization use a consultant to improve its capacities. The organization's administrators can then become change leaders in introducing to staff the need for capacity building, showing its value to the organization, creating urgency if needed, and implementing a change process.

Needs for capacity building at the organizational level can become apparent in several ways. Opportunities for capacity building can emerge when a major problem becomes evident within the organization. Some examples were given in Chapter 1. An incidence of a child client death in child welfare can force an agency to look at what went wrong and needs to be corrected. In a more proactive way, someone in the agency can identify a need or opportunity of any scope for improvement and seek capacity building help.

According to Light and Hubbard (2004), "Most capacity building approaches are characterized by either a focused, problem-centered approach or a broader commitment to work on a range of organizational issues" (p. 6). A foundation providing funding for a nonprofit may make available or require that the agency take advantage of capacity building to address a weakness seen by the foundation. Some foundations accept requests and support capacity building from any agencies that meet certain criteria (e.g., being funded by that foundation or having a mission in alignment with the mission of the foundation). A government funding organization can also require or offer technical assistance capacity building for its funded agencies.

While research on capacity building effectiveness is limited, some studies have found that capacity building can improve management capacity in areas such as program development, leadership development, and program evaluation. For capacity building to be impactful, it needs to go beyond short or limited activities such as a workshop and should include involvement of both management and front-line staff (Despard, 2016; Minzer et al., 2014; National Council of Nonprofits, n.d.-a).

Assessing Capacity Building Needs

McKinsey and Company has developed a useful capacity assessment tool for nonprofit organizations. Their capacity assessment grid (McKinsey & Company, n.d.) includes these factors:

- Aspirations: mission, vision, goals
- Strategy: overall strategy, performance targets, programs, funding model
- Organizational skills: performance management, planning, fundraising, external
- Human resources: staffing, board, senior management
- Organizational structure: governance, organizational design coordination, job design
- Culture: shared values, beliefs, and practices

This is a well-regarded tool that can be used as a self-assessment checklist regarding your possible needs for technical assistance. You will need to assess your organization's capacities to conduct such an assessment with existing staff expertise, perhaps with assistance from an outside consultant (e.g., from a consulting firm or a local university).

Two other tools are the elements of an effectively managed organization in the second edition of Allison and Kaye's (2005) book on strategic planning for nonprofit organizations, and the Management Audit in Appendix 2. These suggest best practices with reference to leadership and management functions. They are both in checklist form, allowing each function to be rated regarding the extent to which it is present and functioning at an adequate level. Such assessments can be conducted internally, assuming you have competent managers who are willing to be self-critical regarding their own operations. An employee survey can be designed to include many of these items if staff are in a position to observe management and leadership processes in operation. The results can be used to identify needs for improvement. Next steps would then be organizational changes at whatever level of change is warranted.

Finally, for organizations considering engaging in formal capacity building, Bartczak and Hyman (2005, pp. 3–8) highlighted several "success factors" to consider:

- Depth and breadth of skill needed
- Commitment and buy-in
- A well-tested framework
- Accurate and complete information
- Confidentiality and ownership of findings
- Clear expectations regarding use of findings.

Some of the material on selecting consultants in Chapter 10 may also be relevant here.

Improving Organizational Capacity

There are many organizations devoted to providing capacity building (sometimes known as technical assistance) through training, consultation, and written resources. In the child welfare field, the National Child Welfare Workforce Institute (https://ncwwi.org/) has extensive resources available. The National Staff Development and Training Association (NSDTA; https://www.aphsa.org/NSDTA), an affiliate organization of the American Public Human Services Association (APHSA), offers many web-based resources and an annual conference. APHSA also offers organizational effectiveness services. NSDTA's journal *Training and Development in Human Services* (Curry, Basso, & Jones, 2011) had a special issue on organizational development that included five case examples and other resources for capacity building. The National Council of Nonprofits and affiliate organizations in many states offer a wide range of resources that can help nonprofit organizations become more effective. The major consulting firm McKinsey & Company noted previously has practice arenas, including the public and social sectors (https://www.mckinsey.com/industries/public-and-social-sector/how-we-help-clients) with a wide range of resources offered.

Barbara Blumenthal, an early leader in capacity building for nonprofit organizations, wrote a book (2003) on capacity building that was primarily for funding organizations but that also has useful information for organization executives and managers. She made the important point that assessments with recommendations made by "expert" consultants (as I contrasted with process consultants in Chapter 10), are likely not to have the support of the client organization. This can be prevented or minimized if you as an administrator use a process consultant who will provide expertise in the use of an assessment tool but will not tell the organization what it should do as a result of an assessment. If you are working with a funding organization that has made an arrangement for capacity building, you will, of course, need to work closely with the funder, using the suggestions above by Bartczak and Hyman. Blumenthal also asserted that organizations need to better develop their learning capacities in order to effectively use capacity building. This point was amplified in a later article by Austin, Regan, Samples, Schwartz, and Carnochan (2011) who noted, in the context of a leadership development program, that Blumenthal later (2007) highlighted four components that shape the design of a management training program that seeks to expand organizational capacity:

1) making explicit the organizational capacity-building goals;
2) creating a supportive practice environment within the training program and in the agency;
3) training approaches that include multiple approaches to learning, e.g., didactic, experiential, reflective, self-assessing, and life-long learning; and
4) the use of different training tools such as self-assessment inventories, online resources, videotapes, observational checklists, etc. (Austin, et al., p. 262)

These components seem worth considering in other capacity building initiatives. Even for a technical change such as a new information system, attending to these training dynamics would be appropriate.

Executives and other managers of HSOs should be constantly looking for opportunities for change. The strategic planning techniques of SWOT (strengths, weaknesses, opportunities, threats) and PESTL (political, economic, social, technological, legal), mentioned in Chapter 5, are examples. I quoted Tom Peters in Chapter 1, who said, "If it ain't broken, you just haven't looked hard enough." If an organization has developed excellent capacities for organizational learning, any staff member can be looking for opportunities for improvement.

Since I am trying hard to make a case for executives and managers asking for capacity building, I should also note that some may feel that asking a funder for such help might be seen as a sign of dependence, incompetence, or something equally undesirable. I know this is easy for me to say as an outsider, but do consider that asking for assistance can be seen as a sign of your thoughtfulness and awareness of an area for improvement, your desire to make your organization more effective, and your commitment to transparency and collegiality with your funder.

Best Practices and Benchmarking

After you asses your organization's current operations and identify areas for improvement, one step you may want to take before developing a change plan is to identify best practices that may be appropriate for your organization to adopt. *Best practices* for the human services, which can apply to both management practices and service delivery models as discussed in the next section, can be defined as "identifying high quality practice interventions and promoting these as the 'best' or most appropriate responses in given situations in a particular field of practice" (Hughes & Wearing, 2016, p. 26). At an organizational level, this process is sometimes known as *benchmarking*, which became popular in the manufacturing sector but has since been adopted in other sectors, including HSOs.

Benchmarking basically involves comparing an organization's current process or practice, such a program model, an information system, or a human resources system such as performance appraisal, with a standard or best practice. In an excellent review of this practice for application to nonprofit organizations, Grobman (1999b) defined benchmarking as involving "collecting and analyzing data to determine how well a business process, policy, or program is performing, and whether modifying it based on the experience of similar organizations will improve outcomes." *Internal* benchmarking involves collecting and analyzing data on a process within your organization, such as how long an intake process takes. Total Quality Management or Continuous Quality Improvement methods covered in Chapter 14 can be useful for such analysis. *External* benchmarking involves collecting data from an organization or program similar to yours. For example, if you are operating a job skills development program, you could try to gather data from similar programs to see which have the best outcomes and which are the most efficient. As is the case with implementing an evidence-based program, you may need to make adaptations of the process or program to fit the uniquenesses of your own situation. For example, a job development program for adults may need to be adapted for use in a program for adolescents. There may also be cultural considerations in adapting a program for a particular immigrant or cultural group.

An Internet search using keywords or, for more academic sources, specifically using Google Scholar, might identify some promising models for your area of interest. Professional organizations and technical assistance organizations such as those mentioned in Chapter 10 on consulting can also be excellent sources. The California Evidence-Based Clearinghouse for Child Welfare (https://www. cebc4cw.org/) is an excellent resource for EBPs in child welfare. The federal Substance Abuse and Mental Health Services Administration site (https://www. samhsa.gov/multi-site-search?search_api_fulltext=evidence-based+) is a good resource for mental health and substance abuse programs.

If you have identified a need for change that involves improving or adding a new process or program to your organization, benchmarking to identify a relevant best practice can provide a great deal of structure for implementation of a change plan. On the other hand, your change goal may not have an obvious solution in terms of simply adapting something that works well elsewhere. In that case, your change process would involve a lot more analysis, brainstorming, and problem-solving to, with involvement of staff, create and implement the best solution.

Next, we look at implementing a very specific change goal: adopting an EBP for one of your programs. Treat what follows as a menu. Given your situation, you can consider which of these seems to be a good fit for your organization. I briefly describe the models to give you a sense of what each entails. All these should involve the use of consultants who are experts in their use.

Evidence-Based Practice Implementation and Implementation Science

To improve organizational capacity at a program level, implementing EBPs is a rapidly growing area of organizational change in HSOs. The broader term for this is *implementation science*, which "seeks to inform how to deliver evidence-based interventions, programs, and policies in real-world settings so their benefits can be realized and sustained" (Proctor & Bunger, 2020). Specifically, IS

(1) identifies quality gaps (assesses the degree to which services delivered in the real world are consistent with standards of care or EBPs); (2) explores implementation barriers and facilitators; (3) examines factors associated with implementation outcomes; and (4) tests implementation strategies (deliberate methods or interventions for integrating EBPs). (Bunger & Lengnick-Hall, 2019, p. 258)

A particularly rich literature is growing in this area, notably represented by an open access journal of that name. This literature often focuses only on implementation of EBPs, with less consideration of other aspects of organizational change.

Proctor (2014) made an important distinction between the EBP to be implemented and the "implementation strategies" used to put them into practice in an organizational setting. Based on her review, she suggested that implementation strategies should be "multifaceted or multilevel (if appropriate); robust or readily adaptable; feasible and acceptable to stakeholders; compelling, saleable, trialable, and observable; sustainable; and scalable," with budget impact also being a consideration.

Proctor's suggestions were reinforced by work of the California Evidence-Based Clearinghouse (Walsh, Rolls Reutz, & Williams, 2015), which discussed issues relating to EBP implementation failure that include *fidelity* (a model not being implemented as designed, *sustainment* (the model doesn't last long enough to see meaningful change), and *scale* (implementation is done on a scale too small to see impact in a service delivery system). Based on their experiences, their four key lessons are

- Careful planning is necessary, especially problem identification stage.
- It is essential that decisions on choosing a practice be data driven.
- Referral systems with other agencies need to be developed before implementation.
- Not only initial training but also ongoing support (e.g., through coaching and mentoring) will be needed.

Besides technical considerations in implementing a new service delivery method and the importance of organizational culture change, which is discussed later in the chapter, another consideration is the required organizational resources for implementation. In this regard, Proctor and Bunger (2020) have noted that "implementing new interventions often requires financial resources for consultation, supervision, and infrastructure changes."

The focus here is not on a particular EBP, but on processes to be used in implementing an EBP.

There is a growing number of models. I mention here a few that should have the most relevance for organizational change leaders.

EPIS: Exploration, Adoption/Preparation, Implementation, and Sustainment

Aarons, Hurlburt, and Horwitz (2011; see also Walsh et al., 2015) developed perhaps the most elaborate model for describing EBP implementation. Their model has four stages: *exploration, adoption decision/preparation, active implementation, and sustainment* (EPIS).

At each stage, they identified factors to consider. *Outer context* factors include the agency's sociopolitical context, funding, client advocacy, and interorganizational networks. *Inner context* factors include organizational characteristics such as knowledge and skills, readiness for change, culture, climate, leadership, innovativeness, fidelity monitoring, supportive coaching, and individual staff characteristics. This framework provides a structure for looking for challenges and opportunities during implementation. One important factor, embedding a culture that will be supportive of EBPs, was addressed in Chapter 15. What follows is a brief summary of the stages, with some detail on the relevant outer and inner context issues.

- At the *exploration stage*, leaders in the organization note a need for change that may come from, for example, a funding organization that requires the use of an EBP. Assessment of organizational capacity and readiness for the change begins at this stage and needs continuing attention through implementation.
  - Outer context factors to consider include relevant legislation and policies that might be driving change, including expectations of funders, and how funding can be acquired and maintained. Client advocacy issues or the organization's relationship with other organizations (including professional organizations or technical assistance providers) may be relevant here.
  - Inner context factors include the organization's readiness for this change, perceived need for the change, organizational culture and climate, and leadership. Some of these were covered in detail in Chapter 5.
- At the *adoption/preparation phase*, the organization's leaders decide to implement an EBP, giving particular attention to the allocation of necessary resources and creating a culture and climate "conducive to the adoption of service innovations and in taking ownership of the process of advancing a specific innovative practice" (Aarons, Hurlburt, & Horwitz, p. 11).
  - Outer context factors to be addressed at this stage may include client advocacy issues and interorganizational forces such as partnerships.
  - Inner context factors will be addressed by developing plans to deal with readiness and capacity issues using tactics such as those in the develop and maintain support step in Chapter 8. A force field analysis would be an example.
- The *active implementation* phase typically involves allocation of implementation roles for involved staff and intervention developers who offer expertise regarding the practice to be implemented, including ensuring fidelity to the model.
  - Outer context issues include acquiring funding and addressing expectations of key external stakeholders, collaborating with them and gaining their support.

- Inner context issues can be addressed through the development of the action system and change processes discussed in Chapter 7.
- After the practice has been implemented, continued use of it needs to be ensured through *sustainment* of the practice, including ensuring ongoing fidelity to the model and institutionalizing it in the organization's policies, practices, and culture.
  - External context issues include maintaining funding and ensuring adherence to any external policy directives to ensure that eternal stakeholders remain satisfied.
  - Internal context dynamics can be handled through institutionalization of the change, including through organizational culture, and ongoing monitoring and evaluation, making adjustments as needed.

These stages align well with the stages of generic organizational change described in Section 3 and will continue to be informed by the growing body of research on the specifics of IS.

LOCI: Leadership and Organizational Change for Implementation

Aarons and colleagues (2015) have also developed a training intervention, leadership and organizational change for implementation (LOCI), which actually includes aspects of organizational change, to train agency leaders to assist in implementing EBPs. They use the full-range leadership (FRL) model, which includes transformational and transformational leadership (covered here in Chapter 4), which is incorporated into a training program that includes

- a 360-degree assessment (including FRL, implementation leadership, and implementation climate),
- a 2-day group-based interactive and didactic training session with leadership development planning,
- weekly coaching,
- organizational strategy development with the first-level leader and organizational upper and middle management,
- one in-person group booster session, and
- graduation. (p. 3)

Notably, this model also uses an implementation climate scale (Egeland et al., 2019; Ehrhart, Aarons, & Farahnak, 2014) that has subscales to measure support for EBP implementation: a focus on EBP, educational support for EBP, recognition for EBP, rewards for EBP, selection for EBP, and selection for openness.

Using an elaborate research design, they concluded that LOCI "was judged to be feasible and acceptable and to have utility for developing leaders with the potential to support EBP implementation in organizations" (Aarons, Ehrhart, Farahnak, & Hurlburt, 2015, p. 8).

NIRN: National Implementation Research Network

Another prominent IS model was developed, after an extensive review of the literature, by Fixsen and colleagues at the National Implementation Research Network (NIRN) (https://nirn.fpg.unc.edu). This model includes four stages of implementation: exploration, installation, initial implementation, and full implementation. The model also gives special attention to *implementation drivers* (Bertram, Blasé, & Fixsen, 2015). *Competency drivers* include coaching, training, and staff selection. *Organization drivers* include systems level integration, facilitative administration, and a decision support data system. *Leadership drivers* attend to both technical (traditional management under conditions of certainty) and adaptive (complex conditions with less certainty and agreement) leadership.

Some of the activities at the four implementation stages are:

EXPLORATION
Exploration involves an assessment of assets and needs of the focus population, fit of the program or practice with those needs and assets and feasibility of implementation.

INSTALLATION
Installation involves building the infrastructure necessary to implement the program or practice, which includes building practitioner and organizational capacity.

INITIAL IMPLEMENTATION
Initial implementation includes the initial efforts of staff to use the program or practice, with attention to using data for continuous improvement.

FULL IMPLEMENTATION
Full implementation occurs as staff use the program or practice (National Implementation Research Network, 2020, p. 2).

CFIR: Consolidated Framework for Implementation Research

Damschroder et al. (2009) researched existing models and developed the consolidated framework for implementation research (CFIR) as "an overarching typology to promote implementation theory development and verification about what works where and why across multiple contexts." This model has five major domains: intervention characteristics, outer setting, inner setting, characteristics of the individuals involved, and the process of implementation. Each characteristic has a number of specific "constructs." Some of these are listed below.

Intervention characteristics:

A Source: The intervention is externally or internally developed
B Evidence strength and quality: Stakeholders' perceptions of the viability of the intervention
C Relative advantage: Stakeholders' perception of the advantage of implementing the intervention
D Adaptability: The degree to which an intervention can be adapted to meet local needs
E Trialability: The ability to test the intervention on a small scale in the organization
F Complexity: Perceived difficulty of implementation
G Design quality and packaging: Perceived excellence in how the intervention is presented
H Cost

Outer setting:

A Patient needs and resources: Patient needs are accurately known and prioritized
B Cosmopolitanism: The organization is networked with other external organizations
C Peer pressure: Mimetic or competitive pressure to implement an intervention
D External policy and incentives: Includes policy and external mandates

Inner setting:

A Structural characteristics: Age, maturity, and size of an organization
B Networks and communications: Formal and informal communications
C Culture: Norms, values, and basic assumptions of a given organization
D Implementation climate: Absorptive capacity and receptivity for change

Characteristics of individuals:

A Knowledge and beliefs about the intervention, familiarity with the intervention
B Self-efficacy: Individual belief in their own capabilities to achieve implementation
C Individual stage of change: Characterization of the phase an individual is in (e.g., enthusiastic)
D Individual identification with organization
E Other personal attributes, such as tolerance of ambiguity

Process:

A Planning: The degree to which plans are developed and their quality
B Engaging: Attracting and involving opinion leaders, formally appointed internal implementation leaders, champions, external change agents
C Executing: Carrying out or accomplishing the implementation according to plan
D Reflecting and evaluating: Feedback and debriefing

The CFIR can be used in two valuable ways: in initial assessment of preconditions (readiness and capacity) and as a checklist to ensure that all are addressed in an implementation plan or to identify ones that should be attended to for improvement.

These models outline factors to consider and processes to be used to implement EBPs. I hope some of the elements in these models look familiar, as they have been included in the model in Section 3. Some factors here are specific to implementing EBPs, but others are generic factors that would be relevant in assessment and implementation for any organizational change initiative.

Given the increasing popularity of EBPs, some words of caution are also worth mentioning. In a thoughtful critique of the "what works" movement, which promotes the use of EBPs, Mosley, Marwell, and Ybarra (2019) reminded us that we should not neglect the important principles of "valuing community-based knowledge; preserving staff autonomy and a pipeline for social work trained managers; and making program decisions with a thorough understanding of organizational and community context" (p. 326). They suggested these probing questions to ask when implementing or testing new intervention models:

1. Is the model of evaluation being used privileging certain kinds of interventions, organizations, and capacities?
2. Does building evidence about this particular intervention diminish investments in other, competing, interventions that remain untested?

3. Are you giving "bottom-up" solutions as much of a chance to demonstrate their efficacy as "top-down" solutions?
4. What are you doing to build capacity in community-based organizations serving unique populations or needs?

They also suggested the use of organizational learning principles (discussed in the next section) to guard against an uncritical adoption of an EBP, perhaps to appease a funding organization. And one of their conclusions reinforces the importance of participative decision-making: "Organizational change is more likely to succeed when the diverse strengths of managers, front-line workers, and communities themselves are seen as assets, rather than potential impediments, to incorporating evidence for improved practice" (p. 331).

In an interesting discussion of occasional "deimplementation" of an obsolete or now ineffective or culturally inappropriate practice, Pinto and Park (2019) offered another reminder about the importance of the inclusion of stakeholders, particularly community members, with particular attention to cultural compe-tence, cultural humility, and social justice as EBP adoption or deimplementation are being considered.

Plath (2017, p. 6) has offered another creative overlay to a generic change model for EBP implementation, suggesting a variation of the traditional practitioner-oriented perspective to an organizational approach, with these steps:

1. Define key practice questions for the organization.
2. Use internal and external resources to generate evidence that will inform answers to the practice questions.
3. Ensure that research evidence is appraised critically for strength and suita-bility to the practice context in the organization.
4. Engage staff with new knowledge and decision-making about effective programs and interventions to be offered by the organization.
5. Establish a systematic approach to monitoring service user outcomes and evaluating programs.

Next, we look at another growing area of organizational change in HSOs: cre-ating learning organizations and developing knowledge management systems that can help an organization manage regular change.

Learning Organizations and Knowledge Management

First popularized by Peter Senge's (1990) classic *The Fifth Discipline*, learning or-ganizations and organizational learning have received growing attention in the

HSO field. Recently organizational learning has been directly connected with organizational change, with Bess, Perkins, and McCown (2011) noting that a growing number of writers "argue that learning—individual and/or organizational—is an essential ingredient in the implementation of planned organizational change" (p. 37). This field originated in the general management literature and is receiving increasing attention in HSOs. More specifically, these principles are also relevant regarding implementing EBPs and, to some extent, other content areas of organizational change, such as improving organizational culture or diversity practices.

Definitions of these terms and the distinctions between them are still evolving. In the simplest terms, a learning organization is "an organization that is 'skilled at creating, acquiring, and transferring knowledge, and at modifying its behavior to reflect new knowledge and insights'" (Garvin, cited in Maynard, 2010, p. 309). The literature on organizational learning highlights two key components: a supportive organizational culture and structural supports for learning (Sabah & Cook-Craig, 2013). Here, culture includes

- beliefs about innovation (sharing and using new ideas),
- feelings of safety to try new ideas,
- commitment to setting goals and objectives, and
- leadership that supports and rewards new ideas.

Structural aspects include learning mechanisms such as

- collaboration—staff regularly meet to learn from each other and review program progress measures,
- planfullness—staff set measurable outcomes to be achieved and make sure plans and activities link to outcomes,
- diffusion—staff actively share their program successes with each other and with other related organizations, and
- infrastructure—organizational resources and time are set aside to promote learning.

Garvin (cited in Maynard, 2010) suggested these steps to create a learning organization:

1) fostering an environment that is conducive to learning by providing time for reflection, planning, and assessing current work systems;
2) "open up boundaries that simulate the exchange of ideas"; and
3) create activities that foster learning that are designed with "explicit learning goals in mind" and "requiring employees to wrestle with new knowledge and consider its implications." (p. 91)

DiBella and Nevis (1998) provided more detail in their steps. First, information is gathered about conditions outside the work unit, followed by an assessment of the identified gap between current and desired performance. Discussion about how key factors are defined and measured ensues, followed by discussion of creative new ideas. The organization must foster a climate of open communication and provide resources necessary for continuous education. Members must be open to the consideration of new and different ideas and methods, and leaders need to be personally and actively involved in maintaining the learning environment. Finally, a systems perspective (Senge, 1990) is necessary to recognize interdependence among units.

Maynard (2010) suggested that principles of learning organizations may facilitate the implementation of EBPs, noting some of the implementation challenges, including staff being concerned that risks outweigh benefits; not having a "a change oriented culture, information technology support, performance monitoring and outcome measurement, alignment with quality improvement strategies, organizational flexibility, recognition and rewards for staff, retention of staff and support of internal or external change agent" (p. 306); and a lack of training, commitment, support, or resources. Beyond EBP implementation, learning organizations are likely to enhance readiness and capacity for change of any kind.

A book by Austin and Hopkins (2004) was a major addition to the HSO literature on organizational learning, with its emphasis on the importance of the development of a learning culture in an organization, with particular attention paid to the role of supervisors. Austin and others (Austin, 2012) in a special issue of *Evidence-Based Social Work*) further advanced this method by reframing organizational learning in terms of creating knowledge-sharing systems to support EBP implementation and have staff use relevant research in their work. That issue included 12 case studies and useful guidelines for enhancing organizational learning and building knowledge management capacities.

Based on their analysis of 12 cases of knowledge-sharing systems, Lee and Austin (2012) found the following "intermediary outcomes" that contribute to the development of a knowledge-sharing system. These, with some examples, are

- *Transparency*: Encouraging more open and proactive communication, greater discussion of topics previously given limited public attention, and encouraging greater interpersonal interaction and contact
- *Self-assessment*: Assess the status of agency operations and services in order to find ways to improve effectiveness and efficiency of the organization
- *Dissemination and utilization of knowledge*: A staff role to provide for the interpretation and communication of data to share with staff, a knowledge management leadership team, a senior management position to build structures and facilitate processes in support of knowledge management

Setting up systems for organizational learning and knowledge management is in itself an organizational change, and it also creates systems that make it easier to identify future organizational change opportunities. This is also a significant culture change of an organization, itself a commonly identified organizational change need.

Summary

We began this chapter with a discussion of capacity building in HSOs. Capacity building has been a significant field of practice for nonprofit organizations, with many training and consulting organizations and some funding organizations helping HSOs improve their operations. Best practices and benchmarking are tools that can be used at the level of the entire organization or for specific service delivery practices to search for models that can be adapted to another organization.

The notion of EBP is becoming increasingly common in HSOs, and I discussed it briefly here as an arena for organizational change. IS has emerged as a dynamic field that is studying the implementation of EBPs. We looked at several formal EBP models and the field of IS generally.

The concept of learning organizations has also become increasingly better known in HSOs and actually represents an arena of organizational change that can help organizations develop ongoing methods for continuous improvement.

18
Change Models for Human Service Organizations

> Organizations can motivate and inspire us, or they can demoralize and disappoint us. In the same way, organizations that provide human services affect the behavior, functioning, and being of those who are served.
>
> —Hemmelgarn and Glisson (*Building Cultures and Climates for Effective Human Services*, 2018, p. 1)

Previous chapters covered generic change processes that originated for use in for-profit organizations, but that have obvious uses in nonprofit and governmental human service organizations (HSOs). This chapter will addresses processes and models that have unique relevance for HSOs. I start with a discussion of four change models that are unique to HSOs: the ARC (availability, responsiveness, and continuity) and sanctuary models, getting to outcomes, and design team. They are presented without a lot of detail, but I hope with enough detail for you to understand their basic elements so you can pursue them in more detail if they may have relevance for your organizational situation. After that, I discuss a growing field—social innovation and intrapraneurship—which can be seen as representing organizational change methods. We then look at a more problem-based change process: cutback management.

I hope you'll see how aspects of these models align with the model covered in Section 3. In fact, I made a point to include some tactics, such as addressing team development and conflict management from the ARC model, into my generic model. The other models discussed here may be of particular interest to a change leader depending on the situation being faced.

Change Models for HSOs

There must be a countless number of "official" change models, from books for the generic management audience to models used by individual consultants. My main criteria for selecting the ones I cover here is that they apply to HSOs

Organizational Change for the Human Services. Thomas Packard, Oxford University Press. © Oxford University Press 2021. DOI: 10.1093/oso/9780197549995.003.0019

specifically, and they have been covered in the academic literature. That suggests that they have been subjected to blind peer review by people not affiliated with that particular model and, to the extent that they have been evaluated, have shown their value and relevance to a broader audience. The level of evidence for such models can range from a single case study to multiple randomized control trials and meta-analyses. Most of those discussed here are closer to the randomized control trial end, but not there yet.

These would all require the use of a consultant with knowledge and skills for the particular method. They are described here mainly to give you an overview of the methods to see which look promising for your situation. They all offer processes and principles that might be relevant on other organizational change initiatives.

The ARC Model

The ARC organizational intervention model is a "team-based, participatory, phased process designed to improve organizational culture and climate in mental health and social service organizations, support innovation, and remove barriers to effective service" (Glisson & Williams, 2015, p. 512). It is an elaborate, precisely developed model with a notable and growing evidence base (Hemmelgarn & Glisson, 2018). The model has supporting manuals and a facilitator's guide and definitely requires a qualified consultant to aid with its use.

It emphasizes the importance of organizational social context (OSC; covered in more detail in Chapter 16 as aspects of organizational culture change). In the ARC model, OSC includes culture, climate, and work attitudes.

The key components of the model are three overall strategies. The first strategy includes the following five principles:

- be mission-driven not rule-driven, ensuring that all actions and decisions contribute to clients' well-being;
- be results-oriented not process-oriented, measuring success by how much client well-being improves;
- be improvement-directed not status quo–directed, continually working to be more effective in improving clients' well-being;
- be participation-based not authority-based, ensuring that policy and practice decisions that affect client well-being involve everyone with a stake in the decision; and
- be relationship-centered not individual-centered, focusing on networks of relationships that affect services and clients' well-being. (Glisson & Williams, 2015, p. 513)

The second strategy includes 12 "organizational component tools" to address barriers to effective services (Hemmelgarn & Glisson, 2018, Chap. 7):

1. *leadership development* to help leaders articulate a vision of high performance
2. *personal relationships* among team members to improve organizational culture and climate
3. *network development* to promote boundary spanning within parts of the organization and with external stakeholders
4. *team building* to facilitate participation and information sharing among staff
5. *information and training* on the ARC model and other aspects of best practices
6. *feedback* about program performance and outcomes to identify needs for change
7. *participatory decision-making* to support innovation and input from staff members
8. *conflict management* training to address inevitable conflicts resulting from the change
9. *goal setting*, using feedback from client assessments to set performance criteria
10. *continuous improvement* technique to facilitate innovation
11. *job redesign* to eliminate service barriers and improve outcomes for clients
12. *stabilization* of innovations to ensure that they continue

The ARC model has four phases: exploration, adoption, implementation, and sustainment, with the following components:

Collaboration:
    Forming relationships between the ARC specialist and all levels of staff
    Providing information and expectations about staff roles and responsibilities
    Network development among key stakeholders

Participation:
    Building teamwork and openness to change
    Using meeting and planning tools to increase effectiveness
    Developing team members knowledge and skills for participatory decision-making and problem-solving

Innovation:
    Address service barriers
    Implement new treatment models
    Ongoing process of improvement

The third strategy is shared mental models to support service innovation and service improvement (Hemmelgarn & Glisson, 2018, Chap. 8). Mental models are deeply held beliefs and mindsets about how organizations operate. Staff are encouraged to share and examine their mental models in order to develop new assumptions, such as being open to change and feeling psychological safety to speak up.

Model implementation roles include an ARC specialist (an external consultant), an ARC liaison (filling the internal champion role), an executive leadership team, an organizational action team, and front-line teams.

The Sanctuary Model

The sanctuary model (Esaki et al., 2013) is a treatment model as well as another model of organizational change in HSOs. It includes training, skill development through technical assistance and consultation, and the use of tools, including fidelity checklists and manuals.

The conceptual model has the following inputs:

Assessment:
- Assessment of organizational readiness for the sanctuary model (best practices pretraining)
- Certification/recertification (assessment for adherence to standards)

Training:
- 5-day leadership
- Core team
- General staff
- Clients/families
- Stakeholders
- New hire orientation
- Boosters (refreshers of model materials)

Skill Building:
- On-site technical assistance
- Phone technical assistance
- Implementation manuals
- Practice-based learning materials
  - Sanctuary network days (annual best practice conferences)

Tools:
- Sanctuary model toolkit (10 tools)
  - Fidelity checklists
- Psychoeducation training manuals

The model describes activities at the individual, interpersonal, organizational, and community levels that lead to a range of outcomes, including an increased sense of physical and psychological safety, improved treatment outcomes for clients, improved stress management by staff, improved staff recruitment and retention, and staff and client satisfaction.

There is a growing literature on the use of this model (e.g., Elwyn, Esaki, & Smith, 2017; Purtle, 2020).

Getting to Outcomes

The getting to outcomes model was designed to help public child welfare systems that wanted to adopt evidence-based practices (EBPs) such as solution-based casework (Barbee, Christensen, Antle, Wandersman, & Cahn, 2011). It is also designed to be used to implement other best practices. The framework uses a "10 step accountability approach that we have applied to the challenges a child welfare system faces when adopting a practice model into their system" (Barbee et al., 2011, p. 624). The steps are as follows:

1) Identifying needs and resources,
2) Setting goals to meet the identified needs,
3) Determining what science-based, evidence-based (EBP) or evidence-informed practices or casework practice models exist to meet the needs,
4) Assessing actions that need to be taken to ensure that the EBP fits the organizational or community context,
5) Assessing what organizational capacities are needed to implement the practice or program,
6) Creating and implementing a plan to develop organizational capacities in the current organizational and environmental context (including training on the new model, financial resources, information systems, and caseload sizes),
7) Conducting a process evaluation to determine if the program is being implemented with fidelity,
8) Conducting an outcome evaluation to determine if the program is working and producing the desired outcomes,
9) Determining, through a continuous quality improvement (CQI) process, how the program can be improved and
10) Taking steps to ensure sustainability of the program (Barbee et al., 2011, p. 625)

This model is especially valuable in addressing barriers or challenges regarding outcomes measurement by helping an HSO focus its program design, build staff skills in evaluation, define outcome measures, and assess how organizational processes are linked to outcomes (Acosta & Chinman, 2011).

Design Team

The design team model, a facilitated, participatory process for identifying and solving agency problems, has been used in child welfare agencies. The design team intervention intends to

> enhance the quality of the workforce, specifically through improved job satisfaction and reduced turnover. The intervention introduced members of the agency to the participatory design team model in which all "levels" of the agency identified and prioritized issues, and were represented in the solution and implementation of the decision-making processes. (Claiborne, Auerbach, Lawrence, McGowan, & Lawson, 2014, pp. 3–4)

The model includes seven steps (Strolin-Goltzman et al., 2009, p. 154):

(1) Clearly identifying the problem and/or need
(2) Assessing causes of problem
(3) Evaluating its effects on retention and workforce stability
(4) Pondering the ideal situation
(5) Discussing solutions already in place
(6) Developing new feasible solutions
(7) Identifying specific action steps that team members had to complete prior to the next meeting

According to Lawrence, Claiborne, Zeitlin, and Auerbach (2016), during the intervention, organizations identify a change initiative related to organizational function rather than a change in service model or practice approach, and a design team of employees works with an external facilitator to design and implement the change initiative. As a team of employees is empowered to propose and implement a change to how the organization functions, the design team intervention, in theory, may increase organizational change (p. 41).

Innovation and Intrapraneurship

This section deserves special attention for several reasons. First, it treats innovation and intrapraneurship as opportunities for the use of organizational change

tactics and methods. Also, it suggests that any HSO administrator would benefit from building innovation and intrapraneurship into one's regular thinking.
Finally, it is an excellent example of leading an organizational culture change to
build these into the daily life of the organization.

Intrapraneurship derives, of course, from the more common practice of entrepreneurship, which in recent years has become much more common in the social
sector, usually referred to as social entrepreneurship. It has been most prominent
in international nongovernmental organizations (which can be either nonprofit
or for profit) that provide a wide range of economic development, community
development, environmental, and other consultation and technical assistance
services to countries around the world.

A recent book (Berzin & Camarena, 2018) provided a detailed model to enable an organization to create innovations and an organizational culture that
has innovation built into it. It has many valuable and useful activities and assessment tools to enable full use of the model and its related principles. Their
book addresses nonprofit organizations, but their model could be used in
other HSOs as well. These definitions provide both context and focus for our
discussion here:

- *Innovation* is a process, method, product, or outcome that is new and creates
  an improvement.
- *Social innovation* is an umbrella term that encompasses multiple pathways
  and processes that address the root causes of social injustices. The solutions
  are more effective, efficient, and/or sustainable—socially, economically, and
  environmentally—than previous solutions and as a result of collaboration
  with diverse stakeholders.
- *Social entrepreneurship* at its heart is formed by an entrepreneur (typically
  an individual or small group) starting a business or organization for social
  purposes. While social entrepreneurship has taken on a broader definition
  about transformative solutions to social problems using entrepreneurial
  principles (including risk-taking, innovative approaches, change orientation, and the sustainable business model) it most typically is portrayed as
  starting of forming something new.
- *Social intrapreneurship* is the use of entrepreneurial principles *within existing organization or institution* to solve social problems. (p. 6, italics in
  original)

There is obviously a lot packed into these definitions. To keep our focus on organizational change, I need to provide here only their basic model for social
innovation within an HSO. Change leaders engaging in social innovation can

be seen as intrapreneurs at whatever level of the organizational hierarchy they occupy.

Berzin and Camarena (2018) listed their "right conditions for innovation." I see these as preconditions. To the extent that they do not exist in your organization, developing them would be a good initial change activity. They are

- People
  - Leaders who can set the context and establish a culture that embraces innovation
  - Powerful teams, with members using their unique capacities and also ensuring a variety of perspectives
  - Meaningful partners such as collaborators from other organizations
- Tools
  - A variety of communication tools, including nonverbals such as drawings, photos, or videos
  - Design thinking—a powerful new concept that essentially includes principles such as a "human-centered approach (taking the user's perspective), visual activities, and prototyping to solve complex problems"
  - Extensive use of information and communication technologies
- Mindset
  - A "beginner's mindset," enabling staff to always be learning and seeing things in new ways
  - Maintaining a focus on social problems and social justice
  - Empathy, especially regarding the marginalized groups that many HSOs serve
  - A willingness to tolerate failure
  - The ability to plan with purpose

Their model has four steps: initiate, investigate, innovate, and integrate.

Initiate

The initiate step basically establishes the preconditions, especially creating a culture of innovation and preparing for the forming and training of "innovation teams" (an example of the generic action teams in Chapter 7). Change leaders can mobilize innovators by talking about innovation, holding workshops, showing executive commitment, and setting goals and expectations. Their book (Berzin & Camarena, 2018) has a very useful innovation audit to assess and build an innovation culture.

Investigate

With training of staff and the formation of innovation teams, some opportunities for innovation may have already emerged. Teams can look for areas needing improvement and begin problem analysis, including identifying criteria for a good solution (e.g., it is practical, it addresses root causes) and then using brainstorming and maybe using a SWOT analysis (examining organizational strengths, weaknesses, opportunities, and threats), defining an ideal future, researching best practices, interviewing stakeholders, holding focus groups, or conducting a staff survey. Findings can be synthesized, refining the problem if needed, and shared, especially with anyone who needs to be brought on board to support the innovation process. At this point team members should also take time to question their assumptions.

Innovate

At the innovate stage, teams can "ideate" possible solutions, again using brainstorming, picking the best ideas from best practices or ideas developed by the team. Solutions—an "alpha prototype"—can be tested with stakeholders and critiqued. Based on feedback, a "beta prototype" (small scale, cheap, and functional) can be tested and redesigned as needed. When the idea is ready, it can be taken to the organization's decision-makers for approval to implement. Berzin and Camarena (2018) gave an example of a homeless shelter that proposed a 2-month training for residents, which could lead to a social enterprise to sell goods to the public.

Integrate

In the integrate step, full implementation of the innovation can use traditional project management tools such as logic models, Gantt charts, and a budget, but it should also "continue to be fun, visual, and participatory" (p. 142). As many stakeholders as possible should be involved. A formative evaluation can be used to track implementation and make adjustments as needed, and, later, an outcome evaluation can be used to assess impact on the original problem. It should be formalized (or institutionalized, to use the term in our model) through agency policies, procedures, and budgets. If appropriate, the innovation can be "scaled" to other programs or settings. Successes can then enhance the emerging innovation culture.

This summary of course does not do full justice to the model, but I hope it gives you a sense of its basic design and its possibilities for organizational improvements. In addition to their excellent book, the Center for Social Innovation at Boston College (Berzin, Dearing, Mathews, & Choi, & Pitt-Catsouphes, 2018; also at http://center4si.com/) builds innovation capacity for agencies through research, training, and consultation. Another recent book (Nandan, Bent-Goodley, & Mandayam, 2019) includes related detail on social enterprise, social innovation, social value creation, and design thinking.

Cutback Management

Cutback management, in its simplest terms, involves "managing" cuts in funding to ensure that expenses are no greater than revenues. It is more complicated than that, of course. It can be framed in varying ways, as the result of making immediate cuts in a budget because a significant deficit has been discovered or because of a significant drop in funding from grants, contracts, donations, or other sources. It is not necessarily an official change method in the sense that the other models in this chapter are, but it is an important subject regarding organizational change. A technique of cutback management, downsizing, was mentioned in Chapter 14 in a discussion of business process reengineering.

Administrators and other staff hope, of course, that they will never be confronted with funding cuts so severe that formal cutback management must be used. Good administrative practice, including ongoing, strategic management that includes monitoring predictions of environmental trends and effective financial management systems, including rigorous cost analysis, maintaining prudent reserves, attention to maintaining staff skills and morale; and strong relationships with external stakeholders, including boards and funders, may help an agency be as well prepared as possible for severe funding cuts.

Cutback management writing has focused mainly on governmental organizations, but there has been some attention to it for nonprofit organizations.

One recent framework (Schmidt, Groeneveld, & Van de Walle, 2017) uses the concepts of context, content, process, outcomes, and leadership. This model suggests that organizational leadership plays a key role in managing the context (the environment that is requiring cutbacks) and the process and content of the changes, leading to desired or undesired outcomes in terms of balanced budgets, at least adequate performance and morale or their opposites. Process and content here have the same meanings as used in our organizational change process. Content is what people usually think of first, so I briefly address that before moving on to processes, which are at least equally important for change leaders to attend to.

Cutbacks: Content

Angelica and Hyman (1997), in an older but still relevant book for nonprofit organizations, outlined a thoughtful process for addressing cutback challenges. They suggested starting with an assessment of the organization's mission, values, competencies, and visions and an assessment of the agency's community conditions to use as criteria to assess possible strategies. Decisions need to be made about which staff, board members, and community members should be involved. After the problem is clearly defined and criteria for a successful outcome (e.g., alignment with mission vision, and values, financial parameters, staffing and services) are determined, brainstorming of possible strategies can be done. The authors grouped cutback strategies for consideration into three categories: financial strategies, including cost-cutting and revenue increases; structural strategies, such as modifying the organization's mission, structure, or culture; and engagement strategies, such as becoming more involved with community. Strategies are then selected based on identified criteria, and action planning can begin.

In the for-profit sector, a related concept is downsizing, later euphemistically called "right-sizing."

Another important aspect of criteria for cutback decisions is the use of ethics principles. In an old but still relevant article, Reisch and Taylor (1983) listed the following guidelines for cutback decision-making from a distributive justice perspective:

1. Programs that benefit the least well-off should be retained
2. Provide services based on need, not cost benefit
3. Use a unitary, as opposed to a two-tiered system in which the least advantaged receive lower quality services
4. Use distributive justice rather than a strictly utilitarian approach when considering trade-offs between programs
5. Avoid cutting or reducing programs for the least powerful
6. Administrators should be politically active in advocating for socially just programs and policies

More recently, the simple term *cost-cutting* is being used. As a cautionary note, a recent international study by the McKinsey consulting firm found that most cost-cutting efforts failed, noting that "governments that make big budget cuts simply to 'force' efficiency improvements are less likely to deliver and sustain the intended cost reductions" (Allas, Dillon, & Gupta, 2018, p. 1). On the other hand, they found that successful efforts had assigned sufficient staff to the effort, relied on data and advanced analytics, and used cost savings to further other reforms.

Whereas cutback management in the nonprofit and government sectors is typically driven by funding cuts by governmental or other funding sources, downsizing can also be based on a company's change in strategy or a changing market. Cummings and Worley, in their well-regarded book on organization development and change (2015, pp. 359–361) included downsizing in their Restructuring Organizations chapter. They listed three areas of downsizing tactics:

- *workforce reduction*: attrition, transfers, outplacement, retirement incentives, buyout packages, and layoffs
- *organization redesign*: eliminate functions, merge units, eliminate layers, eliminate products, redesign tasks
- *systemic redesign*: change responsibility, involve all constituents, foster continuous improvement and innovation, simplification, downsizing as a way of life

Workforce reduction is traditional cutback management, while organization redesign and systemic redesign are basically organizational change, such as culture change to foster continuous improvement and innovation. These are mostly process strategies, which I cover next. Of course, I would suggest that cutback management, if necessary, be conceptualized as organizational change, and therefore that generic tactic and methods should be used as needed.

Cutbacks: Processes

In a study of nine county human service agencies in Southern California, colleagues and I (Packard, Patti, Daly, Tucker-Tatlow, & Farrell, 2008) found that content changes such as transfers of staff were typically embedded in eight larger management strategies or themes: the processes of change. Our major themes are listed here.

Collaborative Leadership: Directors demonstrated effective leadership through behaviors encompassing collaboration rather than competition and compassion rather than judgmental attitudes. Examples included collaborating with peers within and outside the agency to advocate for their agency's needs and expressing confidence in the leadership abilities and efforts of their staff. Other useful behaviors included displaying enthusiasm and optimism and creating a problem-solving climate. In several agencies, department heads formed strong collaborations with one another and presented information to the county leadership on how to make cuts that would have the least impact on services while maximizing state and federal fund drawdowns.

To advocate for their agency's needs, many directors reported that it was essential to present their cases for avoiding or minimizing cuts to the county administrative officers (CAOs) and the board of supervisors in areas such as mandated matches, the extent to which county general funds are used to leverage state and federal revenue, and the consequences of various funding scenarios. Alliances with directors of other county agencies, for example, probation and public health, served to build credibility with CAOs and supervisors and strengthen relations with colleagues.

A "Big Picture" Approach: Leadership was also reflected when directors and deputies tended to think and act in a system-wide context. The big picture approach was manifested through shifting and sharing of employees across programs, leveraging categorical funds in collaboratives to serve shared clients across departments, and pursuing cross-agency collaborations in service delivery. In many cases, funding allocations reflected a broader based view of the team, as opposed to the individual worker, and the region as a whole, rather than one office. This enabled work to be more effectively distributed, with more proactive planning. Cross-training staff and transferring them across programs also helped mitigate staff reduction. In cases where it did not look likely that a staff member would return from a long-term leave of absence, agencies brought on staff members who had lost their positions in other programs.

Maintaining Focus Through Strategic Planning: Alliances with directors and community stakeholders were supported when new initiatives were aligned with county strategic goals. Many counties reported that existing strategic plans and the mission-critical services defined therein were useful in prioritizing programs. Budget decisions were made based on compatibility with the agency's mission-critical services or higher priority functions, and low-value activities were, in many cases, eliminated. This is consistent with Cummings and Worley's (2015) recommendation that downsizing should be focused on achieving strategic objectives.

Developing Relationships With Key Constituencies: Agency directors and staff spent much of their time communicating with and working with community stakeholders and informing policymakers of the likely effects of cuts in particular programs. Tactics included outreach to get the informed perspective of community stakeholders in creating budget strategies and sharing information and exchanging ideas about alternatives for dealing with reductions. These helped foster alliances, deepening community awareness and securing future support for clients who might go underserved without community involvement. Alerting all constituencies as early as possible about the potential magnitude of the cuts and their implications was especially important.

Communication With Staff: The agencies devoted extensive energy to keeping employees informed of the budget situation and actions that were being taken. Most counties reported using comprehensive communication strategies to build staff understanding, acceptance, and support of budget cuts. Communicating how and why budget decisions were made was important to demystify the decision processes, counteract unfounded rumors, and show concern for staff and clients. Being sensitive to staff needs made a significant difference in how smoothly adjustments occurred. Communication was most effective when it consistently involved all parties who were impacted, used a variety of venues and channels, and was mindful of staff stress and burnout. Executives shared budget development principles with managers and lower level staff to show how and why budget decisions were made. Conveying to staff the efforts that were made to protect jobs and help with transitions to other jobs was important to staff morale and to management–labor relations. Most directors and managers were proactive in convening staff in forums for the sharing of information and problem-solving. These sometimes served as opportunities for employees to engage in problem-solving discussions on streamlining work processes, time management, and reorganizations. Cummings and Worley (2015) noted the importance of communicating frequently with staff and also suggested reminding staff that downsizing is part of a plan to improve organizational performance.

Preserving Staff Capacity: Efforts to retain staff expertise and minimize disruptions were a high priority for executives. Special efforts to help workers transition to other jobs, such as hosting job fairs, employee option meetings, and counseling sessions, were important ways of showing commitment to employees. Directors cited a variety of recognition programs, both formal and informal. Ongoing recognition programs for exemplary staff performance were important for morale and contributed to a culture that values achievement. Expressions of concern for staff who were laid off, such as presenting layoff notices in person rather than through the mail, were not only important to those impacted but also often had positive symbolic value to others who remained. Modeling compassion toward surviving employees during budget crises made it easier for them to focus on maintaining the level of services provided to clients.

Cummings and Worley (2015) offered several related suggestions regarding effects on staff. For survivors, recognize their stress over workload changes, possible additional tasks, and survivor guilt and focus on future goals and visions and their connections with these. For those who leave, consider outplacement, severance packages, other counseling, and support for job searches.

Decentralizing Decision-Making: A notable aspect of cutback management was the involvement of staff in creating solutions, getting lower level employees involved in decision-making regarding program priorities and improving program efficiencies. In several counties, decentralized fiscal management was seen as particularly useful. For example, several departments directed division managers to work with stakeholders to develop their funding priorities. This theme aligns with the use of participative strategies described in Chapter 4. Typically, county leaders set the targets for budget cuts, but then delegated to department heads the discretion regarding where the cuts should occur. Directors would then initiate workgroups consisting, in some cases, of program staff, which would propose various percentage reduction scenarios to the directors for approval.

Managers in this study tended to favor decentralized decision-making for several reasons. First, those who are knowledgeable about the programs and closest to the client contributed significant value to an informed decision-making process. Second, program staff recommended cuts that would have the least impact on service delivery. Finally, participation at the program level built support for difficult budget decisions. One county solicited input from labor management committees, comprising representatives from organized labor unions and agency management, to identify potential areas to cut. Staff were also presented with a survey asking them how resources could be shifted to manage budget cuts more effectively. Taking decentralized decision-making to the community level, one county built community support by involving community stakeholders in developing resource allocation recommendations for the board of supervisors through a series of 14 facilitated meetings using consensus decision-making.

Notably, in her summary of over 20 years of research on empowerment, Spreitzer (2008) concluded that "empowerment has also been shown to be particularly important to preserve the hope and attachment of survivors during times of organizational downsizing" and that empowerment helps staff adapt "where they need to be more proactive in making sense of the situation and determining the appropriate course of action" (p. 60).

One possible ethical dilemma is worth mentioning here. I have mentioned several times the value of participative decision-making, in our study here described in terms of decentralized decision-making. If cutback brainstorming begins to look at eliminating programs or positions, having employees make recommendations about which staff or units should get eliminated puts them in a jam that they should not have to deal with. I have talked to my students about administrators not having employees make self-inflicted wounds, and they should not be expected to suggest the layoffs of colleagues. In our study, positions were eliminated, but efforts were taken to minimize the effects. In addition to outplacement services, some agencies arranged part-time scheduling, voluntary work furloughs, and counseling sessions for supervisors who had to lay off staff. In at least one county, reductions were made in higher level staff to maintain front-line staff. Some other options for dealing with layoffs were covered in the reengineering section of Chapter 15. Managing the tensions of employee participation and the actual recommendation of position cuts should be handled very thoughtfully.

Using Data to Guide Decisions: Both executive and program managers relied heavily on information and data analysis to inform their decisions. Agencies used their staff in both finance and program areas to clearly describe programs and administrative processes to guide analysis and decision making. One manager noted that it was especially useful to train program staff on fiscal processes and to make fiscal staff more aware of program issues to facilitate their working together. Directors relied on a variety of data sources, such as worker-to-client ratios, time study results, and work participation rates, to better understand how funding cuts would impact service delivery. These data were useful later as well. When directors presented their cases regarding budgets to their chief administrative officers and elected officials, they were able to use these data to document anticipated impacts of cuts and to support their decisions to continue or cut programs based on their documented effectiveness.

In a similar study of 11 California county HSOs located in the San Francisco Bay area, Graaf, Hengeveld-Bidmon, Carnochan, Radu, and Austin (2016) identified several factors that helped minimize the impacts of budget cuts. Contextual factors or preconditions were important:

Supportive boards and chief administrative officers increased the ability of leaders to develop innovative revenue-generating solutions, to create new internal and external partnerships that expanded services with little or no increase in costs, and to engage in collaborative planning with their own staff and other organizations. The hands-off relationships that these boards developed over time with their HSO leadership, which implicitly communicated respect and trust, may provide a model of leadership that HSO managers channel to empower their own staff to find new ways to generate revenue or reduce program costs. Further, empowering boards and collaborative unions may have allowed these HSO leaders to innovate with their staff, plan ahead more carefully, and create new partnerships by minimizing approval processes and reducing barriers to change (Graaf et al., 2016, p. 166).

Formal guiding principles, typically mission related, such as preserving services to children and families, preserving direct service positions, maintaining quality, increasing efficiency, and staff morale were used.

Financial models and time studies were used to assess various budget reduction scenarios. Restructuring (eliminating or reformulating programs, reducing infrastructure; covered here in Chapter 14) was the most common strategy for budget reductions. New and reconfigured partnerships with community organizations were used to maintain services with less funding. Partnerships with other county divisions were used, for example, to transfer programs to another division. As might be expected, reducing or eliminating spending was frequently used.

In another study focusing on organizational communications during cutbacks, Graaf, Hengeveld-Bidmon, Carnochan, Salomone, and Austin (2018) noted the importance of first-line supervisors in providing support to their staff and all leaders demonstrating respect, support, empathy and communicate good and bad news in a timely manner.

One final overriding observation is worth noting. Consistent with the Graaf et al. (2016) findings regarding preconditions, we observed in the agencies we studied some themes related to organizational preconditions that seemed to be important. These organizations generally had existing strategic plans, at both the county and agency level, and they were clearly used to guide decision-making regarding cutbacks. Second, the agency executives appeared to be positively regarded by their own staff as leaders with a history of collaborative behavior seemed to have a positive effect on management and staff morale, lessening the negative impacts of inevitable budget cuts. A major study of downsizing (Mishra, Mishra, & Spreitzer, 2009, also mentioned below) found that survivors who had high trust in their management and felt empowered by management were more optimistic and willing to actively engage in continued problem-solving.

In looking beyond addressing cutback conditions, many of these cutback management strategies, including positive and visionary leadership, ongoing communication with staff and outside stakeholders, strategic management, zero-based budgeting, performance-based management, collaboration, and searching for new revenues, can be seen as useful at any time, not just when budget stress is the greatest. In that sense, organizations that have these characteristics and capabilities can be expected to do well on an ongoing basis. Even when times are good, these strategies can help the organization get ready for the next challenging budget cycle.

In addition to all the negative effects of downsizing on staff, clients, and communities, organization development writers Cummings and Worley (2015, p. 363) concluded that, "The empirical research on downsizing is mostly negative," including "negative productivity and employee consequences," and also negative results on financial performance. "One survey of 1,005 companies that used downsizing to reduce costs reported that fewer than half of the firms actually met cost targets." These findings need to be interpreted cautiously: Some human resources staff surveyed may have been inclined to see downsizing as negative, some companies may have been poorly managed to begin with, and downsizing may have been poorly done. For example, some studies found that when formal organizational change methods are used, there have been more positive results for individuals and the organization.

To end this section on a more positive note, I share some of the findings of researchers who studied downsizing in a range of sectors for 20 years (Mishra et al., 2009). They reported three success factors that are important to successful downsizing:

- Organizations must become more flexible (e.g., cross training staff, giving managers assignments in other departments).
- They must become more innovative and creative (trust and empowerment are critical here, and "managers must instill hope and craft a credible vision of the future," with hopeful messages that are "neither glib nor naïve but incorporate present realities," such as the need to work harder in the short term (p. 40).
- They must improve their communications with stakeholders who are increasingly skeptical of downsizing efforts (being transparent and giving consistent information to all stakeholders; having in-person, two-way communication as much as possible).

The authors also mentioned the importance of training and empowering middle managers and supervisors *before* crises such as downsizing occur, so that they have leadership skills that will be especially valuable in difficult times.

Summary

The four organizational change models discussed here that are specific to HSOs would typically require expert consultants. Innovation and intrapreneurship are also important as organizational change models but would typically not require the use of consultants. These were all presented as brief overviews: a menu of options for you to explore and dig deeper if they seem appropriate for your situations.

Because the funding environments of HSOs have been so unstable in recent years, I thought it would be helpful to review some research on how HSOs can prepare for and manage major funding cuts. This is an example of organizational change that is dictated by outside forces.

The change model covered in Section 3 includes many aspects of these approaches, and some of the tactics in the model could actually be used in concert with any of them.

19

Staff-Initiated Organizational Change

> Ask forgiveness, not permission.
> —Mark Homan (*Promoting Community Change*, 2016, p. 515)

One final method of organizational change, very different from others, warrants attention. Often, employees at the front-line staff level see a need or opportunity for change before administrators do. Change strategies that are initiated by lower level employees have been called "change from below" (Brager & Holloway, 1978) or "change from within" (Resnick, 1978; Resnick & Patti, 1980). I use here the term used by Holloway (1987), which offers a fairly precise description of the approach: *staff-initiated organizational change* (SIOC). A good definition of this process was originally offered by Resnick (1978) as

> a series of activities carried out by lower or middle-echelon staff in human ser-
> vice organizations to modify or alter organizational conditions, policy, pro-
> gram, or procedures for the ultimate improvement of service to clients. The
> activities engaged in are legitimized by professional purposes as well as by or-
> ganizational norms. (p. 30)

SIOC Models

While this is primarily focused on front-line staff, note that the definition also includes "middle-echelon" staff. So, you can look at this as a form of upward influence, from whatever level you are located in the hierarchy. Related to this, the influence skills mentioned in Chapter 3 regarding you as a change leader can be used by someone using SIOC.

In this chapter, then, "you" typically refers to you as a lower level staff person wanting to create change upward. Nevertheless, I encourage managers and executives to read this chapter as well so you will be prepared if any of your staff seem to want to present, or do present, ideas for organizational change. If this happens, you might even suggest elements of this model for them to use. Of course, I hope you will use a participative leadership style in letting them come up with creative ideas, within the minimum critical specifications that I discussed in

Organizational Change for the Human Services. Thomas Packard, Oxford University Press. © Oxford University Press
2021. DOI: 10.1093/oso/9780197549995.003.0020

Chapter 15. Also, if you as a change leader have established a culture of employee involvement and empowerment and mechanisms for ongoing organizational learning, dynamics in this process will seem appropriate and even normal.

After some publications in the 1970s and 1980s and some recent attention by Hyde and others, this model has been rarely discussed in the professional literature. And, as noted in some of that literature, there is not much of an empirical basis for these principles. Most of the writing was based on theory, with occasional reference to case studies (M. Cohen & Hyde, 2014a). This is admittedly a more difficult change method to be studied than more popular ones such as organization development, partly because there is not yet an agreed-on model to test, and there are challenges in finding examples of its use for more detailed research. So, what is presented here should be considered to be based on a relatively low level of evidence and used with that in mind. On the other hand, in addition to the theoretical underpinnings of this work, there is notable consistency across sources about key steps and principles to use for this type of change.

Hyde (2018) used the term *low-powered actors*—"organizational members with relatively little formal authority but who nonetheless influence organizational processes and outcomes in ways disproportionate to their official role" (2018, p. 53)—to describe this change agent role. One of her studies of low-power actors examined applications of "multicultural organizational development" ("a means of becoming more culturally responsive to the client/constituent base and of diversifying the workforce"; 2018, p. 54) initiatives. In most of the cases, the change results were seen as modest, especially in larger or more bureaucratic organizations. The organizational contexts, and especially leaders who were comfortable with the current state of organizational cultures and structures, were often inhibiting factors.

Another model offered primarily for the front-line staff level (Rae & Nicholas-Wolosuk, 2003) focuses specifically on changing organizational *policy* (an example of the *content* of change—what needs to be changed), but it can be used for other content change goals, such as implementing a new program, improving cultural competence, becoming skilled at cultural humility, or changing organizational culture. These authors also used the term *bottom-up* for their model.

Their model has the following steps:

- Dream about agency policy change (e.g., a better way of serving clients) and discuss with coworkers
- Analyze the policy situation related to the change idea (e.g., an agency policy that needs to be changed or written) and consider possible undesirable consequences and resistance to the idea

- Develop a plan of action (including rallying allies and assessing the target system [e.g., agency administrators] and selecting a change strategy [cooperation, campaign, or contest])
- Implement the change strategy, including presenting the proposal to administrators and obtaining approval

You'll see that this model has a lot in common with the one I present here.

Levin, Goor, and Tayri (2013) proposed a similar model, which they called "agency advocacy," or AA. The main goals of agency advocates

are to deal with social agencies that provide inadequate services to their clients, professionals that treat clients disrespectfully, professional networks that do not communicate beneficially with one another, services that are not accessible to certain clients, insufficient investment of resources in prevention and outreach activities, and the suggestion or implementation of organisational policies that harm clients. This is generally achieved through the initiation, implementation and assessment of services and professional networks that ensure a just, equally accessible and financially efficient provision of services. (2013, p. 524)

Key tactics of AA include assessing a problem, developing a plan and evaluating it, and creating task forces or coalitions, sometimes including clients and staff from other agencies. The authors found that AA tactics combined with methods of organization development (covered in Chapter 10), including action research, participatory decision-making, and attention to organizational culture issues led to notable successes in two case studies.

In an article looking at conditions in which public sector managers favor and pursue organizational change, Fernandez and Pitts (2007) asserted that "some research on organizational change and innovation indicates that employees at the bottom of the organization can be catalysts for change," adding that small "pockets of continuous change spawn innovations that are implemented throughout the entire organization" (p. 331). Managers with more participative styles are more likely to create such conditions.

Another organizational change model (Netting et al., 2017) takes the perspective of those at lower levels in the organizational hierarchy. It focuses specifically on front-line staff that have identified a way, perhaps a new program model, to improve services to clients. It has the following steps:

1. Develop the intervention hypothesis by analyzing a client problem and developing the best service intervention to address it.
2. Define participants and build support for the idea by selecting people who can support and lead the initiative, as well as noting clients and others who could benefit from the new idea. This also includes identifying the

target system (the people, groups, or structures that need to be changed) and the *action system*, such as a steering committee that can oversee the change effort.

3. Determine openness and commitment to change, including assessing the system's capacity for change (similar to Step 5 in the change model in Chapter 6).

4. Strengthen collective identity by identifying people and groups who could support the change idea and identify communication mechanisms (e.g., social media) for generating support.

5. Identify outside opposition, including using a force field analysis of driving and restraining forces as discussed in Chapter 5.

6. Assess political and economic feasibility and consider the sense of urgency felt by key stakeholders and sources of support as well as anticipated costs to the organization.

7. Select a change approach: a focus on policy change, a program change, a short-term project, a personnel approach (considering staff and community members), or a practice approach regarding operations within the organization.

8. Select strategies and tactics. Options including collaboration, campaign, or contest strategies are options. These are covered in the SIOC model discussed next.

9. The next set of steps are essentially developing a logic model for a new program intervention, including refining the original working hypothesis; determining goals, objectives, and activities; and initiating an action plan.

10. Conduct process and outcome evaluations after the new program is implemented.

This process could be used within a full SIOC model, which pays more attention to influencing decision-makers to actually to approve a change suggestion.

A recent contribution to this sparse literature is a book by M. Cohen and Hyde (2014a) that uses the term *change from below* to offer conceptual frameworks and cases to describe this change method. This is based primarily on Holloway, with elements from other sources.

In previous chapters, *change leader* has referred to an organization's executive, or at least someone in an authority position such as a director or division head, who is taking the initiative to lead a planned change process. In this chapter, the change leader is a lower level staff person or, probably in most SIOC initiatives, several people, often referred to in the literature as *change agents*. While the process for SIOC is notably different based on this distinction, there are nevertheless many elements here that are very similar to those in the major change model presented in Section 3. For example, many of the change readiness and change capacity factors covered in Chapter 5 apply here. The focus here is mainly on the readiness and capacity of your target for change: someone or some unit at a higher management level, such as the organization's executive leadership team or the director of your program.

Especially important for consideration will be the organization's overall leadership philosophy, in particular the leadership philosophy of your change targets. Also relevant will be other organizational factors, including the organization's culture and other challenges and priorities that the organization is currently addressing.

SIOC and Worker Empowerment

Actually, SIOC is an example of worker empowerment, although in this case lower level staff initiate the process by empowering themselves, not necessarily with organizational sanction, whereas worker empowerment is more commonly framed as something that leaders who use a participative management style try to create for their staff. In this spirit, B. Cohen and Austin (1997) asserted that empowerment of staff should be formally sanctioned by the organization and built into organizational processes and the worker's job role, with a commitment to individual and organizational learning throughout the change process.

A study by Frohman (1997) of innovation by lower level units in large business organizations supported the notion of officially sanctioning worker input: Success occurred when low-level employees were supported in going outside their job descriptions to suggest changes—a condition that may not be part of the culture of some human service organizations. Frohman added that change proposals were accepted when they directly addressed existing organizational objectives, a point that low-level change agents should keep in mind when developing change ideas.

So, with hopes that your organization has favorable preconditions, including a participative management philosophy, an organizational culture that supports high-quality of working life for staff, a commitment to quality services, and minimal extra challenges such as potential funding or program cuts, we now review a model for SIOC. This model has seven stages: preassessment, assessment, preinitiation, initiation, implementation, institutionalization, and evaluation.

Preassessment

This model includes, as you may expect, *assessment* as a key step. This model also includes not only *initiation* of the change, but also *preinitiation*. In the same spirit, an additional step, *preassessment*, is worth considering in SIOC, where you, as the change agent, occupy a position lower in authority and therefore having some vulnerabilities that executive-level staff do not have. Preassessment here looks particularly organizational at preconditions that can make the organization and its leaders more likely to be open to SIOC. As noted above, we hope that your organization will be led by managers with a participative leadership style, as some research suggests that this is appropriate for organizations with highly trained professional staff who are working in a complex environment with complex service delivery technologies.

Even in the case of an organization that espouses a philosophy of employee empowerment, and certainly in the case of an organization that has a more directive style of leadership, lower level change agents should thoughtfully consider the risks that they may be facing if they go forward. While Homan (2016, p. 515) confidently suggested that you "ask forgiveness, not permission," you would be wise to consider realistic risks and how they can be mitigated in advance or recovered from later. Even Homan noted that you may be risking "interference with career advancement . . . denial of requests for authority support on other matters, or . . . some form of social disapproval" (p. 515). If it is clear to you, and can become clear to the upper level decision-makers, that the change will, in fact, result in improvements in the organization that will outweigh costs (funds, time, etc.), risks can be minimized.

The formula that upper level change leaders were encouraged to apply to their employees in Chapter 8 can be used here. If the change target (in this case, the executive, a management team, etc.):

- perceives a high level of dissatisfaction with the current state,
- sees the desirability of a better future state, and
- sees a change process that will not require excessive time and energy,

then the perceived benefits factored together may be greater than the perceived costs of the change, and the decision-makers will have higher readiness to approve the change, thus eliminating the possible negative consequences for lower level change agents. Using collaborative, rather than conflict, tactics (discussed below) is also likely to lower resistance.

Another aspect that should ideally precede this preassessment is for the change agents to have developed social capital within the organization. You as a worker should, as a normal part of your work, behave in the most responsible and professional manner possible, demonstrating your commitment not only to your professional ethics but also to the organization and its mission. Attributes such as perceived competence, professional knowledge and skill, collegiality, tenure or longevity with the organization, loyalty, and one's social relationships

(M. Cohen & Hyde, 2014b, p. 36) are obviously important aspects of social capital. A lower level change agent who is known by managers and key decision-makers to be high in such social capital will likely be perceived more favorably when submitting a change proposal than would someone who is seen as only a modestly committed worker or, even worse, apathetic or a complainer.

It may be wise to consider how your supervisor should be involved in the process that you have in mind. According to Homan (2016, p. 111), there are several basic approaches you can take to begin to gain acceptance for your change idea. First, you can get permission in advance from your supervisor to begin your analysis of a problem and develop a change plan. Second, you can do some preliminary work on your own and then go to your supervisor for permission to do further work on it. Or, you may simply start the process without getting permission and let your role as a change agent evolve until it becomes accepted. Homan stated a personal preference for the second option. He suggested these steps to gain support from you supervisor:

1. Describe the issue as you see it, using available data to document the problem.
2. Suggest, at least at this point in general terms, what you think would be an appropriate response to address this issue.
3. Emphasize your thinking about wanting to address this issue, and how your involvement will benefit the organization's mission, and perhaps how it is in line with your supervisor's values.
4. Try to get your supervisor to support this idea, and solicit her/his ideas for improving your proposal. (p. 111)

Assessment

For the initial assessment, a problem is identified, an action system consisting of individuals who have a commonality of interests and concerns is formed, data are gathered, a change goal is set, and possible solutions are considered.

Similar to the assessment stage in the model discussed earlier, you can assess both the *content* and the *process* of change.

The Content of the Change

The content of the change includes defining the problem, developing a change goal (a new, ideal future state), considering various ideas for creating the change, and agreeing on a proposal that will solve the identified problem and achieve the desired goal. To assess the content of the change, data collection (through methods including interviews and focus groups with staff and clients, surveys, and review of documents) can be used to refine the problem statement and the change goal. A cost analysis, which ideally will show net cost savings or at least be cost neutral, will be of particular interest to administrative decision-makers.

The problem-solving process covered in Chapter 8 can be used here as well, with the main difference being that in management-led change, a problem group is sanctioned by the change leaders, whereas in the case of SIOC, staff would initiate this problem-solving process on their own.

The problem-solving process includes these steps:

1. Gather information on the current state, using as data sources any staff involved or affected, relevant organizational performance data, and perhaps additional interviews or surveys.
2. Develop a clear problem statement: its effects, who and what is affected, and the like; describe a vision, ideal state, or end result.
3. Develop criteria for a successful solution:
   a. What conditions need to be satisfied?
   b. What budgetary constraints need to be addressed?
   c. What policies or regulations need to be complied with?
   d. What do the key stakeholders and decision-makers need?
4. Analyze potential causes, determine the root cause(s). Total Quality Management techniques, for example, cause-and-effect diagrams, flow charts, Pareto charts, histograms, or control charts, may be useful.
5. Identify possible solutions, using brainstorming:
   a. No evaluation of ideas
   b. Wild ideas are encouraged
   c. Quantity, not quality, of ideas is encouraged
   d. Piggyback on others' ideas
   e. Clarification questions only
6. Refine the brainstorming list and select the best solutions(s):
   a. Adapt, modify, or combine ideas
   b. Now is the time to evaluate ideas, using the criteria from Step 3
   c. Choose the best solutions(s)
7. Develop an action plan for implementation:
   a. Write a detailed plan with action steps, responsible persons or groups, resources needed, cost, and deadlines
   b. Consider possible barriers or challenges to implementation and develop plans for addressing them (e.g., use a force field analysis)
   c. Prepare the plan for review by decision-makers and others whose support will be needed

8. Present the plan to decision-makers (e.g., probably an executive team) for approval or adjustments as needed. (This is actually the *initiation* stage in SIOC. Assuming that the change proposal is approved, the next steps of implementation, institutionalization, and evaluation correspond to the following step of the problem-solving process.)
9. After approval by decision-makers, modify implementation plans as needed and implement. As part of implementation, prepare a process for monitoring progress and evaluating results after implementation.
10. Monitor and evaluate, plan, and take additional actions as needed. Celebrate accomplishments.

During the problem-solving process, particular attention can be paid to the factors mentioned next that are unique to SIOC. These actually involve going from the content of the change to the process for how it will be introduced.

In one of the early works in this area, Patti (1974) provided some concepts that can be used as you assess your change goal in terms of its possible impact. Generally, the broader and deeper the impact of the change on the organization, the greater the concern may be on the part of decision-makers. *Generality* refers to the size of the organizational unit that will be affected. *Component* changes typically affect only a workgroup or perhaps a segment of a program. *Subsystem* changes would be focused on an entire program or perhaps a regional office or another subset of the whole organization. *System* changes would affect the entire organization.

Changes in *depth* can range from *procedural* changes that involve minor changes to existing procedures; to *programmatic* changes involving an entire program, such as implementing a new service delivery model; to *basic* changes that may have implications for the mission or strategies of the organization.

Changes with a larger scope and depth will probably confront greater resistance and require more detailed analysis, more persuasive arguments of the value of the change, and support from broader groups of stakeholders. Depending on the change agents' assessment of the change goals and factors within the organization, if a system level change would be desirable but unrealistic, it may be possible to scale down the change proposal, perhaps treating it as a pilot project or experiment, which can be broadened later if it has been successful.

Patti noted two other factors for consideration. *Sunk costs*, in the case of a change proposal, refer to the ways in which the organization and its key decision-makers have a vested interest in things remaining as they are. People who have put a good deal of time, energy, resources, and personal commitment to getting the organization to its current state may be more resistant to changes in systems they are comfortable with and may have helped develop.

He also noted *organizational distance* as a factor to consider. The more levels in the hierarchy between the change agents and the ultimate decision-makers, the more difficult the effort will be. The change goal may be approved at lower levels, but unless the original change agents stay directly involved as the proposal moves up the bureaucracy, the idea may be modified significantly. Also, decision-makers at different levels may have different criteria for assessing the proposal. If the original change agents are not involved with the steps up the chain of command, they will not have the opportunity to listen to concerns and address them, and decision-makers will lack some of the knowledge that the change agents could convey in meetings.

Patti suggested that considering these factors at the assessment stage can help change agents assess the feasibility of their proposal, consider the best level to target the change, and decide on change tactics.

The Process Aspects of the Change

Assessing the process of change includes identifying key actors within the organization, with particular attention to those in decision-making roles. According to M. Cohen and Hyde (2014b, p. 39), these actors can be classified into three groups. *Critical actors* are decision-makers who have the power to implement the change goal. Their support will be essential. *Facilitating actors* may have formal or informal power in the organization and can be helpful in influencing the decision-makers. *Allies* are staff who can support the change effort in other ways. Homan (2016, p. 512) also suggested that it might be appropriate to involve as allies client partners and/or external advocacy groups.

One way to assess these actors, and particularly the critical actors, will be to determine as much as you can their self-interests, particularly regarding their feelings of "prestige, autonomy, influence, or authority" (M. Cohen & Hyde, 2014b, p. 35). To the extent that these decision-makers see the change proposal as enhancing their self-interest in any of these areas, a favorable decision is more likely. On the other hand, if self-interest is seen as being threatened, resistance is likely.

Resnick and Patti's model includes analyzing resistance at this stage. Here, it will be important to try to identify or predict any concerns that decision-makers may raise regarding your proposal and to address these in a way that minimizes or fully addresses the concerns.

M. Cohen and Hyde (2014b) suggested the use of a force field analysis, described here in Chapter 5, to provide a detailed assessment of actors and other forces: driving forces that can support or facilitate the change and restraining forces that will make the change difficult. Unless restraining forces outweigh driving forces so extensively that the change seems impossible, change agents then determine ways to enhance and use the driving forces and minimize or modify the restraining forces. You as change agents can be seen as an action system: individuals who have a commonality of interests and concerns regarding the problem and change goal.

You as a change agent should also assess the potential influence and, as just mentioned above, social capital that you and allies who will be involved will have. This is another area where materials from a previous chapter may be relevant. Chapter 3, which focused on a manager as a change leader, reviewed some influence tactics that can be used in organizations. Some of these can be used by lower level change agents, including

- Articulate and build commitment to a desirable vision
- Behave in ways that are consistent with the organization's key values and culture
- Use rational persuasion: present facts, data, and a plan to support your proposal
- Use ingratiation: act in a friendly manner prior to making a request, sympathize about the hardships the request may cause, praise the person
- Use positive sanctions: promise desirable rewards
- Use reciprocity: offer something in exchange, remind of past favors, "chits" acquired
- Use coalitions to get others' support
- Use bridging: draw out the other person's needs or perspectives
- Seek participation and feedback from those you are trying to influence
- Get others involved and supportive regarding the idea, use their input and ideas
- Appeal to personal values
- Be assertive and explicit regarding what you want

In addition to assessing and planning for the use of your influence skills, Resnick and Patti (1980) mentioned some other factors (actually forms of social capital) that you can consider that can enhance your ability to influence the decision-makers whose support and sanction will be needed to implant the change. First, consider your *organizational legitimacy*. A primary consideration here is your "ethical obligation to the primacy of client welfare" (p. 14). It will be difficult for an administrator to disagree with the importance of this, so the extent to which you can show that your change proposal will enhance client welfare, it will likely be favorably received. You can also claim legitimacy on "the basis of substantive knowledge regarding the problem at hand" (p. 15). Don't be afraid to point out the expertise of you and other change agents in terms of your hands-on knowledge of the issue you are addressing. Administrators by definition know much less, in a detailed way, about activities at lower levels of the organization. Another source of your legitimacy can be seen as you present your-self as "a preserver of organizational values" (p. 15). Showing how your proposal fits with or even advances the use of the organization's stated values may make it easier to accept.

As part of your plan for the change process, all of the change agents can look for relevant ways that they can draw on their social capital and influence skills with the decision-makers to help frame their change proposal.

Next, based on the force field analysis and analysis of other data gathered, an overall change strategy can be chosen. A collaborative strategy is appropriate where there is high agreement among all actors on the change goal. A campaign strategy may be used when the decision-makers may not see the need for the change, and a conflict strategy may be needed if the decision-makers oppose the change. M. Cohen and Hyde recommended using the "principle of least contest" (2014b, p. 47), which suggests using the least conflictual strategy that can achieve the change goal.

After a strategy is chosen, specific tactics can be developed. These can range from persuasion and presenting data on the problem and proposed solutions to decision-makers (collaborative) to negotiation or threats (campaign), or demands and actions such as protests and strikes (conflict). Drawing on research on advocacy, Seabury, Cohen, and Hyde (2014, p. 61) summarized these tactics based on change strategy:

Collaborative:
- Provide information or documentation on the issue
- Suggest changes or alternatives
- Encourage experimentation

Campaign:
- Be persistent
- Appeal to emotion or conscience
- Point out negative consequences
- Create worst case scenarios

Contest:
- Go over the decision-maker's head
- Confront in public meetings
- Testify in public forums
- Blow the whistle
- Boycott or strike
- Pursue litigation

Preinitiation

The next stage in Holloway's model, preinitiation, involves change agents assessing and developing their influence and credibility (social capital) and inducing or augmenting stress so that the problem will be addressed. Assessing and developing social capital should actually have begun earlier, as discussed at the preinitiation stage. Workers who have been supportive of the organization and in the past have taken initiative to support the organization's strategies will have built up social capital, which should result in upper administration paying more attention to their ideas.

Brager and Holloway (1978) suggested some ways to induce and manage stress to help set up the urgency of a need for change. They noted, to begin with, that "although stress is a necessary condition for successful innovation, it does not necessarily facilitate change and may act to inhibit it" (p. 162). Therefore, planning on the ways to use organizational stress should be very thoughtful. Sources of stress that may serve as driving forces for the change would include, for example, an unacceptable recidivism rate in a program, documented client or community dissatisfaction, and perhaps morale problems in a program or the organization as a whole that could impact quality of services and staff retention. Essentially, documenting and sharing any information that is inconsistent with people's views that things are going well in the organization or program may create some cognitive dissonance that could lead to interest in considering change (Brager & Holloway, 1978, p. 164). Homan (2016, p. 514) suggested creating awareness of the need for change through disseminating symptoms of the problems. Brager and Holloway also emphasized that sharing of problems should be seen as coming from a place of concern for the organization and commitment to its values and mission, rather than as criticism. It will be difficult for a decision-maker to ignore a problem that affects the organization's mission or quality of services.

Even if a collaborative strategy is chosen, and especially if one of the others is chosen, lower level staff should consider the risks they may be facing. Homan (2016, pp. 515–517) suggested several tactics to manage risk:

- Put yourself in a position within the organization that gives you standing to promote change [e.g., being a member of a committee, having social capital] . . .
- Manage the perception of the change effort, particularly as it relates to the motivations of those most highly involved.
- Avoid making a fight without sufficient reason. Avoid making a fight without sufficient resources.
- Keep your discussion related to the beneficial impact of the change. . . .

- Focus on mutual benefits. Whenever appropriate, endeavor to diminish the fears and discomfort of opponents.
- Maintain an awareness of the message your personal demeanor sends. If you act outraged or outrageous, do it on purpose.
- Remember, you work there. The way you pursue change will leave an impression on the organization, your work community. In your selection of strategies, see if you can select an approach that helps you achieve your goal in a way that humanizes this community and makes it more respectful of its members.
- "Keep your nose clean." That is, make sure that you fulfill all of your job responsibilities. . . .
- Follow, but don't necessarily rely upon, appropriate channels. You may need to show them as inadequate for dealing with the situation. . . . Have alternative tactics ready to go to when it is clear that "proper procedures" are clearly problem perpetuators.
- Use your head to avoid unnecessary risks. Don't give opponents added reasons to discredit you.

Initiation

The use of the term *initiation* may be confusing here. This does not mean initiating change, but rather means initiating the process of introducing your change goal and plan to key decision-makers. At this stage, the change goal is introduced to the decision-makers, with consideration of how it will be seen as conforming to their interests. Change agents can draw on any allies identified earlier to develop support and assistance in preparing specific proposals that conform to interests and values of key decision-makers.

At this point, the change agents and any of their allies will select representatives to meet with decision-makers and introduce the change goal and proposal. The social capital and influence skills of the various change agents will be key factors to consider when selecting people to present the proposal.

In anticipation of the meeting, Homan (2016, p. 514) suggested that a change agent should assess possible reasons that decision-makers may resist the change, such as a lack of information, "psychological investment" in some aspect of current operations, or recent major turmoil or current issues causing distractions in the organization, such as budgetary problems. These should be addressed in advance by change agents, by developing rationales for the net benefit of the change *from the point of view of the organization's decision-makers*. While your idea may make total sense from the perspective of a lower level staff person, think about the perspective of the executive or managers who will be considering this change.

They will need to conclude, even if unconsciously, that their concerns or areas of resistance can be adequately addressed in your proposal.

The actual forum for a presentation should be determined based on an organization's existing norms and processes. This may be as an agenda item at a regularly scheduled meeting of an executive team or a special meeting with the change proposal as the only item. The choice of delivery mechanism should also be made with consideration of common practices within the organization. Use a method that has been used with success in the past and that fits with organizational norms. Rae and Nicholas-Wolosuk (2003), in their model of changing policy, listed several mechanisms for delivering the proposal. Typically, at minimum there would be an oral presentation (often including, these days, technology such as PowerPoint and perhaps handouts). If the proposal involves a new program or other initiative, the presentation can be accompanied by a document in the form of a program proposal, with standard elements including a needs assessment, goals and objectives, a program model with staffing and budget plans (i.e., how it could be funded), and an evaluation component. In the case of a formal policy change, a position paper may be appropriate.

Implementation

The change agents will of course hope that their proposal will be accepted by decision-makers, perhaps with modifications that will still ensure goal accomplishment. This may involve multiple levels of review in an organization's hierarchy, ultimately leading to the appropriate level (e.g., the executive team, program directors) approving a plan. When the change goal and plan are approved, the implementation stage includes gaining support and commitment of staff involved and managing their resistance, ensuring that implementation expectations are understood. Some of the same tactics presented in Chapter 8 may be relevant here.

An evaluation and follow-up process should be included in the plan, so that there will be a process, agreed on by the lower level change agents and management decision-makers, to monitor implementation, with a commitment to make adjustments as needed to ensure that the desired outcomes are achieved.

Institutionalization

As in the case of the change model presented in Chapter 9, institutionalization involves making any necessary adjustments to the plan and then developing standardized procedures for the proposal and linking it with other organizational elements (e.g., human resource systems, information systems).

Evaluation

Very similar to the final stage of the model in Section 3, evaluation of the results of the change initiative will be important. Data to evaluate the implementation of the change, both the process that was planned to be used and the desired outcomes, can be gathered at intervals that all stakeholders determine to be appropriate for the change. Consistent with the action research model covered in Chapter 11, this cycle of data collection and analysis, followed by any necessary adjustments, can be repeated as needed.

Summary

Staff-initiated organizational change is different in many ways from the overall change model covered in this book, which assumes that the key change leader is typically at an upper administrative level. There are some similarities, however. Both approaches are intended to improve the functioning of the organization, and both use some of the same processes, such as problem analysis and problem-solving. Also remember that SIOC can be used by people above the line level who might be supervisors or middle managers who want to influence upward.

This approach may present some risk for lower level staff, depending on the leadership styles and philosophies of managers and the overall culture of the organization. Nevertheless, if the process is done thoughtfully, with a lot of dialogue among those at the unit level who are interested in change, it has potential for not only making small improvements but also stimulating changes at a larger level.

Reflection and Focusing Questions

1. What opportunities do you see in your organization to use the SIOC model?
2. What social capital have you developed, or could you develop, to give yourself more credibility in the eyes of administrators?
3. How have executives reacted in the past to suggested changes from lower level staff?
4. Do preconditions that are favorable to SIOC exist in your organization? If not, what could be done to help create these preconditions?

SECTION 6
WRAP-UP

Chapter 20: Where We Have Been and Where You may go

20

Where We Have Been and Where You May Go

Someone's got to do something, and it's just incredibly pitiful that it has to be us.

—Jerry Garcia, the Grateful Dead

Where We Have Been

Looking back over what I've written, I can imagine an overall message that you might be getting is something like, "If you are doing organizational change, be thinking about everything all the time and make sure you do all this stuff." Clearly there is a lot here, and specific principles, methods, ideas, and examples will vary in the value they have for you based on your unique situation at a particular time.

To provide some perspective and a sense of order, I briefly review here where we have been by highlighting some major themes. I end with some reflections that I hope will encourage you to do some reflection as well, about yourself as a potential organizational change leader or participant, and where you see yourself going in this regard.

I include here the conceptual model (Figure 20.1) from Chapter 2, which you can treat as a dashboard for things to pay attention to and address what's needed at present or will be needed in the future.

I briefly revisit the model, but before that, a contextual issue not covered by the model deserves attention here: ethics and organizational change. Actually, leadership and ethics could be a third dimension of the conceptual model, underpinning everything else. I have mentioned ethics in nine chapters. It seems that ethics issues in human service organizations (HSOs) can come up without notice. A well-functioning HSO should have policies and procedures as well as guidelines for identifying and addressing ethics issues. Ideally, the organization would have ethics principles formally stated, perhaps in the context of the organization's statement of values.

Beyond what the organization specifies, administrators who are members of a profession such as social work also have ethics principles to which they must be committed. In the National Association of Social Work Code of Ethics

Organizational Change for the Human Services. Thomas Packard, Oxford University Press. © Oxford University Press 2021. DOI: 10.1093/oso/9780197549995.003.0021

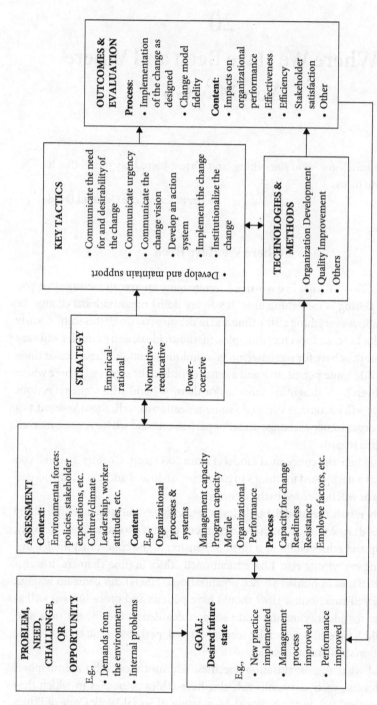

Figure 20.1 A conceptual framework for organizational change.

(https://www.socialworkers.org/About/Ethics/Code-of-Ethics/Code-of-Ethics-English), in addition to noting that administrators should advocate for adequate resources to meet clients' needs, one specific commitment to the employing organization is that social workers should work to "improve their employing agencies' policies and procedures and the efficiency and effectiveness of their services" [Section 3.09 (b)]. This is one way that a prospective change agent, whether at or near the top or the bottom of the hierarchy, can show the importance of organizational change.

A Planned Change Model

After you have considered a change opportunity and decided it is of the scope and importance that would benefit from a formal planned change process, you can use the change model introduced in Chapter 2. It's included here as well. The major steps are as follows:

1. Identify the problem, need, challenge, or opportunity
2. Identify the desired future state: the change goal
3. Assess the present: external and internal factors
4. Determine an overall change strategy
5. Communicate the need for and desirability of the change
6. Create a sense of urgency
7. Communicate the change vision
8. Develop the action system
9. Implement the change
10. Develop and maintain support
11. Institutionalize the change
12. Evaluate the change

Once you have a goal, especially if it is a big goal, spend a lot of time with assessment. Assess yourself as a change leader. Assess your organization's and staff's readiness and capacity for a change. Pick an overall strategy. Normative–reeducative and empirical–rational ones are probably going to be the most appropriate. Then you can design a model with a bunch of steps to take, keeping in mind the tactics. Please don't skimp on any of those. I, and some of my organizational clients, sometimes learned the hard way that it is worth taking the time to go through the steps, including getting all necessary people involved and on board and having a clear process for how the change initiative can unfold.

You will also consider what specific change methods would help: group problem-solving, maybe Total Quality Management or another quality improvement model, team building, employee surveys, maybe some consultant help, or maybe using staff-initiated change tactics.

And, remember that even though this is presented in a linear way, you may be going back and forth, repeating things, and doing different things at the same time. Remember the tent metaphor: you are not setting it up in your living room; you are probably on the side of a hill in the dark and rain. Also remember that things are likely to get worse before they get better, and that things are likely to take longer than anticipated.

Also remember to celebrate accomplishing a change goal and celebrate small accomplishments and growth steps every day.

With hopes that this will not be discouraging, after you accomplish something, big or not, recognize that another opportunity for change will present itself. It's become a tedious but true axiom that change is constant. You don't always have to be acting on opportunities for change. Recognize that no one will be able to do everything. Use self-care and keep things in perspective.

You as a Change Leader

Organizational change, planned and unplanned, is of course happening all the time. Some situations that could benefit from planned change are routine and can be handled as part of people's regular work. Larger and more complicated challenges, requiring transitional or transformational change, could benefit from conscious use of planned change principles and techniques.

There are probably plenty of opportunities for planned organizational change in your organization. If you are scanning the organization's internal and external environments on a regular basis, you should be able to see problems or potential problems and new opportunities to take advantage of. An updated strategic plan will certainly suggest opportunities for organizational change.

If you see something needing change, envision how it would operate if things were going really well—an appreciative inquiry approach. Think in terms of the outcome, the ideal future: how effective a program or an administrative operation would be, and how motivated and committed staff would be, after the change.

Support your staff in thinking this way as well. Be humble enough to recognize that all the good ideas don't need to come from you. That should actually make your job easier. By using a participative leadership style on a regular basis, you can create a climate and culture in which creativity, innovation, and employee empowerment are valued and even normal practice.

Thinking of this brought to mind for me Stephen Covey's second of his seven habits from his classic book (Covey, 1989) about leadership and life: Begin with the end in mind. And as I looked at the habits again, I think they are all worth mentioning since I see them all as relevant to someone who wants to be a change leader at work. Here they are, with my short elaborations:

1. **Be Proactive:** Always be looking for opportunities to improve: yourself, your team, the organization.
2. **Begin With the End in Mind:** Envision how your organization, program, or team will be operating after a change.
3. **Put First Things First:** Be alert to what's important, even if it is not urgent. It's easy to be consumed with little urgent things.
4. **Think Win–Win:** The leadership and change behaviors I have been writing about start from a place of collaboration and how changes can benefit all involved.
5. **Seek First to Understand, Then to Be Understood:** Empathy is of course a core skill for human service professionals. Seek other points of view on the problem and goal, and new, good ideas can emerge. Especially understand the perspectives of those staff at lower levels in the organization: their concerns, possible reasons for resistance, and their own ideas that can help the change be successful.
6. **Synergize:** Getting more people committed to a common goal will make it easier to achieve.
7. **Sharpen the Saw:** Keep being a lifelong learner and help your organization become an explicitly learning organization.

The oft-quoted retired chief executive officer Max De Pree famously said that "the first responsibility of a leader is to define reality. The last is to say thank you. In between the two, the leader must become a servant." (De Pree, 2004, p. 11). I would add that all three responsibilities can be ongoing. As I noted in the Introduction, there are multiple views of organizational reality. A change leader should pay particular attention to discussing with others the current realities of the organization, including weaknesses or challenges as well as strengths and potentials. And while I didn't mention servant leadership as a key one for change leaders, it can be a powerful force in organizational change. As summarized by East (2019, p. 80), servant leaders "support, enable, and promote the work of others in accomplishing the goals of the organization or community." Regular "thank yous" can be helpful as well.

And I must make space for at least one quotation from baseball legend Yogi Berra: "You can observe a lot by watching" (Berra & Kaplan, 2001, p. 64[1]).

---

[1] Also known for "when you come to a fork in the road, take it," "ninety percent of the game is half mental," and other fractured wisdom.

Especially when you are under a lot of pressure, it's easy not to notice what's happening around you. So, occasionally take time to pause, see what others are doing and saying, and consider how you can use what you see and hear to recalibrate, or maybe to simply acknowledge others. You might also want to recognize and appreciate all the good that the staff of your organization is doing at the moment, even as you are focusing on difficulties and challenges.

Remember also that in the words of one of social work administration's key thought leaders, HSOs are *moral organizations* (Hasenfeld, 2015). Zeke Hasenfeld reminded us that "the human services field is expected to embrace values that enhance human dignity, counter discrimination and social stigma, and offer services to reduce suffering and social inequality" (p. 1). He also reminded us to be alert to excessive uses, or misuses, of models from the for-profit sector and the popular new public management philosophy that I mentioned in Chapter 1. He asserted that HSO administrators "have to acknowledge that they operate in a highly politicized environment in which management ideologies and practices are an expression of the power relations in the organizational field in which they are located" (p. 3). He also asserted that "managers need to be reflective and be critical about their own organizational practices" (p. 4) and maintain open dialogue with staff and clients so that they are able to give feedback to the organization.

Practice principles including entrepreneurship and performance-based accountability systems are, I believe, legitimate and appropriate, with the latter sometimes being essential, in our organizations. But, if our organization receives inappropriate expectations or demands from a funder or other stakeholder, we should be mindful of our ethical obligations to our professions, our clients, and our communities. We are accountable to them as well as to funding organizations. Also remember that ethics are the *essence* of human services leadership (Manning, 2003, pp. 6–7).

While most of this book has presented organizational change in fairly traditional ways, all that material is bracketed by coverage in the first chapter and this last chapter regarding two increasingly urgent crises: racial justice and Covid-19. The latter raises issues of health-care adequacy and the need for prevention but has also made vividly clear how the deep inequalities of class and race impact not only healthcare but also life prospects more broadly for vulnerable populations. This is important on two levels. First, in times of crisis, traditional organizational change principles need to be modified to respond effectively and quickly, and organizations should pay more attention to using organizational change to anticipate and prevent problems and challenges rather than always reacting to new internal and external demands. Second, some organizational problems need to be addressed at the broader policy level in terms of prevention, resource adequacy, and social and racial justice.

Leaders in the human service professions should keep social justice principles near, and sometimes at the forefront of, our consciousness, in spite of the intense day-to-day demands to be accountable to a complex and sometimes contradictory set of stakeholder expectations. This is likely to involve as a regular part of an administrator's job some amount of involvement with advocacy to impact policies and practices that affect our organizations and communities.

Managing and leading one's organization or a part of it while also maintaining awareness of the larger contexts in which our organizations exist is a huge and ongoing challenge. Meg Wheatley, who did seminal work in applying principles of quantum physics, self-organizing systems, and chaos theory to organizations (Wheatley, 2006), offered more recently some vivid descriptions of some of the "extraordinary leaders" that she encountered over her nearly 50 years of consulting with organizations.

These leaders cannot prevent the unraveling of our global civilization, and that is not their ambition. They know they can make a profound difference locally, in the lives of people in their communities and organizations.

They also know that their successful initiatives that took such dedication and endurance to create are vulnerable to the destructive politics and behaviors too familiar in today's culture. At any moment, they or their programs may be swept away or severely hampered by thoughtless or venal political decisions. There are no assurances they will achieve long-term impact or be rewarded for success from the leaders above them who are possessed by fear and panic.

And yet they persevere because they are committed to doing the best they can for people. They have learned that nearly all people desire to do good work in good relationships with their colleagues. In full awareness of the trials and tribulations that will not cease, they offer their leadership skills to create islands of sanity, places of possibility and sanctuary where the destructive dynamics of this time are kept at bay.

They continue to persevere in the face of obstacles, setbacks, slander, and hate. They have made a choice to do the right thing, clear about their values, connected to those they lead, unwilling to succumb to fear or aggression. They are committed to staying in their work, exemplars of integrity and possibility no matter what is occurring in the external environment. (Wheatley, 2017, pp. 40–41)

I hope you can see yourself, now or in the future, to some extent in this description, and that you may also use other thoughts in this chapter as parts of your own visions for yourself and your work. I also hope that to the extent that you can identify with these leaders you will also take this as validation and appreciation for the work you do every day in very challenging environments and circumstances.

Some Final Thoughts

In looking back over the content of this book, it occurred to me that I haven't counted the number of times I have told you, the reader, what to do about organizational change and how often I have used the word *should*. In my early training as a counselor, we were told that we should avoid saying "you should" to clients. (I know, there's a paradox there.) Regardless, the message was clear, and appropriate. I found that client-centered practice seemed to work best when the counselor asked questions and helped the client explore options, possible outcomes, and consequences, rather than when the counselor told the client what to do. As movie producer Sam Goldwyn once put it, "For your information, I would like to ask a question."

I also recognize that I have presented principles, tactics, and methods in their ideal sense. I used the metaphor of a pup tent in Chapter 2 to recognize that we cannot always implement plans with perfection. I'll reiterate that with another story. People of a certain age may remember comedy albums by Bob Newhart. (If you missed them, check some out at YouTube.) One of his common scenarios was to talk as if he were on a phone call talking to another person. In one of these, he played a police chief telling a police officer over the phone how to disarm a bomb. He told him that "according to the manual, this is very important: use a LT507 screwdriver with a plastic handle and a demagnetized head." When the officer told him he did not have that tool, the police chief told him to "use a coin" (laughter here). As a change leader, you will clearly need to improvise on occasion and may need to implement change tactics with less than perfection. There will be judgment calls, and there are no firm guidelines regarding when something has to be done in a certain way and when it can be modified. Just do your best within the circumstances you have.

Social work writer and researcher Brene Brown has used the term *disruptive engagement*, asserting that "to reignite creativity, innovation, and learning, leaders must re-humanize education and work" (2012, p. 187). In her book, she focused on shame, vulnerability, and blame. The whole book is worth reading, but for our purposes here, she said that we can be driven by emotions and behaviors beyond those. She challenged us to "dare greatly and facilitate honest conversations" (p. 196), which can apply to *any* difficult issue, potentially leading to personal or organizational change. For Brown, a "*daring greatly* culture is a culture of honest, constructive, and engaged feedback" (p. 197, italics in original). This could be a powerful culture change goal for an organization, in service of better performance and a higher quality of working life for staff.

When I began studying organization development and practicing as a consultant, it occurred to me that organization development consulting (described in Chapter 10 as *process*, rather than *expert*, consulting) was a lot like client-centered counseling. I occasionally described my work to people in the helping professions as "counseling with organizations." When I was a consultant with the city of San Diego, a lot of my work was process consulting with individual managers. They generally seemed a bit surprised that we, part of the Financial Management Department's Organization Effectiveness Program, were not there to tell them what to do, but rather to help them assess what they expected of themselves, their staff, and their programs and what others, including their supervisors, expected of them. We then helped them decide what to do regarding issues facing themselves and their areas of responsibility. One manager told me that I was like the chaplain he had in the Army, who would basically listen and be supportive and not give orders or advice.

I conducted many team-building sessions in which I was hugely grateful for my social work background in group facilitation and family counseling, in settings from inpatient psychiatry to crisis intervention with runaways and families. Things went a lot better when we facilitated, rather than directed, team members in figuring out for themselves what they were dealing with and what they wanted to do. A big part of our role was helping them work well together and helping ensure that they were clear on the agreements and action plans they were making and helping them develop ways to follow through on what they planned and agreed to do.

All this is to help make the point that I have approached my work as a writer, teacher, consultant, and researcher with humility. I have had enough of "management by bestseller" books full of authoritative statements on what someone should do in their organization. And I realize I have given you a lot here. Treat what I have shared as menus or sets of resources, using what seems appropriate for you and your organization in a particular situation. Where possible, I have used research (mine and others) to support what I have said. At the end of the last session of my advanced social work administration classes, I tell my students to carefully scrutinize all the advice they receive, including the advice I am giving them at that moment.

For an additional observation, if not piece of advice, I again share some words from Jaiya John (2016), who has a rich way of describing the work we do and the potentials we have.

> Our workplace does not have to be a dungeon, and we do not have to be its morose dungeon guards. We have it in us to change the culture, it is possible for the places where we work and serve to feel like an artist colony. A workshop where compassion sparks fly, a bright fireworks to our passionate industry. Those who work here and come here to be aided can feel the warmth of our caring, liberated by our own permission to let our truer rivers flow. (pp. 196–197)

Where Do You Want to Go From Here?

Any employee in a HSO has many things to think about and deal with every day, and organizational change is probably not something you think of when preparing for your workday. I challenge you to regularly look hard for opportunities, large and small, for change and improvement. You will be able to deal with some of these easily as part of your regular work. Others will require taking some extra time, whenever you can find it, for more thinking about whether or not it should be addressed and, if so, how. Dialogue with colleagues can be very helpful in mulling over such opportunities and deciding what to do.

I clearly know nothing about the situations that you are facing in your work and cannot presume to expect that any particular thing in this book will be the right thing for you and your situations. I trust that you will use your judgments, insights, knowledge, and skills in adopting and/or adapting anything here as you and others in your organizations see fit.

Since you have been reading this book, I assume you are considering the notion that you are a lifelong learner, or at least a career-long learner, and that you want to continue to get better at what you do. If you have been required to read this as part of a class, you are furthering your education, which I hope will give you greater capacity to help change the world in your own small-to-large ways. In any case, your enhanced capacities can be a benefit to the clients and communities that your organization serves. You can also benefit those working in your organization through your enhanced leadership and organizational change skills.

Organizational change is mostly internal to the organization, but it is directed toward larger purposes: the provision of outstanding services to clients and communities and a secondary purpose of providing a high quality of working life for staff and volunteers. A third purpose served by positive results of organizational change may be at the policy level: showing governments, foundations, and the public at large the value of impactful programs.

In a book from the early days of the "alternative agency" movement of the 1970s, the authors asserted that

> Social service is treated like an eccentric uncle living in the attics of capitalism. He must be fed and clothed, because he is, after all, family. But he certainly is unproductive and better be grateful for what he gets. (Holleb & Abrams, 1975, pp. 102–103)

I hope we can keep working to change our national attitudes and policies to give more respect and support to the vulnerable populations in our midst. One way administrators can advance this effort is to ensure that our organizations are well run, by competent and committed staff, and are achieving valuable outcomes for clients, communities, and society at large.

Because HSOs serve so many with limited financial resources and political power, there are always struggles for funding. Advocacy can and should emphasize moral and humanitarian values that most citizens allegedly hold, but our arguments also need to emphasize the value that our programs add to society in terms of the long-term cost effectiveness and cost benefits of our services. We need outstanding programs, staff, information systems, and evaluation designs to demonstrate our value to those whose higher priorities may be financial. Policy advocates will have more credibility if they are known to be operating highly impactful and cost-effective organizations, not to mention holding social justice values.

Our clients and communities deserve the best services that we can provide. In order to do this, our staff deserve the best quality of working life that an organization can provide. Many of the challenges we face in addressing these expectations are in the policy arena and beyond the scope of this book. We can, however, improve the organizations in which we work and the services we provide and then show the value of these improved services not only to clients but also to policymakers and society at large.

I wish you the best in your endeavors. I will be interested in how things go for you.

Reflection and Focusing Questions

1. What are the key insights about yourself as a current or potential organizational change leader that have occurred to you based on this book?
2. Can you see yourself being a change leader in an organization? If so, what would that look like?
3. Is there something that you'd like to work on now?
4. Would it help to talk to others about this? Maybe you can help bring out greatness in not only yourself but also others.

Leader Development Plan

Goals/Desired Outcomes	Due Dates
1.	
2.	
3.	
Activities to Work Toward Goals/Outcomes	**Due Dates**
1.	
2.	
3.	
Support/Resources Needed (e.g., training, mentoring, workshops, etc.)	

Evidence of New/Increased Skills or Knowledge (i.e., how will you know you have accomplished the goals?)

1.

2.

3.

Management Audit

Adapted from Lewis, J., Packard, T., & Lewis, M. (2012). *Management of Human Service Programs*, 5th Ed. Belmont, CA: Thompson/Brooks Cole.

Indicate the degree to which each factor is present in your organization. Use a rating of "4" if all aspects are fully present with positive effect; use a "1" when the factor is absent or not at all effective; use a "2" or "3" to reflect relative amounts of the factor being present/ effective or problematic.

Planning

1. ____ The organization has a clearly defined mission that is well known, well understood, and well accepted by staff.
2. ____ The organization has and uses a current and relevant strategic plan.
3. ____ There is a written annual operational plan that includes timelines and identification of responsible persons for all outcomes and activities.
4. ____ The strategies, goals, and objectives of the organization are based on the mission.
5. ____ The goals and objectives are complete and clear.
6. ____ The objectives reflect measurable client benefits and other outcomes.
7. ____ The plans of the organization are used on a regular basis.

Management of the Environment

8. ____ The problems or needs the organization is intended to address are clearly identified and documented.
9. ____ The target populations (e.g., demographics, geographic boundaries) the organization is intended to serve are clearly identified and documented.
10. ____ Key stakeholders (funders, other agencies, regulators) are satisfied with the organization's programs and services.

Client Relations

11. ____ Clients' perceptions of their needs are clearly known by the organization.
12. ____ Clients are satisfied with the services as delivered by the organization.
13. ____ Policies and procedures regarding confidentiality and reporting requirements (e.g., abuse, dangers posed by clients) are compliant with laws and clear to clients and staff.

Program Design/Technology

14. _____ Service delivery technologies are appropriate to the achievement of the mission, strategies, and objectives.
15. _____ All services use explicit logic models of cause and effect, which are based on evidence-based practices.
16. _____ Each service is effective in accomplishing its stated goals and objectives.
17. _____ There are clear program standards that describe the quality and types of services delivered.
18. _____ The organization specifies objectives and outcomes for each client.

Structure and Design

19. _____ All staff members' roles and performance expectations are clear and agreed to.
20. _____ The organizational structure and reporting relationships are clear to all.
21. _____ The organization has clear, written policies and procedures that are consistent with the mission and goals and that drive expected behavior.
22. _____ The organization's structure is clearly aligned with strategy.
23. _____ The organization's structure is flexible and minimally bureaucratic.
24. _____ The organization's structure facilitates cross-function communication, coordination, collaboration, teamwork, and support.
25. _____ The organization has communication mechanisms to keep all staff informed about current and anticipated activities or developments.
26. _____ Decision-making processes support decision implementation and include clarity regarding who has input and who has responsibility for making decisions.
27. _____ Decision-making is appropriately decentralized to lower level staff.

Management Information System

28. _____ The organization has a computerized client data collection and processing system for demographic, services, and outcome data.
29. _____ The information system can identify and aggregate client outcome data (effectiveness).
30. _____ The information system has clearly defined units of service and service completions that can be used to measure the types and amounts of services provided and their unit costs (efficiency).
31. _____ The information system can measure cost effectiveness.
32. _____ There are clear performance standards for which aggregated client data are used in ongoing service monitoring and feedback.

Budget and Financial Management

33. _____ All programs and cost centers have clearly defined budgets.
34. _____ A budgeting process is in place that ensures the effective allocation of resources.

35. ____ A realistic short-term and long-term fund development or budget management program is in place.
36. ____ Financial reports provide managers with complete, accurate, and timely information.
37. ____ Expenditures consistently match program budgets and actual income.
38. ____ An external audit has been conducted within the last year, results have been shared, and identified problems have been corrected.
39. ____ Administration and program budgets are clearly aligned with strategies and objectives.

Staffing and Human Resources Management

40. ____ All staff are fully trained and qualified to perform their duties.
41. ____ All staff are fully oriented on hiring and are regularly supervised.
42. ____ There are appropriate and adequate staff development opportunities for staff.
43. ____ The organization recruits and selects staff whose professional ideology and training are compatible with the mission and values of the organization.
44. ____ The organization has a formal performance appraisal system that is appropriate and regularly used.
45. ____ There are appropriate rewards and recognition for all personnel.
46. ____ Comprehensive personnel policies and procedures are in compliance with relevant employment laws, regulations, and industry standards.

Leadership and Ethics

47. ____ Leaders help develop and articulate an inspiring and shared vision, purpose, and mission that drive strategy and programs for the organization.
48. ____ The organization has clearly defined values that are well known, well understood, and well accepted by staff.
49. ____ Leaders project a positive attitude (e.g., trust and respect) toward staff.
50. ____ Leaders in the organization use appropriate management styles that support and motivate staff to achieve high performance.
51. ____ Leaders clearly articulate high ethical standards and ensure that they are maintained.
52. ____ The organization has clearly identified standards and procedures for addressing key ethical issues, including confidentiality, client self-determination, respect of clients' social and cultural norms, and protecting clients from harm.

Organizational Culture and Change

53. ____ Managers create an organizational culture conducive to organizational effectiveness.
54. ____ Managers pay attention to informal group and organizational processes that affect the organization's operations.
55. ____ People feel free to express unusual or unpopular views without fear of personal attack or criticism.

56. ____ There are opportunities for staff to discuss what changes should be made to improve organizational operations or processes.
57. ____ The organization's mechanisms and processes for organizational change are known by and used by staff.
58. ____ Staff feel empowered to take initiative, be creative, and solve problems.
59. ____ Team spirit within and among departments is encouraged and supported.

Program Evaluation

60. ____ The impact of programs compared to the need for programs (program adequacy) is evaluated.
61. ____ The organization gathers data from consumers to assess satisfaction and the long-term effects of the services.
62. ____ Each program is formally evaluated regarding effectiveness and efficiency on a regular basis.
63. ____ Data and the results of program evaluations are used to make changes.
64. ____ All relevant accreditation, licensing, or regulatory standards are met.

Quality of Working Life

65. ____ Salaries provide adequate and fair compensation.
66. ____ The organization provides safe and healthy working conditions.
67. ____ The organization provides adequate and appropriate work areas and necessary supplies and equipment for all staff.
68. ____ The organization allows for individual worker autonomy.
69. ____ Jobs permit the learning and exercise of a wide range of skills and abilities.
70. ____ Job assignments contribute to employees expanding their capabilities.
71. ____ The organization provides upward mobility.
72. ____ The work environment provides supportive groups.
73. ____ The organization possesses a sense of community that extends beyond face-to-face workgroups.
74. ____ The organization allows for free speech and provides the right to personal privacy.
75. ____ The organization provides procedures for due process and access to appeals.
76. ____ The organization provides equitable treatment in all matters.
77. ____ The demands made by the organization allow for a balanced role of work that allows the worker to have leisure and family time on a regular basis.

Diversity, Cultural Competence, and Cultural Humility

78. ____ Organizational environment: Visual representations, policies, vision and mission statements, language training, and accessibility demonstrate the valuing of diversity.
79. ____ Community relations: Board membership, informational materials, special events, and community partnerships show that diversity is valued.

80. ____ Human resources: Diversity, cultural competence, and cultural humility training are offered regularly; staff are culturally appropriate and competent to work with communities served; and policies (e.g., bilingual pay) are regularly assessed and revised for cultural competence.

81. ____ Service delivery: Written materials are screened for cultural appropriateness, culture and other relevant variables are analyzed and used in services planning and design, and services are tailored to population groups served.

82. ____ Policies and procedures are fully compliant with all laws and regulations related to equal opportunities and disability issues, and staff are aware of these policies and procedures.

83. ____ The organization has and follows clear policies for enhancing diversity, equity, inclusion, and social justice considerations among all levels of staff.

Risk Management

84. ____ The agency is fully compliant with laws, regulations, and industry standards regarding insurance and liability related to staff, clients, volunteers, and facilities.

85. ____ Records management procedures are compliant with relevant laws, regulations, and standards, including confidentiality and backup capability.

86. ____ Policies and procedures are in effect to prevent and deal with workplace hazards including safety, crises such as client violence, Occupational Safety and Health (OSHA) criteria, and ergonomics.

87. ____ The organization has a disaster management plan that outlines staff and the organization's responses to disasters to ensure staff and client safety and services to the community; staff are aware of the plan and adequately trained to implement it.

Governance and Accountability

88. ____ The organization's governance structure (e.g., board) and systems are clearly defined and in compliance with relevant laws.

89. ____ The governance system provides appropriate oversight of the chief executive, finances, and operations.

90. ____ Organizational systems enable fulfillment of all of the organization's grant and contract requirements.

Sources

Some items are adapted from the following references:

Allison, M., & Kaye, J. (2005). *Strategic planning for nonprofit organizations* (2nd ed.). New York: Wiley.

Daft, R. (2010). *Organization theory and design* (10th ed.). Mason, OH: South-Western Cengage Learning.

Jones, J. (1981). *Principles of organizational structure*. San Diego, CA.

Kettner, P., Moroney, R., & Martin, L. (2017). *Designing and managing programs* (5th ed.). Thousand Oaks, CA: Sage.

Kurzman, P. (2006). Managing risk in nonprofit settings. In R. Edwards & J. Yankey (Eds.), *Effectively managing nonprofit organizations* (pp. 275–290). Washington, DC: NASW Press.

La Frontera Inc. (n.d.). *Building bridges: Tools for developing an organization's cultural competence*. Tucson, AZ: Author.

Martin, L. (2001). *Financial management for human service administrators*. Boston: Allyn & Bacon.

Sugarman, B. (1988). The well-managed human service organization: Criteria for a management audit. *Administration in Social Work, 12*(4), 17–27.

Walton, R. (1975). Criteria for quality of working life. In L. Davis & A. Cherns (Eds.), *The quality of working life: Volume 1: Problems, prospects, and the state of the art* (pp. 91–118). New York: Free Press.

Role Functions Worksheet

Role being discussed (person and job title): _____

List each of your major functions (responsibilities) and indicate for each whether or not you want to change the amount of time you spend on it.

Function	% Time Spent on This at Present	Continue As Is	Do More Of or Add	Do Less Of or Stop
1.				
2.				
3.				
4.				
5.				
6.				
7.				
8.				
9.				
10.				
11.				
12.				
13.				
14.				

Responsibility Chart

Your name: _____

Program or Project: _____

In the left column, list each function or task of any member of the workgroup.

In the top row, list all staff roles involved with the functions or tasks listed.

Under each role, indicate that person's involvement with a function or task using the Key below.

FUNCTIONS OR TASKS   ROLES

Key

D,   Director: general responsibility, sets policy, establishes criteria

DM, Decision-Maker: has the authority to make decision

S,   Supervisor: assigns, supervises, and ensures completion

W,   Worker: does the work

CI, Consult/Imperative: must be consulted

CO, Consult/Optional: may be consulted

NI, Notify/Imperative: must be notified

A,   Approves: must approve or disapprove completed task

Adapted from Helen Reynolds & Mary Tramel, *Executive Time Management*. Prentice Hall, 1979, p. 32.

Transition Management: Team Member

1. What are your areas of responsibility?
2. What concerns do you have about this transition?
3. The word(s) that best describes me as a person is/are
4. The word(s) that best describes me on the job is/are
5. My chief strengths are
6. My chief limitations are
7. My pet peeves are
8. How I act when I am angry or upset is
9. How would you describe your management style?
10. What management style should the new manager use with you?
11. My top personal values are
12. What should be the major goals over the next year be for
    a. Your area of responsibility?
    b. The whole agency or program?
13. What should the new manager know about how rewards and recognition are handled in this organization?
14. What should the new manager know about communication and decision-making processes in this organization?
15. What should the new manager know about the culture and climate of this organization?
16. What should the new manager know about the current performance of this organization (e.g., status on goals and objectives, financial status, quality, reputation)?
17. What could be done to improve the organization's management operating processes?
18. What problems or obstacles do you anticipate in the coming months in accomplishing your goals and the organization moving forward?
19. What support do you need to maintain and improve your effectiveness?
20. If you were the new manager, what things would you
    a. Start doing?
    b. Stop doing?
    c. Continue doing?
21. What is the one most resolvable problem around here?
22. What are the most effective things this workgroup accomplishes?
23. What are the problems or issues you see in this workgroup?
24. What questions do you have for the new manager?

Transition Management: Team Leader

1. The word(s) that best describes me as a person is/are
2. The word(s) that best describes me on the job is/are
3. My chief strengths are
4. My chief limitations are
5. My pet peeves are
6. How I act when I am angry or upset is
7. I would describe my management style as
8. My top personal values are
9. The concerns I have entering this organization/team are
10. This team can help me by
11. What I expect and need from my subordinates are
12. People will know I am satisfied or appreciative by
13. People will know something is important if
14. People will know I am dissatisfied by
15. My philosophy about working hours, time off, flex time, and the like is
16. The ground rules about calling me at home should be
17. If a subordinate wants to raise a concern with me, I prefer this be done by
18. Negotiation with me is permitted or expected when
19. Negotiation with me is not permitted, and obedience and loyalty to the decision made are expected, when
20. If subordinates think I am making a mistake, they should
21. The amount of information I need from subordinates should be based on
22. I prefer oral communication on
23. I prefer email communication on
24. I prefer written communication (memos, reports, etc.) on
25. I provide performance counseling by
26. My philosophy on delegation and participative decision-making is
27. Key behaviors I expect of subordinates include
28. I would like my relationships with subordinates to include
29. Actions that are unacceptable and unforgivable include
30. I prefer to handle conflict by
31. Subordinates can earn my trust by
32. Other things my subordinates should know about me are

Source: Unknown

Organizational Change
Tactics Questionnaire

The Organizational Change Tactics Questionnaire (OCTQ) questionnaire will gather information on your observations of an organizational change process that you have witnessed at work. Ideally, the change effort would have been at a broad level: a department or the whole organization. Examples of such changes would be initiatives to improve service outcomes, implement a major new policy, improve a data collection system, conduct a major restructuring, improve quality or efficiency, or address significant budget cutbacks. Please consider such an organizational change process that you have observed or been part of at work. You will then respond to this survey with that change in mind. Do not select a change initiative for which you had the major leadership implementation responsibility, but do select one in which you participated and/or were able to closely observe.

[NOTE: Instructions can be adapted to address a particular change initiative. Another version of the OCTQ enables respondents to rate two similar organizational change initiatives—one seen as successful and one seen as unsuccessful—that they have experienced.]

Your responses are anonymous. No information on this survey will identify you or your organization. This survey should take no more than 10–15 minutes to complete. All you need to do to send the survey is click on DONE on the last page.

1. How many years of management experience have you had? _____

       None   1–5   6–10   11–15   16–20   21 or more

---

2. State in your own words, as specifically as you can, the goal for this change initiative. What was this change process designed to accomplish?

---

3. What type of organization was this?

       Government   Nonprofit   For profit

4. What was the scope of this change process?

   Entire Organization   Entire Department   Entire Division   Specific Program

5. What was the type of organization, department, division, or program?

Department of Social Services		Human Services Agency
Child Welfare	TANF/Welfare to Work	Aging/Adult Services
Employment Services	Behavioral Health	Mental Health Substance Abuse
Food Stamps/SNAP	Medicaid or Medicare	Admin Services (e.g., HR, Finance)

Other (please specify): _____

6. Approximately how many employees were in the department, division, or program?

0–99   100–199   200–299   300–399   400–499   500–999   1,000 or more

7. Approximately how long did this initiative last, from the time it was announced to the time it was considered completed?

0–6 months   7–12 months   13–24 months   25 months or more

8. What was your position at the time of this change?

Executive management (CEO, Executive Director, Assistant Director, Deputy Director)

Middle management (e.g., Assistant Deputy Director, Division Director, District Director, Division or Section Chief, Program Manager, Program Coordinator)

Supervisor

Frontline staff (e.g., counselor, caseworker)

Analyst/staff support

Other (please specify):

9. What was your extent of involvement with this change process?

3 Regular involvement in change implementation activities (e.g., meetings, task forces, etc.)

2 Occasional participant in change implementation activities (e.g., meetings, task forces, etc.)

1 Not involved in the process but affected by it

4 Other (please specify): _____

10. Approximately how many meetings per month did you attend in which you were involved with

Planning and making decisions regarding the project's change activities:____

Working on change activities such as problem identification or analysis, group problem-solving: ____

Receiving training, briefings, or updates on the change process: ____

SCALE: 1 None/Was not involved   2 Fewer than one per month   3 One per month
4 Two per month   5 Three per month   6 Four per month   7 Five or more per month

Change Tactics

11. Following are several things that might have been present in the change process that you experienced. Now, still thinking about this change process, please indicate the extent of your agreement or disagreement with each statement on the scale indicated, or select Don't Know if you had no experience with that factor. Then, if you agreed or strongly agreed with the statement, rate the extent to which you think it was a factor in the success of the change initiative.

SCALE: Strongly agree   Agree   Neutral   Disagree   Strongly disagree Don't know

<FOR STRONGLY AGREE OR AGREE ON ANY ITEM, SKIP PATTERN TO FACTOR SCALE FOR THAT ITEM.>

FACTOR SCALE: 4 To a large extent   3 To some extent   2 To a small extent   1 Not at all

1 I clearly understood the need and desirability for the change ___
2 I clearly understood the urgency for the change ___
3 Change leaders shared information to document the change problem to be addressed ___
4 I clearly understood the vision and outcomes for the change ___
5 I understood the plan for how the change initiative would be implemented (including basic activities and who would be involved) ___
6 Top management showed support and commitment, including a skilled senior individual or group to champion the cause for change ___
7 A cross section of employees was selected as a change team to guide the change process ___
8 I had the information and training that I needed to implement the change ___
9 Change leaders solicited my support for the change process ___
10 There was widespread participation of staff in the change process ___
11 There were adequate opportunities for team building and conflict management ___
12 The change was supported by the organization's governing body (e.g., Board of Directors, Board of Supervisors, or Commissioners) ___
13 The change was supported by organizations with whom we collaborate and other community partners ___
14 I clearly understood the progress on the change process as it was occurring ___
15 We had sufficient resources (staff time, necessary funding) for the change process ___
16 Any of my concerns were addressed by the change leaders ___
17 Monitoring tools were used to track progress and results ___
18 Project activities were revised as appropriate based on new information or changing conditions ___
19 The results of the change initiative were institutionalized through formal changes in policies and procedures, training, new or modified staff roles, permanent funding, etc. ___
20 The results of the change process were evaluated using data (e.g., pre–post data) ___
21 I was made aware of the results of the change initiative ___

12. As you look back on this change process, please list here the key accomplishments or results that you observed: _____
13. As you look back at this change process, please indicate here the extent to which you believe the goals for this change process were achieved. Goals were fully achieved, Goals were mostly achieved, Goals were only partly achieved, Goals were minimally or not at all achieved.
14. Please add here any other comments regarding factors that you observed as being important for the success a major change process: _____

THANK YOU for your time and participation. If you have any questions about this survey, please contact... _____

DONE

APPENDIX 8

Organizational Change Research: Some Challenges and History

I hope some readers might be curious to dig a bit deeper into what has been written, mainly in the professional literature, about organizational change in human service organizations (HSOs). This might be useful to you in at least three ways. First, this may give you an appreciation of the time span and the scope of research that has been reported in the literature regarding organizational change in HSOs, reinforcing its importance and relevance as an issue worth consideration. Second, you may learn some things about past change efforts that could be useful in your own work in the future. Third, it should become clear that there is a great deal that we don't yet know about organizational change, which can help us to be both cautious about how we engage in organizational change and confident that there is a good amount of evidence and practice wisdom that can be valuable in spite of their limitations.

I start with a general discussion of the quality of research on organizational change in general and then offer a brief history of the research regarding HSOs. The dynamic areas of implementation science and implementing evidence-based practices (EBPs) in general as well as other works cited in the book aren't necessarily covered here.

Limitations and Challenges Regarding Organizational Change Research

A vast literature on organizational change, mainly in the general business or organizational behavior fields, has become even more extensive and complex in recent years, ranging from books in the popular management press to scholarly articles. An expert in the field of organization development, Warner Burke (2018), listed several "sources of knowledge" regarding organizational change. First, there are books on theory (especially subfields of organizational behavior and organizational change). I would add to this category the academic literature from journals, including the *Journal of Change Management* and the *Journal of Organizational Change Management*. Much of this literature consists of theory development, studies examining only a limited number of possible variables or individual case studies, many of which offer limited guidance to actual practice. An exception is a relatively rare quantitative study with multiple variables (Parish, Cadwallader, & Busch, 2008), that examined relationships among individual-level variables, including job motivation, role autonomy, commitment to change, and perceived change outcomes. There is a growing literature on change readiness (Holt et al., 2007) and capacity for change (Judge & Douglas, 2009), but these studies do not often include variables regarding change interventions or outcomes.

Next is a category that Burke called the "trade literature." In my reading of some of this literature, also sometimes known as the "guru literature" or "management by bestseller," I have found that the books are typically based on only authors' experiences as consultants or on profiles of allegedly successful change leaders, with little empirical support beyond case narratives and limited or nonexistent conceptual models. Burke concluded that

> the problem here is that by using popular, actual organization cases as the base from which to derive principles, sooner or later—and today it is much sooner rather than later—the organizations studied and showcased no longer illustrate the principles because things have changed. (pp. 2–3)

He eloquently represented my thoughts on this literature in our current concern for EBPs (in this case, the practice of organizational change) this way: "Without independent verification and validation that what these authors recommend actually works under a variety of circumstances, however, leaves me with some concerns and skepticism" (p. 4).

Burke defined another category as the "story book," with the famous *Who Moved My Cheese?* as an example. I must say that I have spent very little time with such books. His final category includes books with a combination of trade book features and academic research, with Foster and Kaplan's *Creative Destruction* (2001) as an example. I hope that future books go in the direction of better use of high-quality and relevant research with an emphasis on practical application.

Other eloquent criticism of this "trade literature" was offered by K. Parry (2011) and Hughes (2015). Hughes focused specifically on the modern classic *Leading Change* by Kotter (1996), which I have cited in several places in this book. One of Hughes's most notable points is that in the second edition of this book (Kotter, 2012) there are essentially no updates except for a new Preface. Hughes's critique of Kotter's book also applies to other books in this field, reinforcing the skepticism of Burke. Appelbaum, Habashy, Malo, and Shafiq (2012) surveyed the literature to see what support they could find for Kotter's famous eight steps. They found that "not many studies set out to validate the full eight steps" (p. 776).

These literatures include, but rarely in the same source, conceptual frameworks, theoretical considerations, studies of selected variables in the change process, qualitative and quantitative methods, and practice guidelines. Conceptual frameworks (e.g., Burke, 2018) have been developed, but these are not often used to guide research. Practice guidelines are often presented without a conceptual framework and with evidence limited to the author's authority and experiences as a consultant or to findings from a single case study. Specific organizational change strategies, tactics, and methods are rarely examined in a detailed and systematic way.

K. Parry (2011; cited in Hughes, 2015, p. 10) offered this summary:

> "Organizational change" has become an interest for organizational consultants more so than for empirical researchers. There are many more books and articles on practitioner or conceptual scholarship than on theoretical or empirical scholarship. Much of the practitioner work is case study-based, and anecdotal and not rigorous in its conduct.

Leadership as a concept itself shows up a lot in organizational change. Hughes (2016) completed an extensive review of the literature on leadership in organizational change. Besides the usual conclusion that more research is needed, he also asserted that the field needs a "more fundamental rethink of the assumptions and paradigms influencing leadership and organizational change understanding" (p. 218).

Additionally, defining and measuring success are particularly complex and challenging, and perhaps for that reason success is rarely documented adequately. For example, in a study by Parish et al. (2008), the variables of "implementation success" and "improved performance" were based on only respondent opinion statements on a Likert scale.

Because there is not a commonly agreed on conceptual framework to guide research, this literature remains fragmented, with few ways to easily connect elements of new knowledge.

Paul Gibbons (2015), who had a long career as a consultant with a major international firm and is now focusing more on the science of organization change, has offered a lot of criticism of the evidence base for organizational change and some ideas on where to go from here. He made an important point regarding cause-and-effect problems in the literature:

> People who make strong causal claims about what they do and company performance are guilty of two logical fallacies: *post hoc ergo propter hoc* (it happened before it, so it caused it) and causal reductionism (reducing to a single cause something that could have been caused by many things). (pp. 7–8; italics in original)

Gibbons also noted some valuable distinctions between validity and usefulness:

> In the business world (especially in HR/change), we have a war, between the "validity people" and the "usefulness people." The validity people berate the usefulness people for lack of evidence and pseudoscience. The usefulness people, when they do not just ignore the researchers, respond, "Leave me alone, I have a job to do." The usefulness people, in their desire to get on with things, are guilty of dropping rigorous evidential standards, hence we get fads, pseudoscience, antiscience, and lack of accountability. They then berate the validity people for not "being in the real world." This theory-practice war destroys value and not just in business. (pp. 10–11)

I actually saw this as a major theme in my reviews of both the general management and HSO literatures. There are valid but not particularly useful studies in peer-reviewed journals regarding variables in organizational behavior and organizational psychology, but these usually do not offer much guidance to practitioners. There is allegedly useful writing on subjects such as performance pay, engagement surveys, strategy/change models, and large group interventions that seem useful but are not particularly valid (i.e., they are lacking strong research support).

Gibbons (2015) concluded that "change management culture needs to move toward increased validity and accountability even though it will take decades" (p. 10). To help this process, he created a "pyramid" of evidence for evidence-based management that has many parallels with traditional hierarchies of evidence for HSOs (pp. 274–281). At the bottom is professional experience, followed by expert opinions, case studies, surveys, and benchmarking. He did note that benchmarking is weak in the sense that it doesn't account for contextual factors, making adoptions across different organizations a bit risky. Cohort studies such as the classic *In Search of Excellence* and the more recent *Built to Last* and *Great by Choice* have lots of data but say nothing about cause and effect. Observational studies (e.g., surveys measuring variables that correlate with employee engagement) are better but, again, do not show causality. Just as with HSOs, randomized controlled trials [RCTs] are the gold standard, but "at the scale of entire businesses, the precision of a well-controlled RCT is impossible" (p. 281). He did add that RCTs can work for smaller units such as teams. One of his final assertions was "few practitioners read the well-conducted research studies. Stories sell more books" (p. 281).

He did offer some good suggestions for change leaders (with my additions):
Individual leaders can start small with some of these steps:

1. observe where knowledge and expertise come from... [what sources do we trust, and what are our standards?]
2. learn the essentials of what constitutes good, mediocre, and no evidence
3. challenge consultants and advisors... [e.g., "what is the evidence?"]
4. use critical thinking... [e.g., is the "burning platform" a valid metaphor?]
5. confirm, verify, and criticese theories.
6. be truthful about the scientific status of what we do... [we have to act without a lot of evidence]
7. hold ourselves to higher standards of evaluation... [did something really improve?]
8. base what we do upon the best science available and not myth, pseudoscience, pop science, or fad theories...
9. create cultures that insist on the scientific mindset, and using the scientific method. Gary Loveman, CEO [chief executive officer] of Caesars Entertainment, says "you can get fired for three things, stealing, sexual harassment, and running an experiment without a control group."
10. steer management reading and management education toward evidence-based books and away from the feel-good, or guru books. (pp. 283–284)

His final conclusion was that "with the *gradual raising of standards*, individual managers can begin to transform their practices, and over time, entire organizations may be shifted in this helpful direction" [italics in original] (p. 284).

In addition to the limitations in the research in this field, there has been one other area of criticism. It has become axiomatic in this field that up to 70% of organizational change efforts fail (e.g., Judge & Douglas, 2009; Pasmore, Woodman, & Shani, 2010), although a recent study found no evidence for these common assertions (Hughes, 2011). Paul Gibbons asserted that "dozens of surveys place the actual failure rate at around 50%. . . . These surveys are not robustly scientific, but they are the best that is available in this arena" (2015, p. 19). From another perspective, Stouten et al. (2018) found in their survey of the literature that only a third of executives thought their change initiatives succeeded, and in another study, only 38% of executives thought the change led to higher performance.

In perhaps the most ambitious attempt to summarize the best research on organizational change, ten Have et al. (2017) surveyed the literature and identified 18 "key assumptions" or assertions regarding organizational change. This list included the axiom that 70% of change efforts fail and assertions that factors including a clear vision, a sense of urgency, trust in the leader, a guiding coalition, participation, and emotional intelligence are essential to success. They found studies that tested the assumptions and drew conclusions about each. It was difficult to find good studies that directly and adequately tested the factors, so many of their conclusions should be treated as guarded. For example, they concluded that "a sense of urgency is related to change, but not necessarily as a precondition" (p. 81) and "the fact that no high-quality studies were found does not mean that a guiding coalition has no effect" (p. 111). What emerged overall was the paucity of good research on success factors.

By (2005) noted the weaknesses in current approaches, suggesting exploratory studies to identify critical success factors for change management. Pettigrew, Woodman, and

Cameron (2001) eloquently discussed some of these issues and made suggestions for advancing research in this area, some of which is addressed here. Regarding perhaps the most promising area for study, organizational change tactics, there is still a great deal to be learned about which factors are essential or valuable in creating successful organizational change, and which activities, in what sequences, contribute to success.

The weaknesses regarding conceptual frameworks, practice guidelines, and the evidence base, especially in books and case studies, point to a pressing need for increased knowledge regarding what factors are, in fact, most relevant in implementing successful change. Thoughtful and learning-oriented practitioners, typically agency administrators needing to change or improve some aspect of their organizations, want to know what "works" in organizational change, and researchers can help by providing valid, relevant, evidence-based knowledge for such practitioners.

The fragmented nature of this literature suggests that this topic warrants much more attention than it receives. With some exceptions, the evidence in this literature that can guide practitioners or consultants wanting to change organizations must be considered to be limited according to EBP standards that are applied to service delivery programs and to principles of evidence-based management (Briggs & McBeath, 2009).

Before we move on to the HSO literature, I offer another perspective: in addition to practitioners paying attention to research, practitioners can start producing better evidence on their own, perhaps guiding researchers on what they should do to build on practice knowledge. This will have to go beyond just telling "success" stories to using evidence standards in the academic literature. Practitioners are probably aware of successful programs, and if they can study them and describe their findings in valid ways, they can make notable contributions to the knowledge base. Researchers could lend their expertise to help practitioners examine their own work to create generalizable, practice-relevant knowledge.

One recent and comprehensive review of both the practitioner-oriented and scholarly literatures (Stouten et al., 2018) found disagreements even among commonly stated axioms regarding assessing the opportunity for change, creating a sense of urgency, formulating and communicating a compelling vision of the change, the role of a guiding coalition, mobilizing energy for the change, empowering employees, monitoring the change process, and institutionalizing the change. Nevertheless, they did feel confident in articulating these 10 principles:

- get facts on the nature of the problem
- assess and address the organization's readiness for change
- implement evidence-based change interventions
- develop effective change leadership throughout the organization
- develop and communicate a compelling change vision
- work with social networks (e.g., teams and professional groups) and tap their influence
- use enabling practices: goal setting, group and team learning, employee participation, fairness and justice principles such as respect for staff and transitional structures such as task forces
- promote experimentation in task groups
- assess change progress and outcomes
- institutionalize the change

They concluded that "at present, practicing managers appear to make little use of available scientific evidence in making decisions or changing their organizational practices" (p. 780), and of course, they "promote the ability of practitioners, educators, and scholars to better appreciate and access the available knowledge base regarding organizational change—and to recognize what remains unknown or untested" (p. 780).

Another major contribution to the organizational change literature, this with a particular emphasis on the evidence base, is a two-volume book edited by Hamlin, Ellinger, and Jones (2019). The first section of Volume I has nine chapters that lay out some conceptual foundations ranging from the challenges of evidence-based research on organizational change to specific change technologies, including action research, appreciative inquiry, culture change, and employee participation. Section 2 contains nine chapters written by organizational change practitioners from Australia, Brazil, Germany, Italy, Palestine, and the United Kingdom. Many of these are case-based reflections on key issues in the field. In Volume II, one section includes not only 33 case histories, mostly from the United States and the United Kingdom, but also 15 from other countries, including Germany, Honduras, India, Lebanon, Malaysia, Singapore, and the United Arab Emirates. Most involved for-profit organizations, but nine were in governmental organizations, and three were in nonprofit organizations. A final section includes a chapter on the challenges of conducting and studying EBPs in organizational change and some suggestions for addressing them. The final chapter summarizes the case research in previous chapters with some common insights and lessons learned. It ends with a conceptual process model for bridging the research–practice gap.

Organizational Change in Human Service Organizations

Before examining in more detail the academic literature regarding HSOs, it is worth mentioning here Mary Parker Follett, a social worker from the profession's settlement house days who actually became much more famous and influential in the general business and industry sector than in social work as what we call today a major "thought leader" in the field. Her work regarding employee participation in decision-making was particularly notable. One of her writings that touches specifically on organizational change is mentioned here. In 1949, when discussing the role of staff in organizational improvement, she noted that

in looking at almost any business we see many suggestions coming up from below. We find sub-executives trying to get upper executives to install mechanical improvements, to try a new chemical process, to adopt a plan for increasing incentives for workers, and so on. (Graham, 1995, p. 171)

This suggests the model of staff-initiated organizational change, although her focus was on leadership style, and how upper managers should get their staff more involved in providing input for making organizational improvements.

In HSOs, formal writing on organizational change began mostly in the 1970s. An annotated bibliography of *Management Practice in Social Welfare* (Patti & Osborne, 1976) reviewed the literature from general management studies and the human services. This included a classic book on organizational change by Bennis et al., which published its first edition in 1961, and a few articles or books that touched on organizational change. Also in the 1970s, several well-focused articles (Brager & Holloway, 1978; Patti, 1974; Patti & Resnick, 1985; Resnick, 1978; Resnick & Patti, 1980) appeared in the social work literature. Employee participation as a change method was fully described in a book by Toch and Grant (1982). They based their practice prescriptions solidly on earlier studies of the human relations movement, which included McGregor's famous Theory X and

Theory Y model, and also on the quality of working life movement that showed significant successes, mainly in the manufacturing sector, from the 1940s to the 1980s.

The *Encyclopedia of Social Work* has included some articles on administration that mentioned organizational change. Stein (1965) encouraged participation in decision-making, and Friesen (1987) mentioned participative management, but neither directly covered organizational change. Staff-initiated organizational change had its own article in 1987 (Holloway, 1987). Three relatively recent articles were on organizational change specifically (Packard, 2008, 2014, 2020).

A special issue of *Administration in Social Work* (Bargal & Schmid, 1992) summarized other work in this area.

An annotated bibliography of writing on organizational change includes a main emphasis on social work's principle of system change (Guerrero & Fenwick, 2014).

A special issue of *Training and Development in Human Services* (Curry et al., 2011) included studies of change initiatives in settings including child welfare and economic security. The issue also included articles on competencies for change agents and challenges in evaluating organizational change.

By (2009) edited a comprehensive book covering organizational change in the public sector. Osborne and Brown (2005) wrote a similar book on managing change and innovation in public service organizations.

Other examples of organizational change in HSOs include implementing evidence-based practices (Johnson & Austin, 2008); implementing knowledge management processes (Lee & Austin, 2012; Winship, 2012); and implementing new information systems (Gillingham, 2015; Lyons & Winter, 2010).

Some articles covered organization development methods in HSOs (e.g., Latting & Blanchard 1997; Norman & Keys, 1992; Packard, 1992; Resnick & Menefee, 1993). DuBrow, Wocher, and Austin (2001) described the use of organization development in a county human services agency. One case study of organizational change included the use of an organization development consultant supported by a visionary agency director to build a learning culture in a county human service agency (Lindberg & Meredith, 2012). Amodeo, Ellis, Hopwood, and Derman (2007) described the use of organization development principles, including forming change teams, gathering data, and empowering staff in a change process, in a substance abuse treatment agency.

There is a growing literature on organizational change in the nonprofit sector. Eadie (2006) outlined a model for change and innovation in nonprofit organizations. Allen, Smith, and Da Silva (2013) examined the relationships among leadership style and climate related to change readiness and creativity in churches, and McMurray, Islam, Sarros, and Pirola-Merlo (2013) examined relationships among leadership, climate, and innovation. Becker, Antuar, and Everett (2011) described implementation of a performance management system in which leaders consulted with staff on its design. Ramos (2007) noted the value of consultation and the involvement of executive and management staff in change success in a community agency in Hawaii. In a case study of an organizational redesign in a nonprofit child welfare organization (Ezell et al., 2002), a staff survey revealed perceptions of successful implementation and the solving of some problems, but no changes in staff performance. Whittaker et al. (2006) described an implementation of EBP in a nonprofit child mental health agency, noting the importance of logic modeling, partnerships with researchers, and ongoing evaluation. Callahan (2009) described her experiences as a change agent at a community mental health center. Kerman, Freundlich, Lee, and Brenner (2012) offered a rich case study of a major programmatic change in a child welfare agency and some useful recommendations for organizational change implementation. Vito (2019) provided a good review of current research to introduce findings from a detailed case study of an organizational change initiative in a large mental health and development services agency that offers valuable opportunities for debriefing and learning.

Research focusing on the *content* of organizational change has been conducted in several practice settings. Change efforts in public child welfare have been described (e.g., Cohen, 1999; McBeath, Briggs, & Aisenberg, 2009). Regarding welfare reform, Austin (2004) and others described 21 cases in content areas, including workforce participation, self-sufficiency programs, behavioral health, and community partnerships where organizational change occurred. A similar, more recent, edited volume (Carnochan, DuBrow, & Austin, 2019) covered a range of change initiatives, focusing mostly on the content of the changes (e.g., community relations and financial literacy). It also included a section on knowledge sharing to support EBP implementation and several chapters on leadership and career dynamics for managers.

In the homeless services field, Guarino, Soares, Konnath, Clervil, and Bassuk (2009) developed a toolkit for agencies to use to implement trauma-informed care. The manual includes not only detail on principles of trauma-informed care but also organizational change steps to take to ensure implementation. A similar manual (Zvetina, 2009) offers detailed guidelines on both implementation of a housing first model and also organizational change tactics to facilitate implementation. Gao, Waynor, and O'Donnell (2009) described an organizational change process to implement a supportive employment program in a supportive housing agency.

Summary

There is an extensive literature on organizational change in the business and organizational studies fields. The evidence base of much of this work is not strong, and there is limited consideration of conceptual frameworks and theories, many studies of only selected variables in the change process, and studies that generally do not build on or connect with relevant earlier research or models. Several authors have reported very low success rates of organizational change initiatives. Practicing managers seem to not pay much attention to good evidence that does exist.

The literature on organizational change in HSOs has some of the same limitations noted in the organizational change literature in general. Glisson (2012) eloquently summarized the limitations in this literature, from poor specification of intervention strategies to inadequate outcome measures. With exceptions, including the research on ARC (availability, responsiveness, and continuity) by Glisson and colleagues (e.g., Hemmelgarn & Glisson, 2018) and implementation science research, much published research involves individual case studies, often with weak theory, and quantitative studies that generally do not build on or connect with relevant earlier research or models. It is difficult to derive generic practice principles from this work.

APPENDIX 9

Evidence for The Model

> If we knew what we were doing, it wouldn't be called research, would it?
>
> —Anonymous

I summarize here some findings from several studies that colleagues and I have done regarding the use of change tactics that guided my writing and then suggest some ideas for future research.

In my search of the literature, I noted and saved (skimmed many of them) over 500 articles, books, monographs, or book chapters that I thought had some practical relevance for my research on human service organizations (HSOs) specifically. I found a lot of material that supported my research and the key sources that my work was built on. Some seemed too esoteric to offer useful practice guidelines. If I saw something relevant with at least some empirical support, I built it into the material included in the book, mostly in Section 3.

Within my limits of time, energy, and intellect, I did the best I could to draw conclusions from what I found. As I noted in the Introduction, a reviewer discussing the work of an Italian Renaissance art expert who had to identify the artists of paintings cited this description by John Pope-Hennessy: "His success was due not to the belief that he was necessarily right but to the knowledge that, of available opinions, especially on great artists, he was least likely to be wrong" (Kaiser, 2013, p. 13). Finding and analyzing data and drawing conclusions in work such as mine may never lead to the level of definitiveness of an art expert identifying an artist, but the sense of not being "wrong," whatever that means, is something I strive for.

The work colleagues and I and other researchers have done regarding change tactics is clearly at a rudimentary level, but I think what we have found is encouraging and worth a good deal more study. I include some implications for further research at the end of this appendix item.

A Content Analysis of the Literature

As I became familiar with the literature on organizational change, and specifically in HSOs, it seemed to me that, besides all the limitations covered in Appendix 8, there was very little attention given to specific tactics that change leaders could use to enhance the prospects of success of change initiatives. To explore this further, Amber Shih and I (2014) conducted a content analysis of the literature, starting with a review summarized in a public administration journal (Fernandez & Rainey, 2006) and then the HSO literature, with particular attention to research methods and the use of change tactics.

Our study included a content analysis of two related streams of literature on organizational change, with quantification of several aspects of both the research methods used in these studies and the research findings. The first stream of research was derived from a thorough and eloquent narrative review by Fernandez and Rainey (2006) in *Public Administration Review*, which had a particular focus on the public sector, a common arena for HSOs. Fernandez and Rainey conducted a review and content analysis, "providing an overview of the vast literature on organizational change that demonstrates its complexity but that also helps to bring some order to the literature" (p. 2).

They summarized their findings as factors contributing to successful organizational change with 8 propositions and 22 subpropositions, which identified

> points of consensus in the literature on successful implementation of such changes. These points serve as testable propositions for researchers to examine in future research, and as major considerations for leaders of change initiatives in public organizations. (p. 2)

They discussed the use of these propositions with a primary focus on public sector organizations. They concluded that

> a number of empirical studies have supported many of the propositions from these models and frameworks. This suggests a pattern of consensus about what accounts for successful implementation of planned change. We examined streams of research relating to organizational change, including work on public sector reform and innovation and policy implementation, to distill a set of factors that contribute to successful implementation of organizational change in the public sector. (p. 6)

From this set of propositions and subpropositions, they created a list of 22 change tactics. This list formed the structure for categorizing tactics mentioned in the references selected and described below.

For the first analysis, we reviewed references in the Fernandez and Rainey (2006) article that appeared, based on the contexts in which they were described in the article, to address organizational change tactics, using the methods described below.

For a second content analysis, we focused specifically on the literature from 2005 to 2011 in HSOs. Many of the abstracts we found only mentioned organizational change in passing, often noting that there were "implications for organizational change" or simply mentioned the benefits and risks of organizational change, without discussing any specific tactics.

In the first analysis, using the Fernandez and Rainey (2006) article, we identified 85 references that actually mentioned change tactics. Of the 85 references, 42 each were journal articles and books, and 1 was a monograph. In the study of human services references, 38 were from journals and 1 was a monograph. The contrast between the two sources could be expected, with the former explicitly using any source (e.g., book or journal), while the automated search of the HSO literature was much more likely to identify articles rather than books. In fact, while there have been hundreds of books published on organizational change in general, primarily in the business and government sectors, there had been very few such books (e.g., Bloom & Farragher, 2013) published in the human services during the period we studied.

Both sets of data were assessed to identify the sector that was studied in each reference. Most Fernandez and Rainey references were in the government/public sector, while the human services references were nearly equally divided among government/public, nonprofit, and a combination of sectors.

For both the Fernandez and Rainey and HSO references, the most common evidence base was literature reviews (29% for Fernandez and Rainey; 28% for HSOs). Multiple case studies also represented 28% of HSO references, and this method was found in 26% of Fernandez and Rainey references. Single-case studies (24%), the author's authority as a consultant (14%), and the author's authority as a researcher or teacher (13%) were the next most common sources in Fernandez and Rainey. Of these, only the single-case study (21%) was found in the human services references, probably reflecting a stronger evidence base in refereed journal articles showing up in an automated search, compared to the Fernandez and Rainey data, which included many books. In some references, more than one evidence source was apparent. For example, a book might have used as the evidence base both the author's experiences and a survey of the literature. In those cases, more than one evidence base was recorded.

Qualitative methods were used in 76% of Fernandez and Rainey references and 58% of HSO references. Studies using both qualitative and quantitative methods were the next most common, followed by studies using strictly quantitative methods.

Thirty-two percent of the Fernandez and Rainey references mentioned a specific theory or model, while 21% of the HSO references did so. Only 8% of the references from Fernandez and Rainey articles reported statistically significant findings, while in the human services literature, 10% reported statistically significant findings.

The key section of this research is the assessment of the extent to which the references mentioned any of the 22 change tactics that were based on Fernandez and Rainey's (2006) article.

The most frequently mentioned tactics were support and commitment from top management (mentioned by 66% of Fernandez & Rainey references and 59% of HSO references). The organization providing sufficient resources for the change initiative was the second most commonly mentioned tactic (in 61% and 46% of references, respectively). Two tactics were the third most often mentioned in Fernandez and Rainey, clearly communicating the vision and desired outcomes for the change and having a clear and specific plan for how the change initiative would be implemented (59%). In HSOs, the third most common tactic was widespread participation of staff in the change process (40%).

The Fernandez and Rainey references mentioned an average of 6.64 tactics each, and the HSO references mentioned an average of 5.13 tactics each. There were two Fernandez and Rainey references that mentioned 18 tactics, and two mentioned 17 tactics. The HSO reference with the most tactics mentioned 16, with the next highest mentioning 12 tactics. In several references in each group, no change tactics could be found.

Several factors beyond the 22 being studied were occasionally mentioned. Factors mentioned more than once included management being trusted, rewards for staff, a change-oriented culture, and getting support from outside and internal stakeholders.

This study provided a useful but necessarily preliminary overview of the extent to which tactics are mentioned in the literature and the evidence supporting them. As may be expected, tactics were more commonly mentioned in the Fernandez and Rainey references, which were the basis of the list of change tactics. In the Fernandez and Rainey references, 7 of the 22 tactics were mentioned in over 50% of the references, and an additional 10 were mentioned in 40%–49%.

In the human services literature, only one tactic was mentioned by over 50% of the references, and two tactics were mentioned in between 40% and 49% of the references. Both sets of references had most frequent mentions of the same top two tactics.

Because there is no standard for what could be expected here, it can't be said that the fact that a tactic was mentioned by a particular percentage of writers validates theory or is necessarily essential or important in organizational change. Further research, using more systematic methods, will be needed to learn which tactics, and in what combinations, really are associated with successful organizational change.

Overall, many of the articles and books contained tactics that were not well supported by higher levels of evidence in the evidence-based practice (EBP) hierarchy, perhaps due to the difficulty in carrying out such research and the lack of well-developed research designs when the works were written.

Literature reviews, case studies, and authority-based assertions were the most common sources of evidence, suggesting that a greater use of quantitative methods such as surveys of all employees in an organization experiencing formal organizational change could augment rich and detailed case studies to develop new knowledge that can better guide researchers and practitioners as they work to improve organizational effectiveness.

This assessment of the literature on organizational change can be viewed from several perspectives. First, a study of organizational change could be assessed from a hierarchy of evidence perspective. Johnson and Austin (2008), in an article focusing on EBP implications for organizational change, listed the following levels:

- Systematic reviews and meta-analyses
- Randomized control trials
- Cohort studies
- Case–control studies
- Cross-sectional surveys
- Case reports

Of course, randomized control trials are not possible when studying organizational change, and meta-analyses are not currently possible due to the limited number of studies using similar methods. However, case–control studies (matching and studying cases, e.g., regarding organizational change, comparing successful and unsuccessful organizational change interventions) could be adapted to research on organizational change. Cross-sectional surveys and case reports are frequently used to study organizational change, and if enough such cases are studied using similar methods, systematic reviews may be possible.

Another perspective, according to Johnson and Austin, is to consider "the multiple sources of knowledge that are available to practitioners who seek to engage in evidence-based practice" (2008, p. 244). From this perspective, the occasional systematic review, existing case reports, authority-based books by consultants, quantitative studies, and other sources could be assessed as a group to identify the best available evidence to guide an organizational change intervention. The value of using multiple sources has also been noted (Dixon-Woods, Agarwal, Jones, Young, & Sutton, 2005; Rozas & Klein, 2010).

The literature can also be assessed in terms of the variables being studied. In the current study, the small number of references that explicitly mentioned theory suggests that future work in this area could be strengthened by using a theory or model (Burke, 2018, e.g., offered several), and ideally by using common models across studies. Comprehensive models of change include more variables than a typical researcher studying HSOs could easily manage logistically, ranging from environmental forces and structure to dynamics of leadership and organizational culture and climate, organizational processes such as reward systems, and service delivery technologies. Some research on organizational dynamics in HSOs has looked at a wider range of variables (e.g., Hemmelgarn & Glisson, 2018; Jaskyte, 2011; Yoo et al., 2007), but research on organizational change has not typically reached this level of comprehensiveness.

The Use of Organizational Change Tactics: Preliminary Studies

Based on this review of the existing literature on organizational change, I developed a conceptual model for organizational change (Packard, 2013) and an instrument, the Organizational Change Tactics Questionnaire (OCTQ), to enable staff respondents (staff in HSOs) to indicate the extent to which they observed change tactics that came from the literature review I just described. There are two versions. On the first, respondents are asked to retrospectively assess two organizational change processes with which they were familiar: one that was successful and another that was unsuccessful. In the other version, they are asked only about one organizational change that they recently experienced.

For the successful and unsuccessful change efforts, respondents describe the change goals and indicate the extent to which they observed 22 organizational change tactics. For the process they saw as successful, they are also asked to indicate the extent to which each tactic was a factor in the success. Demographic data include the respondent's position, the program in which they worked, and their role in the change process; agency size; and the use of consultants.

The original version of the survey asked respondents to indicate in a yes/no format whether or not they observed each change tactic. This version was used with a youth and family services agency (Packard, 2017) and also with participants in a leadership development program for county managers that I was involved with, and with several cohorts of students in a social work administration class that I taught. The first study (Packard & Gibson, 2014), described in more detail below, used this version of the survey.

After those uses of the instrument, several changes were made. In the original version, tactics were worded as abstract principles to be followed, so that a respondent could simply indicate whether or not they were observed. For the next three studies, one with child welfare workers in 13 Colorado counties (Packard et al., 2015), one with staff of a large homeless shelter (Packard, 2019), and a third with members of the Network for Social Work Management (Packard, 2016), the response scale was changed from yes/no responses regarding whether or not the respondent observed a particular tactic to a Likert scale from 1 (*strongly disagree*) to 5 (*strongly agree*), showing the extent to which the tactic was observed. Along with this change, 11 questions were reworded to enable a respondent to answer in the first person on the extent to which one experienced the tactic. For example, "The vision and outcomes for the change were clearly communicated" was reworded to "I clearly understood the vision and outcomes for the change." Three questions were deleted, and three were added.

I first summarize the findings from the study of youth agency staff, leadership development program participants, and social work administration students. Then, I mention the study with the Colorado child welfare workers, the homeless shelter study, and the survey of the Network for Social Work Management (Packard, 2016). Two of these, the homeless services program and the youth and family agency (Father Joe's Villages and San Diego Youth Services, respectively) are used as examples in Section 3.

County Managers, Master's of Social Work Students, and Community Agency Staff

Data from the first study are from survey administrations to three sets of subjects (Packard & Gibson, 2014). One set of subjects ($N = 153$) was a group of middle managers in eight county human service agencies in Southern California who were participating in a leadership development program that included a day on organizational change. Another set of subjects were master's in social work students ($N = 45$) in a social work administration class that included coverage of organizational change. The third group of subjects were staff of a youth and family service agency ($N = 129$), resulting in a total of 327 subjects.

Change goals were quite varied, ranging from improving program operations (e.g., changing data systems) or procedures (e.g., child abuse risk assessment tools) to improving efficiency.

Regarding the use of specific change tactics (see Table A9.1), there were statistically significant differences between successful and unsuccessful initiatives on each of the tactics. It should be noted that one tactic noted by Fernandez and Rainey, the use of coercion or threats, was stated as one to avoid. This was presented in the OCTQ in a neutral sense, simply asking respondents to indicate whether or not it was observed. There were no significant differences between successful and unsuccessful changes on this item. This may be used as a check for response set bias: The fact that response patterns were different on this question may suggest that this bias was not a factor.

The youth and family service agency mentioned here was San Diego Youth Services, one of the case examples used in Section 3. In addition to the quantitative data summarized here, I did a fuller analysis of quantitative and qualitative data from that study (Packard, 2017). Ten of the 22 tactics were observed by at least 50% of the respondents. Change goals were seen as fully or mostly achieved by 95% of the respondents. According to a content analysis of an open-ended question regarding change results, responses typically showed results reflecting accomplishment of the stated goals. Eighteen of the tactics were seen as change success factors to a "great extent" or "some extent." Examples of the use of many of the tactics were provided in an interview with the chief executive officer and a focus group of two staff members.

Colorado Child Welfare Workers

The Colorado child welfare workers sample consisted of child welfare staff who responded to an online survey 3 years into the organizational change effort. The study was part of a larger evaluation of organizational change that occurred between 2009 and 2012.

We found that individuals who reported higher use of change tactics also reported significantly higher ratings that the initiative achieved its goals, indicating that staff who perceived change tactics as being used also perceived the initiative as more successful. We also found that individuals who participated more frequently in change activities (planning and decision-making meetings) showed higher perceptions of change success, and

Table A9.1 Percentage of Respondents Who Observed Change Tactics in a Successful Organizational Change

The need and desirability for the change were clearly and persuasively communicated by leaders	91%*
The urgency for the change was clearly and persuasively stated by leaders	87%*
Top management showed support and commitment, including a senior individual or group to champion the cause for change	84%*
A cross section of employees was selected for a team to guide the change	63%*
The change team was seen as legitimate by most members of the organization	77%*
Key individuals and groups affected by the change were involved and solicited for their support	80%*
There was widespread participation of staff in the change process	76%*
The vision and outcomes for the change were clearly communicated	85%*
The change was supported by political overseers (e.g., board or CAO/CEO) and external stakeholders	59%*
Progress on the change process was clearly communicated throughout the organization	69%*
Criticism, threats, or coercion were used to reduce resistance to the change	16%
The organization provided sufficient resources (staff time, necessary funding) for the change effort	75%*
Change agents gathered information to document the change problem to be addressed and shared this with staff	69%*
There was a clear plan for how the change initiative would be implemented (schedule, strategy, who would be involved, and who would be accountable for planned activities)	81%*
The change strategy was based on a sound causal theory for how the results would be achieved	63%*
Potential sources of resistance (individuals or groups) were identified, and strategies for addressing resistance were developed	52%*
Monitoring tools were used to track progress	67%*
Project activities were revised as appropriate based on new information or changing conditions	69%*
The change was comprehensive and integrated, so that relevant subsystems (e.g., HR, finance, programs) were compatible or congruent with the overall change	64%*
The results of the change initiative were institutionalized through formal changes in policies and procedures, new or modified staff roles, permanent funding, etc.	86%*
The results of the change effort were evaluated using data (e.g., pre–post data)	58%*
Staff were made aware of the results of the change initiative	76%*

CAO, county administrative officer; CEO, chief executive officer; HR, human resources.

*Statistically significant difference between successful and unsuccessful change efforts.

individuals who received regular training, briefings, or updates also perceived the initiative as more successful.

Homeless Services Program

The agency, Father Joe's Villages, had recently completed a major organizational change that involved creating a new services model featuring multidisciplinary teams. I was able to ask staff to complete an online survey in which they could share their observations of the change initiative. The main part of the survey was the new version of the OCTQ.

As shown in Table A9.2, respondents tended to strongly agree or agree that tactics were observed, with only three averaging below the neutral level of 3, and one of those was clearly undesirable. Respondents were also asked about the extent to which each tactic was a factor in success, on a 3-point scale with 3 indicating *to a large extent* and two indicating *to some extent*. For all tactics except two, the mean score was over 2.00. Sixty percent of respondents indicated that the change goals of the successful change were fully or mostly achieved. Forty percent saw the goals as partly achieved.

Network for Social Work Management

In another study (Packard, 2016), using the later version of the OCTQ, members of the Network for Social Work Management were surveyed. An email announcement was sent to all members of the organization, asking them to respond if they had experienced organizational change processes at work. One hundred forty-seven responded, with 95 (65%) indicated having experienced both successful and unsuccessful organizational change processes. Of these, there were 33 matched pairs of responses for both successful and unsuccessful changes.

Examples of successful and unsuccessful change processes included

Successful change	Unsuccessful change
Restructuring care management requirements and procedures	Implement a new service delivery model
Increase staff morale, better interdepartmental communication, strengthen ease-of-use of IT	Redesign organization with an outdated mission and business model
Enhance teamwork, develop new initiatives	Improve the quality of services

IT, information technology.

As shown in Table A9.3, there were statistically significant differences regarding the extent to which each tactic was observed, with the tactics being seen more often in the successful change processes.

Respondents were also asked about the extent to which each tactic was a factor in success, on a 4-point scale with 4 indicating *to a large extent* and 3 indicating *to some extent*. For all tactics except three, the mean score was over 3.00. Seventy-five percent of respondents indicated that the change goals of the successful change were fully or

Table A9.2 Observation of Change Tactic, Change Tactic as a Success Factor

Change Tactic (Ranked by Most Observed)	Observed Tactic[a]	Factor[b]
The results of the change effort were evaluated using data (e.g., pre–post data)	4.19 (0.834)	2.27 (0.647)
The change was supported by the agency's board of directors	4.09 (0.539)	1.92 (0.729)
I clearly understood the need and desirability for the change	4.08 (1.06)	2.29 (0.588)
I clearly understood the vision and outcomes for the change	3.96 (0.871)	2.47 (0.624)
Top management showed support and commitment, including a skilled senior individual or group to champion the cause for change	3.95 (0.999)	2.27 (0.458)
The results of the change initiative were institutionalized through formal changes in policies and procedures, training, new or modified staff roles, permanent funding, etc.	3.90 (0.684)	2.31 (0.630)
I clearly understood the urgency for the change	3.81 (1.06)	2.18 (0.636)
A cross section of employees was selected as a change team to guide the change effort	3.80 (0.941)	2.00 (0.632)
Project activities were revised as appropriate based on new information or changing conditions	3.80 (0.616)	2.33 (0.492)
Monitoring tools were used to track progress and results	3.60 (1.06)	2.10 (0.738)
There was widespread participation of staff in the change process	3.57 (1.08)	2.00 (1.04)
Change leaders shared information to document the change problem to be addressed	3.54 (0.932)	2.27 (0.884)
I understood the plan for how the change initiative would be implemented (including basic activities and who would be involved)	3.46 (1.10)	2.07 (0.829)
Any of my concerns were addressed by the change leaders	3.39 (1.03)	2.30 (0.483)
I clearly understood the progress on the change process as it was occurring	3.33 (0.917)	2.0 (0.793)
There were adequate opportunities for team building and conflict management	3.30 (1.22)	1.77 (0.725)
I had the information and training that I needed to implement the change	3.26 (1.05)	2.07 (0.884)
The change was supported by organizations with whom we collaborate and other community partners	3.25 (1.04)	2.25 (0.500)

Table A9.2   Continued

Change Tactic (Ranked by Most Observed)	Observed Tactic[a]	Factor[b]
I was made aware of the results of the change initiative	3.25 (1.15)	1.92 (1.24)
Change leaders solicited my support for the change effort	2.95 (1.29)	1.78 (1.09)
We had sufficient resources (staff time, necessary funding) for the change effort	2.84 (1.26)	2.13 (0.354)
I experienced criticism, threats, or coercion to reduce resistance to the change	2.04 (1.20)	1.29 (1.38)

Mean, (SD)

Ranked by mean score on observed.

[a] Observed the tactic: 1 = strongly disagree; 2 = disagree; 3 = neutral; 4 = agree; 5 = strongly agree.

[b] Tactic was a success factor: 3 = to a large extent; 2 = some; 1 = small; 0 = not at all.

mostly achieved. Twelve percent saw the goals of the unsuccessful change fully or mostly achieved.

These studies shared some common limitations. Respondents might have had faulty recall of earlier events, possibly overstating or distorting tactics reported or perhaps recalling and reporting tactics that actually occurred. Because of the small samples in these studies, these results must be considered preliminary. Also, qualitative data gathered through interviews with agency respondents cannot be fully representative of what actually happened.

Implications for Further Research

Armenakis and Bedeian (1999) asserted that "research reporting what processes have been used to implement changes should be extended to include how well and when specific tactics and strategies for change have been successful" (p. 312). My research has been intended to respond to that suggestion.

While notable progress has been made in extracting new knowledge and practice principles from case studies (e.g., Austin, 2004), research that can show relationships between change interventions and specific aspects of organizational performance are still rare and represent opportunities for further research.

Comprehensively studying organizational change could include a number of organizational variables, including those listed above and also staff and organizational readiness (Holt, Armenakis, Feild, & Harris, 2007) and capacity for change (Judge & Douglas, 2009). The last two have been extensively studied in the organizational change literature but have not often been studied in relation to organizational change tactics and outcomes of an organizational change initiative. All of these areas represent rich opportunities for further study, ideally by examining relationships among different combinations of important variables.

Table A9.3 Observation of Change Tactic, Change Tactic as a Success Factor: Successful and Unsuccessful Change Processes: Means and Differences Between Them

Tactic	Successful Mean	Unsuccessful Mean	Difference	Significance
I clearly understood the need and desirability for the change	4.61	4.11	0.494	0.01
I clearly understood the urgency for the change	4.39	4.00	0.391	0.055
Change leaders shared information to document the change problem to be addressed	3.76	3.00	0.761	0.049
I clearly understood the vision and outcomes for the change	4.13	3.44	0.689	0.021
I understood the plan for how the change initiative would be implemented (including basic activities and who would be involved)	3.93	2.91	1.020	0.003
Top management showed support and commitment, including a skilled senior individual or group to champion the cause for change	3.91	2.97	0.942	0.018
A cross section of employees was selected as a change team to guide the change effort	3.24	2.37	0.868	0.006
I had the information and training that I needed to implement the change	3.61	2.46	1.152	0.001
Change leaders solicited my support for the change effort	3.61	2.97	0.637	0.118
There was widespread participation of staff in the change process	3.26	2.24	1.026	0.005
There were adequate opportunities for team building and conflict management	3.27	2.23	1.038	0.006
The change was supported by the agency's board of directors	4.02	3.06	0.965	0.005
The change was supported by organizations with whom we collaborate and other community partners	3.89	2.20	1.691	0.001
I clearly understood the progress on the change process as it was occurring	3.59	2.89	0.701	0.037
We had sufficient resources (staff time, necessary funding) for the change effort	3.30	1.91	1.390	0.000

Table A9.3   Continued

Tactic	Successful Mean	Unsuccessful Mean	Difference	Significance
Any of my concerns were addressed by the change leaders	3.53	1.94	1.590	0.000
Monitoring tools were used to track progress and results	3.20	2.29	0.910	0.037
Project activities were revised as appropriate based on new information or changing conditions	3.63	2.26	1.373	0.000
The results of the change initiative were institutionalized through formal changes in policies and procedures, training, new or modified staff roles, permanent funding, etc.	3.67	2.43	1.245	0.002
The results of the change effort were evaluated using data (e.g., pre–post data)	3.33	2.34	0.983	0.017
I was made aware of the results of the change initiative	3.78	2.94	0.840	0.002

Observed the tactic: 1 = strongly disagree; 2 = disagree; 3 = neutral; 4 = agree; 5 = strongly agree.

Perhaps the most promising factors to study together are organizational readiness and change capacity, change leader behaviors, change tactics and methods, and results in terms of both implementation of the change and client outcomes. There are existing measurement tools for these variables and information systems to measure client outcomes, but relationships among them are not often examined in the same study.

Possible research questions include

- What preconditions (e.g., organizational history, readiness, capacity, climate) affect the successful use of particular change tactics? How should tactics be adjusted based on these contextual factors?
- Do certain styles of leadership interact with particular tactics to enhance prospects for success? For example, measures of leadership (e.g., Bass & Avolio, 2006; Kouzes & Posner, 2017) could be correlated with data on organizational change tactics used and change results to assess the effects of leadership.
- What specific change tactics, and in what combinations, are more likely to be successful, generically or with reference to unique conditions such as the change goal and organizational climates and cultures?
- What change methods, such as organization development, are successful and under what conditions?
- How is success impacted by contextual factors such as type of program, agency size or structure, environmental context, staff, or clients?

- What direct connections can be made among preconditions, change activities, and organizational outcomes?

Relationships among variables such as these could be studied by surveying employees to see if organizational conditions and the use of particular change tactics are more prominent in successful than in unsuccessful initiatives, as the literature suggests. Variations in the success of change initiatives could also be studied when a new program is implemented statewide. Individual counties could be studied to compare the extent of new program implementation, change variables such as organizational change tactics used, and client outcomes.

As conceptual models are further refined and success factors are more definitively identified, future research can be more precisely based on this prior work, helping to unify this growing body of knowledge.

I do recognize the complexity related to how all these variables may be connected and how difficult it would be to do such large-scale studies. For example, challenges of connecting specific change initiative results to client outcomes can be daunting. Measuring the effects on client outcomes of implementation of a new program in child welfare, for example, would involve assessing not only organizational preconditions and the extent of implementation of the intervention itself, but also waiting for a year or more to assess effects on clients, such as family reunification or avoidance of further abuse and neglect.

The literature reviewed here was based almost entirely on allegedly successful cases of organizational change, often using data provided by the author as a consultant or in case studies where the data may come only from selected administrators, who were often the change leaders, and therefore represent a limited and perhaps one-sided perspective on what actually occurred. Future research should go beyond gathering data from only a few managers or allegedly successful cases. Contrasting equivalent successful and unsuccessful organizational change initiatives could greatly strengthen the evidence base in this area.

Rather than the common approach of gathering data from only a few managers or allegedly successful cases, mixed-methods studies, using both qualitative methods such as observation and interviewing and quantitative methods such as surveys of participants and organizational outcomes data should strengthen the evidence base, providing practitioners such as agency administrators acting as change agents with stronger and more useful evidence to guide them as they work to improve the effectiveness of their organizations.

Collaboration between researchers and practicing administrators and other HSO staff is especially important when studying organizational change—a subject that can affect any employee of an HSO. I conducted one such project through an "intermediary organization" for practice research (Austin & Carnochan, 2020): the Southern Area Consortium of Human Services (SACHS, n.d.; https://theacademy.sdsu.edu/programs/sachs/), a collaboration between the SDSU School of Social Work's Academy for Professional Excellence and eight Southern California county human service directors. As part of the SACHS leadership development program, participants completed the OCTQ, with results fed back at an all-day session on organizational change to link participants' real practice experiences with a model of organizational change. (This research was described above, with the studies of master's in social work students and community agency staff.) Austin and Carnochan's book offers many more models of collaborative practice research.

In spite of all the challenges in doing this work, I hope policymakers, foundations, organizational leaders, and researchers will see the value of such research and keep taking steps to advance the knowledge base, to the benefit of HSOs and their clients and communities.

About the Author

Tom Packard is a professor emeritus in the School of Social Work at San Diego State University, with teaching specialties in administration, macro practice, and social policy. For 15 years, he was a faculty consultant with the school's Academy for Professional Excellence, providing research, consultation, and training support to the Southern Area Consortium of Human Services, which includes the directors of eight Southern California county human service agencies. He has 20 years of experience as an organization development consultant specializing in government and nonprofit organizations ranging in size from 10,000 to 5 employees. He was an organization effectiveness specialist for 6½ years in the city of San Diego's Organization Effectiveness Program, which he managed for 1½ years. Prior to entering teaching, he was the manager of two nonprofit human service agencies and was a program evaluator for San Diego County. He received his doctorate in social welfare at UCLA, where he also studied in the Graduate School of Management and the Center for Quality of Working Life.

References

Aarons, G., Ehrhart, M., Farahnak, L., & Hurlburt, M. (2015). Leadership and organizational change for implementation (LOCI): A randomized mixed method pilot study of a leadership and organization development intervention for evidence-based practice implementation. *Implementation Science, 15*, 1–12.

Aarons, G., Hurlburt, M., & Horwitz, S. (2011). Advancing a conceptual model of evidence-based practice implementation in public service sectors. *Administration and Policy in Mental Health and Mental Health Services Research, 38*(1), 4–23.

Abdul-Jabbar, K., & Walton, A. (2004). *Brother in arms: The epic story of the 761st tank battalion, WWII's forgotten heroes.* New York: Broadway Books.

Abrams, L., & Moio, J. (2009). Critical race theory and the cultural competence dilemma in social work education. *Journal of Social Work Education, 45*(2), 245–261 https://doi.org/10.5175/JSWE.2009.200700109

Ackerman Anderson, L. (2020). *Launching successful transformation.* Being First, Inc., Brandman University, January 19, 2020

Acosta, J., & Chinman, M. (2011). Building capacity for outcomes measurement on human service originations: The getting to outcomes method. In J. Magnabosco & R. Manderscheid (Eds.), *Outcomes measurement in the human services* (2nd ed., pp. 73–87). Washington, DC: NASW Press.

Adams, S. (1996). *The dilbert principle.* New York: HarperBusiness.

Administration for Children and Families. (2012). *Information memorandum.* Retrieved from http://www.acf.hhs.gov/sites/default/files/cb/im1207.pdf

Agency for Healthcare Research and Quality. (n.d.) *Plan-do-study-act cycle.* Retrieved from https://innovations.ahrq.gov/qualitytools/plan-do-study-act-pdsa-cycle

AI Commons. (n.d.). *5-D cycle of appreciative inquiry.* Retrieved from https://appreciativeinquiry.champlain.edu/learn/appreciative-inquiry-introduction/5-d-cycle-appreciative-inquiry/

Akingbola, K., Rogers, S., & Baluch, A. (2019). *Change management in nonprofit organizations.* Cham, Switzerland: Palgrave Macmillan.

Alfes, K., Truss, C., & Gill, J. (2010). The HR manager as change agent: Evidence from the public sector. *Journal of Change Management, 10*(1), 109–127.

Al-Haddad, S., & Kotnour, T. (2015). Integrating the organizational change literature: A model for successful change. *Journal of Organizational Change Management, 28*(2), 234–262.

Allas, T., Dillon, R., & Gupta, V. (2018, April). A smarter approach to cost reduction in the public sector. *Public Sector Practice.* McKinsey & Company. Retrieved from https://www.mckinsey.com/industries/public-and-social-sector/our-insights/a-smarter-approach-to-cost-reduction-in-the-public-sector

Allen, S., J. Smith, & Da Silva, N. (2013). Leadership style in relation to organizational change and organizational creativity: Perceptions from nonprofit organizational members. *Nonprofit Management and Leadership, 24*(1), 23–42.

Allison, M., & Kaye, J. (2005). *Strategic planning for nonprofit organizations.* 2nd ed. New York: Wiley.

Amodeo, M., Ellis, M. A., Hopwood, J., & Derman, L. (2007). A model for organizational change: Using an employee-driven, multilevel intervention in a substance abuse agency. *Families in Society, 88*(2), 223–232.

Anderson, D. (2015). *Organization development: The process of leading organizational change* (3rd ed.). Thousand Oaks, CA: Sage.

Anderson, D. (2017). *Organization development: The process of leading organizational change* (4th ed.). Thousand Oaks, CA: Sage.

Anderson, D., & Ackerman-Anderson, L. (2010). *Beyond change management* (2nd ed.). San Francisco: Pfeiffer: An imprint of Wiley.

Anderson, D., & Ackerman-Anderson L. (2011). Conscious change leadership: Achieving breakthrough results. *Leader to Leader*, Fall, 51–58.

Anderson, D., & Ackerman-Anderson, L. (n.d.) *Ensuring your organization's capacity to change.* Retrieved from http://changeleadersnetwork.com/free-resources/ensuring-your-organizations-capacity-to-change

Angelica, E., & Hyman, V. (1997). *Coping with cutbacks: The nonprofit guide to success.* St. Paul, MN: Amherst H. Wilder Foundation.

Annie E. Casey Foundation. (n.d.). *Race matters: Organizational self-assessment.* Retrieved from https://ncwwi.org/files/Cultural_Responsiveness__Disproportionality/RACE_Matters_Organizational_Self-Assessment.pdf

Appelbaum, S., Habashy, S., Malo, J., & Shafiq, H. (2012). Back to the future: Revisiting Kotter's 1996 change model. *Journal of Management Development, 31*(8), 764–782. http://dx.doi.org/10.1108/02621711211253231

Araque, J., & Weiss, E. (2019). *Leadership with impact: Preparing health and human service practitioners in the age of innovation and diversity.* New York: Oxford University Press.

Armenakis, A., & Bedeian, A. (1999). Organizational change: A review of theory and research in the 1990s. *Journal of Management, 25*(3), 293–315.

Armstrong, C., Flood, P., Guthrie, J., Liu, W., MacCurtain, S., & Mkamwa, T. (2010). The impact of diversity and equality management on firm performance: Beyond high performance work systems. *Human Resource Management, 49*(6), 977–998.

Aronowitz, S., De Smet, A., & McGinty, D. (2015, June). Getting organizational redesign right. *McKinsey Quarterly*, pp. 1–14.

Ashkenas, R. (2013, April 16). Change management needs to change. *Harvard Business Review.* Retrieved from https://hbr.org/2013/04/change-management-needs-to-cha

Ates, N., Tarakci, M., Porck, J., vab Knippenberg, D., & Groenen, P. (2019, February 28). Why visionary leadership fails. *Harvard Business Review.* Retrieved from https://hbr.org/2019/02/why-visionary-leadership-fails

Austin, M. (2004). *Changing welfare services: Case studies of local welfare reform programs.* New York: Haworth Press.

Austin, M. (2012): Introduction, *Journal of Evidence-Based Social Work, 9*(1-2), 1-2 http://dx.doi.org/10.1080/15433714.2012.636305

Austin, M., Brody, R., & Packard, T. (2009). *Managing the challenges in human service organizations: A casebook.* Thousand Oaks, CA: Sage.

Austin, M., & Carnochan, S. (2020). *Practice research in the human services: A university-agency partnership model.* New York: Oxford University Press.

Austin, M., & Claassen, J. (2008). Impact of organizational change on organizational culture: Implications for introducing evidence-based practice. *Journal of Evidence-Based Social Work, 5*(1/2), 321–359.

Austin, M., & Hopkins, K. (Eds.). (2004). *Supervision as collaboration in the human services*. Thousand Oaks, CA: Sage.

Austin, M., Regan, K., Gothard, S., & Carnochan, S. (2013). Becoming a manager in nonprofit human service organizations: Making the transition from specialist to generalist. *Administration in Social Work, 37*(4), 372–385. doi:10.1080/03643107.2012.715116

Austin, M., Regan, K., Samples, M., Schwartz, S., & Carnochan, S. (2011). Building managerial and organizational capacity in nonprofit human service organizations through a leadership development program. *Administration in Social Work, 35*(3), 258–281

Balogun, J., & Hope Hailey, V. (2004), *Exploring strategic change* (2nd ed.). London: Prentice Hall.

Barbee, A. P., Christensen, D., Antle, B., Wandersman, A., & Cahn, K. (2011). Successful adoption and implementation of a comprehensive casework practice model in a public child welfare agency: Application of the Getting to Outcomes (GTO) model. *Children and Youth Services Review, 33*(5), 622–633.

Bargal, D., & Schmid, H. (1992). Special issue: Organizational change and development in human service organizations. *Administration in Social Work, 16*(3/4) 1-214.

Bartczak, L., & Hyman, V. (2005). *A funder's guide to organizational assessment: Tools, processes, and their use in building capacity*. St. Paul, MN: Fieldstone Alliance Publishing Center.

Basford, T., Schaninger, B., & Viruleg, E. (2015, September 1). The science of organizational transformations. McKinsey & Co. Retrieved from http://www.mckinsey.com/business-functions/organization/our-insights/the-science-of-organizational-transformations

Bass, B., & Avolio, B. (2006). *Transformational leadership* (2nd ed.). Mahwah, NJ: Erlbaum.

Battilana, J., Gilmartin, M., Sengul, M., Pache, A., & Alexander, J. (2010). Leadership competencies for implementing planned organizational change. *Leadership Quarterly, 21*, 422–438.

Becker, K., Antuar, N., & Everett, C. (2011). Implementing an employee performance management system in a nonprofit organization. *Nonprofit Management and Leadership, 21*(3), 255–271.

Beckhard, R., & Pritchard, W. (1992). *Changing the essence*. San Francisco: Jossey-Bass.

Benschop, Y., & Van Den Brink, M. (2018). The holy grail of organizational change: Toward gender equality at work. In J. Messerschmidt, M. Messner, R. Connell, & P. Yancey Martin (Eds.), *Gender reckonings: New social theory and research* (pp. 193–210). New York: New York University Press.

Bernotavicz, F., Dutram, K., Kendall, S., & Lerman, D. (2011). Organizational development specialist competency model. *Training and Development in Human Services* [Special issue: Organizational Development], 6(1), 20–36.

Bernotavicz, F., McDaniel, N., Brittain, C., & Dickinson, N. (2014). Leadership in a changing environment: A leadership model for child welfare. *Administration in Social Work, 37*(4), 401–417.

Berra Y., & Kaplan, D. (2001). *When you come to a fork in the road, take it.* New York: Hyperion.

Bertram, R., Blasé, K., & Fixsen, D. (2015). Improving programs and outcomes: Implementation frameworks and organization change. *Research on Social Work Practice, 25*(4), 477–487.

Berzin, S., & Camarena, H. (2018). *Innovation from within: Redefining how nonprofits solve problems*. New York: Oxford University Press.

Berzin, S., Dearing, T., Mathews, O., & Choi, Y., & Pitt-Catsouphes, M. (2018). The center for social innovation at boston college. *Journal of Evidence-Informed Social Work, 15*(4), 473–480. doi:10.1080/23761407.2018.1455615

Berzin, S., Pitt-Catsouphes, M., & Gaitan-Rossi, P. (2015). Defining our own future: Human service leaders on social innovation. *Human Service Organizations: Management, Leadership & Governance, 39*(5), 412–425.

Bess, K., Perkins, D., & McCown, D. (2011). Testing a measure of organizational learning capacity and readiness for transformational change in human services. *Journal of Prevention & Intervention in the Community, 39*(1), 35–49. doi:10.1080/10852352.2011.530164

Best-Giacomini, C., Howard, A., & Ilian, H. (2016). A racial equity and staff development strategy for public human service organizations. In A. Carten, A. Siskind, & M. Greene (Eds.), *Strategies for deconstructing racism in the health and human services* (pp. 286–308). New York: Oxford University Press.

Billings, D. (2016). Deconstructing white supremacy. In A. Carten, A. Siskind, & M. Greene (Eds.), *Strategies for deconstructing racism in the health and human services* (pp. 91–100). New York: Oxford University Press.

National Implementation Research Network (2020). *Implementation Stages Planning Tool.* Chapel Hill, NC: National Implementation Research Network, FPG Child Development Institute, University of North Carolina at Chapel Hill. Retrieved from https://nirn.fpg.unc.edu/resources/stages-implementation-analysis-where-are-we

Blitz, L., & Kohl, B. (2012). Addressing racism in the organization: The role of White racial affinity groups in creating change. *Administration in Social Work, 36*(5), 479–498. doi:10.1080/03643107.2011.624261

Bloom, S., & Farragher, B. (2013). *Restoring sanctuary: A new operating system for trauma-informed systems of care.* Oxford, England: Oxford University Press.

Blumenthal, B. (2003). *Investing in capacity building: A guide to high-impact approaches.* New York: Foundation Center.

Blumenthal, B. (2007). *A framework to compare leadership development programs.* New York: Community Resource Exchange.

Borland, M. (2019). The leadership challenges in transforming a public human services agency. In S. Carnochan, A. DuBrow, & M. Austin (Eds.), *Guiding organizational change: A casebook for the executive development program in the human services* (25th Ed., pp. 150–174). Berkeley, CA: Bay Area Social Services Consortium, University of California, Berkeley.

Bouckenooghe, D., Devos, G., & Van den Broeck, H. (2009). Organizational change questionnaire-climate of change, processes, and readiness: Development of a new instrument. *Journal of Psychology, 143*(6), 559–599.

Bowditch, J., Buono, A. & Stuart, M. (2008). *A primer on organizational behavior* (7th ed.). Hoboken, NJ: Wiley.

Brager, G., & Holloway, S. (1978). *Changing human service organizations: Politics and practice.* New York: Free Press.

Brannen, S., & Streeter, C. (1995). Doing it with data. In B. Gummer & P. McCallion (Eds.), *Total Quality Management in the social services: Theory and practice* (pp. 72, 74). Albany, NY: Rockefeller College Press.

Brennan, D. (2020, June 15). Schools consider how to support student mental health amid distance learning. *San Diego Union-Tribune.* Retrieved from https://www.sandiegouniontribune.com/communities/north-county/story/2020-06-15/schools-consider-how-to-support-student-mental-health-amid-distance-learning

Bridges, W., & Bridges, S. (2016). *Managing transitions: Making the most of change* (4th ed.). Boston: Da Capo Press.

Briggs, H., Briggs, V., & Briggs, A. (2019). *Integratve practice in and for larger systems*. New York: Oxford University Press.

Briggs, H., & McBeath, B. (2009). Evidence-based management: Origins, challenges, and implications for social work administration. *Administration in Social Work, 33*(3), 242–261.

Brimhall, K., & Mor Barak, M. (2018). The critical role of workplace inclusion in fostering innovation, job satisfaction, and quality of care in a diverse human service organization. *Human Service Organizations: Management, Leadership, & Governance, 42*(5), 474–492.

Briner, R., Denyer, D., & Rousseau, D. (2009). Evidence-based management: Concept clean-up time? *The Academy of Management Perspectives, 23*(4), 19–32.

Brown, B. (2012). *Daring greatly*. New York: Gotham Books.

Brown, J., with Isaacs, D., and the World Café Community. (2005). *The World Café book: Shaping our futures through conversations that matter*. San Francisco: Berrett-Koehler.

Brown, M. Treviño, L., & Harrison, D. (2005). Ethical leadership: A social learning perspective for construct development and testing. *Organizational Behavior and Human Decision Processes, 97*(2), 117–134.

Bryson, J. (2018). *Strategic planning for public and nonprofit organizations: A guide to strengthening and sustaining organizational achievement* (5th ed.). Hoboken, NJ: Wiley.

Buchanan, D., & Badham, R. (2008). *Power, politics, and organizational change* (2nd ed.). Thousand Oaks, CA: Sage.

Buckingham, M. (2007). *Go put your strengths to work: 6 powerful steps to achieve outstanding performance*. New York: Free Press.

Buckingham, M., & Clifton, D. (2001). *Now, discover your strengths*. New York: Free Press.

Buckingham, M., & Coffman, C. (1999). *First, break all the rules*. New York: Simon and Schuster.

Bucy, M., Hall, S., & Yakola, D. (2016). *Transformation with a capital T*. New York: McKinsey & Company.

Bunger, A., & Lengnick-Hall, R (2019). Implementation science and human service organizations research: Opportunities and challenges for building on complementary strengths. *Human Service Organizations: Management, Leadership & Governance, 43*(5), 258–268. doi:10.1080/23303131.2019.1666765

Bunker, B., & Alban, B. (2014). Large group interventions. In Jones, B & Brazzel, M. (Eds.). *The NTL handbook of organization development and change: Principles, practices, and perspectives* (2nd ed.), (pp. 407–427). San Francisco: Wiley.

Buono, A. F., & Kerber, K. W. (2010). Intervention and organizational change: Building organizational change capacity. *EBS Review, 27*, 9–21.

Burke, W. (2018). *Organization change: Theory and practice* (5th ed.) Thousand Oaks, CA: Sage.

Burnes, B., Hughes, M., & By, R. (2016). Reimagining organizational change leadership. *Leadership, 1*(18), 1–17.

Bushe, G.& Kassam, A. (2005). When is appreciative inquiry transformational? *Journal of Applied Behavioral Science, 41*(2), 161–181.

Bushe, G., & Marshak, R. (2015). *Dialogic organization development: The theory and practice of transformational change*. Oakland, CA: Berrett-Koehler.

By, R. (2005). Organisational change management: A critical review. *Journal of Change Management, 5*(4), 369–380.

By, R. (2009). *Managing organizational change in the public sector*. London: Routledge.

Callahan, A. (2009). Growing through organizational change. *Families in Society, 90*(3), 329–331.

Calzada, E., & Suarez-Balcazar, Y. (2014). *Enhancing cultural competence in social service agencies: A promising approach to serving diverse children and families* (OPRE Report #2014-31). Washington, DC: Office of Planning, Research and Evaluation, Administration for Children and Families, US Department of Health and Human Services.

Cameron, K., & Quinn, R. (2011). *Diagnosing and changing organizational culture: Based on the competing values framework* (3rd ed.). San Francisco, CA: Jossey-Bass.

Carnochan, S., & Austin, M. (2004). Implementing welfare reform and guiding organizational change. In M. Austin (Ed.), *Changing welfare services: Case studies of local welfare reform programs* (pp. 3–26). New York: Haworth Press.

Carnochan, S., DuBrow, A., & Austin, M. (Eds.). (2019). *Guiding organizational change: A casebook for the executive development program in the human services* (25th ed.). Berkeley, CA: Bay Area Social Services Consortium, University of California, Berkeley.

Carten, A. (2016). Preface. In A. Carten, A. Siskind, & M. Greene, M. (Eds.), *Strategies for deconstructing racism in the health and human services* (pp. xv–xx). New York: Oxford University Press.

Carten, A., Siskind, A., & Greene, M. (2016a). Closing thoughts from the editors. In A. Carten, A. Siskind, & M. Greene (Eds.), *Strategies for deconstructing racism in the health and human services* (pp. 309–314). New York: Oxford University Press.

Carten, A. Siskind, A., & Greene, M. (2016b). *Strategies for deconstructing racism in the health and human services*. New York: Oxford University Press.

Carucci, R. (2016, October 24). Organizations can't change if leaders can't change with them. *Harvard Business Review*. Retrieved from https://hbr.org/2016/10/organizations-cant-change-if-leaders-cant-change-with-them

Carucci, R. (2017, February 10). Most reorganizations aren't ambitious enough. *Harvard Business Review*. Retrieved from https://hbr.org/2017/02/most-reorgs-arent-ambitious-enough?referral=00563&cm_mmc=email-_-newsletter-_-daily_alert-_-alert_date&utm_source=newsletter_daily_alert&utm_medium=email&utm_campaign=alert_date&spMailingID=16544207&spUserID=MjE3Nzk0NDU0NzMxS0&spJobID=960974229&spReportId=OTYwOTc0MjI5S0&utm_source=General+Email+Marketing+List+-+ALL&utm_campaign=d6f85a4a89-SMB+02_24_17&utm_medium=email&utm_term=0_e8af03eabe-d6f85a4a89-72534645

Casey Family Programs and the National Child Welfare Resource Center for Organizational Improvement. (2005). Using continuous quality improvement to improve child welfare practice. Retrieved from https://ncwwi.org/files/Data-Driven_Decision_Making__CQI/Using_Continuous_Quality_Improvement_to_Improve_CW_Practice.pdf

Catalyst. (n.d.). Engaging men in gender initiatives. Retrieved from https://www.catalyst.org/research-series/engaging-men-in-gender-initiatives/

Choflet, A., Packard, T., & Stashower, K. (in press). Rethinking organizational change in the Covid-19 era. *Journal of Hospital Management and Health Policy*.

Choi, M., & Ruona, W. (2011). Individual readiness for organizational change and its implications for human resource and organization development. *Human Resource Development Review, 10*(1), 46–73.

Claiborne, N., Auerbach, C., Lawrence, C., McGowan, B., & Lawson, H. (2014). Design teams as an organizational intervention to improve job satisfaction and worker turnover in public child welfare. *Journal of Family Strengths, 14*(1), 69–80.

Clarke, N., & Higgs, M. (2019). Employee participation in change programs. In R. Hamlin, A. Ellinger, & J. Jones (Eds.), *Evidence-based initiatives for organizational change and development* (pp. 179–199). Hershey, PA: IGI Global.

Clifton, J., & Harter, J. (2019). *It's the manager.* Washington, DC: Gallup Press.

Cohen, B. (1999). Fostering innovation in a large human services bureaucracy. *Administration in Social Work, 23*(2), 47–59.

Cohen, B., & Austin, M. (1997). Transforming human services organizations through empowerment of staff. *Journal of Community Practice, 4*(2), 35–50.

Cohen, M., & Hyde, C. (2014a). *Empowering workers & clients for organizational change.* Chicago: Lyceum Books.

Cohen, M., & Hyde, C. (2014b). Organizational assessment for change. In M. Cohen & C. Hyde (2014). *Empowering workers & clients for organizational change* (pp. 34–51). Chicago: Lyceum Books.

Coloma, J., Gibson, C., & Packard, T. (2012). Participant outcomes of a leadership development initiative in eight human service organizations. *Administration in Social Work, 36*(1), 4–22.

Conger, J., Spreitzer, G., & Lawler, E. (Eds.). (2008). *The leader's change handbook.* San Francisco: Jossey-Bass.

Connor, P., Lake, L., & Stackman, R. (2003). *Managing organizational change* (3rd ed.). Westport, CT: Praeger

Cooperrider, D., Whitney, D., & Stavros, J. (2003). *Appreciative inquiry handbook.* San Francisco: Berrett-Koehler.

Correll, S. (2017). SWS 2016 feminist lecture: Reducing gender biases in modern workplaces: A small wins approach to organizational change. *Gender & Society, 31*(6), 725–750.

Council on Social Work Education. (2015). *Educational policy and accreditation standards.* Retrieved from https://www.cswe.org/Accreditation/Accreditation-Process/2015-EPAS

Covey, S. (1989). *The seven habits of highly effective people.* New York: Simon & Schuster.

Crosby, B, & Sherer, J. (1981). Diagnosing organizational conflict-management climates. In J. Pfeiffer & L. Goodstein (Eds.), *The 1981 annual for facilitators, trainers, and consultants* (pp. 100–109). San Diego, CA: University Associates.

Crossroads Ministry. (n.d.). *Continuum on Becoming an Anti-Racist Multicultural Organization.* Adapted from original concept by Bailey Jackson and Rita Hardiman, and further developed by Andrea Avazian and Ronice Branding; further adapted by Melia LaCour, PSESD. Chicago: Author. Retrieved from https://ncwwi.org/files/Cultural_Responsiveness__Disproportionality/Continuum_AntiRacist.pdf

Cummings, T., & Worley, C. (2015). *Organization development and change* (10th ed.). Stamford, CT: Cengage Learning.

Curran, C., & Bonilla, M. (2010). Taking OD to the bank: Practical tools for nonprofit managers and consultants. *Journal for Nonprofit Management, 14*, 1–7.

Curry, D., Basso, P., & Jones K. (2011). Organizational development [Special issue]. *Training and Development in Human Services, , 6*(1).

Daft, R. (2010). *Organization theory and design* (10th ed.). Cincinnati, OH: South-Western College.

Damschroder, L., Aron, D., Keith, R., Kirsh, S., Alexander, J., & Lowery, J. (2009). Fostering implementation of health services research findings into practice: A consolidated framework for advancing implementation science. *Implementation Science, 4,* 50. doi:10.1186/1748-5908-4-50. Retrieved from http://www.implementationscience.com/content/4/1/50

Deming, W. E. (1982). *Out of the crisis.* Cambridge, MA: Massachusetts Institute of Technology, Center for Advanced Educational Services.

Dent, E., & Galloway Goldberg, S. (1999). Challenging resistance to change. *Journal of Applied Behavioral Science, 35*(1), 25–41.

De Pree, M. (2004). *Leadership is an art.* New York: Currency Doubleday.

De Smet, A., Lavoie, J., & Hioe E. (2012, April). Developing better change leaders. *McKinsey Quarterly,* pp. 1–6.

Despard, M. (2016). Strengthening evaluation in nonprofit human service organizations: Results of a capacity-building experiment. *Human Service Organizations: Management, Leadership & Governance, 40*(4), 352–368. https://doi.org/10.1080/23303131.2016.1140101

DiBella, A., & Nevis, E. (1998). *How organizations learn.* San Francisco: Jossey-Bass.

Dickinson, N. (2014). Child welfare leadership development to enhance outcomes for children, youth and families. *Human Service Organizations: Management, Leadership & Governance, 38*(2), 121–124.

Dixon-Fyle, S., Hunt, V., Dolan, K., & Prince, S. (2020, May 19). Diversity wins: How inclusion matters. McKinsey & Company. Retrieved from https://www.mckinsey.com/featured-insights/diversity-and-inclusion/diversity-wins-how-inclusion-matters#

Dixon-Woods, M., Agarwal, S., Jones, D., Young, B., & Sutton, A. (2005). Synthesizing qualitative and quantitative evidence: A review of possible methods. *Journal of Health Services Research and Policy, 10*(1), 45–53.

Dryburgh, A. (2016, February 28). Change management: "Everything needs to change so that everything can remain the same." *Forbes.* Retrieved from http://www.forbes.com/sites/alastairdryburgh/2016/02/28/change-management-everything-needs-to-change-so-that-everything-can-remain-the-same/#37ee7a3046bd

DuBrow, A., Wocher, D., & Austin, M. (2001). Introducing organizational development (OD) practices into a county human service agency. *Administration in Social Work, 25*(4), 63–83.

Dyer, W. (1995). *Team building: Current issues and new alternatives* (3rd ed.). Reading, MA: Addison-Wesley.

Dyer, W., Dyer, J., & Gibb, D. (2013). *Team building: Proven strategies for improving team performance.* Hoboken, NJ: Wiley.

Eadie, D. (2006). Building the capacity to lead innovation. In R. Edwards & J. Yankey (Eds.), *Effectively managing nonprofit organizations* (pp. 29–46). Washington, DC: NASW Press.

East, J. (2019). *Transformational leadership for the helping professions.* New York: Oxford University Press.

Eckstrand, K., Lunn, M., & Yehia, B. (2017). Perspectives: Applying organizational change to promote lesbian, gay, bisexual, and transgender inclusion and reduce health disparities. *LGBT Health, 4*(3), 174–180.

Egeland, K., Solheim, A., Endsjø, M., Laukvik, E., Bækkelund, H., Babai, A. . . . Aarons, G. (2019). Testing the leadership and organizational change for implementation (LOCI) intervention in Norwegian mental health clinics: A stepped-wedge cluster randomized design study protocol. *Implementation Science, 14*, 28. https://doi.org/10.1186/s13012-019-0873-7

Ehrhart, M., Aarons, G., & Farahnak, L. (2014). Assessing the organizational context for EBP implementation: The development and validity testing of the Implementation Climate Scale (ICS). *Implementation Science, 9*, 157.

Ehrhart, M., Schneider, B., & Macey, W. (2014). *Organizational climate and culture: An introduction to theory, research, and* practice. New York: Routledge.

Elwyn, L., Esaki, N., & Smith, C. (2017). Importance of leadership and employee engagement in trauma-informed organizational change at a girls' juvenile justice facility. *Human Service Organizations: Management, Leadership & Governance, 41*(2), 106–118. doi:10.1080/23303131.2016.1200506

Esaki, N., Benamati, J., Yanosy, S., Middleton, J., Hopson, L., Hummer, V., & Bloom, S. L. (2013). The sanctuary model: Theoretical framework. *Families in Society, 94*(2), 87–95.

Ezell, M., Casey, E., Pecora, P., Grossman, C., Friend, R., Vernon, L., & Godfrey, D. (2002). The results of a management redesign. *Administration in Social Work, 26*(4), 61–79.

Fernandez, S., & Pitts, D. W. (2007). Under what conditions do public managers favor and pursue organizational change? *American Review of Public Administration, 37*(3), 324–341.

Fernandez, S., & Rainey, H. (2006). Managing successful organizational change in the public sector: An agenda for research and practice. *Public Administration Review,* March/April 66(2), 168–176.

Ferris, G., Treadway, D., Kolodinnsky, R., Hochwarter, W., Kacmar, C., Douglas, C., & Frink, D. (2005). Development and validation of the political skill inventory. *Journal of Management, 31*(1), 126–152.

Finch, J. (2016). Theoretical perspectives for transformation. In A. Carten, A. Siskind, & M. Greene, M. (Eds.), *Strategies for deconstructing racism in the health and human services* (pp. 101–124). New York: Oxford University Press.

Flinchbaugh, J. (2007). Five principles of lean manufacturing from toyota production systems. *Lean Learning Center.* Retrieved from https://www.pfonline.com/articles/lean-is-born-from-how-we-think.

Ford, J., & Ford, L. (2009). Resistance to change: A reexamination and extension. In R. Woodman, W. Pasmore, & A. Shani (Eds.), Research in organizational change and development (Vol. 17, pp. 211–239). Burlington, VT: Emerald Group.

Ford, J., Ford, L., & D'Amelio, A. (2008). Resistance to change: The rest of the story. *Academy of Management Review, 33*(2), 362–377.

Foronda, C., Baptiste, D. L., Reinholdt, M. M., & Ousman, K. (2016). Cultural humility: A concept analysis. *Journal of Transcultural Nursing, 27*(3), 210–217.

Foster, R., & Kaplan, S. (2001). *Creative destruction.* New York: Penguin Random House.

Freeman, S. (1999). The gestalt of organizational downsizing: Downsizing strategies as packages of change. *Human Relations, 52*(12), 1505–1541.

French, W., & Bell, C. (1995). *Organization development* (5th ed.). Upper Saddle River, NJ: Prentice Hall.

French, W., & Bell, C. (1999). *Organization development* (6th ed.). Englewood Cliffs, NJ: Prentice Hall.

Friesen, B. (1987). Interpersonal aspects. In A. Minahan (Ed.), *Encyclopedia of social work* (18th ed., pp. 729–736). Washington, DC: NASW Press.

Frimpong, J., & Guerrero, E. (2020). Management practices to enhance the effectiveness of substance use disorder treatment. IntechOpen. doi:10.5772/intechopen.91054.

Retrieved from https://www.intechopen.com/books/effective-prevention-and-treatment-of-substance-use-disorders-for-racial-and-ethnic-minorities/management-practices-to-enhance-the-effectiveness-of-substance-use-disorder-treatment

Frohman, A. (1997). Igniting organizational change from below: The power of personal initiative. *Organizational Dynamics, 25*(3), 39–53.

Galbraith, J., Downey, D., & Kates, A. (2002). *Designing dynamic organizations: A hands-on guide for leaders at all levels.* New York: AMACOM.

Galpin, T. (1996). *The human side of change.* San Francisco: Jossey-Bass.

Garrow, E., & Hasenfeld, Y. (2010). Theoretical approaches to human service organizations. In Y. Hasenfeld (Ed.), *Human services as complex organizations* (2nd ed., pp. 33–57). Thousand Oaks, CA: Sage.

Gao, N., Waynor, W., & O'Donnell, S. (2009). Creating organizational commitment to change: Key to consumer employment success in a supportive housing agency. *Journal of Vocational Rehabilitation, 31,* 45–50.

Germak, A. (2015). *Essential business skills for social work managers: Tools for optimizing programs and organizations.* Philadelphia: Routledge.

Gibbons, P. (2015). *The science of successful organizational change.* New York: Pearson.

Gill, R. (2003). Change management—or change leadership? *Journal of Change Management, 3*(4), 307–318.

Gillberg C., & Jones G. (2019). Feminism and healthcare: Toward a feminist pragmatist model of healthcare provision. In P. Liamputtong (Ed.), *Handbook of research methods in health social sciences* (pp. 1–16). Singapore: Springer.

Gilley, A., McMillan, H., & Gilley, J. (2009). Organizational change and characteristics of leadership effectiveness. *Journal of Leadership & Organizational Studies, 16*(1), 38–47.

Gillingham, P. (2015). Electronic information systems and human service organizations: The unanticipated consequences of organizational change. *Human Service Organizations Management, Leadership & Governance, 39*(2), 89–100.

Glisson, C. (2012). Intervention with organizations. In C. Glisson, C. Dulmus, & K. Sowers (Eds.), *Social work practice with groups, organizations, and communities* (pp. 159–190). Hoboken, NJ: Wiley.

Glisson, C. (2015). The role of organizational culture and climate in innovation and effectiveness. *Human Service Organizations: Management, Leadership & Governance, 39*(4), 245–250. doi:10.1080/23303131.2015.1087770

Glisson, C., & Williams, N. (2015). Assessing and changing organizational social contexts for effective mental health services. *Annual Review of Public Health, 36*(1), 507–523.

Graaf, G., Hengeveld-Bidmon, E., Carnochan, S., Radu, P., & Austin, M. (2016). The impact of the great recession on county human-service organizations: A cross-case analysis. *Human Service Organizations: Management, Leadership & Governance, 40*(2), 152–169.

Graaf, G., Hengeveld-Bidmon, E., Carnochan, S. Salomone, M., & Austin, M. (2018). Change communication in public sector cutback management. *Public Organization Review, 19*(4), 453–472

Graham, P. (1995). *Mary Parker Follett: Prophet of management.* Boston: Harvard Business School Press.

Grantmakers for Effective Organizations. (2015). *Strengthening nonprofit capacity.* Washington, DC: Author.

Greene, M., & Levine, P. (2016). Promoting organizational and systemic change. In A. Carten, A. Siskind, & M. Greene (Eds.), *Strategies for deconstructing racism in the health and human services* (pp. 3–17). New York: Oxford University Press.

Grobman, G. (1999a). Business process reengineering. In *Improving quality and performance in your non-profit organization* (Ch. 3). Harrisburg, PA: White Hat Communications. Retrieved from http://www.socialworker.com/topics/improving-quality-and-performance-in-your-non-profit-organiz/

Grobman, G. (1999b). Benchmarking. In *Improving quality and performance in your non-profit organization* (Ch. 4). Harrisburg, PA: White Hat Communications. Retrieved from http://www.socialworker.com/topics/improving-quality-and-performance-in-your-non-profit-organiz/

Grobman, G. (1999c). Introduction to large group intervention. In *Improving quality and performance in your non-profit organization* (Ch. 6). Harrisburg, PA: White Hat Communications. Retrieved from http://www.socialworker.com/topics/improving-quality-and-performance-in-your-non-profit-organiz/

Grobman, G. (2008). *The nonprofit handbook* (5th ed.). Harrisburg, PA: White Hat Communications.

Guarino, K., Soares, P., Konnath, K., Clervil, R., & Bassuk, E. (2009). *Trauma-informed organizational toolkit for homeless services*. Rockville, MD: Center for Mental Health Services, Substance Abuse and Mental Health Services Administration. Retrieved from https://communityactionpartnership.com/external_resources/trauma-informed-organizational-toolkit-for-homeless-services/

Guerrero, E., & Fenwick, K. (2014). Organizational development and change. In *Oxford bibliographies in social work*. In E. Mullen (Ed.), New York: Oxford University Press. Retrieved from https://www.oxfordbibliographies.com/view/document/obo-9780195389678/obo-9780195389678-0176.xml?rskey=18cXWc&result=2&q=organizational+change#firstMatch

Guerrero, E., & Khachikian, T. (2020). Leadership approaches to developing an effective drug treatment system. IntechOpen. doi:10.5772/intechopen.91055. Retrieved from https://www.intechopen.com/online-first/leadership-approaches-to-developing-an-effective-drug-treatment-system

Guerrero, E., Khachikian, T., Frimpong, J., Kong, Y., Howard, D. L., & Hunter, S. (2019). Drivers of continued implementation of cultural competence in substance use disorder treatment. *Journal of Substance Abuse Treatment, 105*, 5–11. https://doi.org/10.1016/j.jsat.2019.07.009 Retrieved from https://www.sciencedirect.com/science/article/abs/pii/S0740547218305889

Hamlin, B. (2016). HRD and organizational change: Evidence-based practice. *International Journal of HRD Practice, Policy and Research 1*(1). 7–20. doi:10.22324/ijhrdppr.1.102

Hamlin, R. (2016). Evidence-based organizational change and development: Role of professional partnership and replication research. In C. Hughes, C., & M. Gosney (Eds.), *Bridging the scholar practitioner gap in human resources development* (pp. 120–142). Hershey, PA: IGI Global. doi:10:4018/978-1-4666-9998-4.ch007

Hamlin, R. (2019). Organizational change and development: The case for evidence-based practice. In R. Hamlin, A. Ellinger, & J. Jones (Eds.), *Evidence-based initiatives for organizational change and development* (pp. 1–29). Hershey, PA: IGI Global.

Hamlin, R., Ellinger, A., & Jones, J. (Eds.). (2019). *Evidence-based initiatives for organizational change and development*. Hershey, PA: IGI Global.

Hamlin, R., & Russ-Eft, D. (2019). Evidence-based organizational change and development: Organizational understanding, analysis, and evaluation. In R. Hamlin, A. Ellinger, & J. Jones (Eds.), *Evidence-based initiatives for organizational change and development* (pp. 30–51). Hershey, PA: IGI Global

Hammer, M., & Champy, J. (1993). *Reengineering the corporation.* New York: HarperBusiness.

Hardy, K. (2016). Antiracist approaches for shaping theoretical and practice paradigms. In A. Carten, A. Siskind, & M. Greene (Eds.), *Strategies for deconstructing racism in the health and human services* (pp. 125–139). New York: Oxford University Press.

Harvard Business School (2005). *The Essentials of managing change and transition.* Boston: Harvard Business School.

Hasenfeld, Y. (1980, December). Implementation of change in human service organizations: A political economy perspective. *Social Service Review,* pp. 508–520.

Hasenfeld, Y. (2015). What exactly is human services management? *Human Service Organizations: Management, Leadership, & Governance, 39*(1), 1–5.

Hassan, S. (2013). The importance of role clarification in workgroups: Effects on perceived role clarity, work satisfaction, and turnover rates. *Public Administration Review, 73,* 716–725.

Heckelman, W., Garofano, C., & Unger, S. (2013). Driving cultural transformation during large-scale change. In L. Carter, R. Sullivan, M. Goldsmith, D. Ulrich, & N. Smallwood, N. (eds.). *The change champion's field guide: Strategies and tools for leading change in your organization* (2nd ed., pp. 29–37). New York: Wiley.

Heifetz, R., & Laurie, D. (1999). Mobilizing adaptive work: beyond visionary leadership. In J. Conger, G. Spreitzer, & E. Lawler (Eds.), *The leader's change handbook* (pp. 55–86). San Francisco: Jossey-Bass.

Hemmelgarn, A., & Glisson, C. (2018). *Building cultures and climates for effective human services: Understanding and improving organizational social contexts with the ARC model.* New York: Oxford University Press.

Hengeveld-Bidmon, E. (2015). *An after action review of a research project team: A teaching case.* Berkeley, CA: Mack Center on Nonprofit and Public Sector Management in the Human Services School of Social Welfare, University of California, Berkeley.

Heritage, B., Pollock C, & Roberts, L. (2014). Validation of the organizational culture assessment instrument. *PLoS One, 9*(3), e92879. doi:10.1371/journal.pone.0092879

Herold, D., Fedor, D., & Caldwell, S. (2007). Beyond change management: A multilevel investigation of contextual and personal influences on employees' commitment to change. *Journal of Applied Psychology, 92*(4), 942–951.

Hersey, P., Blanchard, K., & Johnson, D. (2013). Management *of organizational behavior: Leading human resources* (10th ed.). Upper Saddle River, NJ: Prentice Hall.

Higgs, M., & Rowland, D. (2010). Emperors with clothes on: The role of self-awareness in developing effective change leadership. *Journal of Change Management, 10*(4), 369–385.

Holleb, G., & Abrams, W. (1975). *Alternatives in community mental health.* Boston: Beacon Press.

Holloway, S. (1987). Staff-initiated organizational change. In A. Minahan (Ed.), *Encyclopedia of social work* (18th ed., pp. 729–736). Washington, DC: NASW Press.

Holt, D., Armenakis, A., Feild, H., & Harris, S. (2007). Readiness for organizational change: The systematic development of a scale. *Journal of Applied Behavioral Science, 43*(2), 232–255.

Homan, M. (2016). *Promoting community change* (6th ed.). Belmont, CA: Brooks/Cole.

Huggins, C. (2016). Systems serving ethnically diverse older adults. In A. Carten, A. Siskind, & M. Greene. (Eds.), *Strategies for deconstructing racism in the health and human services* (pp. 169–190). New York: Oxford University Press.

Hughes, M. (2011). Do 70 per cent of all organizational change initiatives really fail? *Journal of Change Management, 11*(4), 451–464.

Hughes, M. (2015). Leading changes: Why transformation explanations fail. *Leadership 12*(4), 449–469.

Hughes, M. (2016). *The leadership of organizational change.* New York: Routledge.

Hughes, M., & Wearing, M. (2016). *Organisations & management in social work: Everyday action for change* (3rd ed.). Los Angeles: Sage.

Hyde, C. (2018): Leading from below: Low-power actors as organizational change agents. *Human Service Organizations: Management, Leadership & Governance, 42*(1), 53–67. doi:10.1080/23303131.2017.1360229

Institute of Medicine (IOM). (2015). *Psychosocial interventions for mental and substance use disorders: A framework for establishing evidence-based standards.* Washington, DC: National Academies Press. https://doi.org/10.17226/19013

Jacobs, C., van Wittleloostuijn, A., & Christe-Zeyse, J. (2013). A theoretical framework of organizational change. *Journal of Organizational Change Management, 26*(5), 772–792.

Jacquemont, D., Maor, D., & Reich, A. (2015, April 1). How to beat the transformation odds. McKinsey & Company. Retrieved from http://www.mckinsey.com/business-functions/organization/our-insights/how-to-beat-the-transformation-odds

Jamieson, D., & Rothwell, W. (2016). The convergence of organization development and human resource management. In W. Rothwell, J. Stavros, & R. Sullivan (Eds.), *Practicing organization development: Leading transformation and change* (4th ed., pp. 384–392). Hoboken, NJ: Wiley.

Jaskyte, K. (2011). Predictors of administrative and technological innovations in non-profit organizations. *Public Administration Review, 71*(1), 77–86.

John, J. (2016). *Your caring heart: Renewal for helping professionals and systems.* Camarillo, CA: Soul Water Rising.

Johnson, M., & Austin, M. J. (2008). Evidence-based practice in the social services: Implications for organizational change. *Journal of Evidence-Based Social Work, 5*(1–2), 239–269.

Jones, J. (1978). Role clarification: A team building activity. In J. Jones & W. Pfeiffer (Eds.), *Structured experiences* (Vol. 5, pp. 136–137). San Diego, CA: University Associates.

Judge, W., & Douglas, T. (2009). Organizational change capacity: The systematic development of a scale. *Journal of Organizational Change Management, 22*(6), 635–649.

Kaiser, W. (2013, September 21). The passions of Bernard Berenson. *New York Review of Books*, pp. 66–68.

Katz, J., & Miller, F. (2016). Leveraging diversity and inclusion for performance. In W. Rothwell, J. Stavros, & R. Sullivan (Eds.), *Practicing organization development: Leading transformation and change* (pp. 366–375). Hoboken, NJ: Wiley.

Kerman, B., Freundlich, M. Lee, J. M., & Brenner, E. (2012). Learning while doing in the human services: Becoming a learning organization through organizational change. *Administration in Social Work, 36*(3), 234–257.

Khan, S., Vendermorris, A., Shepherd, J., Begun, J., Lanham, H., Uhl-Bien, M., & Berta, W. (2018). Embracing uncertainty, managing complexity; applying complexity thinking principles to transformation efforts in healthcare systems. *BMC Health Services Research, 18*, 192.

Knoster, T., Villa, R., & Thousand, J. (2000). A framework for thinking about systems change. In R. Villa & J. Thousand (Eds.), *Restructuring for caring and effective education: Piecing the puzzle together* (pp. 93–128). Baltimore: Brookes.

Kotter, J. (1990). *A force for change: How leadership differs from management.* New York: Free Press.

Kotter, J. (1996). *Leading change.* Boston: Harvard Business School Press.

Kotter, J. (2008), *A sense of urgency.* Boston: Harvard Business Press.

Kotter, J. (2012). *Leading change, with a new preface by the author.* Boston: Harvard Business Review Press.

Kouzes, J., & Posner, B. (2002). *The leadership challenge* (3rd ed.). Hoboken, NJ: Wiley; p. 64.

Kouzes, J., & Posner, B. (2017). *The leadership challenge* (6th ed.). Hoboken, NJ: Wiley.

Kraut, A. (2009). An overview of organizational surveys. In W. Burke, D. Lake, & J. Paine (Eds.), Organizational change: A comprehensive reader (pp. 300–309). San Francisco: Jossey-Bass.

LaPiana, D. (2020, June 4). COVID-19's impact on nonprofits' revenues, digitization, and mergers. *Stanford Social Innovation Review.* Retrieved from https://ssir.org/articles/entry/covid_19s_impact_on_nonprofits_revenues_digitization_and_mergers#

Latting, J., & Blanchard, A. (1997). Empowering staff in a "poverty agency": An organization development intervention. *Journal of Community Practice, 4*(3), 59–75.

Lawrence, C., Claiborne, N., Zeitlin, W., & Auerbach, C. (2016). Finish what you start: A study of Design Team change initiatives' impact on agency climate. *Children and Youth Services Review, 63,* 40–46.

Lee, C., & Austin, M. (2012). Building organizational supports for knowledge sharing in county human service organizations: A cross-case analysis of works-in-progress. *Journal of Evidence-Based Social Work, 9*(1–2), 3–18.

Lehman, W., Greener, M., & Simpson, D. (2002). Assessing organizational readiness for change. *Journal of Substance Abuse Treatment, 22*(4), 197–209.

Levin, L., Goor, Y., & Tayri, M. (2013). Agency advocacy and organisational development: A feasible policy practice alliance. *British Journal of Social Work, 43,* 522–541. doi:10.1093/bjsw/bcr200

Lewin, K. (1951). *Field theory in social science: Selected theoretical papers.* New York: Harper & Row.

Lewis, J., Packard, T., & Lewis, M. (2012). *Management of human service programs* (5th ed.). Belmont, CA: Thompson/Brooks Cole.

Light, P., & Hubbard, E. (2004). The capacity building challenge: part I: A research perspective. Retrieved from https://www.issuelab.org/resource/the-capacity-building-challenge-part-i-a-research-perspective.html?_gl=1*x4hgqq*_ga*MTM5MzY4MT QxOS4xNjE0MjAxNjM4*_ga_5W8PXYYGBX*MTYxNDIwMTYzNy4xLjEuMTYx NDIwMjAyNy4w&_ga=2.3286192.188781343.1614201638-1393681419.1614201638

Likert, R. (1967). *The human organization: Its management and value.* New York: McGraw-Hill.

Lindberg, A., & Meredith, L. (2012). Building a culture of learning through organizational development: The experiences of the Marin County Health and Human Services Department. *Journal of Evidence-Based Social Work, 9*(1–2), 27–42.

Lindsey, M., & Watson, A. (2016). Barriers to mental health treatment among urban adolescent and emerging adult males of color. In A. Carten, A. Siskind, & M. Greene (Eds.), *Strategies for deconstructing racism in the health and human services* (pp. 191–205). New York: Oxford University Press.

Linn, S. (2000). *Agency change plan.* Unpublished manuscript, San Diego State University.

Linton, K. (2013). Developing a social enterprise as a social worker. *Administration in Social Work, 37,* 458–470.

Livne-Tarandach, R., & Bartunek, J. (2009). A new horizon for organizational change and development scholarship: Connecting planned and emergent change. *Research in Organizational Change and Development, 17,* 1–35.

Lopez, M., Hofer, K., Bumgarner, E., & Taylor, D. (2017). *Developing culturally responsive approaches to serving diverse populations: A resource guide for community-based organizations* (Publication # 2017-17). National Research Center on Hispanic Children & Families. Retrieved from https://www.hispanicresearchcenter.org/?s=culturally+responsive+approaches

Luthans, F., & Avolio, B. (2003). Authentic leadership development. In K. Cameron, J. Dutton, & R. Quirm (Eds.), *Positive organizational scholarship* (pp. 241–261). San Francisco: Berrett-Koehler.

Lyons, P., & Winter, C. (2010). Data management system selection in a family service agency. *Families in Society, 91*(4), 440–446.

Mallon, G., & McRoy, R. (2016). Children, youth, and family serving systems. In A. Carten, A. Siskind, & M. Greene (Eds.), *Strategies for deconstructing racism in the health and human services* (pp. 143–168). New York: Oxford University Press.

Manning, S. (2003). *Ethical leadership in human services: A multi-dimensional approach.* Boston: Pearson Education.

Marshall, C., & Nielsen, A. (2020). *Leaders of change: How MI can help leaders in social services, health care and helping organizations to listen, understand and guide their employees and organizations towards change.* New York: Guilford Press.

Mathews, B., & Linski, C. (2016). Shifting the paradigm: Reevaluating resistance to organizational change. *Journal of Organizational Change Management, 29*(6), 963–972.

Maynard, B. (2010). Social service organizations in the era of evidence-based practice: The learning organization as a guiding framework for bridging science to service. *Journal of Social Work, 10*(3), 301–316.

McBeath, B., Briggs, H, & Aisenberg, E. (2009). The role of child welfare managers in promoting agency performance through experimentation. *Children and Youth Services Review, 31,* 112–118.

McBeath, B., Mosley, J., Hopkins, K., Guerrero, E., Austin, M., & Tropman, J. (2019). Building knowledge to support human service organizational and management practice: An agenda to address the research-to-practice gap. *Social Work Research, 43*(2), 115–128.

McKinsey & Company. (2015). *The science of organizational transformations.* Retrieved from https://www.mckinsey.com/business-functions/organization/our-insights/the-science-of-organizational-transformations

McKinsey & Company. (n.d.). *Capacity Assessment Grid.* Retrieved from https://uconn.edu/search/?cx=004595925297557218349%3A65_t0nsuec8&q=capacity+assessment&sa=&cof=FORID%3A10&ie=UTF-8

McMurray, A., Islam, M., Sarros, J., & Pirola-Merlo, A. (2013). Workplace innovation in a nonprofit organization. *Nonprofit Management and Leadership, 23*(3), 367–388.

Miles, R. (1965). Human relations or human resources? *Harvard Business Review, 9*(43), 148–152.

Miles, R. (1975). *Theories of management: Implications for organizational behavior and development.* New York: McGraw Hill.

Miller, J., Bogatova, T., & Carnohan, B. (2011). *Improving performance in service organizations.* Chicago: Lyceum Books.

Minzer, A., Klerman, J., & Markovitz, C. (2014). The impact of capacity-building programs on nonprofits: A random assignment evaluation. *Nonprofit and Voluntary Sector Quarterly, 43*(3), 547–569.

Mishra, A., Mishra, K., & Spreitzer, G. (2009). Downsizing the company without downsizing morale. *MIT Sloan Management Review, 50*(3), 39–44.

Mohr, B. (1989). High-performing organizations from an open sociotechnical systems perspective. In W. Sikes, A. Drexler, & J. Gant (Eds.), *The emerging practice of organization development* (pp. 199–211). Alexandria, VA: NTL Institute.

Mor Barak, M. (2017). *Managing diversity: Toward a globally inclusive workplace* (4th ed.). Thousand Oaks, CA: Sage.

Mor Barak, M., Lizano, E., Kim, A., Duan, L., Rhee, M., Hsiao, H., & Brimhall, K. (2016). The promise of diversity management for climate of inclusion: A state-of-the-art review and meta-analysis. *Human Service Organizations: Management, Leadership, & Governance, 40*(4), 305–333. doi:10.1080/23303131.2016.1138915

Morgan, G. (2006). *Images of organization* (Updated edition). Thousand Oaks, CA: Sage.

Mosley, J. E., Marwell, N., & Ybarra, M. (2019). How the "what works" movement is failing human service organizations and what social work can do to fix it. *Human Service Organizations: Management, Leadership & Governance, 43*(4), 326–335. doi:10.1080/23303131.2019.1672598

Mosley, J. E., & Smith, S. R. (2018). Human service agencies and the question of impact: Lessons for theory, policy, and practice. *Human Service Organizations: Management, Leadership & Governance, 42*(2), 113–122.

Nandan, M., Bent-Goodley, T., & Mandayam, G. (2019). *Social entrepreneurship, intrapreneurship, and social value creation: Relevance for contemporary social work practice.* Washington, DC: NASW Press.

National Child Welfare Workforce Institute. (2010). *Systems and organizational change resulting from the implementation of systems of care.* Washington, DC: US Department of Health and Human Services Administration for Children and Families Administration on Children, Youth and Families Children's Bureau.

National Child Welfare Workforce Institute. (2011). *Leadership competency framework.* Washington, DC: US Department of Health and Human Services Administration for Children and Families Administration on Children, Youth and Families Children's Bureau.

National Child Welfare Workforce Institute. (2019). *Racial equity discussion guide.* Washington, DC: US Department of Health and Human Services Administration for Children and Families Administration on Children, Youth and Families Children's Bureau.

National Child Welfare Workforce Institute. (n.d.). *Gaining buy-in from the front line during times of change.* Washington, DC: US Department of Health and Human Services Administration for Children and Families Administration on Children, Youth and Families Children's Bureau. Retrieved from https://www.childwelfare.gov/pubPDFs/GainingBuy-InFromtheFrontLine.pdf

National Council of Nonprofits. (n.d.-a). *What is capacity building?* Retrieved from https://www.councilofnonprofits.org/tools-resources/what-capacity-building

National Council of Nonprofits. (n.d.-b) *Why diversity, equity, and inclusion matter for nonprofits.* Retrieved from https://www.councilofnonprofits.org/tools-resources/why-diversity-equity-and-inclusion-matter-nonprofits

Netting, E., Kettner, P., McMurrtry, S., & Thomas, M. L. (2017). *Social work macro practice* (6th ed.). Boston: Pearson.

Niven, P. (2008). *Balanced scorecard:Sstep-by-step for government and nonprofit agencies*, 2nd Ed. .Hoboken, NJ: John Wiley & Sons.

Norman, A., & Keys, P. (1992). Organization development in public social services—the irresistible force meets the immovable object. *Administration in Social Work, 16,* 147–165.

Northouse, P. (2019). *Leadership: Theory and practice* (8th ed.). Thousand Oaks, CA: Sage.

O'Connor, M., & Netting, E. (2009). *Organization practice: A guide to understanding human service organizations* (2nd ed.). Hoboken, NJ: Wiley.

O'Looney, J. (1996). *Redesigning the work of human services.* Westport, CT: Quorum.

Oreg, S., Vakola, M., & Armenakis, A. (2011). Change recipients' reactions to organizational change: A 60-year review of quantitative studies. *Journal of Applied Behavioral Science, 47,* 461–524.

Organization Development Network. Home page. (n.d.). Retrieved from http://www.odnetwork.org

Ortega, R. M., & Coulborn Faller, K. (2011). Training child welfare workers from an intersectional cultural humility perspective: A paradigm shift. *Child Welfare, 90*(5), 27–49.

Osborne, S., & Brown, K. (2005). *Managing change and innovation in public service organizations.* New York: Routledge.

Ouellette, R., Goodman, A., Martinez-Pedraz, F., Moses, J., Cromer, K., Zhao, X.,.., & Frazier. S. (2020). A systematic review of organizational and workforce interventions to improve the culture and climate of youth-service settings. *Administration and Policy in Mental Health and Mental Health Services Research, 47,* 764–778. https://doi.org/10.1007/s10488-020-01037-y

Owen, H. (2008). *Open space technology: A user's guide* (3rd ed.). San Francisco: Berrett-Koehler.

Packard, T. (1989). Participation in decision making, performance and job satisfaction in a social work bureaucracy. *Administration in Social Work, 13*(1), 59–73.

Packard, T. (1992). Organization development technologies in community development: A case study. *Journal of Sociology and Social Welfare, 19*(2), 3, 15.

Packard, T. (1993). Managers' and workers' views of the dimensions of participation in organizational decision making. *Administration in Social Work, 17*(2), 53–65.

Packard, T. (2001). Enhancing staff commitment through organizational values: The case of a homeless shelter. *Administration in Social Work, 25*(3), 35–52.

Packard, T. (2008). Organizational development and change. In T. Mizrahi & L. Davis (Eds.). *Encyclopedia of social work* (20th ed., pp. 324–327). New York: Oxford University Press.

Packard, T. (2012). Organizational change in nonprofit organizations: Implications for human resource management. In R. Burke & C. Cooper (Eds.), *Human resource management in the nonprofit sector: Passion, purpose and professionalism* (pp. 221–240). Cheltenham, UK: Elgar.

Packard, T. (2013). Organizational change: A conceptual framework to advance the evidence base. *Journal of Human Behavior and the Social Environment, 23*(1), 75–90.

Packard, T. (2014). Organizational change in human service organizations. In *Encyclopedia of Social Work.* doi:10.1093/acrefore/9780199975839.013.272

Packard, T. (2016). *Organizational change tactics: Successful and unsuccessful interventions from a survey of NSWM members.* Network for Social Work Management Annual Conference, Los Angeles, June.

Packard, T. (2017). Tactics for successful organizational change in a youth and family services agency. *Children and Youth Services Review, 81,* 129–138. http://dx.doi.org/10.1016/j.childyouth.2017.07.028

Packard, T. (2019). Organizational change tactics in a homeless services agency. *Nonprofit Management and Leadership, 30*, 353–363. https://doi.org/10.1002/nml.21386

Packard, T. (2020). Organizational change. In C. Franklin (Ed. in Chief), *The encyclopedia of social work*. Retrieved from https://oxfordre.com/socialwork/view/10.1093/acrefore/9780199975839.001.0001/acrefore-9780199975839-e-272?rskey=V7RFRG&result=1

Packard, T., & Gibson, C. (2014). *Organizational change in human services organizations: Comparing successful and unsuccessful interventions*. Network for Social Work Management Annual Conference, Boston, June.

Packard, T., Jones, J., & Nahrstedt, K. (2006). Using the image exchange to enhance interdisciplinary team building in child welfare. *Child and Adolescent Social Work Journal, 23*(1), 86–106.

Packard, T., McCrae, J., Phillips, J., & Scannapieco, M. (2015). Measuring organizational change tactics to improve child welfare programs: Experiences in 13 counties. *Human Service Organizations: Management, Leadership, & Governance, 39*(5), 444–458.

Packard, T., Patti, R., Daly, D., & Tucker-Tatlow, J. (2012). Organizational change for services integration in public human service organizations: Experiences in seven counties. *Journal of Health and Human Services Administration, 34*(4), 471–525.

Packard, T., Patti, R., Daly, D., & Tucker-Tatlow, J. (2013). Implementing services integration and interagency collaboration: Experiences in seven counties. *Administration in Social Work, 37*(4), 356–371.

Packard, T., Patti, R., Daly, D., Tucker-Tatlow, J., & Farrell, C. (2008). Cutback management strategies: Experiences in nine county human service agencies. *Administration in Social Work, 32*(1), 55–75.

Packard, T., & Reid, R. (1990). OD in a fire department: Lessons in using parallel structures and institutionalization. *Consultation, 9*(2), 167–184.

Packard, T., & Shih, A. (2014). Organizational change tactics: The evidence base in the literature. *Journal of Evidence-Based Social Work, 11*(5), 498–510.

Palmer, I., Dunford, R., & Akin, G. (2017). *Managing organizational change: A multiple perspectives approach* (3rd ed.). Boston: McGraw-Hill.

Parish, J. T., Cadwallader, S., & Busch, P. (2008). Want to, need to, ought to: Employee commitment to organizational change. *Journal of Organizational Change Management, 21*(1), 32–52.

Parry, C. (2011). Evaluating organizational effectiveness in human services: Challenges and strategies. *Training and Development in Human Services,* Special Issue: Organizational Development, 6(1), 37–49.

Parry, K. (2011). Leadership and organization theory. In A. Bryman, D. Collinson, K. Grint, et al. (Eds.), *The SAGE handbook of leadership*. 53–70. London: Sage.

Pasmore, W., Woodman, R., & Shan, A. (Eds.). (2010). Preface. In *Research in organizational change and development* (Vol. 18). Oxford, UK: JAI Press, ix-xi.

Patti, R. (1974). Organizational resistance and change: The view from below. *Social Service Review, 48*(3), 367–383.

Patti, R., & Osborne, P. (1976). *Management practice in social welfare: An annotated bibliography*. New York: Council on Social Work Education.

Patti, R., Packard, T., Daly, D., Tucker-Tatlow, J., & Farrell, C. (2003). *Innovative approaches to managing with less*. A report commissioned by the Southern Area Consortium of Human Services,. San Diego, CA: San Diego State University Academy for Professional Excellence.

Patti, R., & Resnick, H. (1985). Leadership and change in child welfare organizations. In H. Laird & C. Hartman (Eds.), *Handbook of child welfare* (pp. 269–288). Glencoe, IL: Free Press.

Peters, T. (1988). *Thriving on chaos*. New York: Knopf.

Pettigrew, A., Woodman, R., & Cameron, K. (2001). Studying organizational change and development: Challenges for future research. *Academy of Management Journal, 44*(4), 697–713.

Pfeffer, W., & Jones, J. (1974). Intergroup meeting: A image exchange. In W. Pfeffer &, J. Jones (Eds.), *A handbook of structured experiences for human relations training* (Vol. 3, pp. 81–82). San Diego, CA: University Associates .

Pine, B., & Healy, L. (2007). New leadership for the human services: Involving and empowering staff through participatory management. In J. Aldgate, L. Healy, B. Malcolm, B. Pine, W. Rose, & J. Sedens (Eds.), *Enhancing social work management: Theory and best practice from the UK and USA* (pp. 35–55). Philadelphia: Kingsley.

Pinto, R.,& Park, S. (2019). De-implementation of evidence-based interventions: Implications for organizational and managerial research. *Human Service Organizations: Management, Leadership & Governance, 43*(4), 336–343. doi:10.1080/23303131.2019.1672599

Plath, D. (2017). *Engaging human services with evidence-informed practice.* Washington, DC: NASW Press.

Price, R. (2019). *The politics of organizational change.* New York: Routledge.

Proctor, E. (2014). Dissemination and implementation research. In *Encyclopedia of social work.* doi:10.1093/acrefore/9780199975839.013.900

Proctor, E. (2017). The pursuit of quality for social work practice: Three generations and counting. *Journal of the Society for Social Work and Research, 8*(3), 335–353. doi: 10.1086/693431.

Proctor, E., & Bunger, A. (2020). Implementation science. In C. Franklin (Ed. in Chief), *The encyclopedia of social work.* Washington, DC: Oxford University Press & NASW Press. Retrieved from https://doi.org/10.1093/acrefore/9780199975839.013.1338

Proehl, R. (2001). *Organizational change in the human services.* Thousand Oaks, CA: Sage.

Purtle, J. (2020). Systematic review of evaluations of trauma-informed organizational interventions that include staff training. *Trauma, Violence, & Abuse, 21*(4), 725–740. doi:https://doi.org/10.1177/1524838018791304

Pynes, J. (2009). *Human resource management for public and nonprofit organizations* (3rd ed.). San Francisco: Jossey-Bass.

Rae, A., & Nicholas-Wolosuk, W. (2003). *Changing agency policy: An incremental approach.* Boston: Allyn and Bacon.

Rafferty, A., Jimmieson, N., & Armenakis, A. (2013). Change readiness. *Journal of Management, 39*(1), 110–135.

Ramos, C. 2007. Organizational change in a human service agency. *Consulting Psychology Journal: Practice and Research, 59*(1), 41–53.

Ramsdell, P. (1994). Staff participation in organizational decision making: An empirical study. *Administration in Social Work, 18*(4), 51–71.

Ratcliffe, S. (Ed.). (2017). Essays (1580, ed. M. Rat, 1958) bk. 3, ch. 12. *Oxford Essential Quotations* (5th ed.). New York: Oxford University Press.Retrieved from https://www.oxfordreference.com/view/10.1093/acref/9780191843730.001.0001/q-oro-ed5-00007567

Reisch, M., & Taylor, C. (1983). Ethical guidelines for cutback management: A preliminary approach. *Administration in Social Work, 7*(3–4), 59–72.

Reisner, R. (2011). *A leader's guide to transformation: Developing a playbook for successful change initiatives.* Washington, DC: IBM Center for the Business of Government. Retrieved from http://ncwwi.org/files/LeaderCompFrame5-31-2011.pdf

Resnick, H. (1978). Tasks in changing the organization from within. *Administration in Social Work, 2*(1), 29–44.

Resnick, H., & Menefee, D. (1993). A comparative analysis of organization development, with suggestions for what organization development can do for social work. *Journal of Applied Behavioral Science, 29*(4), 432–445.

Resnick, H., & Patti, R. (1980). *Change from within.* Philadelphia: Temple University Press.

Rice, C. (2020, June 8). Op-Ed: The LAPD won't stop traumatizing black Angelenos until it abandons its "warrior culture." *Los Angeles Times* Retrieved from https://www.latimes.com/opinion/story/2020-06-08/op-ed-lapd-protests-warrior-culture

Rieckhoff, K., & Maxwell, J. (2017). Organizational agility in the public sector: How to be agile beyond times of crisis. McKinsey & Company. Retrieved from http://www.mckinsey.com/industries/public-sector/our-insights/how-the-public-sector-can-remain-agile-beyond-times-of-crisis

Rofuth, T., & Piepenbring, J. (2020). *Management and leadership in social work: A competency-based approach.* New York: Springer.

Ross, M. (1982). Coping with conflict. In W. Pfeiffer & L. Goodstein (Eds.), *The 1982 annual for facilitators, trainers and consultants* (p. 264). San Diego, CA: University Associates.

Ross-Sheriff, F., & Orme, J. (2017). Mentoring and coaching. In C. Franklin (Ed.), *Encyclopedia of social work.* Washington, DC: NASW Press and Oxford University Press. doi:10.1093/acrefore/9780199975839.013.1146.

Rozas, L., & Klein, W. (2010). The value and purpose of the traditional qualitative literature review. *Journal of Evidence-Based Social Work, 7*(5), 387–399.

Ruble, T., & Thomas, K. (1976). Support for a two-dimensional model of conflict behavior. *Organizational Behavior and Human Performance, 16,* 145.

Sabah, Y., & Cook-Craig, P. (2013). Organizational learning. In C. Franklin (Ed.), *Encyclopedia of Social Work.* Washington, DC: NASW Press and Oxford University Press. doi:10.1093/acrefore/9780199975839.013.273

SACHS. (n.d.). *The Southern Area Consortium of Human Services.* San Diego State University School of Social Work. https://theacademy.sdsu.edu/programs/sachs/

Samuels, J., Schudrich, W., & Altschul, D. (2009). *Toolkit for modifying evidence-based practice to increase cultural competence.* Orangeburg, NY: Research Foundation for Mental Health.

Sanders, D. (2016). Influencing change: Leadership from a foundation's perspective. *Human Service Organizations: Management, Leadership & Governance, 40*(4), 302–304.

Schalock, R., Lee, T., Verdugo, M., Swart, K., Claes, C., van Loon, J., & Lee, C. (2014). An evidence-based approach to organization evaluation and change in human service organizations. *Evaluation and Program Planning, 45,* 110–118.

Schein, E. (2014). Culture assessment as an OD intervention. In B. Jones & M. Brazzel. *NTL handbook of organization development and change: Principles, practices, and perspectives* (pp. 340–360). San Francisco: Wiley.

Schein, E. (2017a). A conversation with Edgar Schein: Aligning strategy, culture, and leadership. *People & Strategy, 40*(2), 64–67.

Schein, E. (2017b). *Organizational culture and leadership* (5th ed.). Hoboken, NJ: Wiley.

Schmid, H. (2010). Organizational change in human service organizations: Theories, boundaries, boundaries, strategies, and implementation. In Y. Hasenfeld (Ed.), *Human services as complex organizations* (2nd ed., pp. 455–479). Thousand Oaks, CA: Sage.

Schmid, H. (2013). Nonprofit human services: Between identity blurring and adaptation to changing environments. *Administration in Social Work, 37*(3), 242–256.

Schmidt, J., Groeneveld, S., & Van de Walle, S. (2017). A change management perspective on public sector cutback management: Towards a framework for analysis. *Public Management Review, 19*(10), 1538–1555.

Seabury, B., Cohen, M., & Hyde, C. (2014). Social justice and the ethics of organizational change from below. In M. Cohen & C. Hyde, *Empowering workers & clients for organizational change* (pp. 52–72). Chicago: Lyceum Books.

Senge, P. (1990). *The fifth discipline: The art and practice of the learning organization.* New York: Doubleday Currency.

Shafritz, J., & Ott, J. (2001). *Classics of organization history.* Philadelphia: Harcourt Brace.

Sharif, M., & Scandura, T. (2014). Do perceptions of ethical conduct matter during organizational change? Ethical leadership and employee involvement. *Journal of Business Ethics, 124*(20), 185–196.

Shera, W., & Page, J. (1995). Creating more effective human service organizations through strategies of empowerment. *Administration in Social Work, 19*(4), 1–15.

Siskind, A., & Schenk, T. (2016). Incorporating antiracist work at staff and board levels. In A. Carten, A. Siskind, & M. Greene (Eds.), *Strategies for deconstructing racism in the health and human services* (pp. 18–32). New York: Oxford University Press.

Smith, B. (1994). Building shared visions: How to begin. In P. Senge, C. Roberts, R. Ross, B. Smith, & A. Kleiner (Eds.). *The fifth discipline fieldbook* (pp. 312–328). New York: Doubleday.

Sowa, J., Selden, S., & Sandfort, J. (2004). No longer unmeasurable? A multidimensional integrated model of nonprofit organizational effectiveness. *Nonprofit and Voluntary Sector Quarterly, 33*(4), 711–728.

Spitzmueller, M. (2018). Remaking "community" mental health: Contested institutional logics and organizational change. *Human Service Organizations: Management, Leadership & Governance, 42*(2), 123–145.

Spreitzer, G. (2008). Taking stock: A review of more than twenty years of research on empowerment at work. In J. Barling & C. Cooper (Eds.), *The SAGE handbook of organizational behavior Vol. 1: Micro perspectives* (pp. 54–72). Thousand Oaks, CA: Sage.

Stavros, J., Godwin, L., & Cooperrider, D. (2016). Appreciative inquiry: Organization development and the strengths revolution. In W. Rothwell, J. Stavros, & R. Sullivan (Eds.), *Practicing organization development: Leading transformation and change.* San Francisco: Wiley, 96-116.

Stein, H. (1965). Administration. In H. Lurie (Ed.), *The encyclopedia of social work* (Vol. 15, pp. 58–62). New York: NASW Press.

Stouten, J., Rousseau, D., & De Cremer, D. (2018). Successful organizational change: Integrating the management practice and scholarly literatures. *Academy of Management Annals, 12*(2), 752–788.

Strolin-Goltzman, J., Lawrence, C., Auerbach, C., Caringi, J., Claiborne, N., Lawson, H., . . . Shim, M. (2009). Design teams: A promising organizational intervention for improving turnover rates in the child welfare workforce. *Child Welfare, 88*(5), 149–168.

Substance Abuse and Mental Health Services Administration. (2016). *Improving cultural competence: Quick guide for clinicians.* HHS Publication No. (SMA) 16-4932. Rockville, MD: U.S. department of health and human services Substance Abuse and Mental Health Services Administration Center for Substance Abuse Treatment

Taylor, J., & Felten, D. (1993). *Performance by design.* Upper Saddle River, NJ: Prentice Hall.

ten Have, S., ten Have, W., Huijsmans, A., & Otto, M. (2017). *Reconsidering change management: Applying evidence-based insights in change management practice.* New York: Routledge.

Toch, H., & Grant, J. (1982). *Reforming human services: Change through participation.* Thousand Oaks, CA: Sage.

Truong, M., Gibbs, L., Pradel, V., Morris, M., Gwatirisa, P., Tadic, M., . . . Waters, E. (2017). A cultural competence organizational review for community health services: Insights from a participatory approach. *Health Promotion Practice, 18*(3), 466–475. doi:10.1177/1524839916689546

US Department of Health and Human Services, Administration for Children and Families. (2014). Continuous Quality Improvement in the CFSRs. *Children's Bureau Express, 15*(6). Retrieved from https://cbexpress.acf.hhs.gov/index.cfm?event=website.viewArticles&issueid=158&articleid=4228&keywords=CQI

Van Eron, A., & Burke, W. (2016). Closure: Mobilizing energy to sustain an agile organization In W. Rothwell, J. Stavros, & R. Sullivan (Eds.), *Practicing organization development: Leading transformation and change* (pp. 233–244). San Francisco: Wiley.

Vito, R. (2018a) Leadership development in human services: Variations in agency training, organizational investment, participant satisfaction, and succession planning. *Human Service Organizations: Management, Leadership & Governance, 42*(3), 251–266. doi:10.1080/23303131.2017.1421284

Vito, R. (2018b). Social work leadership revisited: Participatory versus directive approaches during service system transformation. *Journal of Social Work Practice.* 34(1), 7–21. doi:10.1080/02650533.2018.1529026

Vito, R. (2019). Self-directed teams as an organizational change strategy to empower staff: A teaching/learning case study. *Human Service Organizations: Management, Leadership & Governance, 43*(2), 146–151. doi:10.1080/23303131.2019.1614852

Walker, S., Trupin, E., & Hansen, J. (2013). *A toolkit for applying the cultural enhancement model to evidence-based practice.* Department of Psychiatry and Behavioral Sciences, Division of Public Behavioral Health & Justice Policy, University of Washington. Retrieved from https://nicic.gov/toolkit-applying-cultural-enhancement-model-evidence-based-practice

Walsh, C., Rolls Reutz, J., & Williams, R. (2015). *Selecting and implementing evidence-based practices: A guide for child and family serving systems* (2nd ed.). San Diego, CA: California Evidence-Based Clearinghouse for Child Welfare.

Ward, T. (2002). Good lives and the rehabilitation of offenders: Promises and problems. *Aggression and Violent Behavior, 7*(5), 513–528.

Wayne E., Lehman, W.,Smpson, D., Knight, D, & Flynn, P. (2011). Integration of Treatment Innovation Planning and Implementation: Strategic Process Models and Organizational Challenges. *Psychology of Addictive Behaviors, 25*(20, 252-261.

Weisbord, M. (1978). The organization development contract. In W. French et al. (Eds.), *Organization development theory, research, & practice* (p. 323). Dallas, TX: Business Publications.

Wheatley, M. (1992). *Leadership and the new science: Learning about organization from an orderly universe.* San Francisco: Berrett-Koehler.

Wheatley, M. (2006). *Leadership and the new science: Learning about organization from an orderly universe* (3rd ed.). San Francisco: Berrett-Koehler.

Wheatley, M. (2017). Who do you choose to be? An invitation to the nobility of leadership. *Leader to Leader, 2017*(85), 37–41; adapted from Wheatley, M. (2017). *Who do we choose to be?: Facing reality, claiming leadership, restoring sanity.* Oakland, CA: Berrett-Koehler.

Whelan-Berry, K., & Somerville, K. (2010). Linking change drivers and the organizational change process: A review and synthesis. *Journal of Change Management, 10*(2), 175–193.

Whittaker, J., Greene, K., Schubert, D., Blum, R., Cheng, K., Blum, . . . Savas, S. 2006. Integrating evidence-based practice in the child mental health agency: A template for clinical and organizational change. *American Journal of Orthopsychiatry, 76*(2), 194–201.

Wimpfheimer, S., Beyer, K., Coplan, D., Friedman, B., Greenberg, R., Hopkins, K., . . . Tropman, J. (2018). *Human services management competencies: A guide for non-profit and for-profit agencies, foundations, and academic institutions*. Retrieved from https://socialworkmanager.org/competencies/professionals/

Winship, K. (2012). Learning from staff to share knowledge and inform decision-making: The contra costa county experience. *Journal of Evidence-Based Social Work, 9*(1–2), 133–148. doi:10.1080/15433714.2012.636318

Woods. L., & Lee, K. (2012). *Addressing health disparities through organizational change: An evaluation of the Colorado Trust's Equality in Health Initiative*. Denver, CO: Colorado Trust. Retrieved from www.communityscience.com/pdfs/EIH_Final_Report.final.4-9-12.pdf

Woolever, J., & Kelly, J. (2014). Leadership and leadership development. In C. Franklin C. (Ed.), *Encyclopedia of social work*. Washington, DC: NASW Press and Oxford University Press. doi:10.1093/acrefore/9780199975839.013.1138 Retrieved from https://oxfordre.com/socialwork/search?siteToSearch=socialwork&q=leadership+and+leadership+development&searchBtn=Search&isQuickSearch=true

World Café. (n.d.) *Design principles*. Retrieved from http://www.theworldcafe.com/key-concepts-resources/design-principles

Wulczyn, F., Alpert, L., Orlebeke, B., & Haight, J. (2014). *Principles, language, and shared meaning: Toward a common understanding of CQI in child welfare*. Chicago: Center for State Child Welfare Data at Chapin Hall. Retrieved from https://fcda.chapinhall.org/longitudinal-analysis/new-publication-principles-language-shared-meaning-toward-common-understanding-cqi-child-welfare/

Yankey, J., & Willen, C. (2006). Consulting with nonprofit organizations. In R. Edwards & J. Yankey (Eds.), *Effectively managing nonprofit organizations* (pp. 407–428). Washington, DC: NASW Press.

Yoo, J., Brooks, D., & Patti, R. (2007). Organizational constructs as predictors of effectiveness in child welfare interventions. *Child Welfare, 86*(1), 53–78.

Young, M. (2009). A meta model of change. *Journal of Organizational Change Management, 22*(5), 524–548.

Yukl, G. (2013). *Leadership in organizations* (8th ed.). Boston: Pearson.

Zeitlin, W., Altschulb, D., & Samuels, J. (2016). Assessing the utility of a toolkit for modifying evidence-based practice to increase cultural competence: A comparative case study. *Human Service Organizations: Management, Leadership & Governance, 40*(4), 369–381.

Zvetina, D. (2009). *Organizational change: Adopting a housing first approach*. Washington, DC: National Alliance to End Homelessness.

Index

Figures and tables are indicated by *f* and *t* following the page number.